Intellectual Property Rights in China

Intellectual Property Rights in China

Zhenqing Zhang

PENN

UNIVERSITY OF PENNSYLVANIA PRESS

PHILADELPHIA

Published by
University of Pennsylvania Press
Philadelphia, Pennsylvania 19104-4112
www.upenn.edu/pennpress

Printed in the United States of America
on acid-free paper

10 9 8 7 6 5 4 3 2 1

Library of Congress Cataloging-in-Publication Data
ISBN 978-0-8122-5106-7

For my family

CONTENTS

Introduction

A Tale of Two Intellectual Property Rights Enforcement Cases

Intellectual property rights (IPR) are highly controversial in China's rapidly expanding foreign economic relations. As such, I encountered enormous difficulty when requesting interviews from IPR professionals in China. Nevertheless, I also encountered some pleasant surprises. In early March 2008, my interview request received a warm response from Mr. Wu, a legal adviser with the IPR office of the branch office of The China No. 1 Pencil Company in Bilin City in East China's N Province.[1] When I entered Mr. Wu's office, I was immediately attracted to a plaque bearing the title of "Model Unit of IPR Work" (*Zhishichanquan Gongzuo Xianjin Danwei*) hanging on the wall. Mr. Wu proudly told me, "We won this plaque with our hard work." He further added, "Maybe some good luck, too."[2]

As one of the leading pencil producers in the country, Mr. Wu's company has survived and thrived on the enormous market need for double black pencils used for China's standardized tests. Standardized tests are important components of China's talent selection system. Indeed, the tradition can be dated back centuries. It has been estimated that the annual sale of pencils in China can reach as many as 100 million a year. The huge business opportunity has been very tempting for legal pencil producers and counterfeiters.[3]

In May 2005, The China No. 1 Pencil Company identified a large amount of counterfeit double black pencils on the market in Bilin City. This discovery came only forty days before June 7, the day on which the Chinese National College Entrance Exam would take place. This was a very important day for millions of Chinese high school students and their families. If the knockoff counterfeit pencils were used in the exam, there was a very good chance that the scanner would not be able to read the answer sheet because the pencil lead would not be black enough, and thereby, the exam results of millions of high school students would be compromised. Mr. Wu and his colleagues reported this to the Economic Case Investigation Team of the Bilin Public Security Bureau immediately. He told the police, "It is not only our company's business interests that are at stake. That was absolutely unacceptable for the families of those affected high school students, either." The police had no reason to delay in taking action on this case. After a thorough investigation, the police identified an important suspect for the counterfeit activities: Shi Jiatao, a former employee of one of the branch factories of The China No. 1 Pencil Company.[4]

With enough evidence to make a case, the police arrested Shi and his accomplices. According to the interrogation record, after resigning from his previous job, Shi, his wife, and their three friends discovered that producing and selling counterfeit pencils could be a highly lucrative business. Starting in February 2004, Shi purchased semi-finished pencils from East China's Shandong Province and produced a fake trademark. In only one year, Shi and his "team" had produced as many as nine million counterfeit pencils. With a factory based in N Province, the marketing network reached Shangdong, Zhejiang, Jiangxi, and Hebei. Altogether, the Bilin City police destroyed ten underground factories, confiscated three million counterfeit pencils, and arrested ten suspects during the investigation. In October 2005, the case was transferred to the Bilin City People's Court for criminal litigation. In June 2006, Shi Jiatao and his accomplices were sentenced to imprisonment ranging from three to five years.

The IPR enforcement case was one of the most important achievements in the history of the Economic Case Investigation team in Bilin City. The case was rated as one of the "top ten representative IPR enforcement cases" of the year, and the head of the team won a national-level prize. The case also left the Bilin police with a very positive reputation among the public, particularly the high school students and their families. Of course, Mr. Wu and his team won praise from the headquarters of The China No. 1 Pencil Company for their swift action to protect the company's business interests.

Although it has been several years since the successful enforcement, Mr. Wu is still very proud of the case. Toward the end of the interview, he told me, "This case was so successful because it was enforced under the right circumstances. It happened at the initiation of the right complainant, against the right counterfeiter, and, most importantly, at the right time. What do I mean by saying 'the right counterfeiter'? Think about it. If those stupid counterfeiters had infringed on a trivial company rather than ours, would our complaint have been so compelling? Moreover, if the case was not enforced before the National College Entrance Exam, would our company have won so much sympathy from the public?"[5]

I did not ask Mr. Wu if he had reported any unsuccessful cases, although I was pretty sure that he did not have good outcomes every time. Another real-world example I encountered earlier indicated that the successful IPR enforcement case that Mr. Wu took pride in was an exception, rather than the norm, in China.

The beginning of the story is similar to the previous one. In spring 2007, Company C, an architecture material company also located in East China's N Province, detected counterfeit goods on the market in Tiqian City and reported this to the city's IPR enforcement agency. Through an investigation, the IPR enforcement officer discovered that the counterfeit goods were being produced by Company X, a smaller company located in the city's jurisdiction. The IPR agency immediately confiscated the counterfeit goods, which were altogether worth over 1 million RMB (about $160,000).[6] Because the total value of the counterfeit goods far exceeded the minimum amount needed for criminal prosecution, the IPR enforcement agency was ready to bring the case to the city court for criminal prosecution. However, the Party Secretary of the small town where Company X was located lobbied the IPR enforcement team not to sue Company X because it was one of the major contributors to the township's tax revenue. With the help of one of the officials affiliated with the city IPR enforcement squad, I participated in several meetings among the township officials and the squad. The most cited reason by the township Party Secretary to protect Company X from legal punishment was that punishing Company X would reduce Q County's tax revenue and would eliminate job opportunities. These reasons did not convince the Tiqian City IPR enforcement team in the beginning. However, when township officials told the IPR enforcement officers that many workers with Company X were previously laid-off employees of several other local, state-owned enterprises and that economic punishment of Company X would drive those workers to lose their jobs again and thus endanger social stability, the IPR enforcement officers started to soften their position. The township officials' lobbying efforts received reinforcement from several female workers of Company X. When we stepped out of the meeting room after a lengthy round of bargaining that afternoon, several female workers of Company X approached us, grabbed the arms of the IPR enforcement officers, and appealed on behalf of the factory owner. The reason they cited was similar to that of the township Party Secretary: punishing the counterfeit factory would deprive them of their jobs and jeopardize their families' well-being.

The lobbying efforts seemed to be effective because afterward, the legal procedures slowed greatly. Before I left Tiqian City in mid-August, some "insiders" were already predicting that Company X was unlikely to face criminal prosecution and that there would be only slight financial punishment.[7] In November 2007, as expected, Company C and Company X reached an "outside court reconciliation." According to this decision, Company X paid 50,000 RMB ($9,000) to Company C, a result that barely punished the trademark infringer.

Unlike the first case, which had received wide media coverage, the second case was never reported in the media. One can only estimate how many IPR enforcement cases in China are successful and unsuccessful due to the illegal nature of IPR infringement activities. Indeed, the Chinese government would not report accurate statistical data about the number of unsuccessful enforcement cases. However, even the Chinese top leadership does not deny the seriousness of the problem. During a national-level conference held by the Chinese State Council in November 2011, for example, then Chinese premier Wen Jiabao told the participants that "counterfeit activities remain rampant in some regions. IPR protection remains a difficult task."[8]

Research Question and Book Argument

The contrast between the two aforementioned IPR enforcement cases indicates that China respects international intellectual property rights but only in certain circumstances. This invites the primary question that drives this book: why do effective IPR enforcement cases occur in only some cases and not others, even though China's World Trade Organization (WTO) entry in 2001 was supposed to protect all intellectual property rights? To answer the question, we need to examine not only the Chinese state but also the Chinese society, particularly how it interacts with the Chinese state.

This book is about the ways in which the collaboration and competition among various state and society actors in China have shaped the evolution of the Chinese IPR policy. This, in turn, constitutes an important part of the enormous social and political change that China has gone through since the late 1970s. I argue that, aside from Chinese state actors, societal actors, such as domestic and foreign firms operating in China, domestic and foreign business associations, and Chinese consumers, play a significant role in shaping the country's IPR policy. Instead of passively following the state's direction, they vie for more influence in the making of IPR policies. They also try to affect the Chinese state to adopt policies in their favor.

I also argue that the degree of China's (non)compliance with IPR norms should be understood as the result of balancing two factors: the need for short-term economic gains by violating others' IPR and the aspiration for long-term, sustained growth by respecting IPR norms. Chinese IPR policy has emerged within the context of the legacy of the planned economy and an immature market mechanism. In this environment, only a small handful of elite Chinese domestic business actors are actively engaged in innovative activities, such as technological innovation, literary and artistic creation, and brand building. Most firms continue to rely on the input of natural resources and cheap labor to survive market competition. Although most foreign business investors in China hold IPR as a vital component of their competitiveness, Chinese economic nationalists interpret their business activities as exploiting Chinese wealth. As such, under some circumstances, the advocates of IPR norms—those few cutting-edge Chinese companies (such as The China No. 1 Pencil Company in the first case), along with foreign IPR holders—are strong enough to persuade Chinese government officials to comply with the IPR norms and achieve the country's long-term economic development goals. However, in many other circumstances, Chinese local governments (such as the township officials in the second case) protect IPR infringers and ignore IPR norms—even though they possess the enforcement capacity—because of the short-term political interests in raising tax revenue and creating jobs.

The story does not end with IPR enforcement per se. My book also situates the study of Chinese IPR policy against the greater backdrop of China's political and economic reforms. Not only do I study IPR enforcement across different issue areas, but I also trace the development of the Chinese IPR regime over time. I demonstrate that the struggle over IPR enforcement is not only merely an economic or legal issue but also a key manifestation of the gradual political reform in China. The IPR norms rest on protecting intellectual creation as *private* property, and private property constitutes one of the foundations of the Western concepts of civil society and the rule of law. However, in a country such as China that has been dominated for decades by socialist public ownership, the notion of private property has been nonexistent. Until recently, neither private entrepreneurs nor literary or artistic creators have existed as an independent social group in Chinese society. Protecting intellectual property rights also requires protecting important aspects of civil liberty, such as individual autonomy and the free flow of ideas, which, in turn, demands a thorough reform of the political and economic underpinnings of China's communist system. Therefore, in an important way, the evolution of the Chinese IPR regime provides a useful angle to study the evolution of China's political and economic reforms. China's partial compliance with IPR norms reflects the coexistence between an emerging capitalist market economy and one of the world's last remaining communist political systems. The uneven compliance level with IPR norms also reflects the differing thoroughness with which institutional reform has taken place in China.

Existing Explanations for Chinese IPR Policy

The rampancy of IPR infringement in China has attracted a lot of scholarly and political attention since the mid-1990s. Specifically, three dominant categories of theoretical attempts in international relations and comparative politics literature exist to address the adoption and compliance of international IPR norms: an external pressure argument, a culturalist argument, and a bureaucratic politics argument. I will evaluate these three strands of argument in this section. I argue that each of the existing explanations contains a grain of truth and provides a solid foundation for scholars' academic exploration. However, each of those theories falls short at some stage of the analysis. Instead of rejecting the explanations as wrong, I argue that they should be improved so that more attention should be paid to address the role of Chinese societal actors and their interaction with the Chinese state.

External Pressure Argument

The most straightforward and popular explanation of China's IPR policy has dwelled on the role of external pressure. Applying a realist perspective to the analysis of IPR, the external pressure argument holds that, in power-oriented trade diplomacy, the cost of noncompliance with the IPR norm is great; the global trade hegemon will impose punitive tariffs on countries considered serious violators. On the issue of IPR, the United States is the global hegemon in the world trade system and the largest producer of IPR-related products. Therefore, it has stronger bargaining power in IPR negotiations to push China onto the track it designs.[9] Apart from bilateral pressure, multilateral pressure from international organizations such as the WTO also has pressed countries aspiring to join the WTO to revise their IPR legislation to meet the minimum standard of IPR protection required by WTO membership.[10]

Like any popular theory, the external pressure argument certainly captures an important aspect of the making of Chinese IPR policy: the "push-behind" role of the developed countries, mainly the United States, to accelerate China's IPR legislation. However, the external pressure argument deserves improvement on the following fronts: first, while the external pressure argument offers a convincing explanation for the *adoption* of the IPR norm, it has little to say about the *implementation* of IPR norms. Indeed, while the Chinese government constitutes a major defensive line at the negotiation table, external pressure can hardly reach the local government and societal actors behind the Chinese border. It is through those actors that formal IPR agreements are translated into real policy outcomes. Second, and possibly more important, the external pressure argument cannot explain why the Chinese government has taken IPR protection measures under some circumstances even *without* pressure from foreign governments. In the two aforementioned fieldwork examples, the pressure confronting the Chinese state came from within the country. Moreover, even if foreign pressure works under some circumstances, it cannot maintain its presence all the time. On many occasions, foreign pressure influences Chinese decision making in the form of newly emerging foreign policy actors and newly developed ideas, values, and orientations. Therefore, researchers cannot treat China as a unitary state; they must open the black box of the Chinese state to examine the operation of Chinese IPR policy on the domestic arena.

Bureaucratic Politics Argument

In the early twenty-first century, scholarly attempts to open the black box of the Chinese state yielded significant progress. Most prominent among those works are those by Andrew Mertha and Martin Dimitrov.[11] Instead of treating Chinese bureaucracy as a monolithic setup, this strand of argument posits that China's IPR policy implementation is handicapped by administrative and legal decentralization, which creates barriers to the central disciplining of local officials and creates opportunities for local protectionism for IPR infringement.

In his 2005 book, Mertha highlights the role of foreign businesses and private investigation firms operating in China, which he terms "lateral exogenous pressure." He argues that exogenous pressure creates inter-bureaucratic competition between different enforcement agencies, which, in turn, brings about higher volumes of enforcement in certain issue areas in IPR, such as a trademark. Building upon Mertha's work, Dimitrov expands his analysis from foreign-owned IPR to Chinese-owned IPR, from the volume of IPR enforcement to the quality of IPR enforcement, and from administrative enforcement organs to other enforcement organs, such as courts, customs, and the police, in his book published in 2009. For him, the quality of IPR enforcement should be measured by consistency, transparency, and fairness. He finds a low volume of high-quality enforcement in issue areas such as patents. However, a very high volume of copyright and trademark enforcement is unfortunately of low quality.

The bureaucratic politics argument is an important stride forward toward a deeper understanding of Chinese IPR policy. When checked with the real-world example above, however, one may find that further analysis should be made to make the bureaucratic politics argument a more complete explanation of the causes for the rampancy of IPR infringement in China.

First, while the bureaucratic politics argument analyzes the relationship between different IPR enforcement organs in China, more emphasis is needed to address the role of societal actors in the implementation of Chinese IPR policy. In the two real-world cases introduced in the beginning, for example, although the IPR bureaucracy conducted the raid, it had to rely on the IPR holder (The China No. 1 Pencil Company in the first case and Company C in the second case) whose business interests were being damaged by the counterfeit goods to obtain clues for enforcement. In fact, the enforcement squad of the Economic Investigation Team of the Bilin City Public Security Bureau consisted of only fifty-two members while the population of Bilin City was over one million in 2008. In the second case, the IPR enforcement squad of Tiqian City had forty-seven members while the population of Tiqian City was 750,000 in 2007. Nationwide, China employs 330,000 enforcement professionals in the country's IPR bureaucracy,[12] the highest number in the world, but these enforcement professionals account for only a tiny portion of the 1.3 billion Chinese. It, therefore, would be impossible for enforcement officers to keep an eye on the consumption behavior of the Chinese populace even if they worked seven days a week, twenty-four hours a day. Since the business community's interests are most directly affected by counterfeits, the IPR enforcement bureaucracy mainly relies on them to provide information that will help them organize anticounterfeit raids. According to an IPR official, without the clues provided by the business actors, the IPR enforcement bureaucracy is both "deaf and blind."[13] Therefore, while the bureaucratic politics argument is right in stating that politics at the local level determines the eventual policy outcome, it should go further to examine how the local societal actors interact with the local bureaucratic institutions.

Second, although part of the bureaucratic politics argument acknowledges the impact of societal actors—namely, IPR holders and IPR infringers —it has not sufficiently considered the power ratio between the IPR holders and IPR infringers. While it is true that the local protectionism forged between the local government and counterfeiters hinders the implementation of IPR policy, is it possible that under some circumstances (such as the first case), IPR holders have the upper hand over the IPR infringers and thus press the local government to take IPR protection measures? While short-term benefits, such as tax revenue and job opportunities from IPR infringers, help local government officials maintain or strengthen their power, what if the benefits come from the innovators or IPR holders? Is it possible that the benefits from the IPR holders are higher than the benefits from having IPR infringers and, therefore, the IPR holders have a stronger voice than the IPR infringers? If yes, what is the mechanism for this to happen? In order to answer these questions, it is not sufficient to explain how local protectionism is forged between the Chinese local government and IPR infringers. It is equally important, if not more, to examine the power relationship between IPR holders and IPR infringers and their relationship with the Chinese state. A clearer picture of that relationship can help to clarify when local protectionism of IPR infringement prevails and when it can be overcome by IPR holders.

Finally, the authors of the bureaucratic politics argument made innovative attempts to study the variation in the quality of IPR enforcement across different issue areas and different enforcement organs.[14] However, in the two real-world examples above, both the successful and unsuccessful cases happened in the same issue area (trademark) and the same geographic region (N Province). A natural question arises: while it is true that effective enforcement is more likely to arise in issue areas where the state capacity is stronger (such as the issue of patent), what explains the variation between effective and ineffective enforcement in the same issue area, where state capacity stays constant? Is it possible that at least under some circumstances, the state *willingly* enforces IPR? Since 2002, the Chinese State Council Intellectual Property Rights Working Group has nominated the top ten representative IPR enforcement cases of the year. Out of the 100 cases from 2002 to 2012, 80 percent were trademark and copyright cases. According to an IPR official, "[During the selection of those representative cases], I understand that people may criticize us as picking up the showcases. They may even criticize us as 'acting' (*zuoxiu*). However, even though it is really acting, I think that it is good acting. We want to demonstrate to the public that even in those difficult issue areas, the situation is not that dismal. There is still hope."[15] I find that even in those issue areas where state capacity is widely regarded as weaker (such as trademark), effective IPR enforcement is still likely to happen when the interests of the Chinese state, business actors, and the public are better aligned with one another. Societal actors do not just exert pressure on the Chinese state to enforce IPR. They also manage to persuade the state that enforcing IPR is to its benefit. While the bureaucratic politics argument deserves credit for offering a more thorough study of the variation of IPR enforcement in China, the analysis could be even more thorough if the variation across different Chinese societal actors was also incorporated.

Culturalist Argument

As one of the pioneering researchers of Chinese IPR policy, William Alford stresses the importance of the historical and cultural contexts in which IPR laws operate in China.[16] This culturalist argument attributes the ineffective enforcement of IPR policy in China to the prevalent ideologies in the country. Specifically, three historical-cultural factors are particularly responsible: the first is the legacy of Confucian culture, which regards copying others' work as a necessary and justified means to disseminate knowledge; the second is China's resentment of the developed countries' forcing China to adopt IPR laws in both the pre-1949 era and the 1980s and 1990s; and the third is the legacy of the planned economy era, when the results of any innovative activities were regarded as collective benefits for the public.

In the early twenty-first century, scholars further developed the aforementioned argument by investigating the role of Chinese consumer culture. Although not supported by sufficient empirical data, Gordon Cheung promisingly pointed out that the Chinese IPR issue should be understood as a "side effect of the general modernization and social changes of China." He argued that the rampancy of IPR infringement in China should be explained as a "culmination of consumer culture with rapid market development and poor administrative implementation of IPR protections."[17] Fan Yang offered a more nuanced analysis of Chinese consumer culture by tracing the interactions between the country's efforts in indigenous innovation (*zizhu chuangxin*) and counterfeit culture. Putting the Chinese IPR issue under the scenario of globalization, Yang argued that IPR infringement in China should be understood as resulting from the unequal relationship between capitalism's global expansion and the Chinese local forces' endeavor to advance their economic gains. As part of the defiance against the global IPR regime, the "copycat brand" phenomenon, also known as *Shanzhai*, in China contains certain elements of creativity although disparaged by the mainstream IPR holders as counterfeiting.[18]

It is true that political and consumer culture exerts an important influence on the formulation of Chinese IPR policy in the contemporary era, but the following significant facts should not be neglected when considering the culturalist argument: culture is constantly changing and is inevitably affected by the political and economic environment from which it originates. One can hardly argue that there have been no significant changes in Chinese political culture from before the late 1970s, when the reform and opening policy was adopted, to the beginning of the twenty-first century. Therefore, a simplistic understanding of culture cannot capture the complexity of culture as a multidimensional phenomenon.

Specifically, both Chinese IPR holders and Chinese IPR infringers share the same Confucian cultural tradition and operate their business in the same market environment, but why do they differ in terms of real IPR actions? If Confucian cultural tradition and market-driven consumer culture in China work against IPR in a uniform way, why do some business actors have a strong inclination to protect IPR while many others do not? Is it possible for Confucian culture to take on new meaning with the introduction of a market mechanism? Is it possible that different actors take different attitudes toward IPR protection because of their different positions in the market environment? The above two real-world examples demonstrate that attitudes vary among the different business actors: the response of IPR holders (The China No. 1 Pencil Company in the first case and Company C in the second case) was serious, but the IPR infringers (such as Company X in the second case) put profit making at the top of their agenda. The IPR holders certainly wanted to protect their intellectual property, but their complaints yielded different results. In that light, Confucian tradition and market-driven consumer culture alone are not sufficient to explain the different actors' attitudes toward IPR. A more sophisticated explanation is desired.

Likewise, many common Chinese people with strong nationalistic sentiments interpret IPR as a means of Western countries' economic invasion. However, the two real-world examples show that the common people's attitude toward IPR is more sophisticated than assumed. While the female workers of Company X in the second case believed that protecting IPR hurt their interests, the high school students and their families in the first case believed that IPR protection was vital to safeguard their interests. The contrast indicates that common Chinese people may interpret IPR in different ways due to their personal relationship with IPR. Researchers will thus invite the following questions: Is it possible that at least some Chinese people are less hostile to IPR because they benefit from observing the IPR norms? Perhaps more important, is it possible that the IPR norms are better observed under some circumstances because the market reform is more thorough and market order sounder? It is, therefore, important to unravel the mechanism that creates the different attitudes.

Culturalist scholars such as William Alford are also right in emphasizing the ideological legacy from the Mao era that works against the diffusion of IPR norms in China. However, China has engaged in market reform since the late 1970s. Although Communist hardliners never ceased to critique the market reform scheme harshly, it is unlikely that China will reverse the trend of economic reform. Therefore, the ideological legacy from the Mao era is not the only ideology that matters in the implementation of Chinese IPR policy. Other scholars such as Fan Yang enriched the culturalist argument by analyzing how various ideas interact with one another over the Chinese IPR issue. Following that analysis, some other questions may arise: If the result of IPR enforcement is dependent on the competition among different ideologies in China, under what circumstances would one ideology take the upper hand over others? Which political and social groups in China are more likely to follow what kind of ideology? What is the power ratio among those groups when it comes to protecting IPR from being infringed? While the culturalist argument rightly brings ideational factors into perspective, further efforts are needed to study the much more pluralistic real situation on the ground.

Hence, my study advocates for an evolutionary perspective over time. For example, during my interview with a prominent IPR scholar with the Chinese Academy of Social Sciences (CASS), the scholar recalled the experience of his mentor, the late Professor Zheng Chengsi (1944–2006), who was respected as a forerunner of IPR studies in contemporary China. According to the scholar, "When Professor Zheng started to study IPR law in the 1980s, there was no meaningful IPR to infringe upon. The notion of IPR was literally nonexistent for most people in China. It was a hard time for him. When I started to study IPR law in the 1990s and educate the younger generation of IPR professionals in the early twenty-first century, my students and I met a lot of difficulty as well because IPR infringement became so rampant. The level of people's respect for IPR is certainly not as high as we desire. But at least the notion of IPR has been growing, which is very different from the situation in the early 1980s."[19] During a follow-up interview with that scholar, he further added, "When we started to advocate IPR protection in the early 1980s, many people thought that we were crazy. They did not even bother to consult us on IPR affairs. Now nobody ridicules us as crazy, but I am obsessed with dealing with IPR complaints every day. The IPR cases that we deal with now are much more complex than before, with the stakes much higher. Different generations of IPR professionals, my adviser, myself, and my students, are encountered with difficult challenges during different phases, except that the challenges are of different nature."[20] In the chapters to follow, I further examine how the evolution of China's political and economic reforms shapes the interaction among different ideas held by different state and societal actors, which, in turn, shapes the outcome of the implementation of IPR norms.

Rationale for Case Selection

Before delving into the empirical chapters, I would like to justify the case selection of this book. Two aspects of the "so what" question are addressed in the following section: Why is China chosen as the specific country under examination? Why is IPR chosen as the specific issue area?

Why China?

According to John Gerring, a case study is "an intensive study of a single unit for the purpose of understanding a larger class of (similar) units."[21] China is chosen as the subject of this study because of its uniqueness and its generalizability.

What comes first is China's uniqueness: with the world's largest population and one of the world's fastest growing economies, China is gaining increasingly more weight in the international political economy. The study of social and political phenomena in China, whose complexity is due a great deal to the country's cultural, historical, and demographic diversity, is able to enrich our understanding of the social world. Here it is also important to note that, with some exceptions, the implementation of IPR laws in China remains underexplored. To the best of my knowledge, in recent years, there have been only a few scholarly attempts to incorporate elements of the Chinese state, society, and foreign pressure to analyze China's IPR policy making and implementation in the past two decades.[22]

Recognizing the uniqueness of the Chinese political economy, researchers should also notice the similarity between China and many other developing and postcommunist countries in the world. Like many other developing countries, in most cases, China regards the unauthorized diffusion of intellectual property as the most efficient way to disseminate knowledge that will eventually lead to economic development and power. As a latecomer to the stage of world economy, China's foreign economic relationship is often plagued by the country's disputes with its trading partners over IPR issues. The debates over IPR that China is engaged with have deeper implications for the study of the political economy of the developing world: whether the IPR notion is really helpful to build the developing countries' innovative capacity and beneficial for their economic development; whether the developing country should comply with the IPR norm in a wholesale manner, as advocated by the developed countries, or should selectively comply with parts of the norm according to its own concrete conditions; and how the interests of foreign investors, domestic companies, and the public should be balanced. Those questions are not unique to China. Recognizing the diversity of the developing world, the conclusions from the study of Chinese IPR policy can help us to achieve better knowledge of other developing countries that are also striving for a higher place in the global political economic setup.

As a postsocialist country, the traditional Chinese approach to IPR is the opposite of the Western capitalist assumption that property rights are the very cornerstone of the establishment of a market economy. Although China has embarked on economic reform since the late 1970s, the notion of protecting intellectual creation as private property remains a hot topic for debate. Although starting from the realm of IPR, those debates have significant implications for the deeper issue underlying the country's political and economic reforms: whether China should further establish private property as the cornerstone of its market reform, whether private entrepreneurs and literary and artistic creators should have a bigger voice in the formulation of the country's policy, whether an authoritarian political system can coexist with the call for individual innovation in a sustainable manner, and whether the encouragement of individual innovation can bring about further social and political liberalization in China. Therefore, the theoretical conclusions generated by the study of China's adoption and compliance with the IPR norms will also deepen our understanding of the political economy in postcommunist polities, many of which are confronted with similar tasks in their political and economic development.

Why IPR?

Since the 1980s, there has been fruitful scholarship on the state-society relationship and its impact on the formulation and implementation of public policy in contemporary China. However, the scholarly community has not studied Chinese IPR policy through the lens of state-society interaction until recently. In international relations literature, much scholarly attention is devoted to the study of de jure compliance. The issue of de facto compliance remains the tricky part, but it is also what makes it the interesting part. Moreover, conventional wisdom holds that the study of IPR is strictly legal and therefore unrelated to the broader study of the political economy. However, I argue that the study of Chinese IPR policy goes beyond the IPR field and has significant theoretical and policy implications.

First, the study of Chinese IPR policy makes substantive contributions to the study of a developing country's compliance with international norms. As Cortell and Davis argued, two shortcomings in the extant literature on a domestic approach to international norm compliance should be redressed. First, insufficient attention has been devoted to the measurement of a norm's strength, legitimacy, or salience in a country's domestic political arena. Second, the mechanisms and processes by which international norms can or cannot attain domestic legitimacy remain underdeveloped.[23] Risse et al. also pointed out that "[a promising avenue for future research will be] to study those cases in which formal organizational structure and political culture do not simply reinforce each other, but where tensions between the two appear."[24] Instead of treating IPR as a monolithic set of norms, I demonstrate that they consist of multiple facets and therefore have multiple meanings to different actors. Instead of merely focusing on state actors, I demonstrate that the impact of societal actors is significant although not necessarily so obvious. My study also demonstrates that, instead of existing in a vacuum, the norm of IPR has to be welded with other types of existing ideologies to be internalized in the Chinese scenario. Those ideologies not only reverberate with the IPR norm but also compete with it under many circumstances. My fieldwork with ordinary citizens in China also illuminates the role of the public in a developing country's compliance with international norms. All of the above not only is relevant to IPR or China specifically but also adds to the general body of compliance literature.

Second, as an interdisciplinary study situated at the intersection of international relations and comparative politics, my project also adds to the comparative politics literature, particularly contemporary Chinese studies, by bringing into perspective an understudied policy area. As one of a small handful of political science studies of the Chinese IPR issue, my research demonstrates that Chinese IPR policy is more than just an economic or legal issue. Neither is it only a foreign policy issue. Instead, so many forces are at play during the making and implementation of IPR policy in China, both because of the complex nature of the Chinese political economy and because of the complex nature of the IPR norm itself. The study of Chinese IPR policy contributes to our understanding of some basic themes in comparative politics, such as the interaction between international and domestic politics, political and economic development, and the state-society relationship. Indeed, throughout my fieldwork, a significant number of findings were gathered from my conversations with people on the ground. My interviewees kept urging me to bear in mind the following important questions while studying the Chinese IPR issue: (1) Through the window of Chinese intellectual property rights policy, what can we infer about the achievements and limitations of China's reform and opening scheme starting from the late 1970s? (2) While domestic reform (*gaige*) and opening China to the outside (*kaifang*) are always juxtaposed with each other in Chinese official policy discourse, what is the relationship between the two?

(3) How does opening to the outside affect China's domestic reform and vice versa?[25] Moreover, during my interviews, a considerable number of Chinese professional elites pointed to the nonobvious link between the issue of IPR and the seemingly unrelated issue of China's political liberalization. In that sense, IPR provide an excellent window to view important themes in the study of international relations and comparative politics as the influence of international norms on domestic politics, the central-local relationship, the growth of civil society and its interaction with the authoritarian state in a transitional economy, and the establishment of rule of law in China, a country that does not have that kind of tradition historically. As far as I know, it is not until recent years that researchers started to explore that orientation, so my study adds a venue for new scholarship to grow.

The policy significance of the Chinese IPR issue is fairly straightforward: innovation constitutes the key aspect of a country's economic competitiveness. With an annual growth rate of 20 percent since 2001, China's total trade volume reached $4.17 trillion in 2013, becoming the world's largest trading power in goods and the second largest trading power in service (only next to the United States).[26] At the same time, however, China has continuously involved itself in trade disputes with the existing powers in the world trade system, mainly the United States. Both China and the United States agree that the issue of intellectual property rights is among the top three most controversial points in the bilateral trade relationship, with the other two being the exchange rate of Chinese currency and the excessive volume of the U.S. trade deficit with China.[27] It is also agreed that the issue of the trade deficit is closely related to intellectual property rights. In all the strategic and economic dialogues between China and the United States from 2006 to the present, the IPR issue has never missed a place on the negotiation agenda. As well, it can be safely predicted that this issue will continue to affect the fast-expanding U.S.-China bilateral trade in the foreseeable future.[28] Therefore, the policy relevance of IPR policy in China goes beyond the legal realm and extends well into other important areas, such as politics, trade, and economic development.

A comment by a Beijing-based IPR scholar aptly summarizes the implications of the IPR issues under study:

> U.S.-China IPR disputes should not only be understood as happening between a group of people debating with each other across the

negotiation table. Instead, that is part of the ongoing bilateral interaction between the world's biggest developed country and the world's biggest developing country, between the world's biggest democracy and one of the world's few remaining communist countries, and probably between the world's incumbent superpower and its ambitious possible successor. A thorough knowledge of that issue can deepen our understanding not only of Chinese and probably American political economy, but also the bilateral relationship between the two countries, which is bound to profoundly influence each other and, quite likely, the entire world.[29]

Chapter Layout

This book aims to unravel the complexities of how various state and societal actors in China compete and collaborate in shaping China's IPR policy. My introduction lays the theoretical foundation for this book with the comparative literature on IPR enforcement and presents the book's main theoretical claim. The six empirical chapters following the introduction are grouped into three parts, respectively addressing China's difficult journey to adopt and implement global patent, copyright, and trademark norms. It is noteworthy that, at least during the early stage of adoption, the Chinese government was a "strategic ratifier" rather than a "sincere ratifier."[30] That is, the Chinese government adopted IPR norms into its domestic legislation not for the sake of enhancing IPR protection but more because it wanted to avoid direct trade conflict with the United States in the early 1990s and to ameliorate its bid for WTO membership in the late 1990s. Thus, although Chinese IPR legislation had already reached the minimum standard set by the WTO during the country's entry in 2001, obstacles remained when it came to the implementation stage.

The first part, consisting of Chapters 1 and 2, focuses on patents, which mainly protect technological and industrial innovation. Chapter 1 examines the evolution of China's patent legislation while Chapter 2 examines the implementation of Chinese patent policy. Instead of rehashing Chinese patent law from one article to another, Chapter 1 examines how various domestic and foreign political/economic forces have led the country's patent regime to its present state. I demonstrate that there was already an incipient notion of protecting technological innovation in China even before the country started its market reform in the late 1970s. Although long suppressed by the dominance of socialist public ownership, Chinese patent legislation gained momentum in the early 1980s. The primary driving forces behind those moves were China's growing recognition of scientific invention and technological innovation as private property and the need to attract foreign investment and technological know-how. Using newly acquired empirical data, I demonstrate how China's expanding interests in foreign trade and international technological exchange helped to overcome the opposition from the antipatent camp in the Chinese government in the 1980s and the early 1990s. Marked by China's WTO entry in 2001, Chinese patent legislation came into full compliance with the global standard.

Rather than focusing on only the patent enforcement bureaucracy, Chapter 2 situates Chinese patent policy against the greater backdrop of Chinese science and technology policy. I argue that China's science and technology reform starting in the late 1970s has produced mixed results. On one hand, an incipient market mechanism was introduced to China's applied research sector; on the other hand, the legacy of the planned economy still continues to influence innovation activities in China. That contributes to different attitudes of Chinese societal actors: both foreign IPR holders investing in China and elite Chinese private companies sincerely adhere to the IPR norm since the norm upholds rewarding their innovation activities with market benefits. But state-owned companies are less enthusiastic about innovation because their profits are backed by the state. For the majority of small and medium-sized private companies that cannot afford to invest in expensive research and development activities, IPR is nothing more than a luxury for the big business players. The small and medium-sized enterprises constitute the majority of IPR violators. Therefore, it can be reasonably concluded that successful implementation of patent policy under some circumstances in China should be attributed not only to efficient coordination between various enforcement branches, as the existing literature argues, but also to IPR holders' active efforts to internalize IPR norms into the government's policy practice for the government to *willingly* enforce them.

Consisting of Chapters 3 and 4, the second part focuses on how China adopted and implemented international copyright norms. Chapter 3 argues that the Chinese copyright regime is embedded in the country's ideology and propaganda policy and is shaped by the combination of domestic demands and foreign pressure for copyright protection. After discussing the intense competition between the procopyright camp and the anticopyright camp within the Chinese government, I demonstrate how the former overcame the opposition of the latter, particularly during the 1990s, and convinced the Chinese top decision makers to integrate into the international copyright regime. I also demonstrate how external pressure hastened the steps of Chinese copyright legislation. That is, both bilateral pressure from the United States and multilateral pressure from the WTO reinforced the already existent, albeit not so powerful, domestic appeal for enhancing copyright protection. Toward the end of Chapter 4, I describe how China's gradually maturing copyright regime during the early twenty-first century witnessed the growing influence of the country's literary and artistic creators, an important part of China's burgeoning civil society.

Chapter 4 moves on to the implementation of Chinese copyright policy. As in the discussion of implementing Chinese patent policy, I do not examine the country's copyright policy in a vacuum. Instead, I put Chinese copyright policy within the greater landscape of the interaction between market reform and the evolving Chinese propaganda and ideology policy. Specifically, my findings suggest that, in making Chinese copyright policy, the Chinese government pursues multiple policy goals: the top priority is to ensure stability in the realm of ideology and cultural life in the country so as to create legitimacy for the rule of the Chinese Communist Party. The second priority is to generate economic benefits from literature and artistic creation as part of the broader scheme of building copyright industries in China. Protecting the economic and moral rights of literary and artistic creators only comes as the third priority. In practice, the first two goals, particularly the first one, often override the third goal. My findings also suggest that the development of the Chinese domestic copyright industry is constrained by the Chinese propaganda state despite three decades of market reform. Specifically, foreign and private capital are allowed only limited access to the production and distribution of copyrighted works in China; the censorship mechanism still shackles the creativity of Chinese copyright owners. Therefore, the Chinese copyright industry possesses neither sufficient financial resources nor legal experience to conduct antipiracy activities. In addition to the economic loss caused by copyright piracy and the challenges posed by the foreign copyright industry, Chinese copyright holders must work within the shackles imposed by the Chinese government. Last but not least, my findings suggest that the majority of the Chinese public does not possess a sufficient level of sympathy for the IPR norm despite the government's repeated advocacy campaigns. Except for some social elites, the majority of the Chinese mass public views the Chinese government's concession on IPR negotiations as betraying China's national interests; like some local officials, they tolerate or even praise IPR infringement as a patriotic act against what they call "foreign economic invasion." Copyright infringers in China not only benefit from an extremely high economic return from piracy but are also backed by consumers who have little sympathy for copyright laws. Only under some rare circumstances could the Chinese copyright bureaucracy win the support of the mass public and successfully enforce copyright norms.

Chapters 5 and 6 focus on the third subcategory of IPR norms—namely, trademark. Specifically, Chapter 5 unravels the close relationship between the evolution of the Chinese trademark regime and its gradual acceptance of the legitimacy of the market economy. I argue that the Chinese trademark holders can advance their agenda with the support of their sympathizers within the Chinese government even though China remains an authoritarian country. I also identify how the U.S.-China IPR negotiation in the 1990s and China's WTO entry negotiation in the late 1990s provided much-needed insights for the Chinese trademark professionals in revising the country's trademark legislation. This ideational change informed Chinese trademark legislation even though trademark was not a salient issue in the negotiation agenda with the developed countries.

Chapter 6 discusses the implementation of Chinese trademark policy. I found varying levels of sympathy for trademarks among different types of business actors in China: first, foreign companies and elite Chinese private companies strongly adhere to trademark protection as an important means of safeguarding their competitiveness. Second, although state-owned companies occupy important positions on the ranking of trademark values in China, the value of their brands lies in their state-sponsored profits rather than in market competition. Therefore, they merely pay lip service to the norm of trademark. Third, millions of small and medium-sized private enterprises are the major contributors to China's position as the world's leading manufacturing power, known as the "world's factory," but their manufactured goods are not independent brands. They either act as the processors of the products already designed by foreign trademark owners or rely on counterfeiting to take a free ride on the good name of established brands. I also trace the mechanism that contributes to the varying levels of trademark sympathy. My findings suggest that different business actors' attitudes toward trademark should be attributed to their differing strategies in building brand recognition and applying brands in their market competition. Although China has installed a complete set of quality control policies since the late 1970s, the policies have been implemented unevenly and resulted in different outcomes among different sets of Chinese business community: foreign enterprises and elite private enterprises comply with the quality control regulations to ensure the quality of their products, but most small and medium-sized private enterprises regard profits rather than quality as their first priority. Moreover, due to the immature nature of the Chinese market mechanism, Chinese domestic enterprises, with the exception of some elite ones, mainly rely on unfair market competition practice, such as price warfare or government connections, to gain consumer recognition. The above mechanism contributes to differentiated levels of brand value among different sets of business actors, which, in turn, contributes to their different attitudes toward trademark. Finally, Chinese consumers' attitudes toward trademark play a significant role as well: my findings suggest that, in purchasing branded products, most Chinese consumers care more about commodity price and quality rather than the authenticity of brands. Chinese consumers' indifference to trademark creates a market for counterfeit goods to grow and survive rounds of government-organized anticounterfeit campaigns.

My conclusion summarizes the theoretical argument and empirical findings. I also offer a series of policy recommendations. I situate my study in the broader context of the interaction between the global political economy and China's domestic political and economic reforms. The conclusion argues that the Chinese government does not enforce IPR just for the sake of it. Their real purpose is to promote the Chinese economy from the early industrialization stage, relying on cheap labor and natural resources, to a knowledge-based, innovative economy. The IPR norm does not enter a vacuum when it enters the country. Instead of following an IPR policy formulated by the central government in a concerted manner, various state and social actors have chosen parts of the IPR norm they consider useful to advance their own political and economic agendas. It is fair to say that there are various IPR policies, rather than one monolithic IPR policy, at work. The outcome of IPR policy implementation is dependent on whether a social consensus can be built to align the interests of different actors—namely, foreign business, domestic society, and the Chinese state. The more successfully that consensus is built, the better the IPR norm is complied with; the more conflicted the relationship among the three is, the less likely it is that the IPR norm will be implemented. As an unintended consequence, the compliance with IPR norms yields deeper implications that extend beyond the realm of IPR. Typically regarded as an important means for industrial upgrades, the growth of IPR in China has also awakened various societal actors' awareness of their own economic and moral rights of their intellectual creation. While the formation of social consensus is essential for high-quality IPR enforcement in the short run, the building of a mature market economy based on more thorough political reform is the essential means to combat IPR theft in China.

Methods and Fieldwork

Since this book emphasizes understanding an interpretive project—that is, how a Western-originated international norm has taken root in China—the data collected for this book are mostly qualitative. The empirical data in this book were gathered from multiple research trips across the Pacific Ocean between May 2007 and January 2014. When I was not in China, I maintained close contact with my interviewees. As my book project proceeded along, I updated the empirical data through emails, phone and Skype conversations, and online chats. Between 2007 and 2010, my field research was conducted in seven provinces or municipalities in China: Anhui, Beijing, Jiangsu, Shanghai, Guangdong, Fujian, and Hong Kong. After 2010, I expanded my fieldwork sites to two inland provinces in China: Shaanxi and Henan.

The fieldwork sites were not randomly chosen. My fieldwork sites covered major geographical regions of China. They varied from the affluent coastal provinces and municipalities (Guangdong, Jiangsu, Shanghai, and Fujian) to the less affluent inland provinces (Anhui, Henan, and Shaanxi), from Beijing, the Chinese capital right "under the emperor's feet," to Hong Kong, the Special Administrative Region (SAR) that is still heavily influenced by its British colonial legacy. This large and heterogeneous sample enables me to develop a comprehensive general picture of the making and implementation of Chinese IPR policy that represents the national pattern. In my original research design, I planned to examine regional variation of support for piracy and counterfeiting and variation by type of products and industry. Findings from my field research, however, demonstrate a much more sophisticated situation. That is, even in the more economically affluent provinces, IPR enforcement can be rendered less effective if the enforcement bureaucracy cannot successfully cooperate with the IPR holders.[31] Even in the less economically affluent provinces, IPR enforcement can reap an effective outcome if the local state can be persuaded that protecting IPR is in their interests.[32]

The empirical data gathered from fieldwork consist of three major components: interviews, archival research, and participant observations. To determine the attitudes of people with different relationships with IPR, I conducted 152 in-depth interviews during my fieldwork trips, including 99 formal interviews and 53 informal ones. Covering all administrative levels of China, the formal interviews were conducted with government officials ranging from one former vice chair of the Chinese National People's Congress and three ministerial-level officials involved in the top Chinese IPR policy, circling all the way down to village-level officials, IPR lawyers and judges, domestic and foreign business professionals, and IPR scholars associated with Chinese think tanks and major universities. Ranging from thirty minutes to two hours, my formal interviews mostly took place in the offices of my interviewees. Some of them were conducted at the dinner table, a place where many Chinese people discuss business matters. I interviewed people with a variety of occupations, including twenty-six interviews with IPR officials at different levels, twenty-nine with domestic and foreign business professionals, nineteen with IPR lawyers and judges, and twenty-five with IPR scholars.

During the early stage of my research, I approached my interviewees through personal connections. As I developed a deeper knowledge of Chinse IPR affairs and my research progressed, I managed to develop my own professional network in the Chinese IPR circle and approached my interviewees by attending academic conferences and government/business meetings. I also started to be more "picky" with my interviewees, based on the level of their expertise and the willingness to share their information. For most of the interviews, I started with a set of general questions, but many interviewees ended up leading the conversation toward the directions that interested them most. That often resulted in unexpected findings that helped me to overcome the selection biases that I originally had. As my research moved on, those interviews with unexpected findings often proved to be most helpful and thus are more frequently quoted in the book chapters to follow. Not all my interviewees welcomed me. Some bluntly asked me, "Are you going to be pro-China or pro-U.S. in your book?" when they encountered what they considered to be thorny questions. Some rejected my interview requests rudely on the phone. Some even questioned the necessity to conduct research on Chinese IPR policy.[33] While not all my interviews succeeded in producing ideal outcomes, the negative interview experiences helped me to get a more complete picture of Chinese IPR policy at the grassroots level and supported my theoretical argument from a different angle.

While formal interviews are important sources for this study, informal interviews play an indispensable role in supplying necessary information. I conducted informal interviews with sellers and buyers of counterfeit/pirated goods, most of whom occupy much lower social positions than the IPR professionals mentioned above. While most of the informal interviews happened in urban areas such as Beijing, Shanghai, and Nanjing, most of the interviewees were migrant workers from inland provinces such as Anhui and Henan. Unlike my formal interviews, the informal interviews were conducted on the street, in stores selling counterfeit and pirated goods, and in basement apartments rented by peasant workers. As a native of East China's Anhui Province, I conducted informal interviews in the local dialect. This proved to be an effective tool to shorten the distance between the interviewees and me as the interviewer. That is, I detected a higher level of trust from street peddlers who were from the same home province but met in a distant urban area such as Beijing and Shanghai. This made them more candid in relating to me their experiences in selling pirated and counterfeit goods. Under those informal circumstances, I could get information that my interviewees would otherwise not divulge on formal occasions.

My fieldwork did not isolate interviews from archival research and participant observations. Instead, they were often combined for the purpose of making better sense of the data acquired. During my fieldwork, I accumulated over 1,000 IPR-related journalistic reports, yearbook articles, leadership speeches, and Chinese government newsletters, some of which were for internal circulation only. Most of those documents were published between 1990 and 2014, with some published in the 1980s or even the 1950s. Admittedly, the Chinese media are still controlled by the government, so many of the reports are filled with bureaucratic jargon, and in many cases, the information is purposefully distorted. I mainly employed the following cross-examination methods to excavate useful information from the bureaucratic jargon. First, at the end of many interviews, my interviewees helped me "read between the lines" to cross-examine the archival documents that I had collected. On the other hand, the archival data also helped me verify the validity, or the lack thereof, of the information gathered from my interviews. Second, consciously aware of the sources of the journalistic reports, I compared and contrasted the information published by different media outlets. For example, the IPR reports from *People's Daily*, the mouthpiece of the Chinese Communist Party (CCP) Central Committee, represents the stance of the Chinese Central Government and State Council. Checking that newspaper with the publications of the various ministries in Beijing, the various provinces, cities, or even counties at the local level and the various domestic and foreign business organizations operating in China, I was able to identify important differences in the attitudes toward IPR held by the Chinese central government and the local government branches. That process of cross-examination was very exhausting, time-consuming, and often frustrating, but it turned out to be an extremely rewarding learning experience.

In August 2007, I participated in several meetings between IPR enforcement officials and several patrons of counterfeiters in a town in N Province during the postraid period.[34] In July 2008, I participated in an anticounterfeit raid conducted in Jiangsu Province. These opportunities made me aware of the political and economic dynamics hindering the implementation of IPR policy at the local government level. Moreover, in the fall of 2007, I had the opportunity to share a basement apartment in Beijing with several street peddlers. During the three weeks of living with them, I observed the workings of a significant portion of the underground pirated/counterfeit goods market: the buying and selling of pirated/counterfeit goods, the cat-and-mouse game between street peddlers and law enforcement officials, and part of the distribution network of pirated/counterfeit goods. After that, I maintained contact with them and visited them for further interviews during the follow-up research trips. As far as I know, this level of access for researchers on Chinese IPR issues, from China's top-level officials to street peddlers selling pirated and counterfeit goods, is very rare.

CHAPTER 1

The Political Economy of Chinese Patent Legislation

Introduction: A Challenging Patent Case and the Adoption of the Chinese Patent Law in the Early 1980s

December 11, 2001, was an important day for the Chinese intellectual property rights (IPR) circle. On that day, China formally acceded to the World Trade Organization (WTO) after fifteen years of painstaking negotiations.[1] As an important part of China's WTO entry negotiations, China signed the Trade-Related Aspects of Intellectual Property Rights (TRIPS) Agreement. That move marked China's de jure compliance with the international IPR regime. Like other issue areas, China reached agreement on IPR after rounds of bitter bargaining. This chapter analyzes the compromises, competition, and controversies among various domestic and foreign interest groups surrounding China's de jure compliance with the international patent norm.

To help understand the convoluted decision-making process that culminated in China's adoption of the IPR norm, I interviewed Ms. Mei, a senior legal adviser at the Chinese State Intellectual Property Office (SIPO). One of the main goals of my interview was to figure out why China decided to adopt an international norm that it had once rejected. In answering my question, Ms. Mei began by explaining a challenging case that she encountered during an early stage of her career. In the late 1970s, a leading bicycle producer in North China's Tianjin Municipality exported folding bicycles to a Southeast Asian country. This type of bicycle had a good reputation among the consumers in that country. However, in 1980, the Chinese bicycle company noticed that some factories in that Southeast Asian country were copying the company's folding bicycles. When the Chinese company complained to that country's government, they got the following reply: "Your home country does not have a patent law to protect the technology to make the folding bicycle. Why should we protect it in our own country?" The case was reported to the newly established Chinese State Patent Bureau (SPB) in Beijing, the predecessor of the Chinese State Intellectual Property Office, where Ms. Mei served as a junior patent agent. Ms. Mei reported the case to the senior leaders of the SPB. The case further reminded Chinese senior decision makers of the imperativeness of adopting a patent law in China.[2]

China eventually has established a sophisticated patent regime over the past three decades. China also joined a series of international IPR agreements. Despite having many critics, it is generally agreed that the standard of patent protection outlined in China's patent legislation has met the minimum level required by international IPR agreements. At the same time, Ms. Mei advanced from being a junior staff member at the State Patent Bureau to one of the leading IPR experts in China. Shortly after Ms. Mei retired in 2009, I spoke with her on the phone. Recalling the aforementioned case in the early stage of her career, she told me,

> [The case that I mentioned two years ago] was the first, but certainly not the last, challenging case that I encountered during my career. It is not pleasant to encounter these embarrassments. But isn't it also a great growing experience to handle those cases? When I look back at my years in the IPR field, I should probably thank those challenging experiences. Through those experiences, I grew from an inexperienced junior IPR staff to a seasoned IPR professional. China's IPR regime grew from scratch to a sophisticated legal setup. More importantly, China grew from a backward autarkic economy to a vibrant open market economy.[3]

This chapter discusses the "growing experience," in Ms. Mei's words, of China's patent regime. A lot of previous scholarship on Chinese patent law has focused on how those legal provisions impacted the rights of various types of patent holders and the practice of patent litigation in the country.[4] Built on the previous scholarship, my analysis will further analyze how China's evolving political and economic situation shaped the country's patent legislation process in the past decades. This chapter makes the following claims: first, although conventional wisdom holds the adoption of IPR legislation as the result of a decision made at the level of the Chinese central government, the decision-making process was by no means a monolithic one. Different interest groups competed and compromised to influence different parts of Chinese patent legislation. Other than the domestic needs for an IPR regime, foreign influence also has a very important role in shaping the present IPR system in China. There had been an incipient IPR regime in China before foreign pressure was keenly felt, but foreign pressure sped the pace of Chinese IPR regime's merging into the international track from the 1990s on. Second, instead of being a monolithic norm, the IPR legal construct is torn between two aspects: one is to protect IPR; the other is to prevent the abuse of IPR as a weapon against potential business competitors. The realities in China, compounded by the inherent contradiction within the IPR norm itself, make the norm more controversial in the country, even during the adoption stage. Third, during the spread of the IPR norm in China, the norm met strong resistance from different socioeconomic forces in China. Domestic resistance against the IPR norm has never ceased to counteract the influence of the pro-IPR interest groups, even several years after China's accession to the TRIPS Agreement. The adoption stage marked China's strategic compliance with international IPR norms. It constitutes the first step of IPR protection, but it is still a large distance from strategic compliance to the complete internalization of IPR norms. This chapter demonstrates that even this first step was accomplished with much painstaking effort.

This chapter is structured as follows: the first section gives a definition of the patent norm and discusses the two legs of the patent norm. The following four sections analyze four major periods of the history of Chinese patent legislation: the prereform era (1949–1978), the early reform era (1978–1990), the pre-WTO era (1990–2001), and the post-WTO era (2001–present). Although the evolution of the Chinese IPR regime is mainly reflected in the adoption of patent laws and the changing of specific legal provisions, the key task for researchers is to understand how the debates between numerous domestic and foreign interest groups have shaped the patent legislation as reflected on paper. Equally, if not more, important is to tease out how the evolution of China's patent regime reflected the different stages of the ongoing market reform and how deeper integration into the global political economy influenced the evolution of the country's patent regime. The conclusion section links back the empirical materials presented in this chapter to the book's central argument by summarizing how competition among different interest groups influenced the evolution of the Chinese patent regime.

Patent Norm and Its Two Legs

A patent is a time-limited, exclusive right that is granted for an invention. As the TRIPS Agreement states, "Patents shall be available for any inventions, whether products or processes, in all fields of technology, provided that they are new, involve an inventive step and are capable of industrial application."[5]

Patent protection is usually related to technology-intensive innovation and provides inventors with the right of exclusion from the use, production, sales, or import of the product or technology in question. Once a patent expires, the invention enters the public domain. Arguments in favor of patent protection are often centered on the various incentives that patents create for innovative activity.

There are two important aspects of the IPR norm: rewarding human creativity, on one hand, and promoting general social welfare, on the other hand. The two aspects are closely related to each other, but they have also competed with each other for centuries.[6] In fact, because the object of IPR legislation—the output of intellectual creation—is extremely fluid compared to other types of private property such as land, real estate, or monetary income, any patent legislation is perpetually confronted with the task of balancing private rewards for intellectual creation and public benefits. An enormous legal literature points toward the delicate but important relationship between these two legs of the IPR regime.[7]

As a reflection of that relationship, the contemporary IPR regime consists of two legs: one is to protect IPR and the other is to prevent the abuse of IPR as a weapon against potential competitors. Without these two equally strong legs, the IPR legal construct cannot stand steadily.[8] The IPR legal construct in most countries bears the task of regulating the relationship between state, business (including the IPR holder as well as the infringers), and the public that consumes IPR products. Specifically, a full-fledged IPR law has to address the following questions: What kind of intellectual output shall be protected as IPR? What is the boundary between the privatization of intellectual output and fair use of IPR by the general public? What constitutes infringement of IPR? Who is responsible for protecting IPR from possible infringement? How should legal remedies be made in case of IPR infringement?

This general trend also applies to patents. In the past decades, the global diffusion of the patent norm met as much applause as resistance from different socioeconomic forces in different countries. Some praise patents as an effective means of promoting technological innovation. Others criticize contemporary patent legal arrangements as tools to exploit the material wealth of the developing countries.[9] As discussed in the following sections, the journey of the patent norm in China has never been smooth because of both the inherent contradiction within the norm itself and China's specific domestic socioeconomic context.

Chinese Patent Regime During the Mao Era, 1949–1976

This section examines how the dominant ideology during the Mao era impacted China's patent regime. I contend that there was an incipient patent regime during the early period of the People's Republic. However, the dominance of socialist public ownership contradicted the notion of protecting technological innovation as private property. That contradiction rendered China's incipient patent regime largely ineffective.

Policy and Ideological Environment During the Mao Era: "March Towards Science and Technology"

Although the majority of the Chinese Communist Party (CCP) members were workers and peasants during the revolutionary era before 1949, the Party's top leaders were fully aware of the importance of science and technology professionals. In December 1939, for example, the CCP top leader Mao Zedong drafted the Decision on Recruiting Intellectuals at Mass Scale. In that document, he posited that "the Communist Party should recruit intellectuals in order to organize a great revolutionary force. . . . Our revolution is unlikely to succeed without the participation of intellectuals."[10] Under that initiative, the CCP recruited a significant number of technological professionals specializing in ammunition production, communication technology, and medical treatment. In some CCP-controlled areas, the government designed some regulations to provide material rewards for technological innovation in the 1940s.[11]

After the CCP came into power in 1949, the Party continued to uphold the importance of science and technology in numerous leadership speeches. For example, then Chinese top leader Mao Zedong pointed out in a speech that "we have to fight the battle of science and technology. We have no other choice but to win that battle."[12] During the first National Conference on the Issue of Intellectuals, the Chinese Communist Party further called upon the entire nation to "march towards science and technology" (*xiang kexue jishu jingjun*).[13]

The development of China's science and technology during the early period of the Mao era did not stop with those exciting slogans. In 1949, there were fewer than 40 scientific research institutes and fewer than 50,000 technological professionals in China. In 1965, however, China boasted 2.46 million science and technology professionals and 1,714 professional scientific research institutes.[14] Starting from scratch, China built a science and technology system that encompassed such key fields as material science, geology, communication, metallurgy, and chemical engineering.

However, the development of Chinese science and technology in the 1950s and 1960s was guided under a Soviet model. Under that model, protecting the result of technological innovation as private property was diametrically opposed to the notion of socialist public ownership. The products of intellectual invention or creation belonged to all members of the larger society rather than the individual creators. A Beijing-based IPR scholar made a thorough analysis of the prevalent ideology governing Chinese science and technology sector in the 1950s:

> Did you notice a common feature of the blood-burning slogans cited by the Chinese top leaders [during the Mao era]? Be it "Fight the battle of science and technology" or "March towards science and technology," there was a military connotation in these slogans. This means that the Chinese top leaders still regarded technological innovation as a cause similar to their revolutionary enterprise. They just won a revolution. They were so familiar with and so good at revolutionary mobilization. Is there a place for individual benefits in a revolutionary army? Of course not! However, the point is that science and technology professionals were different from revolutionary soldiers. It took the Chinese people quite some time to realize that.[15]

According to the recollection of an electrical engineer,

> When Mao Zedong called upon the Chinese people to "march towards science and technology," I was a college student. At that time I felt as if my blood was burning. Our country had been poverty stricken for so many years. I was willing to sacrifice anything to make our country stronger. The claim of individual benefits should be considered a shame for many of us. We were educated that we should attribute any personal achievement to the great Party and the great leader.[16]

Under that policy environment, protecting technological innovation as private property was heretical in the eyes of the Chinese decision makers. That inevitably impacted Chinese patent legislation in the Mao era.

The Rise and Fall of an Incipient Patent System in China, 1949–1976

Throughout my field research on the Chinese patent regime during the Mao era, I did not encounter much historical record of the debates and controversies about the adoption of those legal arrangements. An analyst at the SIPO offered me a reasonable explanation: "It came as little surprise to me that there were hardly any debates during the adoption of patent laws in the early years of the People's Republic. That is not because everybody agreed to protect technological innovation as patents. Instead, that is because the issue of patent was too trivial to arouse any debates during the Mao era."[17] The analyst's claim is well supported by the evidence from the legal texts of Chinese patent regulations in the Mao era.

Months after the establishment of the People's Republic, the Chinese government adopted the Provisional Regulations on the Protection of Patent Rights adopted in 1950, known as the 1950 Provisional Regulations (*Baozhang Faming Quan yu Zhuanli Quan Zanxing Tiaoli*).[18]

However, a close reading of the 1950 Provisional Regulations reveals a deeply rooted contradiction. First, the crux of the 1950 Provisional Regulations was that patent rights were not protected as the private property of the inventor. Although the 1950 Provisional Regulations granted both proprietary patent rights and nonproprietary financial rights (Articles 6 and 7), Article 8 provided that the invention right (*faming quan*) is only granted if the inventor works with a factory, minefield, scientific research organ, or other research institute. Since these branches handled the majority of scientific research activities in China during the 1950s, invention rights took a de facto precedence over patent rights, although they were given equal weight on paper.

Second, Article 14 provided that "if the central government principal organ deems it necessary for inventions or patent to be transferred to the State for the latter to use and manage, it may ask patent right to be transferred to the state upon consultation with the patent holder."

Under that article, the already vulnerable patent right was subject to the state's seizure if the latter deemed it necessary. Last but not least, Section 3 of Article 7 provided that "others shall not utilize the invention without the authorization of the patent holder; those who break the law shall compensate the patent holder's loss." Article 12 further specified five situations under which patent infringers shall be subject to civil or criminal punishment. However, the following important aspects were not provided: (1) how the patent holder's economic loss should be calculated and (2) who is responsible for enforcing the law in cases where patent infringement happens.

With those inherent defects, the 1950 Provisional Regulations were seldom used. Before the 1950 Provisional Regulations were replaced by the Provisional Regulations on Awards for Inventions, Technical Improvements, and Rationalization Proposals Relating to Production in 1954,[19] known as the 1954 Regulations, only four patents and six invention certificates were approved. In fact, all the four patents were granted in 1953.[20] In that sense, the 1950 Provisional Regulations hardly functioned during their short life span.

In 1963, China issued the Regulations on Invention Awards (*Faming Jiangli Tiaoli*) and Technological Improvement Awards (*Jishu Gaijing Jiangli Tiaoli*), also known as the 1963 Regulations, to replace the 1954 Regulations.[21] By then, China had already established a full-fledged planned economy model dominated by socialist public ownership. The notion of granting property rights to individual inventors was ideologically inconsistent with the predominant socialist ideology at that time. As the title of the 1963 Regulations revealed, the term "patent" was replaced by "invention" and "technological improvements." Inventors were deprived of their patent rights to the invention. The key provision in the 1963 Regulations regarding ownership of the invention is laid out in Article 23: "All inventions are the property of the state, and no person or unit may claim monopoly over them. All units throughout the country, including collectively owned units, may make use of the invention essential to them."

Section 4 of both the 1963 Invention Regulations and 1963 Technological Innovation Regulations implemented a system of nonproprietary monetary awards for scientific inventions. However, in practice, the financial reward warranted by those two regulations did not materialize. According to the memoir of Wu Heng, then vice director of the Chinese State Science and Technology Commission, "During the over 2 years between 1963 and early 1966, the year when the Cultural Revolution broke out, 296 invention certificates were issued by State Science and Technology Commission. However, we neither awarded prize nor convened a national-level conference, except that we mailed invention certificates and medals to the inventors. Our country's first prize-awarding conference for scientific invention never materialized as we planned."[22]

The 1963 Regulations were already a serious step backward on patent protection. The deadliest blow to China's incipient patent regime came from the Cultural Revolution. The Cultural Revolution, a nationwide turmoil caused by internal strife within the Chinese top leadership, broke out in 1966 and plagued China until 1976. During the ten years of turmoil, radically hardline ideology dominated the country's legal and economic activities while the country's formal legal system and most government administrative agencies were completely disintegrated.

The Cultural Revolution exerted a disastrous impact on China's incipient patent regime. In the realm of science and technology, even the system of nonproprietary invention certificates and monetary rewards was terminated. Chinese science and technology professionals were regarded as part of the "bourgeoisie class" and therefore the target of mass criticism. They were even ridiculed as "the stinking ninth class" (*chou lao jiu*). Tens of thousands of scientists and technicians were forced into heavy physical labor. Recognition and reward of intellectual creation was regarded as completely opposed to the country's governing ideology.

Although the Chinese patent regime during the Mao era barely played a meaningful role in promoting the country's intellectual creation, later generations of scholars still praised them as heralding the development of the IPR regime in the reform era, which started during the late 1970s.[23] At least it was established as an appropriate notion that scientific invention should be rewarded. When China started to introduce reform and the opening policy in the late 1970s, the country's patent regime gained the opportunity to reestablish itself.

Chinese Patent Regime During the Early Reform Era, 1978–1990

This section argues that the introduction of reform and opening in the late 1970s gave rise to a set of new social and economic groups calling for patent protection. These factors constituted the key driving force for China's reemerging patent regime in the 1980s. However, the still weak voice of the propatent group contributed to some important limitations of Chinese patent legislation in the early 1980s. Starting from the policy and ideology environment in the early 1980s, I discuss how the changing ideology in China shaped the legal arrangements of the first Chinese patent law adopted in 1984.

Policy and Ideology Environment in the Early 1980s: The Advent of "Spring of Science"

The late 1970s and early 1980s marked the beginning of China's market reform. It is within this context that a patent law was adopted. I contend that while the major driving forces behind Chinese patent legislation came mainly from the domestic front, interaction with the outside world played an indispensable role in the adoption of the country's first patent law. Specifically, on the domestic front, the improvement of the social status of Chinese science and technology professionals constituted the soil within which the Chinese patent regime began to reemerge. The recognition of the legitimacy of the market mechanisms further promoted the legitimacy of the desire of Chinese science and technology professionals' claims of owning their intellectual creation. On the international front, China's opening to the outside world not only attracted a considerable amount of foreign capital but also exposed the country to the internationally prevalent practice in patent affairs.

An important indicator of the improved social status of the Chinese science and technology professionals was Deng Xiaoping's speech at the 1978 National Science and Technology Conference. At that conference, Deng Xiaoping denounced the once prevalent notion that Chinese scientists and technology personnel were part of the "bourgeoisie class." Deng Xiaoping boosted the role of science and technology as the key to China's economic modernization campaign. He further added that "[the Communist Party] should provide logistic support to the scientists and technology personnel and create necessary conditions for them."[24] Deng Xiaoping's 1978 speech received a warm welcome from the long-suppressed Chinese scientists and technology personnel. At the same conference, Guo Moruo, then president of Chinese Academy of Science, announced that "the spring of science is coming!"[25] From then on, the respect for knowledge and knowledgeable talents gradually became a prevalent norm in China.

The improvement of the social and political status of Chinese scientists and technology personnel was but the first step. In the early 1980s, China's reform-minded leaders increasingly recognized that command planning and excessive public ownership seriously impeded China's economic development. Under Deng Xiaoping's reform scheme, private ownership, previously regarded as associated with capitalism and therefore incompatible with the socialist value, gained legitimacy in Chinese society and was allowed to coexist with public ownership. In a meeting with a foreign delegation in 1979, for example, Deng Xiaoping made the following statement: "[Some comrades hold that] market mechanism only exists in capitalist society. This is certainly not right. Why cannot socialist countries practice market economy as well? You cannot call that capitalism. Our country mainly relies on socialist public ownership, but we should incorporate market mechanism, too. That is called 'socialist market economy.'"[26]

Although Chinese decision makers still regarded the private economy as a complement to the Chinese state-owned economy, Deng Xiaoping's statement represented a significant departure from the dominant ideology of excessive public ownership during the prereform era.

The Chinese top leadership's recognition of the legitimacy of private ownership was not translated into state policy until much later. However, even the rumor about that progress stirred an exciting reaction among Chinese intellectuals. According to the recollection of the aforementioned electrical engineer, "When I first heard the news [about recognizing the legitimacy of private ownership], I could not believe my ears. If an entrepreneur can own his own enterprise, can an engineer own his own invention? That sounded insane to me at first. I was really excited [to hear that], but years of past experience reminded me that I should be cautious. It was just rumor, not state policy."[27]

Another important wing of China's economic modernization campaign was the end of the autarkic economy and the opening to the outside world. In 1980, a Hong Kong company established the first China-foreign joint venture, Beijing Aviation Food, Inc., in Beijing, which marked the beginning of a huge inflow of foreign direct investment (FDI) in China.[28] Throughout the 1980s, the total amount of FDI inflow in China reached $16.19 billion.[29] This pushed the Chinese government to adopt a series of laws protecting and promoting foreign investment. For example, in 1986, China promulgated the Law of the People's Republic of China Concerning Enterprises Operated Exclusively with Foreign Capital. Article 5 further provides that "except under special circumstances . . . the state shall not nationalize or expropriate a wholly-owned foreign enterprise. Should it prove necessary to do so in the public interest, legal procedures will be followed and reasonable compensation will be made."[30]

China's open door strategy was not limited to attracting foreign investment. Equally important was the exchange of professional patent personnel between China and foreign countries. Before Deng Xiaoping came into power in 1978, China had its first interaction with the World Intellectual Property Organization (WIPO). In 1973, China sent a small delegation as observers of WIPO's conference in Geneva.[31] After the conference, Ren Jianxin, the head of that delegation, stressed the necessity of reestablishing China's almost nonexistent IPR system in a report submitted to then Chinese premier Zhou Enlai.[32] The end of the Cultural Revolution and the start of Chinese economic reform added momentum to China's interaction with WIPO. In 1979, the general secretary of WIPO, Arpad Bogsch, visited China for the first time. During the visit, Arpad Bogsch discussed the possibility of adopting a patent system in China with Wu Heng, then vice director of the Chinese State Science and Technology Commission. In 1980, China formally joined WIPO.[33] At the same time, China also sent delegations to various foreign countries to study the operation of their patent system between 1978 and 1980. Those countries included not only developed countries, such as the United States, Japan, and West Germany, but also developing and then Communist countries, such as Brazil, Romania, and the former Yugoslavia.[34] The exposure to the practice of peer countries' patent laws helped Chinese decision makers acquire much-needed firsthand knowledge before drafting the first patent law in China.

In a nutshell, Chinese political and economic development irreversibly stepped onto the road to reform and opening, beginning in the late 1970s.

The reintroduction of private property rights in the country's economic functioning and the opening to the outside world have inevitably shaped the reemergence of China's IPR regime in the early reform period. Unlike the prereform era, however, Chinese IPR legislation efforts sparked deep controversies among various interest groups in China during the 1980s.

The Drafting of the 1984 Patent Law

China started drafting its first patent law in 1978 and adopted that law in 1984. Mertha gave a thorough discussion of the debates and controversies in the drafting process, particularly the debates among the leaders of the relevant administrative offices at the first several high-level meetings in 1980. Thorough as Mertha's discussion is, I would add some new findings based on more recently declassified documents, particularly how the voice of the emerging economic groups, such as China's rising export sector, impacted decision makers at the top level.

In 1978, China resurrected the 1963 Invention Regulations. Although that move was regarded as a first step back toward recognition of industrial property rights, the exclusive right to patent was still not recognized. It was still widely believed that granting property rights to scientists and inventors contradicted the underlying principle of socialism. With the introduction of reform and opening policy, Chinese senior leaders decided that a patent system was necessary to speed up scientific development.

In 1979, a group of scholars and officials convened to draft China's first patent law. However, after the drafted version of the patent law was completed, certain ministries voiced skepticism and even opposition to the adoption of a patent law in China. On August 25, 1980, a vice-ministerial official with the Ministry of Machinery Industry wrote a letter to the top Chinese leader, Deng Xiaoping, expressing strong opposition to the enactment of patent law.[35] During several high-level meetings in and after October 1980, those opposition opinions had gained direct access to vice premier of the Chinese State Council, Fang Yi. The opposition opinions centered on the following points: first, the monopoly rights granted to the patent holders went against socialist norms of ownership and production. Second, a patent system would end up only protecting foreign interests during a time when foreign technology led a dominant advantage over Chinese domestic technology. Third, the adoption of a patent law in China would endanger the country's "economic security," particularly with regard to the chemical and pharmaceutical industry.[36]

The propatent opinion prevailed in those meetings after hot debates. On March 7, 1981, the State Science and Technology Commission and the State Patent Bureau submitted the Report on the Patent Law of People's Republic of China to the Chinese State Council.[37] The report recommended that the Chinese legislature adopt the patent law by the end of 1981. When the report was circulated among the different ministries for further discussion, it became bogged down at the Ministry of Machinery again.

This time, the Ministry of Machinery did not oppose the adoption of a patent law. Instead, the ministry put forward over seventy revision suggestions to the draft patent law. Many suggestions touched on fundamental principles of the draft patent law. For example, the draft patent law outlined different kinds of penalties against patent infringement. But the revision suggestions recommended a much lower level of penalty against patent infringement as outlined in the draft patent law. Moreover, the revision suggestions also recommended a much weaker stipulation of the exclusive rights of patent holders on the grounds that it went against the basic principle of socialist public ownership. If those suggestions had been incorporated, the patent law would have been left with only an empty frame.[38]

These opinions stopped the draft patent law from being submitted to the Chinese State Council for further review. Since the Ministry of Machinery possessed the same bureaucratic ranking as the State Science and Technology Commission (SSTC) and the SPB, the SSTC and the SPB could not overcome the resistance of its own bureaucratic mandate. Luckily for the propatent officials, a series of events that happened during China's trade and technology exchange with foreign countries provided the momentum for them in 1981 and 1982. In 1981, for example, a pesticide company in Shanghai copied the technology of a French company and produced an insect killer called phosethyl-al. When it advertised the "new" product, the French company, the French Embassy in Beijing, and the French National Institute of Industrial Property protested against the Chinese side. Eventually, the pesticide company in Shanghai had to stop the production of phosethyl-al. This resulted in a heavy economic loss for the Chinese company. There are no accurate statistical data about how many China-foreign trade disputes were caused by the absence of a patent law in China at that time. For the propatent officials in China, however, the key issue was that the reports of those disputes attracted the attention of the Chinese top leaders. Wu Heng, then director of the Chinese SPB, collected a series of similar trade disputes in a report and submitted the report to Chinese top leaders, including Vice Premiers Wan Li and Gu Mu, Premier Zhao Ziyang, and Communist Party General Secretary Hu Yaobang.[39]

Similar things happened in China's deepened technology exchange with foreign countries. In 1981, for example, a Chinese engineer affiliated with Northern China's Taiyuan Polytechnic Institute invented a new means to produce alloy with mild steel, tungsten, and molybdenum when he was a visiting scholar in the United States. Applying that method at a massive scale in the Chinese metallurgy industry, energy and precious metals would produce significant savings, and the strength of the newly made alloy would be greatly improved. An American professor, who happened to be the collaborator of the Chinese engineer during his visit, identified the value of that technology and proposed they apply for a patent together with his Chinese colleague in the United States. Unfortunately, there were no legal arrangements in China to guide the Chinese engineer to apply for a patent and protect the technology. In fact, nobody in the Taiyuan Polytechnic Institute even thought about the issue in that way. Hence, the Chinese side did not receive any benefit from the technological innovation. A senior correspondent with *Guangming Daily*, China's second largest newspaper, learned of that case and wrote a detailed report. Like the report on the aforementioned trade dispute cases, that report made its way into the internal government news sources (*neibu cankao ziliao*) and was circulated among Chinese senior leaders. That report attracted the attention of Hu Qili, then a member of the Chinese Communist Party Politburo. He commented on the report, "The adoption of a patent law is an imperative task for us. At least we should have a framework to protect our scientific inventions."[40]

After the first director of the Chinese SPB, Wu Heng, retired in spring 1982, his successor, Huang Kunyi, kept pushing for the adoption of the patent law.[41] This time, the propatent voices gained the endorsement of the Chinese top leaders. In December 1982, the Chinese National People's Congress approved the Report on the Sixth Five-Year Plan on National Economic and Social Development, drafted by then Chinese premier, Zhao Ziyang.[42] The report posited that "those regulations that prevent the progress and technology should be abolished. A patent law should be adopted and implemented [in the next five years]."

On January 5, 1983, Chinese state councilor, Bo Yibo, told journalists that "[recently the leaders of the State Council] approved the establishment of a patent system. That is a great thing indeed. Our past experience suggested that there should be legislation to govern the realm of science and technology. Once there is such legislation, we should implement the law seriously."[43] The fact that Bo Yibo participated in the drafting of the 1950, 1954, and 1963 Regulations added weight to his comment.

The endorsement from the Chinese top leadership helped the propatent camp overcome resistance from the antipatent camp. Since the propatent voice came from leaders with higher ranking, the leaders of the Ministry of Machinery told Huang Kunyi and his colleagues that they would no longer raise any objections to a patent law.[44] On September 29, 1983, the draft patent law, which had been bogged down for almost two years, was eventually submitted to the Chinese National People's Congress for the final review. On March 12, 1984, the Standing Committee of the National People's Congress (NPC) adopted China's first patent law, which went into effect on April 1, 1985.

Different from the characteristically brief 1950 Regulations, 1954 Regulations, and 1963 Regulations, the 1984 patent law consisted of sixty-nine articles that covered requirements for the granting of patent rights (Articles 22–25), procedure for application for patent rights (Articles 26–33), process to review patent applications (Articles 34–50), balance of interests in the process of applying for patents (Articles 51–58), and the protection of patent rights (Articles 59–66).[45]

The adoption of the first patent law in China turned out to be a big festival for Chinese science and technology professionals. The State Patent Bureau received 3,455 applications on April 1, 1985, the first day that the SPB started to accept patent applications. According to WIPO, this was a record high compared with patent organizations in other countries.[46] For the rest of 1985, the SPB received a total of 14,372 patent applications. In 1986, the SPB handled the first patent dispute case in China. During the 1980s, the total number of patent applications in China grew at an annual rate of 18.3 percent.[47] The adoption of patent law provided a vital driving force for China's economic development. This was recognized by the former critics of patent law. In December 1989, a former leader of the Ministry of Machinery met one of the original drafters of Chinese patent law. He finally admitted that adopting a patent law in China was "the right thing to do."[48]

Despite these big steps forward, the 1984 Chinese patent law still bore the influence of socioeconomic conditions during the early reform period. The 1984 Chinese patent law was different from patent laws in developed countries, which had been in place for at least a century. These differences are mainly represented as follows.

First, the duration of invention patents in China was fifteen years,[49] as opposed to twenty years in most developed countries. That is, technological innovation can be readily used by the public for free fifteen years after the granting of patent rights. A legal scholar interprets the shorter duration of patents as a move that encourages the dissemination of certain technology. Second, the scope of patentability under the 1984 Chinese patent law was narrower than the laws of the developed countries. Under Article 25 of the 1984 Patent Law, food, beverage, and flavorings, as well as pharmaceutical products and substances obtained through chemical processes, should not be granted patent rights.[50]

As will be discussed later, the articles came under serious attack by the U.S. pharmaceutical industry with an intention to invest in China in the U.S.-China bilateral IPR negotiations in the 1990s.

Chinese Patent Regime's Deeper Integration with the Global IPR Norm, 1989–2001

During the reemergence of China's patent regime in the 1980s, external influence began to be felt with both the increase of China's foreign trade and the growing exchange between China and foreign countries. In the 1980s, the key driving force of China's patent legislation mainly came from within. It was not until the 1990s that bilateral and multilateral pressure on Chinese IPR legislation was keenly felt. The China-U.S. bilateral IPR negotiations and China's WTO entry were of particular importance. In this part of the chapter, I examine how the disputes over specific aspects of Chinese patent law were raised, debated, and resolved. I contend that external pressure played a key role in quickening the Chinese IPR regime's deeper integration with the global IPR regime in the 1990s.

The Rise of China-U.S. IPR Disputes in the 1990s and Its Impact on Chinese Patent Regime

The issue of IPR was already raised shortly after China and the United States opened bilateral trade ties in 1979. On January 31, 1979, China and the United States signed the Implementation Accord on Cooperation in the Field of High Energy Physics. In Article 6, it stated that both sides "recognize the need to agree upon provisions concerning protection of copyrights and treatment of inventions or discoveries made or conceived in the course of or under this Accord."[51] On July 7, 1979, China and the United States signed the Agreement on Trade Relations.[52] In Article 6 of the agreement, it was further stated that "both Contracting Parties in their trade relations recognize the importance of effective protection of patents, trademark, and copyrights." Those were among the first China-U.S. bilateral agreements addressing the issue of intellectual property rights. According to the recollection of a Chinese IPR scholar, the U.S. side insisted that the agreements should include an article addressing IPR protection. However, China had just barely started drafting the patent law. The regulations as outlined in those bilateral agreements remained on paper and were rarely cited in real policy practice. The situation started to change as the U.S.-China bilateral trade ties deepened during the mid- and late 1980s.

Although the U.S. private sector and IPR lobbying groups had already raised complaints about China's insufficient efforts to protect IPR in the mid-1980s,[53] this issue was not brought to the government level until the late 1980s. In 1988, the United States revised its 1974 Trade Act and adopted the Omnibus Trade and Competitiveness Act. Under Section 301 of the 1988 Omnibus Trade Act, the U.S. Trade Representative (USTR) was empowered to identify and investigate countries deemed as doing "unfair trade practices" and impose sanctions where appropriate. Under the lobbying efforts by trade interest groups, the 1988 Omnibus Trade and Competitiveness Act further empowered the USTR to investigate and level trade sanctions against countries considered violators of the U.S. IPR. This part of the 1988 Omnibus Trade Act was later known as "Special 301." China became an important target of Special 301.

In late April 1989, China was put on the "priority watch list" by the USTR for the first time. In May 1989, China sent a delegation to the United States, headed by Zhou Xiaochuan, then vice minister of foreign trade. That round of bilateral negotiation resulted in a draft memorandum of understanding (MOU). The draft MOU did not come into effect, but some scholars regarded it as setting the foundation for the formal MOU reached in the 1990s.[54] In the draft MOU, China promised to finish the revision of the 1984 Patent Law by the end of 1989, expanding the scope of patent goods and extending the duration of patents. China also promised to finish reviewing the country's first copyright law by the end of 1989.[55] The U.S. side also agreed to remove China from the "priority watch list."

After the Chinese delegation returned to Beijing, however, they were confronted with harsh domestic critiques. Some criticized the draft MOU as lacking a firm stance against U.S. pressure. Others even asked the delegation members whether they were "real patriots or selling out national interests." At that critical juncture, then general secretary of the State Council, Luo Gan, stood on the side of the Chinese delegation team and praised them because they "did a lot of hard work under harsh conditions." That intervention at least temporarily appeased the criticism.[56]

The 1989 U.S.-China negotiation was only the beginning of a series of IPR brawls between the two countries. In 1991, China was confronted with a more serious challenge: it was listed as one of the "priority foreign countries." Under the U.S. Special 301 regulations, a country would not be subject to U.S. trade retaliation if put on the "priority watch list." However, if a country is included as one of the "priority foreign countries," the U.S. government would be authorized to launch trade retaliation if that country was unable to improve its IPR protection in six months. In April 1991, the USTR published a report, pointing at four glaring inadequacies in the Chinese IPR regime: first, the Chinese patent law is flawed in that it does not grant patent rights to pharmaceutical and chemical products; second, Chinese copyright law does not grant protection to American works published outside China; third, Chinese copyright law does not grant copyright protection for computer software; and fourth, China did not grant sufficient protection for trade secrets.[57]

After the publication of the U.S. Special 301 report in 1991, China and the United States went into several rounds of extremely tough negotiations. On several occasions, the two countries almost entered into a trade war with one other. On January 17, 1992, the two sides came to terms, signing the first MOU over the issue of IPR protection (known as the 1992 MOU).

The 1992 MOU was composed of seven parts that covered the revision of Chinese IPR laws (Articles 1–4), the establishment of U.S.-China bilateral dialogue on IPR issues in the future (Articles 5 and 6), and the termination of the U.S. Special 301 investigation against China (Article 7).[58] The core part of the 1992 MOU was China's promise to revise its IPR laws to address the concerns of the United States.

Under Articles 1 and 2 of the 1992 MOU, China agreed to grant patent rights to pharmaceutical and chemical products and extend the duration of invention patents from fifteen to twenty years; China also agreed to increase foreign patent holders' rights by providing nondiscrimination of patent rights regarding compulsory licensing and providing national treatment as well as administrative protection for chemical and pharmaceutical inventions. The other parts of the 1992 MOU focus on the protection of copyright and trade secrets in China. I will discuss these in Chapters 2 and 3.

The 1992 MOU had a tangible impact on China's already existing IPR regime. On June 23, 1992, the director of the Chinese Patent Office, Gao Lulin, reported to the Standing Committee of the Chinese National People's Congress on the revision of the 1984 Chinese patent law.[59] The revised patent law incorporated the spirit of the 1992 MOU by expanding the scope of patent protection, extending the duration of patent protection, and augmenting the protection of imported patent products. In December 1992, China promulgated the Regulations on Administrative Protection of Pharmaceutical Products and the Regulations on Administrative Protection of Agricultural and Chemical Products.[60] Those two regulations improved on the 1984 patent law and extended patent protection to pharmaceutical, agricultural, and chemical products.

The 1992 MOU only briefly covered IPR enforcement and the implementation of IPR laws. This issue turned out to be the core controversy between China and the United States during the two following rounds of IPR negotiations for the rest of the 1990s. In fact, the China-U.S. bilateral negotiations did not solve these issues completely. The issues of enforcement and implementation lasted well into the twenty-first century. I discuss these issues in Chapters 4, 5, and 6.

Revision of Chinese Patent Laws During the Country's Bid for WTO Entry

While bilateral pressure from the United States propelled China to improve its IPR protection levels more quickly, external pressure also came from multilateral sources during the 1990s. The most important of these multilateral sources was the TRIPS Agreement. In 1995, the end of the Uruguay Round negotiation resulted in the establishment of the WTO. An important component of the new international trade arrangements was the establishment of a global regime for IPR governance: the TRIPS Agreement.[61] Unlike the preceding conventions, the basic function of the TRIPS Agreement was to establish and enforce minimum international standards for IPR protection. There were some other significant changes to a number of aspects of the previous international IPR agreements. Specifically, TRIPS gives the governance regime teeth by applying the WTO's dispute settlement mechanism to any international dispute regarding the undertakings within TRIPS.

As part of the multilateral agreements that led to the establishment of the WTO, TRIPS also links IPR to the wider issues of international trade at the WTO. Moreover, TRIPS ushered in a global IPR regime that reached deep into the domestic regulatory environment of states.[62]

China started its bid for General Agreement on Tariffs and Trade (GATT) membership in the mid-1980s. During this process, the Uruguay Round of multilateral trade negotiations incorporated the issue of intellectual property rights at the request of developed countries. In 1993, the TRIPS Agreement was reached and came into effect on January 1, 1995. On the same day, GATT was transformed into a more powerful multilateral trade organ, the WTO. As discussed earlier, the TRIPS Agreement possesses more enforcement power than the previous multilateral IPR treaties. During its bid for WTO entry, China was obliged to meet the minimum standards outlined by the TRIPS Agreement.

Before China acceded to the WTO in 2001, the Chinese National People's Congress made important revisions to the Chinese patent, trademark, and copyright law, adjusting the level of IPR protection to the standard set by TRIPS.[63] Specifically, the Chinese National People's Congress introduced thirty-five revisions to the sixty-nine articles of the Chinese patent law in 2000. The major revisions are as follows: first, the revised version of Article 14 provided that state-owned enterprises, as market entities, should be treated equally as non-state-owned enterprises in terms of their obligations and rights to patent applications. Second, Articles 41 and 46 provided that the authority to grant and invalidate the patent right was shifted from the patent bureau to the Chinese People's Court.[64]

Chinese Patent Regime During the Post-WTO Era, 2001–Present

Policy and Ideological Environment During the Early Twenty-First Century

China's WTO entry did not end the evolution of the country's patent regime. During the early twenty-first century, important changes happened on both international and domestic fronts, which were bound to impact China's evolving patent regime. Internationally, the fourth ministerial-level conference of WTO members was held in Doha, Qatar, in November 2001. Before and during the conference, the developing countries and other nongovernmental organizations (NGOs) collaborated to voice concern over some arrangements in the TRIPS Agreement. Of particular concern for the developing countries was balancing the relationship between TRIPS and public health. For them, the related regulations in the TRIPS Agreement had too much emphasis on the interests of private owners, particularly the Western multinational corporations, and emphasized less the public and social benefits. The Doha Declaration, adopted after the ministerial-level conference, addressed those concerns. The Doha Declaration also incorporated articles concerning the protection of geographical indications, biodiversity, and traditional knowledge.[65] Those new developments reflected the developing countries' efforts toward an IPR doctrine with further consideration of their interests. They also inevitably impacted China's attitude toward the IPR norms during the new century.

Even before China's entry into the WTO, domestic critics in China had complained that too many concessions had been made and that China moved too fast to merge into the international track of IPR protection.[66] The statement by an official that I interviewed expressed sentiments popular among the Chinese social public: "The Americans copied European countries for more than one century; why can't we copy the Americans for twenty years? They just want to impose their standard upon us. But did they follow these standards when they were at our stage of economic development? The U.S. practices double standard on the issue of human rights. They did the same thing on the issue of intellectual property rights!"[67]

The incorporation of related norms embodied in the TRIPS Agreement was not the final settlement for the disputes. According to an official at the Chinese Ministry of Commerce, with China's bid for WTO membership completed, the issue of intellectual property rights in China has passed through the initial stage of adoption and entered into a new stage of "interest games in depth." In his words, "Unlike the 1980s, an IPR regime has already been in place in China for almost twenty years. Even the weaker players in the IPR games would not dismiss IPR laws as unnecessary and unhelpful. However, they want to impact China's IPR legislation in such a way that the legal arrangements can tilt less to the foreign IPR holders."[68] Under such an international and domestic context, foreign IPR holders, who have been stronger players on the IPR field in China, became the targets of the criticism. A new round of interest games began.

Chinese Domestic Business Community and the Revision of the Chinese Patent Law During the Post-WTO Era

After China entered the WTO, foreign influence reached deeper into the Chinese political economy. Chinese domestic companies were put to a more stringent test on IPR issues by their international counterparts. The battles took place on both the international arena and the domestic arena. In 2002, China's leading producer of communication equipment, Huawei, was brought to a patent lawsuit in Texas by Cisco, accusing the former's American branch, Huawei America, of infringing upon the latter's patent.[69] In 2003, General Motors (GM) filed a patent lawsuit in Beijing against Chery, a private auto company based in Anhui, accusing that a type of Chery's auto products, QQ, had copied the industrial design of the auto body of Spark, a type of mini-car developed by GM.[70] These two leading IPR cases indicated that, after China's WTO entry in 2001, the main fighters on the IPR battlefield shifted from states to companies. More important, as leading Chinese domestic companies, both Huawei and Chery are considered strong competitors for multinational corporations such as Cisco and GM. Not surprisingly, the two cases were interpreted by both the Chinese academia and the public as the abuse of intellectual property rights by foreign companies investing in China.[71]

Eventually, both cases ended up in outside court reconciliation,[72] but critics of companies from the developed world have launched accusations of their abuse of intellectual property rights. At the same time, Chinese scholars and policy researchers have published reports on internally circulated materials, warning against the danger of foreign companies' dominance in the Chinese market.[73] These appeals reached the decision makers of the SIPO. In 2004, the Chinese SIPO sent a working group to investigate the patent dispute between GM and Chery. The working group concluded that the real purpose of GM's launching the patent suit against Chery was not to protect its IPR. Instead, GM's real aim was to strangulate its competitor before it grew strong enough.[74]

The working group's report further convinced SIPO that patents were increasingly being utilized by Western companies to maximize their business interests rather than promote China's own innovation ability. According to a document drafted by the Policy Research Office of the State Intellectual Property Office in March 2005,

> Various signs indicate clearly that developed countries intend to control the practice of international patent affairs. . . . In order for our country to avoid being marginalized on the issue of patent affairs, . . . [we have to] summarize the experience of the practice of patent system during the past two decades so that it can better accommodate our country's concrete condition. We should further kindle the passion of innovation by our country's enterprises and individuals and better balance the interests of patent holder and social public.[75]

Under these guidelines, the Chinese SIPO launched the process for the third revision of Chinese patent law in 2005. This process was completed on December 27, 2008, when the Standing Committee of the National People's Congress passed the revised draft of Chinese patent law.[76] According to a Beijing-based IPR judge, the third revision of Chinese patent law was not driven by foreign pressure as much as the previous revisions; instead, the primary driving force was the need for China's own economic development.[77]

On December 27, 2008, the Sixth Session of the Standing Committee of the Eleventh Chinese National People's Congress passed the revised draft of Chinese patent law.[78] Compared with the previous draft, the current draft further increases the financial punishment for patent infringement (Article 63). The current draft also adds provisions that outline the protection of traditional knowledge and genetic resources (Articles 5 and 26). The most significant revision pertains to the conditions that apply to compulsory licensing. According to Article 48, under the condition that patent holders' business behavior is deemed as constituting a monopoly, a compulsory license can be issued by a related state organ to corporate or individual applicants who can use the patent. Under Article 50, patents for pharmaceutical products can be applied for under a compulsory license in the case of a public health emergency. To put it simply, in both cases, patents can be readily used by relevant parties without the authorization of the patent holders. Although the aforementioned development was noted by some foreign businesses as one of the signs that the pendulum of economic nationalist sentiments was swinging back,[79] history is not merely repeating itself. Behind the third revision of Chinese patent law is the interest competition that demarcates a new era, with a more complex set of actors involved.

The third revision of Chinese patent law greatly promoted Chinese society's patent awareness. The issue of patent was linked to economic development more closely than ever before. The number of patent applications was even incorporated into the performance appraisal index of Chinese patent officials.[80] Those policies, however, overemphasized the quantity, rather than quality, of patents. Therefore, Chinese patent law could not fulfill its mission of promoting technological innovation in the country. Moreover, Chinese patent holders complained that, during the process of patent protection, there existed the problems of "hard to adduce evidence, lengthy lawsuit process, high protection cost, low legal compensation, and ineffective enforcement outcome" (*juzheng nan, zhouqi chang, chengben gao, peichang di, xiaoguo cha*).[81]

In light of those problems, the Chinese SIPO launched the fourth revision of the patent law in January 2012. After half a year of research, SIPO completed the first draft of the revised patent law, which was circulated among the IPR judges, business professionals, lawyers, and IPR scholars. On August 9, 2012, SIPO published the draft revisions on its website. In January 2013, the revisions were reported to the Chinese State Council for further examination.[82] In 2014, the Chinese National People's Congress conducted a new round of inspection of patent law enforcement. In the report to the NPC standing committee, it was admitted that "the overall quality of Chinese patents remains low and cannot accommodate the needs of our country's economic and social development; significant gap exists between the outcome of patent protection and the expectation of innovators; the ability to apply patents remains low, which prevents patents from realizing their market values."[83]

Guided by the NPC report, SIPO introduced further changes to Chinese patent law in late 2014, revising eighteen existing provisions, adding eleven new provisions, and deleting one provision. The new revisions also added a special part on the application of patents. On April 1, 2015, SIPO posted the newly revised patent law online.[84] The fourth revision of Chinese patent law entered the final stage of substantive review.

Conclusion

With China's WTO entry in 2001 and a series of revisions of the existing patent legislation, the formal patent laws in China have come into full de jure compliance with international patent norms. The evolution of China's patent regime between 1949 and the present has been a dynamic and complex process, affected by the tensions between the propatent camp and the antipatent camp in the country. Externally, China's patent legislation is impacted by a complex intertwining of bilateral and multilateral negotiations. The influence of the antipatent camp was not only present before Chinese patent law was adopted; they also tried to influence specific parts of the patent law to suit their needs when the adoption of a patent law turned inevitable in the early 1980s. With the patent law taking roots solidly in China's legislative establishment, societal factors such as domestic and foreign business groups influenced the specific parts of the legal arrangements for the purpose of safeguarding their interests during the several revisions. As demonstrated in Chapter 2, the competition and collaboration among different societal actors also contributed to influencing the implementation of the patent norm.

The tensions among various economic and political groups during the evolution of Chinese patent law also reflect the gradual opening of a once tightly controlled authoritarian society. Recognizing the achievements of scientific research and technological innovation as private property during the late 1970s and early 1980s was part of the larger scheme of China's market reform. China's increasingly close ties with international economy cultivated and strengthened the propatent camp during the adoption stage of the country's patent law. The voice of China's rising export sector played a key role in breaking the stalemate between the propatent camp and antipatent camp in the early 1980s. Despite the harsh critique of "lacking a firm stance against the U.S. pressure," the Chinese IPR delegation's substantive concessions during the China-U.S. IPR negotiations in the 1990s constituted a key component of the country's further integration with the world economy. Both domestic reform and opening to the outside world policy in China consolidated the legitimacy of private property, one of the cornerstones of a mature civil society. Although conventionally held as legal and economic matters, the sea changes in Chinese patent legislation represented an inseparable part of the country's gradual liberalization in the past decades.

Looking into the future, it can be safely predicted that, instead of being compelled by the external influences from foreign governments and international organizations, the evolution of Chinese patent legislation in the next decade will be increasingly driven by the appeals of domestic economic and political groups and foreign businesses investing in China. Although the fourth amendment of Chinese patent law has not been completed, Chinese patent professionals at various levels expect that the revisions will focus on offering stronger protection for patent holders, enhancing the application of patents for industrial use, and promoting the quality of patents. With the rapid growth of the number of patent infringement cases, intellectual property offices at the local level are also expected to be granted an increased administrative mandate to enforce patent protection on the spot.[85] Whatever the future outlook of Chinese patent legislation is, the overall direction is clear. That is, Chinese patent legislation must reflect the demands of China's industrial upgrading, under which the country's economic growth increasingly depends on scientific research and technological innovation.

The establishment of a full-fledged patent regime in China is not the end of the story. More important is the implementation of those legal regulations and enhancement of China's scientific and technological innovation. The adoption of the patent norm was already a difficult process given the competition among different actors, mainly at the level of the Chinese central government. The implementation of the patent norm would reach deep into the Chinese society, with the Chinese local government and the Chinese business community involved. In the words of Ms. Mei, "My career in IPR was about handling challenges one after another. When I retire, it is up to the younger generations of IPR professionals facing new sets of challenges. I know that those challenges will be more complex, but we have no other choice except to face them and handle them."[86] The next chapter will address how Chinese patent professionals handle (or mishandle) those new and more complex challenges during the implementation of patent norms.

CHAPTER 2

The Implementation of Chinese Patent Policy

In 2007, I met two young patent officials, Mr. Huang and Mr. Jiang, at a national intellectual property rights (IPR) conference in Beijing. Both of them were from central China's H Province,[1] a province with a reputation for being a center of the production and distribution of counterfeit goods in northern China. A joke I heard from a street peddler from that province exemplifies this reputation. In that peddler's words, counterfeit products in his province ranged from projects "as big as ceramic tiles covering the Great Wall and gauze masks for hippos in Africa, as small as shackles for fleas and condoms for cockroaches."[2] Before I arrived at their hotel room, I called them on the phone to ask if they would like to schedule an interview with me about patent protection (*zhuanli baohu*) in H Province. They replied enthusiastically, telling me that they would love to discuss the issue of patent work (*zhuanli gongzuo*). Too excited to have access to two IPR officials, I almost ignored the subtle but important difference between "patent protection" and "patent work." In the beginning of the interview, I raised the prepared questions, most of which emphasized patent protection. I asked under what conditions effective patent enforcement would mostly likely happen. The two young officials answered my questions in a polite way, but I could easily sense that they were not as interested in my questions as I had expected. When the interview was nearly completed, I raised a question not previously on the top of my list: "As an inland province, your economy is not as export oriented as provinces in East China. Can you describe the patent strategies of the province's export-oriented enterprises, even though there are not as many?" That question suddenly sparked the interest of my interviewees. They enthusiastically described how many patent applications were filed each year under their sponsorship, how many of them were approved, and how the patent application and approval rate grew annually. Without being asked, they singled out a successful example of their patent work: how the intellectual property office (IPO) of Changxi,[3] a city in the northern part of H Province, helped a local company defend itself in a patent lawsuit with a Japanese company, how that company boosted its export volume and grew from being a small business player into a vibrant competitor, how that company's success benefited the local economy, how one of their colleagues won an annual prize for his excellent work to help that company, and even how that achievement helped the Changxi City IPO bargain for a better share of the city's annual budget. The interview lasted another forty minutes. Instead of being frustrated that the interview did not proceed in the direction as planned, I was excited to learn an unexpected, albeit important, finding: there is an important difference between my interests (and probably that of many other observers of Chinese patent policy) and the interests of the Chinese patent policy practitioners on the ground. The former are more interested in "patent protection," that is, how high-quality enforcement can be delivered to protect the interests of patent holders. For the latter, however, patent protection is only one part of "patent work." More important for them is how patent protection can boost their foreign trade and promote local economic development. Indeed, the case of Changxi City that the two officials proudly cited cannot be called an example of "patent protection" in a strict sense. In almost all my interviews with the Chinese patent officials, I was told that patent protection had equal importance in the development of the patent industry. But the finding gained from the two patent officials spoke for itself: there is a hierarchy of importance in their policy agenda between "patent work" and "patent protection." This hierarchy has a tangible impact on how effectively patent cases are enforced.

The greater importance of patent work over patent protection was reinforced during a research trip to H Province in January 2013. I met Mr. Huang and Mr. Jiang again after many years. Having been friends for the past several years, they invited me to dinner. Both Mr. Huang and Mr. Jiang celebrated their promotion several months earlier, but they were assigned to different sections. Mr. Huang's section was in charge of, in his words, the development of the patent industry while Mr. Jiang's section was in charge of overseeing the enforcement of patent laws. I was invited to the guest seat of the dinner table. Mr. Jiang insisted that Mr. Huang should sit at the seat facing the door, known as the "upper seat." Out of

Chinese modesty, Mr. Huang declined. But Mr. Jiang replied, "Of course you should sit at the upper seat. You are our real boss!" Eventually, Mr. Huang took the upper seat. A fine dinner started. In Chinese culture, the dinner table is an important place for people to discuss business matters. The order of the seats at the dinner table is an important indication of the bureaucratic hierarchy.[4] After drinking wine, Mr. Jiang told me half-jokingly, "Did you ask under what conditions effective patent enforcement would happen? How come you smart scholars just like to pose stupid questions? You scholars just view things differently from us. It all depends on our boss." He pointed to Mr. Huang and said, "If our boss wants us to enforce the case in an effective way, that case will be an effective one."[5]

Mr. Jiang had a lot of wine during dinner, but his comment should not be interpreted as due to the wine. His comment indicated that the Chinese government does not protect intellectual property rights for their own sake. Rather, the Chinese government's ultimate goal of IPR work is to build its own IPR industry. IPR protection is not an end in itself. An IPR scholar from the Chinese Academy of Social Sciences (CASS) explained the policy arrangement in a more explicit way. According to him,

> When people talk about IPR, the first thing that comes in mind is how many counterfeit products are seized and how many IPR infringers are brought to justice. But shouldn't we also think about the nonobvious aspects of IPR work? In fact, our work consists of IPR creation, application, protection, and management. IPR protection is only part of that broader scheme, with the other aspects constituting the foundation of IPR activities. If the economic rationale behind IPR theft remains unchanged, we can only expect IPR infringement to happen constantly—no matter how serious we are about IPR protection.[6]

This chapter explores the relationship between patent enforcement and other aspects of, in the patent officials' words, "Chinese patent work," with an emphasis on the mechanisms to bring about effective patent enforcement. I argue that patent enforcement should be understood as occurring at the interface between the Chinese state and societal actors. An overemphasis of one side and ignorance of the other will at best yield an incomplete understanding of the entire picture. As a developing country, China pursues dual goals in implementing its patent policy: (1) upgrading the country's industrial competitiveness through the development of the patent industry and (2) protecting patent holders' interests by punishing patent infringement. The second goal serves the first goal. The more patent protection is believed to serve the overall agenda of "patent work" and help to promote economic development, the more likely effective enforcement will occur. Otherwise, patent enforcement will yield at best a lukewarm result.

This chapter is organized as follows: the first section discusses the implementation of China's patent policy on the state side—namely, IPR special tribunals and IPOs at various levels. On the basis of analysis by other scholars, I argue that enforcing patent laws is only part of the responsibility of the Chinese patent bureaucracy. Equally, if not more, important is to establish a policy environment conducive to supporting the creation of high-quality patents and apply those patents to benefit the market. The second section discusses the uneven results of Chinese patent policy on various Chinese business actors, which in turn creates different attitudes toward patents. The business actors include foreign companies investing in China, Chinese elite domestic private enterprises, Chinese state-owned enterprises, and the majority of Chinese domestic private enterprises. In an important way, their different attitudes toward the patent norm not only influence the effectiveness of patent enforcement but also reflect an uneven level in the thoroughness of the Chinese political and economic transition. I conclude this chapter by connecting the implementation of Chinese patent policy with the country's ongoing institutional reforms.

Chinese Patent System: Enforcement Function and Beyond

This section provides an analysis of the legal and administrative enforcers of Chinese patent policy—namely, the Chinese IPR special tribunals and patent bureau/IPOs. Previous scholars have already offered a thorough analysis of the organizational evolution of the Chinese State Patent Bureau (SPB); its successor, the Chinese State Intellectual Property Office (SIPO); and SPB/SIPO's regional branches. They have also conducted an in-depth discussion of the relationship between the Chinese patent administrative apparatus and IPR courts.[7] Nevertheless, some key issues that influence their enforcement functions remain underexplored: Do Chinese IPR courts and IPOs have any goals other than patent protection? If patents receive due protection, how do the enforcement decisions influence (and are influenced by) the broader political and economic environment in China? This section situates the operation of Chinese IPR courts and patent bureau/IPOs against the greater political and economic backdrop of the country's market reform since the early 1980s. I argue that the Chinese IPR tribunals and patent bureau/IPOs not only enforce patent laws but also design patent policy to serve the general scheme of the country's economic modernization campaign. Hence, the effectiveness of Chinese patent policy is measured by the quantity and quality of enforcement cases and also by its contribution to the country's technological and economic advancement.

Chinese IPR Tribunals: Between Trial and Mediation

As some scholars have rightly pointed out, Chinese IPR courts are the primary venue for delivering patent protection. Over the years, Chinese IPR courts have handled high-quality patent enforcement cases through trials. Building on these scholars' analyses, I demonstrate that, in addition to delivering legal enforcement through a trial, the Chinese IPR tribunals have also increasingly introduced pretrial mediation as an alternative means to resolving patent disputes in recent years. Both trial and pretrial mediation serve China's need to render technological innovation into practical market benefits.

Chinese patent legislation identifies three types of patent violations: patent infringement (*qinquan*), patent counterfeit (*jiamao*), and patent passing off (*maochong*).[8] The 2008 Chinese patent law defines patent infringement (*qinquan*) as "the exploitation of a patent without the authorization of the patentee" for the purpose of making profits.[9] Patent counterfeit (*jiamao*) is defined as counterfeiting the patent certificate or other patent documents belonging to the legitimate holder of the patent. Patent passing off (*maochong*) is defined as selling or producing a nonpatented product as a patented product.[10] When a patent owner identifies a patent violation, the owner can resort to legal protection or administrative protection. Under the current Chinese patent regime, IPR courts are the primary providers of legal enforcement while IPOs at different levels are the primary providers of administrative enforcement. Due to their technical complexity, most patent infringement (*qinquan*) cases are handled through legal channels. Regional patent bureaus or IPOs are mainly in charge of handling the relatively less complex cases of patent counterfeits and patent passing off.

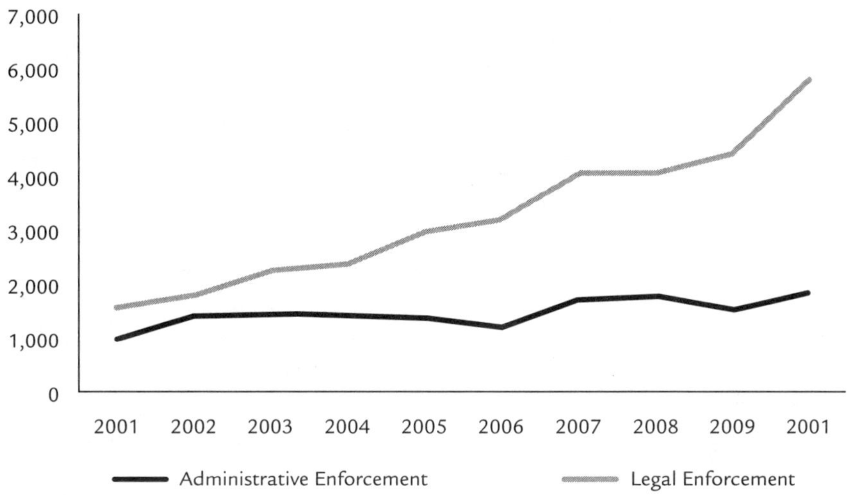

Figure 1. Administrative versus legal enforcement of patent cases in China, 2001–2010. *Chinese Intellectual Property Yearbook* (2002–2011).

According to some scholars of Chinese IPR policy, high-quality enforcement, featuring consistency, transparency, and procedural fairness, has emerged in the Chinese IPR special tribunals. They attribute this to the high qualifications of Chinese IPR judges, the relatively independent status of IPR special tribunals, and the courts' stronger authority to resist local protectionism.[11] These factors have equipped the Chinese IPR special tribunals with the capacity to handle complex patent infringement cases. Chinese IPR judges themselves are also confident of the quality of their legal decisions and are required by the People's Supreme Court to post these decisions online for the general public to review.[12]

Statistical data indicate that, between 2001 and 2010, IPR courts at different levels handled 69.6 percent of the patent disputes while regional IPOs handled 30.4 percent.[13] Further examination of the data reveals that IPR courts in China have witnessed a rapidly growing number of hearings on patent disputes over the past decade (see Figure 1).

Statistical data about Chinese IPR tribunals are telling, and one is tempted to conclude that Chinese IPR special tribunals accomplish all their tasks by offering legal protection to patent holders. But a careful study of the history of Chinese patent dispute settlement indicates that the number of court trials is only a partial reflection of their work. Before China established its first IPR special tribunal in Beijing in 1993, patent disputes were mainly resolved by patent bureaus at different levels. Between 1985 and 1992, the patent bureaus settled a total of 1,858 patent disputes, with 1,400 of the settlements resulting in mediation because the disputes were not high-value cases.[14] According to the recollection of Cheng Yongshun, one of the founding judges of the IPR Tribunal of the Beijing Intermediate People's Court, conducting trials of IPR cases was the main way to resolve IPR disputes during the early years of the IPR tribunals in the 1990s.[15] As the first of its kind in China, the IPR tribunal in Beijing shared its experience with its counterparts in other provinces. As of 2012, China had established 420 IPR tribunals at the basic court (*jiceng fayuan*) level, reaching into some remote provinces such as Xinjiang and Yunnan. The IPR tribunals were staffed by 2,759 IPR judges.[16]

With the rapid growth of IPR special tribunals over the past decade, the complexity and difficulty of patent cases on trial have also increased. Even IPR judges do not deny the challenges that IPR tribunals face. Specifically, these challenges include burdensome evidence collection, expensive lawsuits, lengthy trial processes, and difficulty with calculating economic compensation. These factors make IPR civil enforcement a luxury, particularly for IPR holders with weaker economic status, such as individuals or small and medium-sized companies. Even if companies win the case and the court orders a stop to the patent infringement, the companies may have lost time and business opportunities. As such, they go to court only when absolutely necessary. In light of this, the Chinese IPR special tribunals introduced another important part of their work in the late 1990s and early twenty-first century—the mediation between the different parties involved in the patent cases.

No systematic data exist about when the IPR special tribunals started to adopt pretrial mediation as the major means in the resolution of IPR disputes. Speeches by Chinese judges in the early twenty-first century, however, indicated that the courts increasingly realized the importance of pretrial mediation in solving civil disputes, including IPR cases. For example, in a speech delivered at the annual conference of the presidents of the Provincial High People's Court in 2004, the Chinese People's Supreme Court judge, Xiao Yang, stated that the people's court should "mobilize positive factors in various aspects, explore alternative means other than trials to solve legal disputes, and further improve settlement mechanism of social contradictions."[17] In 2008, Xiao Yang's successor, Wang Shengjun, elaborated that principle as "mediation first and then combine mediation with adjudication" (*tiaojie youxian, tiaopan jiehe*) in handling civil cases.[18] Applying this principle to IPR cases, the newly appointed director of the IPR Tribunal of the Chinese People's Supreme Court, Kong Xiangjun, proposed that disputes between different parties in IPR cases should be mainly categorized as "internal contradictions among the people" (*renmin neibu maodun*). The judge's role should not only be limited to delivering a high-quality trial for individual cases but also should provide a legal basis for resolving plaintiff-defendant contradictions and enhancing the application of technological innovation to promote social and economic development.[19] Under this rationale, mediation mechanisms aim to (1) find common interests between the parties involved, (2) negotiate a technology transfer agreement, and (3) make the parties cooperate. An example cited by an IPR judge in Nanjing illustrates the effect of the mediation mechanism. In 2005, a retired engineer, Mr. Lu (plaintiff), developed a technological innovation that was not put into application until after his retirement. When Mr. Lu discovered this, he was upset to find that his former employer (defendant) had produced goods according to the technological innovation he had designed. As he was about to sue his former employer, the Nanjing IPR court mediated between Mr. Lu and his former employer. Eventually, the two sides reached an "outside court reconciliation" and negotiated a technology transfer agreement, in which Mr. Lu received 110,000 RMB (about $15,000) in economic compensation. After the mediation, Mr. Lu decided to withdraw the lawsuit.[20]

In the early twenty-first century, mediation became an increasingly important way to solve IPR disputes, particularly for those cases of lower financial value. In 2003, 49.4 percent of IPR cases were resolved through pretrial mediation.[21] As of 2010, that number had increased to 57.13 percent.[22] An IPR judge's comment summarized his understanding of Chinese IPR tribunals' work:

> We should not only care about the result of a patent lawsuit. More attention should be paid to the social and economic issues extending out of the lawsuit. A successful judge should not only deliver high-quality trials that can stand the test by the social public but also play his or her own role in directing the healthy development of certain

> industries involved. Our task is to protect inventions, but where do all the inventions come from? If there is not sufficient number of inventions, what should we protect?[23]

While Chinese IPR tribunals handle many more patent disputes than IPOs at different levels and are praised for delivering high-quality enforcement cases, it is unfair to conclude that the Chinese patent bureaus at various levels are weaker on the ground because they handle a lower number of cases. In fact, the IPR special tribunals and regional IPOs shoulder different tasks in the division of labor in Chinese patent work. It is true that IPR special tribunals are focused on dealing with the more complex patent cases, but that should not trivialize the role of patent bureau/IPOs in the implementation of Chinese patent policy. The next section discusses the functions of patent bureau/IPOs at different levels in China. I demonstrate that administrative enforcement is only part of the task of Chinese IPOs at different levels. More important for them is the creation of a social environment conducive to technological invention in the country. In that sense, the IPR tribunals and the patent bureau/IPOs share similar goals in China's "patent work."

Chinese IPOs: More Than Administrative Enforcement?

The primary administrative organ in charge of Chinese patent affairs is the State Intellectual Property Office (SIPO) and its regional offices. Some scholars have examined the organizational evolution of SIPO in a detailed way. That is, SIPO and its predecessor, the State Patent Bureau (SPB), went through several superior or "host" organizations since its establishment in 1980. These organizations include the State Science and Technology Commission (SSTC) from 1980 to 1982, the State Economic Commission (SEC) from 1982 to 1988, and the SSTC again from 1988 to 1993. In 1998, SPB was named the SIPO and acquired the status of a vice-ministerial level organization directly subordinate to the State Council.[24] Scholars such as Mertha attempted to gauge the strengths and effectiveness of Chinese patent bureaucracy through the organizational history of the SPB/SIPO. Using their analysis as a foundation, I examined how the transfer from one superior or "host" organization to another informs the institutional culture of the SPB/SIPO and, possibly more important, how that institutional culture impacts the SPB/SIPO's perception of its role in the implementation of Chinese patent policy. I found that since the early 1980s, the Chinese patent system has performed dual functions: (1) managing Chinese patent affairs in general and (2) providing guidelines for patent protection. The institutional history of Chinese the SPB/SIPO suggests that market reform in the country's science and technology policy introduced in the early 1980s has significantly influenced its operation.

The Chinese SPB was established in 1980, with Wu Heng as its first general director. Wu Heng also held the position of SSTC vice director. As discussed in Chapter 1, the macroenvironment for SPB's establishment was the introduction of reform and opening policy in China. At the ministerial level, the SSTC played a major role in the establishment of the SPB. In 1979, one year before the SPB was formally established, an IPR training seminar was organized to prepare the SPB with the first group of "backbone staff" (*gugan chengyuan*). The seminar participants were young officials and professionals in their late twenties and early thirties, but they became the elites of the Chinese IPR circle thirty years later. Among them were Tian Lipu (SIPO general director from 2005 to 2014), Li Jiahao (former vice director of the Asia Pacific Development and Cooperation Bureau, World Intellectual Property Organization), Lu Xueshi (former director of the Shanghai Branch Office of the Chinese SPB), and many other emerging young professionals who assumed influential positions in Chinese patent affairs in later decades.[25]

Historical archives of the 1979 Training Seminar revealed interesting details that foretold the operation of Chinese patent activities in the decades to come. As the primary organizer of the seminar, the SSTC appointed An Yutao, head of Scientific and Technological Achievement Division, to lead the day-to-day operations. Within the SSTC, some called for patent affairs to fall exclusively under the commission. But those callings met opposition from Wu Heng, the principal designer of the SPB. Wu criticized that opinion as selfish factionalism (*benwei zhuyi*) and insisted that young professionals with expertise in other related fields and from other related ministries should also be included. According to him,

> Comrades of patent work should first have a solid background in science and technology. But that is not enough since patent work is a key component of our country's growing economic modernization scheme. It also has important influence on our country's growing foreign trade. Therefore, we should be well versed in international trade and international commerce. Ideally, our comrades should

> have a good command of at least one foreign language to meet the need for international exchange. In short, our patent cadres should be interdisciplinary talents.[26]

Under that rationale, the first generation of employees of the SPB was recruited from various sources. Cadres from the SSTC constituted the majority of SPB staff, joined by their colleagues from the China Council for the Promotion of International Trade, Ministry of Foreign Trade, Ministry of Education, Chinese Academy of Sciences, and various other ministries of industry. In an official document issued on January 14, 1980, the Chinese State Council clearly delineated the goals to establish the SPB as "promoting and protecting our country's invention and innovation, enhancing international technological exchange, creating conditions for attracting foreign investment and technological knowhow, and quickening the pace of China's economic and technological development."[27]

Work toward these goals was furthered during the first decade of the SPB's operation. By the late 1980s, China had trained over 4,000 patent agents and attorneys, 2,000 corporate patent professionals, and 2,000 patent trade professionals nationwide. As the first-generation practitioners of Chinese patent policy, the young people should be credited for institutionalizing the organizational culture of the Chinese patent system nationwide. That is, while the Chinese science and technology sector has had an indelible influence on the country's patent activities, the country's patent practitioners were also educated to serve the needs of the country's economic development and foreign trade. The back-and-forth transfer from the SSTC to the SEC as the host organization for the SPB in the 1980s and early 1990s helped establish and even reinforce that institutional culture.

The operations of the Chinese patent administration could hardly be detached from the broader scenario of the country's market-oriented reforms introduced in the science and technology sector. While the adoption of Chinese patent law was being hotly debated in the early 1980s, the country was also engaged in a thorough reform of the science and technology system established during the planned economy era. The key components of the Chinese science and technology reforms during that period were twofold: (1) diminish government intervention in the country's science and technology sector to push the sector into the market and (2) create a technology market for transactions between research institutes and industrial enterprises.[28] The establishment of a patent system served that purpose. In an article published in 1986, SSTC Director Song Jian explained the role played by Chinese patent policy in that reform scheme. According to him,

> [As an important part of Chinese science and technology reform], Chinese patent policy serves to establish a technology market in the country and strengthen our enterprises' ability to absorb new achievements in our country's scientific research. In the implementation of Chinese patent policy, we should change the past practice of using the achievements of scientific research for free and guide the science and technology sector from research labs to factories, rural areas, and various corners of our motherland. We should open the gate for our science and technology professionals to the main battlefield of economic modernization.[29]

When Song Jian made that comment, the host organization of the SPB had already shifted from the SSTC to the SEC. Although it was odd for Song Jian, then SSTC director, to comment on the work of the Chinese SPB, an organization that was no longer under his jurisdiction, his comment did not seem to have offended the leadership of Chinese patent policy. Huang Kunxi, then SPB general director, echoed Song Jian's comments in an article published later in 1986. According to Huang,

> The implementation of Chinese patent law is bound to provide strong motivation for our country's science and technological development since it effectively combines the need for economic development with legal practice. The purpose of our work is to coordinate the relationship between the owners of the inventions and their users. . . . There are millions of industrial enterprises, thousands of research institutes, and hundreds of research universities in our country. They are going to produce inventions and utilize inventions as well. At the same time, millions of farmers also need to utilize scientific invention and technological innovation. It is therefore important to create conducive conditions for the technological innovations to be applied and turned into concrete productive forces as early as possible. Our patent work should serve that purpose.[30]

The opinions of Song Jian and Huang Kunyi demonstrate how Chinese patent work was influenced by the general context of Chinese economic reforms. From 1980 to 1998, the SPB shifted from one host organization to another and went through four general directors, but the general goal of Chinese patent work remained unchanged. Shortly after the Chinese SPB was renamed SIPO in 1998, the newly appointed SIPO general director, Jiang Ying, reiterated this goal in an article published in *People's Daily*, the mouthpiece of the Chinese Communist Party. According to her,

> The twenty-first century is an age of knowledge economy. Our main task is to effectively utilize our IPR system and promote the production and dissemination of knowledge. . . . The development of new technology is increasingly gaining pace in the new era. Our work on IPR protection should be adjusted to that new development. We should study the relationship between IPR and knowledge economy in an in-depth manner. That is the requirement of our country's economic development.[31]

Jiang Ying's successors, Wang Jingchuan and Tian Lipu, inherited the rationale elaborated in her article. As China became more deeply involved in the global IPR regime in the late 1990s, the Chinese State Council entrusted SIPO with a more complete set of functions as a vice-ministerial-level organization. Those functions included (1) designing laws and regulations related to patent work and preparing patent legislation; (2) coordinating IPR affairs related to foreign countries, including negotiating with foreign countries and other relevant government ministries and studying the trends of the development of international IPR affairs; (3) organizing and designing development plans for a patent information exchange nationwide; (4) designing the standard for patent validation and infringement and providing professional guidance to local patent bureaus to solve patent disputes and punish patent violations; and (5) educating and training IPR professionals and advocating for patent laws and other regulations.[32]

SIPO was established at a time when China was becoming profoundly integrated into the global economy with its entry in the World Trade Organization (WTO). In the early twenty-first century, Chinese top leadership repeatedly emphasized the importance of technological innovation in the process of upgrading the country's industrial sector and urged the Chinese patent system to play an important role in that grand enterprise. In 2004, former Chinese president Hu Jintao put forward for the first time the notion of "building an innovative country" in an official speech.[33] In 2008, China elevated intellectual property rights to the level of national strategy and adopted the Outline of the National Intellectual Property Rights Strategy, known as the 2008 Outline. The 2008 Outline reaffirmed the goal of building China into an "innovative country" by 2020. To that end, China aimed to "significantly improve the level of independent innovation, further enhance the ability of IPR application to produce knowledge-intensive products, markedly reduce the cost of IPR protection and crack down IPR infringement."[34] It is noteworthy that the 2008 Outline, like other official IPR policy documents, did not downgrade the importance of IPR protection but rather prioritized it lower than IPR creation and application in Chinese IPR work. Leadership speeches and official documents cited above represent the thinking of Chinese patent policy designers. That is, while some scholars focused on patent enforcement, the designers of Chinese patent policy were more interested in how patent enforcement could serve the purpose of transforming science and technology into being the primary engine for the country's economic development. This tendency is also represented in the operation of IPOs at the regional level.

Regional patent bureau/IPOs were being established in the 1980s. As of 2010, all thirty-one provinces/municipalities in China had established a provincial/municipal IPO. Among the provincial/municipal IPOs, nine are at the bureau level (*tingji*) (Beijing, Tianjin, Shanghai, Guangdong, Guizhou, Shanxi, Hunan, Sichuan, and Inner Mongolia), nineteen are at the vice bureau level (*futingji*) (Liaoning, Yunnan, Hebei, Heilongjiang, Jiangsu, Hubei, Ningxia, Xinjiang, Fujian, Jiangxi, Anhui, Shandong, Henan, Chongqing, Jilin, Gansu, Zhejiang, Guangxi, and Hainan), and three are at the section level (*chuji*) (Shaanxi, Qinghai, and Tibet). The IPOs covered the city/prefecture level in twenty-three provinces and reached the county level in thirteen provinces.[35] It is generally agreed that the subnational IPOs have a dependent relationship with the Science and Technology Bureau in their respective provinces. There are also varied budgetary and personnel allocations (*bianzhi*) of the subnational IPOs from one locality to another. Some of them are quite strong and others weak. This coincides with the personnel and budgetary allocations in different provinces/municipalities. The Henan Provincial IPO, for example, only had twenty-five full-time staff when it was established in 2000.[36] In China's capital, Beijing, however, the

Beijing municipal IPO had forty-two full-time staff when it was established in 2002.[37] Scholars also noted that a significant proportion of the staff of the local IPOs come from the Science and Technology Bureau. When the needs for patent enforcement arise, IPOs have to resort to the local Administration for Industry and Commerce (AIC) and Quality and Technology Supervision Bureau (QTSB) for additional help.[38]

A natural question thus arises: under what conditions will the regional IPOs persuade the AIC and QTSB to provide them with necessary help for patent enforcement? The short answer to this question is when the IPOs can convince the AIC and QTSB that patent protection helps to promote local economic development. As indicated by a closer examination of IPO functions, enforcing patent laws is only part of their duties. After the establishment of a complete set of IPR tribunal systems around China in the 1990s, the enforcement function was gradually outsourced to the IPR courts, with the emphasis of the patent bureau/IPOs shifting to the management of patent affairs. Like their counterparts at the central level, the regional IPOs serve to design the regional patent regulations, coordinate the implementation of the intellectual property rights strategy and foreign-related IPR affairs, disseminate patents to enhance the economic development of the area under its jurisdiction, and deliver patent protection through administrative means.[39] Also, like their counterparts at the central level, the regional IPOs never downgraded the importance of patent protection. In practice, however, the development of scientific capacity takes precedence over the enforcement of patent laws. During my research trip to Changxi, an IPR official cited a piece of informal evidence corroborating this. He noted that there are several vice bureau chiefs in the city's IPO, and when the bureau chief and vice bureau chiefs take group photos on formal occasions, the vice bureau chief in charge of the patent industry *always* appears on the right side of the vice bureau chief in charge of patent protection, with the bureau chief in the middle. Due to the lack of institutionalization in Chinese politics, the order that the officials appear in group photos is an important indicator of bureaucratic hierarchy.[40] It is, therefore, no wonder that Mr. Jiang, the official in charge of patent protection, called Mr. Huang, the official in charge of patent industry, "our real boss," even though both of them held the same bureaucratic rank.

With the priority established, the variation in the budgetary and personnel allocations of the regional IPOs only serves as a partial measurement of their capacity and effectiveness. In the affluent provinces/municipalities such as Beijing, Shanghai, and Guangdong, the IPOs can obtain a better share of budgetary and personnel allocations because the tasks of managing patent activities in those regions are more numerous. IPOs in the relatively backward inland provinces may have less of a budget and fewer personnel. As suggested by the example cited at the beginning of the chapter, however, effective patent enforcement is still possible, even in a province that is traditionally regarded as having low respect for IPR. The condition for determining patent enforcement, of course, is whether it is believed to enhance their region's economic development and improve their competitiveness in foreign trade. Some subnational IPOs may be "weak" in the sense that they are not as well financed and well staffed as their counterparts in coastal provinces, but their enforcement efforts can be effective if they can prove that patent protection will benefit the overall economic advancement of the area. This logic holds across inland and coastal provinces alike. The following fieldwork experience further illustrates this point. Before I ended my research trip to Changxi City, Mr. Huang told me,

> Of course we should be better financed and better staffed than before. That is because the likelihood of IPR theft is going to increase with our rapid economic development. Should we be jealous of our comrades in the coastal provinces, who are even better financed and better staffed than us? Maybe, but do not forget that their duty is probably heavier than [ours]. It is not fair to measure the effectiveness of our work according to how many people enforce how many cases. Patent enforcement is part of our work. Our patent work is effective if the patent policy that we designed can serve our economic development and serve it well.[41]

The above analysis indicates that the Chinese patent bureaucracy has never existed in a vacuum. A fuller understanding of patent protection in China should adopt a holistic approach and consider the social, economic, and political environment in which these bureaucracies operate. An integrative approach can yield a more nuanced understanding of the functions of the Chinese patent bureaucracy. In discussing the relationship between patent protection and other aspects of patent work in China, I did not touch on the role of Chinese IPR holders. Although the least parsimonious variable in the equation, patent holders are by no means the least important. In fact, the patent protection apparatus would not exist if patent holders did not feel that their interests were being harmed. The next section discusses the various patent holders.

Chinese Patent Policy and the Societal Actors

The previous section established the principal rationale for designing Chinese patent policy on the state side, and this section studies the effect of Chinese patent policy on the country's various business actors. After all, it is the Chinese business community whose interests are directly affected by the implementation of Chinese patent policy. The following questions guide my discussion: Who creates patents and who holds them? Who infringes upon them? What does the notion of patent mean for patent holders and patent infringers? How important (or unimportant) is the issue of patents for them? Why is the patent issue important for some business actors but not others? During the defense and infringement activities, who are the winners and losers?

I demonstrate that the implementation of Chinese patent policy creates uneven results for different types of Chinese business actors, which in turn shapes their different attitudes toward the international patent norm. That is, foreign companies investing in China and some elite Chinese private companies are very serious about patent protection because it is a key component of their competitiveness. Small and medium-sized private enterprises, which constitute the majority of Chinese private enterprises, adopt an ambivalent attitude toward the patent norm. They understand the importance of patents but cannot afford to invest in expensive research and development activities. State-owned enterprises have been indifferent to patents due to having guaranteed market profits, and they remain at best a clumsy player in the patent game. These different attitudes impact the outcome of patent enforcement in a significant way.

Chinese Patent Policy: Achievements and Limitations

A key component of China patent policy is to create high-quality patents and apply them to market benefits. Chinese patent policy is profoundly dependent on the country's science and technology policy. An in-depth understanding of Chinese patent policy can hardly be achieved without a thorough scrutiny of the country's science and technology reforms. This section demonstrates that China has made impressive achievements in

Table 1. Major National-Level Initiatives on Chinese Science and Technology Reform (1985–2008)

Date	*Major Initiatives on Science and Technology Reform*
June 10, 2008	Outline of National Intellectual Property Rights Strategy
January 26, 2006	State Middle and Long Term Science and Technology Development Guidelines (2006–2020)
August 20, 1999	Decision to Strengthen Technological Innovation Work and Industrialize High Technology
September 15, 1996	Decision to Deepen Science and Technology Reform
June 6, 1995	Decision on Accelerating Science and Technological Progress
May 3, 1988	Decision on Several Issues in Deepening Science and Technology Reform
March 13, 1988	Decision on the Reform of Science and Technology System

building its science and technology capacities, which have made the country a major player in global patent affairs. However, serious limitations remain as barriers to China's efforts at becoming a leading innovator in the world. Both the achievements and limitations of Chinese patent policy provide a useful perspective to examine the thoroughness of the country's ongoing political and economic reforms.

A restructuring of the Chinese science and technology sector started in the mid-1980s. Over the past several decades, Chinese decision makers have increasingly realized that China must place a greater emphasis on intellectual property rights if the country is to maintain its sustainable growth. To that end, China has issued a series of initiatives since 1985 to construct a favorable policy environment for the country's scientific and technological development (see Table 1). Although the wording of the policy initiatives may be different, they are driven by a similar principle, which is to adapt the country's scientific research system to the needs of the market economy. To that end, the Chinese government has attempted to concentrate financial resources on consistently supporting science and technology forces in strategic and basic research areas. Additionally, China's once tightly controlled applied research sector has been pushed to become a market entity and directly face business competition. In the words of a scholar on Chinese science and technology policy, the strategy can be described as "anchoring one end and freeing up the other" (*wenzhu yitou, fangkai yipian*).[42]

The most recent among these initiatives was the 2012 Opinion on Deepening Science and Technology Reform and Accelerating the Construction of National Innovation System, known as the 2012 Opinion. In the 2012 Opinion, the Chinese government reiterated its goal of establishing a full-fledged, market-oriented national innovation system by 2020. According to those guidelines, by 2020, 70 percent of China's gross domestic product (GDP) growth would be due to scientific and technological progress, the research and development (R&D) expenditures would be over 2 percent of the country's GDP, and the cost of importing foreign technology would account for less than 30 percent of the country's total investment in developing new technology.[43]

It is unfair to say that the Chinese governments at various levels were ignorant of the importance of patents. In fact, since China's WTO entry in 2001, various local governments have adopted their own patent strategies to encourage companies under their jurisdictions to apply for patents. This move should be credited for alerting enterprises of the importance of patents and thus causing a rapid increase of patent filings. Nevertheless, significant problems remain because many governmental units seem to equate "patent strategy" with "encouraging patent applications." In some cases, local governments paid patent filing fees for enterprises. Once the patent application was approved, however, the governments refused to pay the patent maintenance fee and asked the enterprises to pay it. Since the enterprises did not know how to utilize the patents, they ceased paying the patent maintenance fee several years after it was granted. In some extreme cases, the enterprises did not even pick up the patent certificates when their patents filings were approved.[44] Chinese patent law provides that an invention patent can be valid for twenty years. But according to Zuo Ye, a deputy of the Chinese People's Political Consulting Conference (CPPCC), in 2012, a province he investigated maintained only nine valid invention patents in 2012, even though that province filed 60,000 new patent applications that year.[45] In that sense, patent strategy became a "face project" (*mianzi gongcheng*) for some local leaders. Despite the Chinese government's repeated call to enhance China's indigenous innovation capability and turn science and technology into a key engine for the country's modernization, both Chinese IPR officials and scholars have expressed reservations about whether China can achieve the goal of building an innovation-oriented country by 2020.[46] According to a Shanghai-based IPR official, "Are you impressed, if not scared, by the rocketing growth of invention patents in China? But do you know that Chinese government units at various levels are good at playing with numbers? Do not forget that grain production in China never declined even during the years of famine. If you do not know the tricks of number games, you do not really understand the Chinese government officials."[47]

The achievements and limitations of Chinese patent policy are further reflected in statistical data released by both the Chinese government and international organizations. As of 2012, China has employed 2.88 million R&D professionals, ranking first in the world. This is an increase of almost three times the number of R&D professionals employed in 2002. The country's R&D expenditures surpassed that of Japan and reached 1,000 billion RMB (about $16 billion), ranking second in the world, behind only the United States. This number accounted for 1.83 percent of China's total GDP. Although this percentage is lower than the 2 percent R&D/GDP ratio of most developed countries in the world, it is the highest among the developing countries.[48] From 2002 to 2011, the number of invention patent filings in China grew at an annual rate of 23.3 percent, far exceeding the worldwide average rate of 4.7 percent. In 2011, China's invention patent filings reached 526,000 and surpassed Japan, the United States, and Korea, ranking highest in the world.[49]

Despite these impressive achievements, China's innovation competitiveness still lags behind developed countries. According to the *Global Competitiveness Yearbook* published by the World Economic Forum in Switzerland, in 2002, China's innovation competitiveness index was ranked as forty-third out of 181 countries under study.[50] Despite the rapid growth of China's patent filings, the newly released *Global Competitiveness Yearbook* for 2012 to 2013 indicated that China's innovation competitiveness index was ranked thirty-third out of the 144 countries under study.[51] Although the ranking is mainly for reference purposes, the data suggest that the growth of China's innovation ability did not progress at a speed commensurate with the country's rapid GDP growth during the past decade.

Because of those limitations, China remains a "big but not powerful country" in the arena of patent affairs worldwide. A closer examination of the quality of Chinese patents may reveal some hard truths disguised by the stunning growth of Chinese patent applications. Under Article 2 of the 2008 Chinese patent law, three types of industrial innovations can be granted a patent in China: invention, utility model, and industrial design. Specifically, an invention patent is for a new technical solution to a product, process, or its improvement; the utility model, popularly known as an "incremental invention" or "minor patent," is a new technical solution to the shape or configuration or their combination of a product, which is industrially applicable; and industrial design is a new design to the shape or pattern of a product, their combination or combination of colors therewith, which is aesthetic and industrially applicable. Judging from the definition of these three types of patents, the invention patent is the most technologically sophisticated, and industrial design is the least sophisticated, with the utility model in between. One cannot dismiss the utility model and industrial design as completely worthless, but the quantity and quality of an invention patent in a country's high-tech industries are a stronger indicator of a country's technological competitiveness. Statistical data, as recorded in the following two figures, reflect both the achievements and limitations of Chinese patent policy. As indicated in Figure 2, invention patents granted to Chinese domestic applicants started to catch up with foreign companies investing in China between 2008 and 2009. However, given the vast number of domestic Chinese companies, most patents granted to Chinese domestic applicants are still concentrated in the areas of utility models and industrial designs (see Figure 3). Therefore, it can be concluded that Chinese domestic companies are still latecomers to the patent game. A long way is still ahead for the Chinese economy to shift from a reliance on cheap labor and mobilization of natural resources toward scientific research and technological innovation.

Business and Government Actors on the Stage of Patent in China: Who Are the Winners? Who Are the Losers?

In business competition, a patent is a very powerful weapon. It serves as both a shield and a spear. It is a shield in that a patent rewards and protects the outcomes of technological innovation and a spear in that a patent helps open new markets for the company's products. In China's business arena, different sets of business actors possess different levels of patent arsenals. They differ from each other not only in terms of the size of their patent arsenal but also in terms of the strategy with which they use their patent arsenal to compete. This, in turn, determines their different attitudes toward patents and therefore the results of patent enforcement. Specifically,

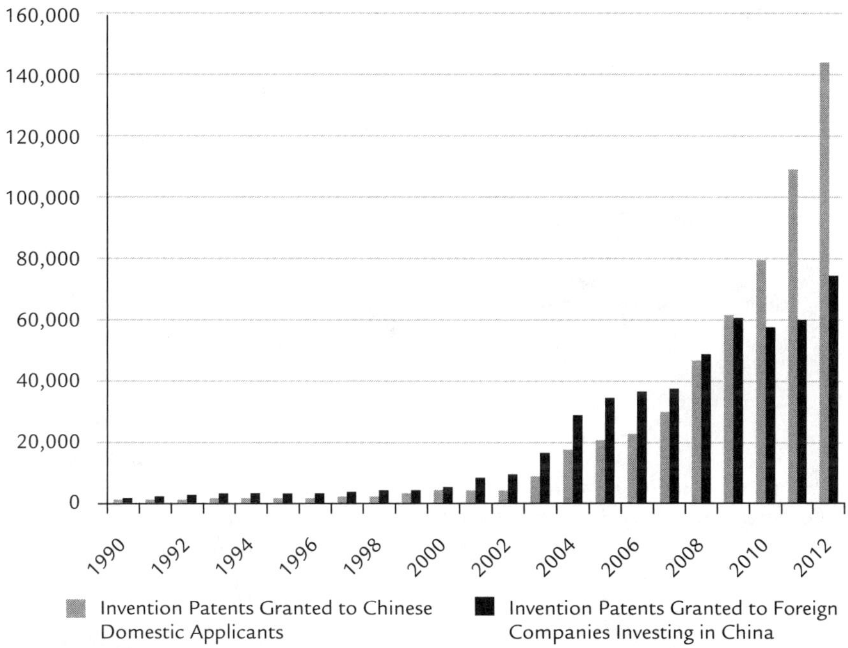

Figure 2. Domestic and foreign invention patents granted in China, 1990–2012. *Statistic Bulletin of the Chinese State Intellectual Property Office (SIPO)* (Guojia Zhishi Chanquan Ju Zhuanli Yewu Gongzuo Ji Zonghe Guanli Tongji Yuebao), January 9, 2013.

three sets of business actors are on the stage: foreign companies investing in China, state-owned enterprises, and domestic private enterprises.

Foreign companies' attitudes toward patents are fairly straightforward. Most foreign companies investing in China originate from developed countries, whose economies have progressed from the industrial age to the information age. Therefore, intellectual property rights constitute a key aspect of their competitiveness. However, as the China branches of their parent companies, the major aspects of their R&D activities happen outside of China's soil. Therefore, the most important aspects of IPR work for foreign companies in China are not the creation and application of IPR. Instead, they mostly concern the protection of their IPR in China and eventually how to maximize their share in the Chinese market. Although foreign companies need to follow the same procedures to apply for patents as their Chinese counterparts, they are much more experienced in utilizing patents

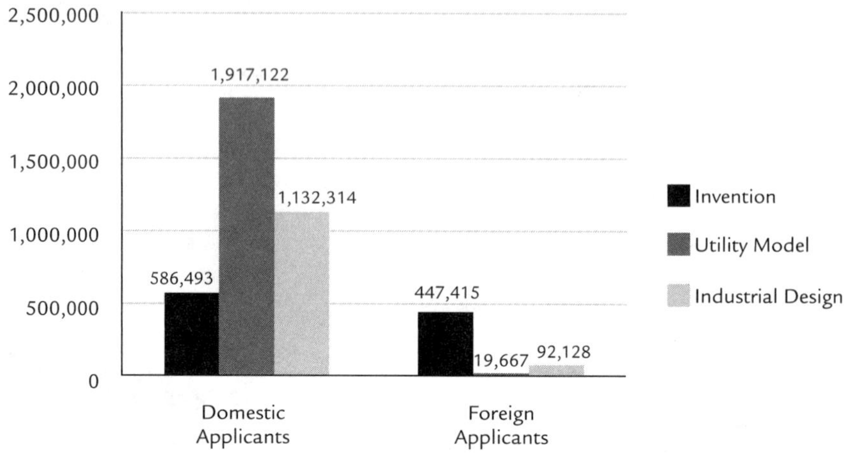

Figure 3. Cumulative number of valid patents in China as of December 2013. *Statistic Bulletin of the Chinese State Intellectual Property Office (SIPO)* (Guojia Zhishi Chanquan Ju Zhuanli Yewu Gongzuo Ji Zonghe Guanli Tongji Yuebao), December 5, 2013.

to maximize their market profits in China. Between 2008 and 2012, foreign-related IPR cases (including Hong Kong and Taiwan related) accounted for only 3.2 percent of the total IPR cases handled by the Chinese court. Since they are more prepared and experienced in dealing with IPR legal matters, foreign IPR holders (including IPR holders from Hong Kong and Taiwan) have won 80 percent of those cases.[52] Not surprisingly, foreign companies' patent activities have raised discontent among China's economic nationalists.

State-owned enterprises constitute the economic foundation of China's socialist system. Starting in the 1980s, China introduced a series of liberalization policies for the country's state-owned enterprises. Under the liberalization policies, the majority of state-owned enterprises turned into market entities. However, the government policy that state-owned enterprises should assume a "leadership role" in the Chinese economy still remains. According to a policy speech delivered by former Chinese president Hu Jintao at the eighteenth Chinese Communist Party National Congress in 2012, the Chinese government should "push state-owned capital to further invest in those important industries and areas key to national security and the life line of national economy, consistently improve state-owned economy's vitality (*huoli*), influence (*yingxiangli*), and ability of control (*kongzhili*)."[53] In 2006, Li Rongrong, former director of the Chinese State-Owned Assets Supervision and Administration Commission (SASAC), already stated that state-owned enterprises should assume "absolute control" over core realms related to the country's economic security. These realms include the production of military industry equipment, electricity supply, petrol and energy, telecommunication services, coal and metal mining, transportation, and machine building.[54] In the past, there consistently were calls to break the monopoly status of Chinese state-owned enterprises. Decision makers, however, seemed to turn a deaf ear to those calls. In 2013, Li Rongrong's successor, Jiang Jiemin, told the press that "[the government should] unswervingly build the state owned enterprises and state owned economy better and stronger."[55] Under this policy, the profits of state-owned enterprises stem more from their monopoly over a certain industry rather than technological innovation. In 2014, of the 106 Chinese companies ranked among the world's *Fortune* 500, 93 were state-owned enterprises. This number was second only to the United States, with 128 companies entering the list. The 93 companies were concentrated in the fields of energy, electricity, telecommunication, and iron and steel, all of which are dominated by the Chinese state-owned economy.[56] Given the monopolistic nature of those industries, most Chinese state-owned enterprises are not as enthusiastic about intellectual property rights as their private counterparts.

Due to their indifference to IPR, many state-owned enterprises have made use of their political advantage and pursued short-term economic interests in areas such as real estate. According to the SASAC, 94 out of 169 central-level state-owned enterprises (SOEs) invested in real estate between 2008 and 2012. Seventy-eight of the central-level SOEs were not previously related to real estate businesses.[57] At the same time, however, the average ratio between R&D expenditures and the total business income of China's central-level SOEs was only 1.5 percent while most of the top 500 companies in the world invest 5 to 10 percent of their business income in research and development.[58] Among the top ten Chinese domestic companies granted invention patents, only one—China Petroleum Co. Ltd.—is state owned (see Table 2).

According to Tian Lipu, then director of the Chinese State Intellectual Property Office, as of 2006, 96 percent of Chinese state-owned enterprises have never applied for patents.[59] In response to these dismal numbers, the

Table 2. Top Ten Chinese Domestic Companies with Valid Invention Patents in 2013

Company	*Number of Invention Patents*
1. Huawei Technology Co. Ltd.	18,880
2. Zhongxin Communication Co. Ltd.	12,902
3. China Petroleum Co. Ltd.	6,416
4. Hongfujin Precision Machinery Co. Ltd. (Shenzhen)	4,877
5. Youda Technology Co. Ltd. (Shenzhen)	4,045
6. SMIC (China) Co. Ltd.	2,327
7. Biyadi Co. Ltd.	2,099
8. TMC (China) Co. Ltd.	1,947
9. Huasan Telecommunication Equipment Co. Ltd.	1,902
10. Hunan Qiuzeyou Patent Strategic Planning Co. Ltd.	1,821

Source: Annual Report on Valid Patents in China, State Intellectual Property Office (2013).

Chinese SASAC included innovation and IPR work in 2007 as part of the evaluation index for the promotion of SOE managers.[60] Chinese state-owned enterprises have started to realize the importance of IPR since then. Nevertheless, a significant problem still remains: they realize the importance of IPR through the SASAC's teachings instead of business competition. During an interview in 2007, a legal representative from a state-owned company asked me why I "bothered to write on such an 'unimportant' topic as intellectual property rights."[61] Harsh realities later educated the SOE employee. In April 2013, the Second Intermediate People's Court in Shanghai published the country's first white paper on an SOE-related IPR trial. According to the white paper, between 2008 and 2012, 76.6 percent of the IPR disputes had SOEs as the defendants, and among those IPR disputes, SOEs lost 88 percent of the cases.[62] Although no national data about SOE-related IPR disputes are available, one can reasonably infer that the bargaining power of SOEs in other provinces was not much stronger than that of their counterparts in Shanghai. When asked for her comment on the white paper, that legal representative said she no longer regarded

IPR as "unimportant." However, her comment indicated that it will require a lot of effort for Chinese state-owned enterprises to fully internalize the patent norm. She stated that "every year we have to include a section on our company's IPR work in the annual report to the SASAC. We do so at their request, not out of our own will. Is IPR more important for us than before? Maybe. But that feeling is more acute for our managers because it is important for their career promotion. For people on the forefront of doing business like us, the importance of IPR remains on paper and would not be felt until business competition reminds us."[63]

Less straightforward is the attitude of domestic private companies. China has nurtured a considerable number of private companies during the countries' three decades of economic reform. As of 2011, there are 10.52 million private companies in China, accounting for 97 percent of Chinese domestic companies. Those 10.52 million private companies contribute about 60 percent of China's GDP, 50 percent of China's tax revenue, 75 percent of employment opportunities, and 65 percent of domestic invention patents.[64] Among the 10.52 million private companies, about 142,000 are startup high-tech enterprises. Out of the 550 "experimental innovative enterprises" designated by the Chinese Ministry of Science and Technology between 2006 and 2011, two-thirds are private enterprises.[65] Private high-tech enterprises are the most responsive actors to market forces and actively engage in innovation activities. As indicated in Table 2, nine out of the top ten domestic companies granted invention patents in 2013 are private high-tech companies. These companies are quickly catching up with their foreign counterparts and becoming increasingly important and skillful players in the patent arena.

However, elite private companies are only a minority of Chinese private companies. Most Chinese private companies still rely on cheap labor, low wages, and heavy inputs of natural resources rather than innovation as the core component of their competitiveness. Years of business competition have educated them about the importance of patents, but heavy investment in R&D and skillful application of patents in business competition are still a luxury for many private enterprises in the early stages of their development. In 2012, Chinese private enterprises only accounted for 15 percent of the country's total investment in research and development, with the majority of research and development funds channeled toward state-owned enterprises. Therefore, Chinese private enterprises' innovation activity is haunted by an embarrassing dilemma: as the most responsive actors to market needs, they have the incentives to innovate, but they do not have sufficient financial aid from the state and have to rely on themselves to engage in research and development projects. Chinese state-owned enterprises worry much less about the funding for innovation, but they are not as enthusiastic about innovation. Due to the lack of a transparent supervision system, much of the state subsidies for innovation channeled to the state-owned research and development units has been wasted.[66] Although the incentives for Chinese private enterprises to engage in innovation activities are predominantly economic, they have to face the harsh reality that they are politically inferior to their state-owned counterparts.

The difficult political and economic environment has created serious barriers for the innovation activities of small and medium-sized Chinese private enterprises. According to Cheng Siwei, former vice chair of the Chinese National People's Congress, "[The small and medium-sized Chinese private companies in China] grow up slowly, live shortly, and die quickly (*zhangbuda, huobuchang, sidekuai*). Due to the high risk involved in the research and development process and the lack of a support network to cushion the risks, many Chinese private enterprises cannot afford to innovate and dare not innovate. If these problems remain unresolved, eventually the consequence is that they do not want to innovate."[67]

A nationwide survey of Chinese private companies by SIPO further illustrates the IPR dilemma faced by Chinese private companies. Ninety percent of the managers of Chinese private companies believed that IPR is "important" or "very important" for their competitiveness. But only 37.5 percent conduct independent research and development activities, and 44.3 percent of their products did not contain any patented technology. Also, 80.2 percent have not established an independent functional department to manage IPR.[68] According to the Chinese People's Supreme Court, as of 2012, more than 90 percent of patent disputes happened between Chinese domestic enterprises.[69] No systematic data are available about who won or lost in those patent disputes, but it is reasonable to conclude that private companies with smaller patent arsenals and less patent lawsuit experience tend to be the weaker side in the disputes.

Foreign companies complain that they have been victims of IPR infringement, often perpetrated by Chinese private companies. But in the long run, the Chinese private companies are not winners either. Due to the unfriendly environment for innovation, many Chinese private enterprises lack their own patents and are content with imitating others. This situation stifles their creativity. In the short term, they may grow quickly in both company size and market share by copying the others, but they also bring attention from their competitors. When their competitors deem the private companies' growth as hurting their interests, a patent lawsuit will be brought forth.[70] Due to their weaker position in the dispute, the Chinese private enterprises are often at a disadvantage. Some are totally unprepared and even do not realize the seriousness of the problem until a lawsuit is brought against them.[71] When they lose the patent cases, they have to pay a high patent fee to the winning side. More important, their creativity gets rusty by relying on the duplication of others' technology, and they lose the ability to grow their companies.

During the current transitional period of the Chinese economy, a lot of private enterprises have reaped business benefits from their innovation efforts and earnestly sought to bring the violators of their IPR to justice when their interests have been hurt by IPR infringement. At the same time, however, private enterprises more or less have depended on copying their more technologically advanced counterparts during the early stages. According to an IPR attorney, "Be it foreign companies, state-owned companies, or private companies; be it established business monster or startup imps, everybody claims to be losers in the IPR game to win sympathy, but nobody in China can claim their hands to be completely clean on the issue of IPR. They can be winners on some occasion[s], but they are losers under other circumstances."[72] Therefore, many Chinese private companies adopt an ambivalent attitude toward IPR. They love it because they have more or less benefited from technological innovation. They also hate it because the costs involved in technological innovation are high and they have a disadvantageous position in IPR competition compared with their foreign counterparts.

As such, according to an IPR official in Shanghai, the Chinese government is often sandwiched between criticism from both foreign and domestic IPR holders who are dissatisfied with them. As expected, foreign IPR holders complain that Chinese bureaucracies only provide lip service and do not offer enough protection of their IPR. Domestic IPR holders complain that the Chinese IPR bureaucracy protects foreign IPR holders' interests over the interests of Chinese domestic businesses. After losing a patent lawsuit, a Chinese domestic IPR holder made the following comment: "The IPR judges praise themselves for delivering high-quality enforcement. They claim that they made the legal decision according to the law and that we are equal with our foreign counterparts before the law. But didn't the foreign companies copy the others during the early stage of their development? We are much later comers to the race. Are we really equal players on the stage?"[73]

Hence, one of the most important obstacles for effective patent enforcement to emerge and be sustained is the weak support from the country's domestic business constituency. As analyzed earlier, obstacles originate in large part from the country's political and economic system: how can one expect a country's societal actors to be innovative if the country's political system does not encourage or even stifles individual creativity? In promoting the effectiveness of patent enforcement, many Chinese IPR professionals, like the two patent officials cited at the beginning of this chapter, share the goals of building China into an innovative country. The building of an innovative country, however, requires bold and sometimes painful reforms, if not a thorough overhaul, of China's political and economic system. The overhaul is so thorough that some of the very basic foundations of China's communist system will inevitably be touched. According to a senior official, who was a prestigious scientist in China before joining government service, insightful people among the country's decision-making circle are already aware of that, but none is bold enough to lay out concrete steps to carry out these reforms because they are also aware that these reforms will become part of a fundamental social change in China that is likely to challenge the rule of the Community Party. In his words,

> In order for patent enforcement to be really effective, state and business actors alike should first agree that technological innovation should be protected as private property. The soul of innovation is freedom—freedom to explore, freedom to experiment, freedom to compete. But that notion goes against the basic principle of Communist belief. Here is the real challenge for the Chinese government: does China want to be built into an innovative country? The answer is yes. But the government has to first recognize the legitimacy of private property and respect the freedom of the Chinese citizens. That move inevitably will plant the seeds for the erosion of the country's Communist system. In that sense, Chinese government is walking on the tightrope.[74]

Conclusion

This chapter demonstrates that the outcomes of Chinese patent enforcement are impacted by the interaction between the country's state and societal actors. The effectiveness of patent protection hinges not only on the capacity of the Chinese state, as previous scholars have argued, but also on how patent holders can persuade the Chinese state to stand on their side. Findings in this chapter also suggest that various branches of Chinese patent bureaucracy hold the promotion of the country's "patent work," rather than just "patent protection," as their top priority. That is, when Chinese patent officials are convinced that protecting patents can help to promote their local economy through industrial upgrading, patent protection efforts are more likely to reap effective outcomes. Otherwise, patent protection efforts will become a mere formality without meaningful outcomes. Different types of business actors—namely, Chinese state-owned enterprises, foreign companies investing in China, elite Chinese private companies, and small and medium-sized domestic companies—assume different positions in the arena of Chinese patent affairs. Their interaction patterns with the Chinese state are different from one another. That further explains why some patent enforcement efforts can yield more effective outcome while the others cannot.

A less obvious, albeit important, aspect of Chinese patent work is how it impacts and is impacted by the country's ongoing political and economic reforms. Conventional wisdom holds that the issue of patents is politically neutral, but this chapter teases out the political logic that impacts the quality of patent enforcement. That is, the designers and practitioners of Chinese patent policy primarily aim to promote the country's economic development with progress in science and technology. But further progress in science and technology requires further political and economic reform, a reform that will challenge the economic foundation of the Chinese communist political system. In seeking to promote the effectiveness of patent enforcement in China, the country should also seek a way to further liberate Chinese people's innovative potential that had once been suppressed by the country's authoritarian political system. However, as the economic foundation of China's authoritarian political system, the country's SOEs are at best mild supporters of patent norms. Even though foreign companies investing in China and Chinese elite private companies strongly advocate the patent norms, the overall level of patent enforcement in China would remain modest if Chinese SOEs could reap guaranteed profits with their dominant position in the country's economy rather than technological innovation. In building an innovative country, however, China should first have the courage to introduce more thorough reforms to remove the political and economic obstacles on the road.

The interaction between Chinese patent policy and Chinese economic development in the past can serve as a useful tool to forecast the country's future development path. After almost a decade of double-digit growth, the annual growth rate of the Chinese economy began to slow down to less than 8 percent in 2014. That growth rate further slowed down to less than 7 percent in 2015.[75] The situation was termed by the Chinese leadership as the "new normal" (*xin changtai*).[76] The "new normal" state of the Chinese economy exposed the old development model as unsustainable and propelled the country to derive its growth momentum from technological innovation rather than mere input of cheap labor and raw materials. That, in turn, pressured the country's patent policy to better serve the needs to build an innovative country. While it is very likely that the Chinese Communist Party (CCP) will still stick to its grip of political power, the further expansion of constituencies for a patent norm in China will require a thorough change in the way in which the CCP governs the country. In fact, in 2015, the Chinese State Council already started a new round of SOE reforms to introduce more private capital into the realms previously dominated by SOEs.[77] Those reforms, known as the "mixed-ownership reform" (*hunhe suoyouzhi gaige*), will thoroughly change the operation of Chinese SOEs and their relationship with their private counterparts. The pattern of implementing Chinse patent policy will inevitably be reconfigured.

In that sense, we can expect that disputes over patents, both among Chinese domestic actors and with foreign countries, will continue well into the future because these disputes are not over the issue of patents per se. In seeking to promote more effective outcomes of patent enforcement, China is also seeking a development model that suits itself and the need to coexist with the rest of the world. In the foreseeable future, that task would remain a critical challenge for the Chinese government.

CHAPTER 3

The Political Economy of Chinese Copyright Legislation

Known for his musical talents since he was a teenager, Shi Guangnan was born in 1940 in southwestern China's Chongqing City. He composed his first song, "Waltz of Tonya," in 1956, which was performed by the prestigious Chinese Central Radio Choir and gained national fame immediately. Shi Guangnan's musical talents were further developed after he was admitted into the Chinese Central Conservatory of Music (CCCOM). While Shi Guangnan was still a college student at the CCCOM in 1961, his musical works won warm praise from the president of the Chinese Musicians Association, Lu Ji, as "representing the new gains of the development of our country's folk music."[1]

In 1966, the Cultural Revolution broke out, marking a decade of long internal political strife due to the power struggles within Chinese top leadership. A year later, Shi Guangnan and other Chinese musicians were driven to the countryside to do forced physical labor. The political persecution, however, did not stop Shi Guangnan from pursuing his dream in music. While living in the rural areas, Shi Guangnan closely interacted with common Chinese people and drew inspiration from their folk music. In 1976, he composed "The Toasting Song" to celebrate the end of the Cultural Revolution. That song established Shi Guangnan as a leading composer in China during the era of market reform. In the 1980s, Shi composed over one hundred songs, most of which were broadcast and well received nationwide. One of the songs, "The Land Full of Hope," won him the Golden Disc Award, the highest award for Chinese composers. The singer who performed that song, Peng Liyuan, was starting to build her fame across the country and later around the globe. In 2006, she became the first Chinese singer to receive the "outstanding artist award" issued by Lincoln Center in New York City.

The material rewards for Shi Guangnan, however, did not match his achievements in music. In 1984, even after Shi Guangnan was elected vice president of the Chinese Musicians Association, his monthly salary was only 105 RMB (about $20). "The Land Full of Hope" won Shi Guangnan the Golden Disc Award, but Shi only received 30 RMB (about $5) as remuneration for that song, which was less than the average price of a concert ticket in Beijing in the mid-1980s. On April 18, 1990, Shi had a stroke and died about two weeks later. While Shi was receiving emergency treatment in the hospital, his wife received the last piece of remuneration via the mail for a song that he had written. The remuneration was only 10 RMB (about $1.5). During Shi Guangnan's funeral, his widow displayed the tape with Shi Guangnan's music and the 10 RMB paycheck.[2] The paycheck was never cashed. Instead, Shi's widow kept it as the evidence of the low esteem for Chinese copyright holders.

Several months after Shi Guangnan's death, China adopted its first copyright law. Wang Liping, a close friend of Shi Guangnan and a member of the Standing Committee of the Chinese National People's Congress, recounted Shi's story to the country's top legislative body.[3] It is generally believed that Shi's story contributed greatly to the adoption of Chinese copyright law.

The life experience of Shi Guangnan is but one example of the fate of Chinese copyright holders. It illustrates the difficulties of the struggle for copyright protection in China over the past six decades. This chapter examines the challenges surrounding China's adoption of the copyright norm. Based on findings derived from interviews and newly declassified archival materials, I advance several arguments in this chapter. First, similar to the patent regime, it is the combination of domestic demands and foreign pressure for copyright protection that has shaped the present Chinese copyright regime. Although the final decision to pass copyright protections was made by the Chinese central government, the process of China's adoption of the copyright norm featured intense competition between domestic and foreign interest groups. Eventually, the procopyright camp overcame the opposition of the anticopyright camp and convinced Chinese top decision makers to follow the track of the international copyright regime. Second, different from the patent regime, which was mainly related to Chinese science and technology policy, the evolution of the Chinese copyright regime reflects China's gradual opening into the realm of ideology and propaganda policy. The adoption of the first patent law in China took four years (1980–1984), but the adoption of the first copyright law in China took a much longer time of ten years (1980–1990). A key reason for this length of time was because the Chinese copyright law regulates not only economic interests but also ideological and cultural affairs, which are more sensitive than merely economic interests.

This chapter is organized as follows: the first section provides a brief definition of the copyright norm and discusses the norm's political implications. The next sections analyze how the evolving political and ideological environments in China affected the evolution of the country's copyright regime in different historical periods. The historical periods include the prereform era (1949–1978), early reform era (1978–1990), pre–World Trade Organization (WTO) era (1990–2001), and post-WTO era (2001–present). The conclusion of this chapter summarizes the evolution of the strength of Chinese copyright holders, from weak to strong, and discusses how that process has impacted China's adoption of the copyright norm.

The Copyright Norm and Its Political Implications

Copyright is traditionally the protection given to creators for their literary or artistic work. Under the Trade-Related Aspects of Intellectual Property Rights (TRIPS) Agreement, copyright protection shall extend to the "*expressions* and not to ideas, procedures, methods of operation or mathematical concepts as such."[4] Computer software has also been included under copyright protection because it is increasingly regarded as a literary work.[5]

Like patents, the goal of copyright protection is to instill incentives to create optimal levels of literary works so as to provide social, cultural, and economic benefits to society. However, because the subject matter of copyright protection is mostly literary material, the theoretical foundation of copyright legislation involves not only economic factors but also social and cultural factors. As argued by a legal scholar, copyright law not only provides economic incentives for authors and publishers but also "encourages creative expression on a wide array of political, social, and aesthetic issues.

The activity of creating and communicating such expression and the expression itself constitute vital components of a democratic civil society."[6]

Although profound socioeconomic changes have taken place in China in recent decades, the country remains an authoritarian country. The government still places many restrictions on the freedom of expression, and advocates of copyright protection in China face this harsh reality. The evolution of the Chinese copyright regime offers a useful perspective to study the struggle for the freedom of expression in a not-yet-democratic country such as China.

Early Years of Chinese Copyright Laws, 1949–1978

This section analyzes the early years of Chinese copyright laws, from 1949 to 1966. I identify two phases during these years. The first phase begins with the success of the Chinese communist revolution in 1949 to the Anti-Rightist Movement in 1957. The second phase is between 1957 and the breakout of the Cultural Revolution in 1966. I argue that there was an incipient recognition of copyright during the first phase of the People's Republic, with a series of legal regulations adopted to protect copyright. However, after the country's general political climate took more stringent control of Chinese intellectuals in the late 1950s, the existing copyright laws were reduced to empty shells and eventually repealed during the Cultural Revolution. Although China's copyright regime was short-lived during the early years of the People's Republic, the early copyright laws planted the seeds for China's copyright regime to reemerge and grow during the market reform era.

The First Phase of Chinese Copyright Legislation, 1949–1957

Although China is the birthplace of printing technology, no official copyright laws existed in the country until the early twentieth century. After being forced to open its door to the outside world in the late nineteenth century, Chinese political and intellectual elites became exposed to the notion of copyright protection. In 1910, 1915, and 1928, the Chinese government successively enacted a series of copyright and publication legal codes.[7] Although those legal codes were not implemented in a meaningful way due to years of political turmoil, civil war, and foreign invasion in China, a key function of the codes was to inform Chinese intellectuals of the importance of protecting their literary and artistic creation. That is, copyrighted works deserved not only material rewards but also moral respect. As a result, the intellectuals became the forerunners of copyright protection in China.

In 1927, a group of Chinese writers, with Hu Yuzhi, Zheng Zhenduo, and Ye Shentao as their leaders, organized the Shanghai Authors Association (*Shanghai Zhuzuoren Gonghui*), one of the first copyright holders' associations in Chinese history. The founders of the Shanghai Authors Association claimed that "authors share the same fate as physical laborers. They are also vulnerable to economic exploitation by the politically and economically privileged. . . . They should establish an organization to change the unfavorable environment."[8] In 1932, the Shanghai Authors Association was upgraded to the China Authors and Writers Association (*Zhongguo Zhuzuozhe Xiehui*). The main goals of the China Authors and Writers Association were to "strive for the freedom of expression and publishing, oppose any form of opposition against the Chinese authors, and improve their working conditions."[9]

When the People's Republic of China (PRC) was founded in 1949, the Chinese Communist Party (CCP) did not immediately establish all-encompassing control over the realm of publishing. In a speech delivered shortly after the establishment of the PRC in October 1949, Lu Dingyi, head of the CCP Propaganda Department, told the representatives of the National Publishing Conference that "[state-owned publishers] should cooperate with private bookstores and publishers in an honest and sincere manner."[10] At the same time, the Chinese government recruited many non–Communist Party intellectuals to participate in the governance of cultural and publishing affairs in the early 1950s. The forerunners in calling for copyright protection in China in the 1920s and 1930s included Hu Yuzhi, who was appointed the first director of the State General Publishing Office, and Ye Shentao, who was the vice director. Also, their colleague at the Shanghai Authors Association in the 1920s, Zheng Zhenduo, became the vice minister of culture. Although these intellectuals did not possess full CCP membership, they were placed in senior positions with real decision-making power. These intellectuals thus had a chance to put their long-held ideals into practice.

In a speech delivered in 1950, Hu Yuzhi put forward the following major proposals to develop China's publishing work. First, "we should uphold the principle of freedom of expression and publishing. The government should refrain from practicing censorship policy unless under extreme circumstances. That is an essential way to respect the authors' moral rights. That is also a responsible attitude towards the readers." Second, "[in order for] the authors and their copyright works to enjoy a relatively high level of respect, our royalty system should balance the interests of authors, readers, and publishers. In order to respect the authors' rights, the royalty rate should be determined after consulting with the authors." Third, "[for that purpose], a clear division of labor between publishing, distributing, and printing sectors should be institutionalized to oversee the publishers' respect for the authors and the readers."[11]

Under these guidelines, the Chinese General Publishing Office successively adopted the Resolution on the Improvement and Development of Publishing Work in 1950 (1950 Publishing Resolution) and the Provisional Regulations on Management of Book and Periodical Publishing, Printing, and Distribution in 1952 (1952 Provisional Regulations).[12] Both the 1950 Publishing Resolution and the 1952 Provisional Regulations emphasized copyright protection for authors. Shortly before the General Publishing Office was fused into the Ministry of Culture in 1954, a draft of the Provisional Regulations on Copyright Protection (1954 Provisional Regulations) was submitted to the State Council. In 1957, the Ministry of Culture formally approved the 1954 Provisional Regulations and issued a more detailed implementation explanation.[13] Shortly before that, a drafting group led by Hu Yuzhi was established to explore the feasibility of adopting a copyright law in China. But a full-fledged Chinese copyright law did not pass until more than three decades later. Chinese copyright legislation in the early 1950s appeared brief and incomprehensive compared with the contemporary Chinese copyright laws. Nevertheless, later generations of Chinese lawmakers respected those forerunner's efforts as courageous experiments to establish a full-fledged copyright regime.[14]

Various specific articles from the early Chinese copyright regulations demonstrated respect for authors' rights. For example, Article 17 of the 1950 Publishing Resolution provided that "the publishing industry must respect copyrights and the right to publish and must not allow unlawful reproduction, plagiarism, tampering and other acts."[15] Under Article 7 of the 1952 Provisional Regulations, the publishers of books and periodicals "must not infringe upon the copyrights and the rights to publish of others to their own works and to publication."[16] The 1957 Provisional Regulations further provided that "copyright holders own the copyright of their works for their entire life. The inheritors of the copyright holders can continue to own the copyright for twenty years after the death of the copyright holders."[17]

Under the early Chinese copyright legislation, authors enjoyed relatively high royalty rates. For example, Article 12 of the 1950 Publishing Resolution provided that "royalty measures shall be determined in consultation with the author, based on the principle of giving consideration to the interests of authors, readers, and publishers. In order to respect the rights of authors, in principle copyrights should not be sold off."[18] The 1950 Resolution also stipulated that "royalty calculation standards should be based in principle on the nature and quality of the work, the number of Chinese characters, and the number of copies printed."[19] Chinese literature and artistic creators welcomed this type of royalty structure because it permitted continuing royalties to authors on a per-copy basis—thereby, not limiting royalties to one-time payments—which resulted in relatively large payments to authors.

Despite the general notions of protecting authors' rights, the 1950 Publishing Resolution did not provide an enforcement mechanism to supervise its implementation. In light of that, the 1952 Provisional Regulations not only reemphasized copyright protection for authors but also for the first time specified the statutory penalties for violations of authors' rights. Under Article 11, "if publishers, printers and distributors fraudulently utilize the name of the work of another or publish, print or distribute in the name of another . . . the publishing administrative organs must revoke that enterprise's permit to publish."[20]

In 1952, the Chinese General Publishing Office ushered in a publisher-author contract system to further clarify the rights and obligations of the parties involved and avoid difficulties with copyrights and royalties. Under this contract system, publishers and authors signed contracts that specified the number of Chinese characters in the original manuscript, the due date for the manuscript, the amount of royalty, and other provisions.[21] The publishing contract system only regulated the relationship between authors and publishers and did not stipulate any effective punishment against unauthorized reproduction by the third parties. Nevertheless, the respect for authors and writers was clearly embodied in those publishing contracts.

Under such royalty regulations, Chinese authors were able to enjoy a relatively high standard of living in the early 1950s. According to the recollection of Zhang Xi, who had served as the secretary general of the Chinese Writers Association (CWA) since 1953, twenty-nine nationally renowned authors were members of the CWA in 1954. With the base royalty and the continuing royalties, an author could make 50,000 RMB after publishing one book. If the book turned out to be a bestseller, an author could make 70,000 to 80,000 RMB.[22] For those authors, the larger royalties not only provided a more comfortable material life, but it also gave them a relatively independent social position. As such, they could focus on their literary creations without following the orders of the Chinese government.

Second Phase of the Early Years of Chinese Copyright Legislation, 1957–1966

The promising situation did not last long. In 1957, the Chinese Communist Party launched a campaign against authors and other intellectuals known as the Anti-Rightist Movement. The country's general policy trend shifted to exert greater control over literature production.[23] With the establishment of a public ownership economy, the Chinese government introduced policies to reduce the income gap between Chinese intellectuals and other citizens and to incorporate the former into the mass public. In that policy environment, China's early copyright laws became an easy target. Advocates for copyright protection in China were either forced to remain silent or had to shift toward the Party line against their will. On September 28, 1958, an editorial in *People's Daily*, the mouthpiece of the Chinese Communist Party, clearly articulated the Party's policy toward the Chinese authors:

> Two different lines struggle with each other during our discussion of adjusting the royalty rates. One is socialist; the other is capitalist. People with their minds filled with capitalistic thoughts would say: how can royalty rates be reduced? If so, who would toil to write books and articles? People armed with socialist and communist thoughts, however, would assert that reducing the royalty rates would not influence literary production. [In our society], communist thoughts have taken the upper hand while capitalistic fetishism is bound to go bankrupt.[24]

This editorial was followed by an official directive by the Chinese Ministry of Culture, entitled the Draft Provisional Regulations on Royalties for Literary and Social Science Works (1958 Royalty Regulations).[25] Under the 1958 Royalty Regulations, per-word and per-copy royalties were cut in half.

In March 1961, while the country's political climate became more stringent, the Chinese Ministry of Culture issued a new directive, known as the 1961 Royalty Directive.[26] According to the 1961 Royalty Directive, book royalties were limited to a one-time payment based on the number of Chinese characters and a vague reference to the "quality of the work." Moreover, authors would not receive royalties for reprinted editions. The 1961 Directive also stipulated that "professional authors" would receive regular salaries and payments under the new restricted system.

The 1961 Directive reflected a tightening of the control over intellectuals, particularly authors and writers, which began after the 1957 Anti-Rightist Movement and the dominant ideology of public ownership in China. The 1961 Directive, combined with the vague provisions for remedying copyright infringement, made the protection of copyright and authors' rights virtually nonexistent. Moreover, the royalty regulations had only covered part of copyright protection. As such, other significant copyright products, such as audiovisual materials, were completely not covered by the country's copyright legislation during this period.

Like the Chinese patent regime, the country's already fragile copyright regime suffered a deadly blow from the breakout of the Cultural Revolution in 1966. During the decade-long political turmoil, tens of thousands of Chinese authors and writers were persecuted, and many lost their lives. At the climax of the Cultural Revolution, the entire country's literary and artistic creations were stifled. From 1966 to 1970, for example, the entire country published only 2,927 new books.[27] China's copyright regime had to wait to reemerge until the Cultural Revolution ended and market reform started in the late 1970s.

The Adoption of the First Chinese Copyright Law, 1978–1990

This section discusses how China's first copyright law muddled through the decade-long debates and controversies during the 1980s and was eventually adopted in 1990. Although foreign countries and international organizations influenced the laws, the drafting of China's first copyright law in the 1980s was mainly a domestic process. Foreign influence did not emerge in the form of external pressure until the 1990s. Therefore, the legal arrangements as outlined in China's 1990 copyright law reflected a compromise between various Chinese domestic branches. The domestic appeal of Chinese copyright holders started to grow in the 1980s, but it remained weak compared with certain government branches. As a result, certain parts of the 1990 copyright law remained problematic and became the target of foreign and domestic critiques as the country was further integrated into the global copyright regime in the 1990s.

Prelude to the Adoption of the First Chinese Copyright Law

The key features of the policy and ideological environment during the late 1970s included the gradual recognition of the legitimacy of private property and respect for knowledgeable professionals. The sea change in the general political climate not only exerted a profound influence on Chinese science and technology professionals but also influenced the country's literary and artistic creators. Based on newly revealed evidence, this section demonstrates that the adoption of China's first copyright law was a complex process. The result was a competition between different state organs. In addition, the voices of Chinese social actors, such as writers and musicians, found their way into the top decision-making circle.

The first step for China to adopt the copyright norm was a restoration of the repealed royalty system. In May 1977, the Chinese State Council appointed Wang Kuang as the director of the State Publication Administration. After consulting with newly rehabilitated veteran authors, Wang Kuang drafted a report to the Chinese State Council proposing to reestablish the almost nonexistent royalty system. In October 1977, the State Council approved Wang's report and issued the Provisional Directive on Remuneration of Press and Publication (1977 Directive).[28] The 1977 Directive did not set the royalty rates as high as that in the early 1950s. Instead, it focused more on the authors' economic rights rather than moral rights. However, the issuing of the 1977 Directive and the other subsequent regulations on improving the authors' payment levels ignited a long-suppressed enthusiasm among Chinese authors. Chinese authors vowed to regain not only economic rights from their work but also their well-deserved moral rights. To that end, merely reinstalling the royalty system repealed during the Cultural Revolution was not sufficient. A copyright law was needed. Among the major advocates for a copyright law was Chen Dengke, a famous writer and a deputy of the Chinese National People's Congress. When the Second Annual Session of the Fifth National People's Congress (NPC) convened in 1979, Chen stated that the "freedom of publishing as enshrined in Chinese Constitution should be further safeguarded by a copyright law, in which authors possess copyright to their works."[29] Chen's proposal received positive feedback from leading Chinese writers and painters, many of whom were Chen's fellow NPC deputies. While there is no hard evidence about the impact of the domestic appeal for a copyright law on the top decision makers in the late 1970s, the mere mention of the "freedom of publishing" and "copyright law" by China's top legislative body in itself indicated an unusual opening to these concepts in China's political and ideological areas.

Another noteworthy development was the external influence from the advanced industrial countries. In 1978, China had its first interaction with the developed world over the copyright issue. In March 1978, a delegation of British publishers headed by Graham Green visited China. During the meeting with Wang Kuang and the senior officials of the Chinese State Publication Administration, the British side expressed a strong interest in cooperating with the Chinese side to introduce British books to China. One of the preconditions for bilateral cooperation was that the Chinese side would either enact a copyright law or join the Universal Copyright Convention. When the Chinese side returned the goodwill visit to Britain in 1979, the British side raised the copyright issue again.[30]

The same issue was raised during China's exchange with the United States. In January 1979, the copyright issue was first mentioned in the Implementation Accord on Cooperation in the Field of High-Energy Physics (known as the China-U.S. High-Energy Agreement) signed between then Chinese State Science and Technology Commissioner Fang Yi and U.S. Energy Secretary James Schlesinger. In the first bilateral trade agreement between China and the United States signed in March 1979, the American side proposed that "[before Chinese copyright law is enacted], both sides should confer rights commensurate with the Universal Copyright Convention to nationals of both countries."[31] Responding to both domestic and external appeals, the Chinese State Publication Administration submitted to the State Council an internal report, proposing that "although conditions are not ripe for our country to join Universal Copyright Convention and sign copyright protection agreement with foreign countries, copyright issue cannot be ignored and active measures shall be taken to handle this issue. At present, we propose to . . . draft copyright law and related regulations so as to get ready for the establishment of special copyright organ and join Universal Copyright Convention in the future."[32]

Adopting the Chinese Copyright Law

In July 1980, a working group was organized to draft the copyright law. Like their colleagues at the State Patent Bureau, the group drafting the copyright law invited foreign copyright experts to organize copyright seminars in China and send Chinese copyright delegations overseas to learn from other countries' copyright experience. On May 2, 1986, after sixteen major revisions, a completed draft of the copyright law was submitted to the State Council. In 1987, the State Copyright Administration and State Council Legal Affair Bureau held more than twenty joint discussion panels in Beijing and asked for opinions from local governments outside Beijing.[33] At the same time, according to the memoir of Song Muwen, then director of the National Copyright Administration (NCA), copyright legislation encountered strong opposition from several other ministries and almost halted the legislative process. On August 8, 1987, the State Science and Technology Commission, State Education Commission, China Science Academy, and China Science Research Society jointly wrote a letter to the State Council, opposing the enactment of the copyright law. For them, "the enactment of Copyright Law will hinder the use of foreign books and magazines and bring significant difficulty for China's scientific research and high education. Moreover, enormous expense of Chinese foreign reserve will be incurred: annual budget to purchase copyrighted foreign works will reach 600 million U.S. dollars."[34]

Therefore, the drafter of the above report proposed that (1) the enactment of the copyright law should be postponed and (2) even though the copyright law is enacted, accession to the Universal Copyright Convention should be postponed. In response to the doubts held by these groups, the Chinese State Copyright Administration submitted three consecutive reports to the State Council on February 26, October 5, and November 2, 1988.[35] On November 18 of that year, Huang Shuhai, vice director of the State Council Legal Affairs Bureau, directly reported to the top leaders of the Chinese State Council, who responded with a positive reply. Huang Shuhai's report summarized the main points in the three reports by the Chinese National Copyright Administration. The report also played a significant role in appeasing the concerns raised by the aforementioned four ministries. According to Huang, the $600 million to purchase copyrighted foreign works was significantly exaggerated. China only spent fewer than $3 million in 1983 and 1986 on foreign copyrighted works. Moreover,

China could purchase the rights to reprint science and technology works from foreign presses. Therefore, the concern that the copyright law would cause difficulty for scientific research and education in China was unwarranted.[36]

On January 15, 1989, General Secretary of the State Council Luo Gan further commented on Huang's report, stating that "it is inevitable to adopt a copyright law. Please distribute the draft law to greater audience and ask for their opinion."[37] On December 14, 1989, Chinese Premier Li Peng submitted the draft of the copyright law to the Standing Committee of the Chinese National People's Congress for legislative review. On December 24, 1989, the Eleventh Session of the Standing Committee of the Seventh Chinese NPC was convened, with the discussion of copyright law on its agenda. Although in principle, different ministries in the State Council agreed that a copyright law was necessary, strong disputes arose among legislators over some specific but important provisions of China's first copyright law. Specifically, the disputes concentrated on whether to grant copyright protection to literary or artistic works prohibited from publication under Chinese mainstream ideology; whether or not Chinese radio or TV stations should pay royalties under the circumstance of playing audiovisual materials for noncommercial purposes; whether computer software should be protected as copyright work and, if yes, how should it be protected; and so on.[38]

These issues were bitterly debated for several months during the Twelfth, Fourteenth, and Fifteenth Sessions of the Standing Committee of the NPC. According to a former official of the Chinese National Copyright Administration, although the drafting committee attempted to pass a law that would provide a higher level of copyright protection, the vice chair of the Legal Affairs Commission of the Standing Committee of the NPC, Song Rufen, passed a short note to then chair of the Drafting Committee as well as the director of National Copyright Administration, Song Muwen, advising him not to get stuck on secondary issues and let the copyright law pass first.[39] On September 7, 1990, after nearly a decade of legislative effort, the Chinese Copyright Law, featuring thirty major revisions, was adopted.

The 1990 Copyright Law consisted of fifty-six articles, divided into six sections, including issues relating to the scope of copyrightable works (Articles 2–8), the scope of copyright (Articles 9–19), the duration of copyright (Articles 20–22), the fair use of copyright (Articles 23–44), and the remedy for and protection against copyright infringement (Articles 45–50).[40] With the adoption of the 1990 Copyright Law, a full-fledged copyright regime was established in China. However, controversies over some specific provisions of the 1990 Copyright Law, particularly over the protection of computer software, during the drafting stage remained unresolved. This issue became one of the focal points during the China-U.S. IPR negotiations. Moreover, regulations concerning the relationship between Chinese copyright holders and performing units, such as radio and TV stations, remained unclear under the copyright law. This issue aroused intense debates between Chinese copyright holders and the country's radio and TV branches. The issue was not addressed until China engaged in the WTO entry negotiations in the late 1990s.

Chinese Copyright Legislation in the 1990s: Torn Between Foreign Pressure and Domestic Appeal

Like patents, Chinese copyright legislation also encountered enormous foreign pressure from both bilateral and multilateral sources during the 1990s. The bilateral pressure mainly came from China-U.S. IPR negotiations during the early 1990s while the multilateral pressure mainly came from China's WTO entry during the late 1990s. As preceding scholars, particularly Mertha (2005), rightly pointed out, the copyright issue was the most contentious part during the U.S.-China bilateral IPR negotiations because of the lobbying efforts of the copyright interest groups in the United States. Mertha also noted that, due to foreign pressure, foreign copyright holders enjoyed greater legal protection under China's copyright law than China's own citizens.[41] Given this, a number of questions arise: How did the Chinese domestic copyright holders and their sympathizers within the Chinese government view the supernational treatment of their foreign counterparts? Did they allow that situation to continue to exist throughout the 1990s? If not, how did they manage to change that situation?

This section demonstrates that, different from in the 1980s, foreign pressure on Chinese copyright legislation reached unprecedented levels in the 1990s. At the same time, Chinese domestic copyright holders adopted an ambivalent attitude in the face of rapidly growing foreign influence on Chinese copyright legislation. While growing foreign influence on Chinese copyright legislation made them uncomfortable as Chinese nationals, further exposure to the global copyright norms lent them a deeper understanding of international common practice as well as a good opportunity to push for further revisions of the Chinese copyright law.

China-U.S. IPR Negotiations and the Chinese Copyright Regime

Mertha provides a thorough analysis of how U.S.-China bilateral IPR negotiations impacted the Chinese IPR regime in the 1990s in his 2005 book.[42] The most important result of the U.S.-China bilateral IPR negotiations was a series of memoranda of understandings (MOUs) reached in 1992, 1995, and 1996, with the 1992 MOU explicitly touching upon Chinese copyright law. Article 3 of the 1992 MOU held that China agreed to accede to the Berne Convention for the Protection of Literary and Artistic Works (Berne Convention) and the Geneva Convention for Protection of Producers of Phonograms (Geneva Convention). China also agreed to adjust its copyright law to the standard determined in these two conventions. Moreover, China agreed to protect software as literary works.[43]

The 1992 MOU accelerated China's participation in the international copyright regime. On July 10, 1992, China acceded to the Berne Convention. On October 15, 1992, the Berne Convention took effect in China.[44] On July 30, 1992, China acceded to the Universal Copyright Convention.[45] On January 5, 1993, China acceded to the Geneva Convention.[46] On September 25, 1992, China promulgated the Regulation on Implementing Universal Copyright Convention, which included related content of the 1992 MOU, such as the protection of foreign computer software as literary works for fifty years and the protection of foreign audiovisual materials.[47]

Such legislative changes represented an unusually big step forward for the Chinese copyright regime. For example, the Berne Convention was signed in September 1886. As a developed country with a much stronger copyright industry, the United States did not accede to the Berne Convention until 1989. When China adopted its first copyright law in 1990, the country's copyright industry was barely emerging. But China acceded to the Berne Convention three years after the United States. That step ignited another strong wave of domestic criticism, accusing the negotiators as "selling out China's national interests."[48] According to a journalist's recollection of the China-U.S. IPR negotiation team, during an internal meeting of the Chinese negotiation team after they returned from the United States, officials from the other government branches asked a series of sharp questions, including, "Why did you make such big concessions? Why should we fear the threat of trade sanctions from the United States? Can't China retaliate with countersanctions?" Even the vice foreign trade minister and the head of the negotiation team, Wu Yi, was concerned that China's promise to increase the level of copyright protection would hurt the development of the country's domestic copyright industry.[49] What was the mechanism, then, that had pushed China to such big concessions?

Newly revealed historical evidence indicated that, several years before the China-U.S. IPR negotiation in the early 1990s, a Japanese author, Toyoko Yamasaki, had already raised the issue of China's accession to the international copyright treaties during her meeting with the Chinese Communist Party general secretary, Hu Yaobang, in 1984. Hu Yaobang responded to Toyoko Yamasaki's concern with a positive reply, promising that "I will keep this issue in mind and work out a solution soon."[50] During a small group meeting with the Chinese Communist Party Central Secretariat held on June 24, 1985, Hu Yaobang further reiterated his support for China's accession to the Universal Copyright Convention.[51] Since China did not have any copyright laws in 1985, Hu Yaobang's positive wishes were not materialized in the 1980s.

Hu Yaobang was ousted from the position of CCP General Secretary for his reformist stance in 1987 and died of a heart attack in 1989, but the general direction for China to merge into the international track of copyright protection remained unchanged. On September 18, 1991, a Chinese copyright delegation headed by the vice director of the National Copyright Administration, Liu Gao, visited Geneva to discuss China's accession to the Berne Convention with Arpad Bogasch, secretary general of World Intellectual Property Organization. Bogasch suggested that China should allow itself a grace period before the Geneva Convention took effect in China. After the visit to Geneva, the Chinese delegation also visited Paris and met senior officials at UNESCO to discuss China's accession to the Universal Copyright Convention.[52] In the words of Liu Gao, "[After the two visits], China was destined to join the two international copyright conventions. The only thing in question is the exact time for China's accession."[53]

The U.S.-China IPR negotiation provided the answer to the timing question. Starting in February 1991, China and the United States engaged in eight rounds of IPR negotiations, with a significant part of the debate focusing on copyright issues. Several times, the two sides were on the brink of a trade war with one another. When the Chinese delegation was on the way to the United States on January 9, 1992, for the last round of negotiations, they realized that they were walking on a tightrope. In the words of a member of the Chinese delegation, "If we make concessions and reach agreement with the U.S., we would probably be accused of selling out China's national interests. If we fail to reach the agreement and allow [a] trade war to break out, we would be criticized as lacking political wisdom. That was a real dilemma."[54] As the weaker party at the negotiation table, the Chinese side was fully aware of the serious consequences of a failure to negotiate. Specifically, the punitive tariff imposed by the U.S. side would deal a serious blow to China's export industry. More important, China's negotiation to recover its membership as one of the founding countries of the General Agreement on Tariffs and Trade (GATT) would be seriously delayed. After a thorough discussion with the other members of the Chinese side, the head of the Chinese negotiation team, Wu Yi, decided to accept the conditions put forth by the United States.[55]

No hard evidence about how the Chinese delegation corresponded with the country's top decision makers about their negotiation stance is currently available. Indeed, the details of the correspondence remain classified even twenty years after the U.S.-China bilateral negotiations. Based on available archival evidence, however, researchers can safely conclude that the Chinese top leadership at least did not oppose the concessions made at the negotiation table. In the words of Liu Gao, the vice director of the Chinese delegation, "The Chinese delegation conducted the negotiations under the direct guide of the Central Leadership and the State Council. The concessions made by the Chinese side represented their serious decision after balancing the benefits and costs."[56] In a report to the Chinese NPC Standing Committee about the decision to quicken China's accession to the international copyright conventions on February 18, 1992, Liu Gao further explained the rationale behind the decisions of the Chinese negotiation team. According to Liu,

> In September 1991, [the] Chinese copyright delegation had discussed the issue of China's accession to the international copyright conventions with related international organizations. It has already been our internal consensus that China will accede to Berne Convention and Universal Copyright Convention at the same time. Our point of departure was more than China-U.S. copyright relationship.
>
> It is necessary for us to promulgate a special regulation on the implementation of these copyright conventions. Since the new regulations are only applicable to foreign copyright works, that would

> cause unequal treatment to domestic and foreign copyright works. That situation is inevitable and should not last long. The real solution is to revise our copyright law and enhance the level of domestic IPR protection to the international standard.
>
> Under the general background of opening to the outside, we would make the concessions [to the foreign countries] sooner or later. The only difference is that the concessions were made earlier than expected. That was not only a kind of pressure for us, but also a motivation to enhance our copyright work.[57]

In 1995 and 1996, China and the United States engaged in two more rounds of IPR negotiations. This time, the legal arrangement of the Chinese copyright regime was no longer the focus of the controversy. Instead, the controversy centered on the implementation of those laws. After the two rounds of bilateral negotiations in 1995 and 1996, the United States temporarily ceased pressuring China on the IPR issue.

When recalling the experience of serving as a legal adviser of the Chinese IPR negotiation team in the 1990s, an IPR scholar told me,

> Our feelings towards the U.S. side during the IPR negotiations were rather ambivalent. On one hand, nobody liked to make concessions under the other country's pressure. The Americans were quite domineering on the negotiation table. On the other hand, however, the pressure from the U.S. side reminded us of our own weaknesses. We realized that there was no choice other than enhancing our own IPR work and strengthening our bargaining ability on the negotiation table. In that sense, we should probably thank the Americans for their threat of using trade sanctions against us on the IPR issue.[58]

Chinese Copyright Regime on the Eve of the Country's WTO Entry

Despite the big step forward after the U.S.-China IPR negotiations in the early 1990s, a number of inconsistencies between the Chinese copyright regime and international copyright conventions, particularly the TRIPS Agreement, remained. At some important points, the revised Chinese copyright law granted more protection to foreign copyright holders than their Chinese counterparts.[59] This section demonstrates how the Chinese copyright community, mostly domestic copyright holders, used China's

WTO entry negotiation in the late 1990s to push for the revision of the country's copyright law and harmonize with WTO regulations.

A number of obstacles stood in the way as China revised its copyright law to meet the standard outlined by the TRIPS Agreement in the late 1990s. The most difficult task was the revision of Article 43 of the 1990 Copyright Law. Under Article 43 of the 1990 Copyright Law, "A radio station or television station that broadcasts, for non-commercial purposes, a published sound recording needs not obtain permission from, or pay remuneration to, the copyright owner, performer or producer of the sound recording."[60] That arrangement in the 1990 Copyright Law reflected the power ratio between the Chinese copyright holders on one side and the Chinese state-run media outlets, mostly radio and TV stations, on the other side. Backed by the powerful CCP Central Propaganda Department, the latter possessed a much stronger influence than the former during the drafting stage of the 1990 Copyright Law. Because foreign copyright works did not enter China on a massive scale during the late 1980s and early 1990s, that article was only applicable to Chinese domestic copyright works, not those of their foreign counterparts. That is, Chinese radio and television stations were allowed to use Chinese domestic copyright works at a very low cost or even for free, but they had to pay for foreign copyright works according to the standard set by the Berne Convention, which China joined in 1992. Under that article, Chinese copyright owners had inferior protection to their foreign counterparts on their own territory.

The inequitable treatment of domestic and foreign copyright holders attracted harsh criticism from Chinese copyright holders, particularly artists, composers, and published authors. In the 1990s, they found support within the Standing Committee of the Chinese NPC, with some artists and authors even gaining membership to the country's top legislative body. They proposed a revision of Article 43 and an adjustment of Chinese domestic law to the standard set forth in international copyright treaties. As Mertha pointed out, NPC supported the prorevision side, while the radio and TV station branch, backed by the Central Propaganda Department, opposed the revision. As Mertha (2005) also noted, the two sides were evenly matched, which made the debates even harder to settle.[61] How did the hard debates get settled? The primary factor that tipped the balance was China's appeal to join the WTO, which added weight to the prorevision side.

The first bullet was fired during a joint seminar held in central China's Wuhan City between June 11 and 13, 1996. Jointly held by the NCA and the Education, Science, Culture, and Health Subcommittee of the Chinese NPC, the main purpose of the seminar was to discuss revisions to Chinese copyright law. The joint seminar laid out seven key points for the revision. The first among them was to "solve the contradictions between international copyright treaties and our country's domestic law, particularly the super-national treatment granted to foreign copyright works."[62] After those key points were outlined during the 1996 joint seminar, the NCA established a small working group on copyright law revisions, drafted a new version of the 1990 Copyright Law, and distributed the revisions to copyright professionals in relevant provinces for further reading. On September 22, 1997, another seminar was convened in northeast China's Shengyang City to further discuss copyright law revisions. This time, seminar participants included the provincial-level Copyright Administration, the People's Congress, and IPR scholars. Based on the outline developed during the Wuhan Seminar, the Shenyang Seminar suggested 115 specific revisions to forty-two different parts of the 1990 Copyright Law. The summary of the Shengyang seminar reiterated the need to revise Article 43 and was reported to the Chinese State Council Legal Affairs Office on January 8, 1998. On March 10, 1998, when the first Annual Session of the Ninth National People's Congress was in session, the State Council Legal Affairs Office officially put forward the Proposal to Speed up the Revision of Copyright Law.[63] That proposal received an endorsement from 123 NPC deputies. Many of those NPC deputies took prestigious political and academic positions in China, including Song Muwen (former director of the National Copyright Administration), Fan Jingyi (former editor-in-chief of *People's Daily*), Gu Jianfen (a famous composer), and Fan Fangping (chief judge of Liaoning Provincial High People's Court).[64] According to one of the initiators of the proposal, it was predicted with optimism that the revision could be completed in 1999.[65]

The optimistic prediction, however, proved to be premature. After the proposal was submitted to the National People's Congress, the Ministry of Radio, Film, and Television raised objections. For the Ministry, media outlets in China, such as radio and television stations, served as the bridge between the Chinese Communist Party and the public and operated on a nonprofit basis. For many years, Chinese radio and TV stations broadcast their programs for free and relied on the government's fiscal support. Paying remunerations to the authors would further burden their already dwindling budgets and increase their operational costs. Second, writers and composers in China were still regarded as "state cadres" who received salaries from the Chinese government. Since the Chinese state was already paying remuneration to the authors in the form of a salary, it was unnecessary for the radio and TV stations to pay remuneration to them.[66] This opposition from the Ministry of Radio, Film, and TV halted the progress of the 1990 Copyright Law's second revision. During the Sixth Session of the Ninth NPC Standing Committee held on December 23, 1998, the initiators of the aforementioned proposal were shocked to see that the revision of Article 43 was not even mentioned in the official report.[67] Half a year later, an even worse piece of news came out: on June 13, 1999, the Chinese State Council submitted a letter to the National People's Congress under the initiative of the Ministry of Radio, Film, and TV. In the letter, it was recommended that "the proposal to revise the 1990 copyright law should be withdrawn because important disagreement arose and necessary consensus remains yet to be reached."[68]

The prorevision side could not sit idle and watch as their efforts were crushed. On March 9, 2000, the NPC deputies who drafted the Proposal to Speed Up the Revision of the 1990 Copyright Law drafted the Proposal to Restart the Revision of the 1990 Copyright Law. In that proposal, the initiators rebutted the reasoning of the Ministry of Radio, Film, and TV in an upfront manner. According to them,

> Comrades of the Radio and TV branch oppose the revision of 1990 Copyright Law on the ground that our country's radio and TV stations are non-commercial organizations serving as the mouthpieces of the Communist Party. That reason is not well grounded. As the mouthpieces of the Party, why do you pay fees to use radio and TV equipment, transportation vehicles, water and electricity during your operation, but use copyright works almost for free? Copyright works are similar as radio and TV equipment. . . . They deserve protection as property. . . . As the mouthpieces of the Party, our radio and TV branch should play a leading role in practicing the Party's policy: respect knowledge and protect intellectual property rights.
>
> Some comrades believe that salaries paid by our government to the authors are already sufficient to reward literature and artistic creators. That reason is not well grounded, either. . . . Our country aims to establish a market economy. Under market mechanism, the

> authors' income is directly related to how well received their works are. The more well received, the more market value their copyright works possess. It is certainly unfair to reward a piece of copyright work only with salaries. That practice bears the influence of planned economy and is not compatible with the goal of our country's reform.
>
> In sum, the reasons to keep the original arrangement of Article 43 are specious and unconvincing. The true motivation behind that is the adherence to sectorial interests. In practice, some comrades equate sectorial interests with our country's national interests. That deserves our serious concern.[69]

As the representative of Chinese composers, Gu Jianfen, a member of the NPC Standing Committee, made a speech that, in the words of a personal witness, "smelled like gun powder" during the discussion session. According to her, "Look at our TV programs. Look at the fancy gala on important dates such as Women's Day, Labor Day and National Day. They cost tons of investment. Hundreds of actors, actresses, and working staff got paid. But have you thought about the songs they perform? Why is the mental labor of those people who wrote the songs worth nothing? Do you understand how the unreasonable arrangements hurt our feelings?"[70] These strongly worded appeals saved the revision efforts from the brink of failure. On May 18, 2000, the State Council Legal Affairs Office sent another letter to the NPC Standing Committee, stating that "[our office] will actively participate in the research of important issues related to the 1990 copyright law and will put forward revision suggestions to the State Council at the appropriate time."[71]

The "appropriate time" mentioned in the letter eventually arrived. On October 27, 2000, the leader of State Council Legal Affairs Office visited the NPC Standing Committee and reported the progress of China's WTO entry negotiation. During the report, the State Council Legal Affairs Office explicitly mentioned that China made the commitment to revise its copyright law to adjust to the standards set by the WTO. Two months later, the new director of the National Copyright Administration, Shi Zongyuan, delivered a speech to the Nineteenth Session of the Ninth NPC Standing Committee. According to him, "Our country's WTO entry negotiation has entered the final stage. There is still some gap between certain regulations of our country's copyright law and the major rules of the WTO, particularly the TRIPS Agreement. Our country has promised to implement the TRIPS Agreement after acceding to the WTO. It is therefore an imperative task for us to make necessary revisions to our current copyright law."[72] Shi Zongyuan's speech provided the much-needed steam to move forward with the revisions, which were nearly aborted. After the meeting at the end of 2000, the revised draft of Chinese copyright law was reviewed in April 2001 and October 2001 by the members of the NPC Standing Committee. This time, the prerevision side acquired the support of several top lawmakers of the National People's Congress. Xu Jialu, a vice chair of the Chinese NPC, expressed his support to the revision of 1990 Copyright Law during one of the standing committee's discussions, which lent another important hand to the prorevision camp. According to Xu,

> [After the revision of the copyright law], some branches may go through a period of adjustment. Their operation cost may increase. However, this kind of expense is worthwhile: because of the revision, the entire Chinese society's creativity may be stimulated, with more high-quality copyright work produced. In that way, our radio and TV programs can attract more audience and generate more advertisement income. Why don't we treat that expense as small bait for some bigger fish?[73]

After Xu Jialu had voiced his support, another NPC vice chair, Peng Peiyun, organized a meeting with the Ministry of Radio, Film, and TV and persuaded them to change their position.[74] With the intervention of those two senior Chinese leaders, the antirevision side eventually decided to accept the proposed revision of Article 43. On October 27, 2001, the Twenty-Fourth Session of the Ninth People's Congress Standing Committee finally approved the Decision to Revise Copyright Law. In the revised copyright law, Article 43 was changed to "a radio station or television station that broadcasts a published sound recording, does not need a permission from, *but shall pay remuneration to*, the copyright owner, except that the interested parties have agreed otherwise. The specific procedures for treating the matter shall be established by the State Council."[75] After additional revisions, the Chinese copyright law eventually met the minimum requirement of the World Trade Organization. Two weeks after China adopted the revised copyright law, on November 10, 2001, the WTO Ministerial Conference approved China's accession.

In 2007, the former director of the Chinese National Copyright Administration, Song Muwen, published his memoir and disclosed several details about the controversy over the revision of Chinese copyright law on the eve of the country's WTO entry. Of great interest is his comment about the role of external influence on the revision of China's copyright law: "I felt somewhat uncomfortable that this round of major revision of Chinese copyright law was motivated at least partially by external forces. But that helped many domestic copyright holders to achieve their long held wishes. In fact, our international commitment is not in conflict with domestic appeal in the long run. The ultimate purpose is still to enhance our country's copyright work."[76]

With China's accession to the WTO and the revision of its copyright laws, the Chinese copyright regime finally was in compliance with international copyright norms, at least on paper, by the turn of the century. The Chinese copyright community gained more than a number of legal revisions. After rounds of controversies and debates over the revisions to the Chinese copyright law, they were no longer the obedient "state cadres" following the orders of the government. Instead, they increasingly became part of the burgeoning Chinese civil society struggling for their own rights. Although the voice of Chinese copyright holders was not quite loud, Chinese decision makers could hardly ignore it as the country began integrating into global economy during the post-WTO era.

Chinese Copyright Regime During the Post-WTO Era

Chinese copyright law went through minor revisions in 2010.[77] The call for a major revision of the Chinese copyright law started in early 2011. This time, the initiation mainly came from Chinese copyright holders. On March 3, 2011, Zhang Kangkang, vice chair of the CWA, wrote a letter to Chinese Premier Wen Jiabao, proposing to introduce another round of revisions to Chinese copyright law.[78] One of the key proposals in the letter was that the Chinese copyright law should make further adjustments to protect copyright during the Internet era. To her surprise, Premier Wen Jiabao replied to Zhang Kangkang's letter the next day, urging the Chinese National Copyright Administration to start the third revision of the Chinese copyright law. On July 13, 2011, a small working group of the third revision of Chinese copyright law was established. With the NCA director,

Liu Binjie, serving as the working group's director, Zhang Kangkang was invited to serve as the vice director of the small working group.[79] On March 31, 2012, the revised draft of Chinese copyright law was posted online and aroused another round of criticism from the Chinese music industry.[80] The most controversial part was Article 46 of the draft law. That article enables any record producer to make a recording of a musical work without receiving authorization from the original owner if the content had been published for three months or longer. If the official copyright law included that article, artists would lose control of their copyright work after three months.

On April 12, 2012, the Chinese Music Industry Society organized a news briefing in Beijing. In addition to Gu Jianfen, a veteran copyright defender since the 1990s, a younger generation of Chinese musicians jointly voiced criticisms of the amendment. In the words of Liu Huan, a popular musician and singer, "If we cannot own our copyright work and cannot even ask how our works are used after three months, do we have even the slightest bit of dignity as musicians? . . . I fear that our music industry will encounter an overwhelming disaster if our copyright law is arranged in that way!"[81] During an interview with the state-run Chinese Central Television, another popular musician, Wang Feng, told the press, "For a long time I hesitate to say that I struggle for our interests. Now I can tell you that it is not at all a shame for musicians to engage in composing music for economic rewards. It is about my rights, my inherent rights as a composer!"[82]

The Chinese government could not afford to ignore the opposition of Chinese musicians. On April 24, 2012, Yan Xiaohong, vice director of the NCA, told the press that the third revision of the Chinese copyright law was still in the initial stages. Opinions from various sides, including the opposition, would be reported to the State Council and the National People's Congress for further consideration.[83] While this reply did not appease the Chinese musicians' concerns, the softened stance of the NCA demonstrated the strength of the opposition opinions.

When asked about the new round of controversies, a Beijing-based IPR scholar told me,

> I cannot foresee the result of this round of copyright law revision as of now. But several important things distinguish this round of revision from the previous ones. First, the Chinese top leadership responded to the request of Chinese writers immediately. The NCA asked for opinions of the copyright holders through [the] Internet

> and other multiple channels. That represents a profound change in the decision-making process in China. Can you imagine the Chinese government being nearly as responsive twenty years ago? More importantly, are the Chinese writers, composers, and other copyright holders as obedient to the government regulations as they were twenty years ago? The answer is no! The strong opinions by the Chinese musicians on the April conference literally pointed the finger towards the supervising body of Chinese musicians. That was totally unthinkable in the past. Whatever the ultimate outcome of the third revision is, the Chinese copyright holders, particularly the musicians, are increasingly willing and able to fight for their own rights. That is the most important progress we made.[84]

The debates surrounding the third revision of Chinese copyright law lasted for three years. During the debates, Chinese musicians, artists, movie producers, and journalists voiced their appeals to the legislative organ.[85] In February 2015, the final copy of the revised copyright law was submitted to the Chinese State Council for further review.[86]

Conclusion

This chapter demonstrated that, similar to Chinese patent regime, the evolution of the Chinese copyright regime over the past six decades was also torn by the tensions among various political and economic copyright-related groups. During the adoption of the Chinese copyright law in the 1980s and 1990s, the Chinese copyright community, from being almost nonexistent to having an increasingly strong voice in the decision making of Chinese copyright legislation, had to overcome one political barrier after another to carry forward their policy agenda. At some critical points, foreign pressure played a catalytic role in Chinese copyright legislation. The goal of foreign countries did not necessarily conflict with that of Chinese domestic copyright holders. Instead, the latter was able to use the pressure of the former as an opportunity to push for positive changes in the country's copyright regime. Contrary to the conventional wisdom that those groups should passively follow the Chinese state due to the authoritarian nature of the country's political system, they could manage to have their voices reach the government decision makers and influence the policy outcomes. The current shape of Chinese copyright legislation is determined by the result of those groups' competition and compromise.

Compared with the issue of patent, copyright legislation in China involves culture, ideology, and propaganda, a more sensitive policy issue than science and technology. Behind the copyright norm is the respect for freedom of expression, a notion that is traditionally at odds with the rule of the Chinese Communist Party. Therefore, the debates surrounding China's copyright legislation are more complicated and extended. Although there is still a long way to go for the Chinese copyright holders, their growing policy influence in itself demonstrates China's promising transformation from a closed and repressive regime to a gradually open and liberal one. The achievements and limitations of Chinese copyright legislation mirror the achievements and limitations of the country's political and economic reforms. As part of China's incipient civil society, the influence of social change not only is limited to the economic realm but also has important political implications.

Although the Chinese decision-making elites are still debating about the specific legal provisions of the third revision of the Chinese copyright law, it is generally agreed that the following two aspects will be the key emphasis. The first is to provide stronger protection for copyright holders. The second is to adjust rules for the copyright transaction and authorization mechanism and create a better environment for the circulation of copyright works.[87] To fulfill both purposes, the opinions of Chinese copyright holders will have to gain more weight in the designing of the Chinese copyright regime in the future. That, in turn, will shake the shackles imposed upon them by the country's authoritarian political system. In that sense, the adjustment of the Chinese copyright regime is also a part of the profound liberalization that the country is undergoing.

It is important to note that the complicated struggles documented in this chapter mainly happened during China's de jure compliance with the international copyright norm. That is, it is about Chinese copyright policy on paper. When the policy on paper is translated in real-world implementation, one can only expect even more complicated struggles. Those struggles are discussed in the next chapter.

CHAPTER 4

The Implementation of Chinese Copyright Policy

During my fieldwork in Beijing in 2007, I had planned to ask an official at the Office of the National Anti-Pornography and Anti-Piracy Working Committee (NAPWC), housed at the General Administration of Press and Publications (GAPP), about how the government had reacted to the rampant copyright infringement activities in China. The official worked for a primary organ responsible for conducting antipiracy raids, so I thought that he would be the best source of information. To my surprise, he suggested that it was not advisable to interview only him for a complete understanding of Chinese copyright policy. Instead, he suggested I begin with officials from the neighboring Ministry of Culture (MOC)—in particular, the Cultural and Copyright Industries Division, the primary organ overseeing the industries that depend on copyright as their core competitiveness, such as the publishing industry and entertainment industry. However, my interview with the officials at the MOC's Cultural and Copyright Industries Division led to another surprise because the officials there suggested that to obtain a full understanding of Chinese copyright policy, I should first interview officials from the Chinese Communist Party Central Propaganda Department.

The logic behind that copyright official's suggestion was clear: although antipiracy campaigns are the most salient part of Chinese copyright policy, it is the development of cultural and copyright industries that constitutes the foundation of China's cultural market, where cultural products, such as books and movies, are traded for profits. Without a thorough understanding of how the cultural market operates, it is hard to comprehend the working of cultural market management activities such as antipiracy campaigns.

Moreover, while it is important to interview MOC officials to understand the operation of Chinese copyright policy, both the antipiracy campaign and the development of the copyright industry[1] fall under the guidance of Chinese propaganda policy. That official's suggestion revealed to me a lesser-known aspect of Chinese copyright policy. That is, instead of being treated in an isolated manner, Chinese copyright policy should be understood as growing from the general body of Chinese ideology and propaganda work. In his words, "In order to understand how the child grows up in a specific way, you should first know how the parents raise the child."[2]

The interview was conducted in 2007, but GAPP's firm stance on safeguarding the orthodox ideology of the Chinese Communist Party has remained unchanged over the past years. An editorial in 2014 by the mouthpiece of GAPP, *Chinese Press and Publications News*, illustrated that the implementation of Chinese copyright policy is impacted by not only the economic and legal factors but also the country's ideology and propaganda policy. According to the editorial,

> [Antipiracy personnel] should have the courage to tackle the sensitive and complicated issues in the ideological realm. In implementing their tasks, they should first be aware of their political responsibility. . . . They should keep in mind that in our anti-piracy work, ideological battle comes before market profits, political struggle comes before business competition, politics comes before culture. They should always place on top the crackdown of illegal publications that threaten social stability and endanger national security.[3]

The copyright official did not explain the mechanism for "parents" to raise the "child." This chapter aims to answer that question. This chapter also explores the reasons for the differentiation between the "good children" (i.e., effective enforcement cases) and the "bad children" (i.e., ineffective enforcement cases). In this chapter, I argue that, in implementing Chinese copyright policy, the Chinese government holds multiple policy goals on its agenda: maintaining ideological order, pursuing commercial benefits, and protecting copyright. Despite the reform of China's ideology and propaganda system, the Chinese government's top priority remains maintaining order in the ideological realm, promoting information that the Party deems right, and cracking down on information that the Party believes to be wrong. When necessary, it can override the other two goals. While a consideration of economic benefits comes in second on the Chinese government's policy agenda, copyright protection comes in third.

This practice has a significant influence on the development of the Chinese domestic copyright industry. On one hand, certain parts of the Chinese copyright industry, particularly those parts that have undergone more thorough reform, have witnessed rapid development. On the other hand, the government-imposed constraints prevent most parts of the Chinese copyright industry from realizing its full potential to contribute to China's economic development.

Thus, the uneven development of the Chinese copyright industry shapes the pattern of its interactions with the country's copyright bureaucracies, who are primarily responsible for designing and implementing Chinese copyright policy. Under some limited circumstances, the three policy goals—the maintenance of ideological stability, the pursuit of economic profits, and copyright protection—can be neatly aligned to produce an effective enforcement outcome. In most other cases, however, even though copyright infringement is detected, the enforcement outcome could hardly be a deterrent.

I also demonstrate that other than corporate actors, the players on the stage of Chinese copyright policy should also include the Chinese public, many of whom are either the sellers or the consumers of pirated goods. All the actors in Chinese copyright policy—from copyright officials, to the domestic and foreign copyright business community, to street peddlers and mass consumers—have their own roles in influencing the operation of China's copyright policy. Other than having a cheap price, pirated copyright products also enjoy a more flexible distribution system than legal products, which makes them better able to meet the demands of Chinese consumers. Interestingly, if not ironically, the Chinese propaganda state's overly rigid control of the copyright industry creates space for the growth of an underground market of illegal copyrighted products.

The first section of this chapter discusses the reforms of the Chinese propaganda system since the late 1970s to provide a policy backdrop for the development of the Chinese copyright industry. The second section discusses the achievements and weaknesses of the Chinese copyright industry in recent decades as the result of incomplete reforms in the country's propaganda policy. The third section examines the functioning of the underground market in which pirated copyright products are produced and distributed and the relationship with the legal market for copyright products. I conclude by situating this chapter within the larger scenario of Chinese political and economic reforms, arguing that China's partial compliance with international copyright norms reflects the coexistence between a burgeoning market economy and one of the world's few existing communist political systems.

Reforming the Chinese Propaganda System: The Policy Backdrop of the Chinese Copyright Industry

This section discusses the reform of the Chinese propaganda system since the late 1970s, which constitutes the larger policy scenario within which Chinese copyright policy operates. Various government institutions and their local branches are involved in designing and operating Chinese copyright policy. While the GAPP/National Copyright Administration (NCA), MOC, and their local branches have responsibilities for copyright enforcement, the State Council Information Office (SCIO), Ministry of Industry and Information Technology (MIIT), and State Administration of Radio, Film, and Television (SARFT) are also active participants in designing and operating Chinese copyright policy.[4] In various ways, those government institutions play their own roles in fulfilling the goals of Chinese ideology and propaganda policy. Scholars on Chinese IPR policy have provided a thorough study of the organizational history of the Chinese copyright administration at the state and local levels.[5] Succeeding scholars have added to the literature with an analysis of how various copyright agencies participate in enforcement activities through a dual-track system, combining administrative enforcement with legal enforcement.[6] Their analysis seems to have told all the stories about Chinese copyright policy.

Yet, some key questions remain unanswered: During the evolution of the Chinese copyright administration, which aspect of their ideological principle was changed and what remains unchanged? When enforcing the copyright policy, what types of cases are more likely to get the attention of the Chinese copyright administration and thus are placed at the top of the enforcement agenda? To answer these questions, researchers should first acquire a sound understanding of the evolution of Chinese propaganda policy during the past three decades.

In this section, I argue that the introduction of market mechanisms is a significant factor that has shaped the reform of the Chinese propaganda system in the past three decades. However, even after three decades of market reform, the ideology from the past still maintains its influence on the operation of Chinese cultural affairs. My findings also suggest that, in the crackdown of pirated copyright products, the Chinese government has prioritized the maintenance of ideological stability since the beginning of the reform era. If the content of certain pirated products violates the Party's mainstream ideology, the products would receive a high level of attention from the Chinese government. Otherwise, copyright enforcement would result in, at best, a lukewarm outcome.

An Overview of Chinese Propaganda Policy During the Prereform Period

Scholars on Chinese copyright policy have already noticed its connection with the country's culture and ideology policy. For example, Mertha (2005) argues that Chinese culture and ideology policy is the foundation, or the "mother of all mothers-in-law" in his words, for the country's copyright policy.[7] But it should be stressed that the real designer of Chinese culture and ideology policy is the Central Propaganda Department instead of the Chinese Cultural Bureaucracy. As one of the most important functional organs of the Chinese Communist Party, the Central Propaganda Department has weathered years of reform and has continued to exert its influence in the early twenty-first century. During its more than sixty years of existence since 1949, the basic missions of the Central Propaganda Department have remained unchanged despite the challenges posed by economic reform. The first mission is to disseminate and ingrain information that the Party deems as right, and the second is to crack down on information that the Party believes to be wrong and prevent it from reaching the populace.[8] Although no country can claim that its cultural realm is completely free from government influence, during the post–Cold War era, China has been one of the very few remaining communist countries where the government firmly and directly controls the country's ideological realm.

The organizing principle of the Chinese propaganda system mirrors that of the Soviet Union.[9] The primary responsibility of the Chinese Central Propaganda Department is to oversee the production and transmission of ideas in China and steer the ideas toward the track that the Communist Party deems appropriate. Before China introduced economic reform in 1978, China's propaganda system was administered in a hierarchical way, with societal actors totally excluded from its operation. The production of cultural products was organized in a planned-economy manner. The Communist Party determined the leading personnel of the cultural units and decided what content was published and broadcasted. Instead of being treated as independent market entities, cultural institutions were accessories to different layers of government branches. Instead of marketing their cultural products such as movies, plays, and literature works for economic gain, Chinese cultural institutions relied on subsidies from the government to survive. Instead of being treated as an independent social class, writers, journalists, and movie and TV program makers were "state cadres" receiving monthly salaries from the government payroll. Expression of any unorthodox thoughts would invite harsh retribution from the government.

These policies stifled the development of the Chinese copyright industry. During the peak time of hardline Communist ideology in the late 1960s and early 1970s, the entire cinema system in China was dominated by eight "revolutionary exemplary movies" (*yangbanxi*) endorsed by Mao Zedong's wife, Jiang Qing, who was then a Party politburo member responsible for ideological work.[10] Not only were producers of cultural products, such as writers, actors, and moviemakers, deprived of the freedom to create literature and artistic works of their own right, but the Chinese audience also was forced to accept whatever cultural products the Party state supplied. When asked to comment on the situation of copyright enforcement in China during the prereform era, an IPR scholar told me, "[During that period], it was unnecessary to worry about copyright infringement because there was no meaningful copyright to infringe upon."[11]

When market reform started in China in 1978, throughout the country, there were altogether 125 radio and TV stations, 105 publishing houses producing 14,987 titles, 930 periodicals, 186 newspapers, and 12 movie studios producing 46 movies.[12] For a country of one billion people, such low levels of cultural production fell far short of meeting the cultural needs of the Chinese people. The rigid control of the Chinese propaganda system did not begin eroding until the introduction of market reform in the late 1970s. The competition between the efforts to introduce a market mechanism and the adherence to the orthodox communist ideology has been an important thread flowing through the entire process of reforming the Chinese propaganda policy. The attempt to control the production of literature and artistic goods remains strong despite years of market reform. The Chinese government's control over the production and distribution of copyright goods is a major hindrance to the healthy development of the Chinese copyright industry.

Reforming the Chinese Propaganda Policy, 1978–Present

When China began its market reform in 1978, economic liberalization had created some cracks in the fortress of the Chinese propaganda system. As the country moved along the path of institutional reform, those cracks developed into bigger trends of liberalization. As is convincingly argued by some scholars, the liberalization endeavors, featured by administrative fragmentation, property rights reform, and technological advances, have weakened the Chinese government's ability to control the country's "thought work."[13]

During the past three decades, the Chinese propaganda system has gone through three major phases of reform: the period of early development (1978–1992), the period of further development (1992–2000), and the period of deepening reform (2001–present). The reform of the Chinese propaganda system constitutes the policy backdrop of the development of the Chinese copyright industry.

Phase I (1978–1992): Warm Face, Cold Feet, and "Illegal Publication"

According to a Beijing-based IPR scholar, the early development period (1978–1992) can be described as a "warm face at the local level got stuck onto senior leader's cold feet, eventually the cold feet became warmer."[14] Unlike the reforms introduced in economic sectors, such as agriculture and industry, reform in the Chinese propaganda policy did not become a full-fledged reform project until the early 1990s. In the realm of cultural affairs, reform in the early stages started with policy changes initiated by grassroots practitioners. In March 1980, the first music café in Mainland China started its operation in the Oriental Hotel in the city of Guangzhou, the capital of South China's Guangdong Province.[15] In September 1980, Zhao Dan, one of China's leading movie actors, drafted an article entitled "Literature and Artistic Work Will Turn Hopeless If Too Tightly Controlled" (*Guande Tai-juti, Wenyi Meixiwang*), which sharply criticized the Chinese government's rigid grip on movie production. One month after Zhao Dan died of cancer, his article was released to the public, and it ignited a heated discussion over the prospect of reforming Chinese ideological and propaganda policy, which had long been taboo in Chinese politics. The fact that Zhao Dan had been a supporter of the Chinese Communist Party since the 1930s made his article even more important among China's literary and artistic elites.[16]

Shortly after Zhao Dan's death, the directors of six leading movie studios in China held a conference in Beijing calling for a transformation of the state-controlled movie studios into economic entities with "independent accounting and full responsibility for profits or losses" (*duli hesuan, zifu yingkui*).[17]

In addition to the advocacy by Chinese literature and artistic creators, there was also an eruption in the demands from the Chinese public for a larger quantity of cultural products of better quality. In 1979 alone, the Chinese cinema system recorded an audience of 29.3 billion, which had not been matched before or since. That is, on average, one Chinese person saw movies twenty-eight times in that year.[18] In 1980, the Chinese press and publication system recorded the sale of 4.25 billion books, another unparalleled record in contemporary Chinese history.[19] The Chinese translation of *Gone with the Wind* and *The Count of Monte Cristo*, formerly banned in the Cultural Revolution, sold a record 600,000 and 750,000 copies that year, respectively.[20] The gap between the bursting demand of Chinese consumers and the production capacity of the country's literature and artistic creation units generated the opportunity for the first generation of pirated cultural products to grow. No accurate statistical data exist about the scale of pirated books and magazines during this time period. But a joint report by the Chinese State Publishing Bureau, Ministry of Public Security, State Administration for Industry and Commerce, Ministry of Culture, Ministry of Education, Ministry of Light Industry, and Ministry of Finance admitted that "non-authorized publications overflowed the market. An underground market for illegal publication [was] taking shape."[21] Published in 1980, that report was the first official document to recognize the existence of piracy activities in China.

China did not have a copyright law in the early 1980s. Unauthorized publishing activities described by the aforementioned report were termed "illegal publications" rather than copyright infringements. But experienced Chinese publishing professionals already discerned the mechanism for such a phenomenon to happen. According to Chen Hanbo, then president of the China Publishers Association,

> At least two factors caused [the overflow of illegal publications]. First and foremost, our cultural products cannot meet the demands of the readers. We should be blamed for that. Our comrades should work hard to improve the diversity and quality of our publications.

> The second should be attributed to the residual influence of those people who ignited the Cultural Revolution. They did not respect authors' rights. We have to adopt a copyright law to eliminate their negative impact on our publication work.[22]

Unfortunately, hardliners among China's top political leadership at the time had a different view. In response to grassroots calls for loosening the Party's grip over cultural affairs, Deng Liqun, then director of the Central Propaganda Department, insisted that literature and artistic works should be guided by Communist thoughts.[23] With the support of Hu Qiaomu, the politburo member who had been in charge of ideology and propaganda affairs, Deng Liqun launched an "anti-spiritual pollution campaign" in the early 1980s to fight against what he deemed as "bourgeois thoughts" in China's literature and artistic circles.[24] Even reformists in China's top decision-making circle considered cultural reform to be a lesser priority and preferred to focus on economic affairs instead. At some point, Deng Xiaoping, the initiator of China's economic reform, even supported the "anti-spiritual pollution campaign." According to him, "We do not emphasize that literature and artistic work should follow political needs as strongly as the past. However, that does not mean literature and artistic work can be really separated from politics. In fact, it should serve the needs of the people and the Party."[25]

The mixture between the "warm face" of the policy practitioners and the "cold feet" of the top leaders made the early efforts to reform the Chinese propaganda policy a lukewarm endeavor. On one hand, the government's control of China's cultural life was so stringent that in some cities, even dancing ballrooms were closed at the Chinese government's request.[26] On the other hand, cultural activities outside the official reign organized by the Chinese masses developed like wildfire—when quenched in one place, it would flame in many other places beyond the government's reach. The government simply could not hold its grip on all the cultural activities.

Eventually, Chinese senior leaders had to face reality. In January 1988, Chinese Minister of Culture Wang Meng agreed that reforms of the Chinese cultural sector were inevitable.[27] Later that year, the MOC and the State Administration for Industry and Commerce (SAIC) jointly issued the Notice on Improving the Management of Cultural Market. The document was the first one issued by central-level government branches that explicitly discussed the notion of the "cultural market" in an official document.[28] In

August 1988, literature and artistic elites from more than twenty provinces in China convened the first nationwide symposium on developing the cultural industry.[29] In November 1988, Vice Minister of Culture Gao Zhanxiang published an article entitled "Some Thoughts on Establishing Management Framework of Our Cultural Industry" in the government-run *China Cultural News*, calling for the introduction of a market mechanism into the management of cultural affairs and discarding the planned economy model.[30]

The combined efforts of grassroots practitioners and their sympathizers in the Chinese government released the long-suppressed creativity of Chinese literature and artistic creators. By 1988, 448 publishing houses in China had produced 65,961 titles, an almost six times increase compared with 1978.[31] Twenty-two Chinese movie studios produced 158 feature films, a more than three times increase compared with 1978.[32] Additionally, 531 radio stations and 469 TV stations produced 645 radio programs and 512 TV programs, respectively. These numbers were an increase of ten times the numbers in 1978.[33]

The promising developments came to a temporary slowdown after the 1989 crackdown of the Tiananmen Democracy Movement. After the crackdown, reform-minded senior officials were purged from the decision-making circle. One of the advocates of Chinese cultural reform, Wang Meng, the former minister of culture, resigned three months after the Tiananmen incident due to "health reasons."[34] At the local level, many writers and press editors were either dismissed from their positions or even immigrated overseas to flee from the painful "self-examination under the Party principle." The newly appointed minister of culture, He Jingzhi, accused members of the literature and artistic circles as "being heavily affected by bourgeois liberalization thoughts" and reiterated that literature and artistic work should be the "mouthpiece of the Party and the people."[35] Although the reforms in the Chinese propaganda policy came to a temporary halt, the development of the Chinese copyright industry had already become an unstoppable trend after a decade of development. When recalling the practice of the Chinese propaganda policy during the post–Tiananmen incident era, a former official with the GAPP told me,

> After the Tiananmen incident in 1989, the dominant theme of our work was "Sweeping Away Pornography, Striking Down Illegal Publication" (*saohuang dafei*). The first part of the theme is very

> straightforward: no country can let the spread of pornographic materials go unchecked. But the second part was quite confusing. The term "illegal publication" is a strange one in itself. Didn't the Chinese Constitution guarantee every citizen's freedom of expression? If that is the case, how come some publications are legal while some others illegal? Who set the standard for that? Is that the government or the Communist Party? If so, does that mean the Communist Party is higher than the Constitution? I did not have any answer to that question.[36]

The copyright official was not the only person confused. In fact, his puzzlement pointed to a fundamental question that haunts the implementation of Chinese copyright policy: while a key component of international copyright norm is to protect the freedom of literature and artistic creation, can that freedom coexist with an authoritarian regime forever? The new rounds of reform in the Chinese propaganda system in the 1990s only eased that contradiction temporarily and by no means achieved a satisfactory resolution.

Phase II (1992–2001): Coopting Market Forces Under the Authoritarian Political System

The reform of Chinese cultural and propaganda policy revived after then Chinese paramount leader Deng Xiaoping's visit to the southern provinces of Hubei, Shanghai, and Guangdong in the spring of 1992. During the visit, Deng called for the acceleration of reform and opening.[37] Following Deng's call, in June 1992, the Chinese State Council issued a Decision on Accelerating the Development of Tertiary Industry. In that decision, the development of the cultural industry was once again mentioned.[38] State Council Secretary General Luo Gan edited a book entitled *A Significant Strategic Move* (*Zhongda De Zhanlue Juece*) one month later. In that book, policy consultants with the Chinese State Council further proposed to revive cultural reform in China. That proposal was widely believed to be a sign of restarting cultural reform in China.[39] In fact, this time, the revival happened at a higher level: from the ministerial level in the 1980s to the State Council level in the early 1990s. Compared with the 1980s, the most significant breakthrough in cultural reform of the 1990s was that market mechanisms eventually received legitimacy in the government discourse of Chinese cultural reform. That breakthrough reached some previously untouched deeper-level issues of China's cultural affairs management system.

First, cultural products, such as books, movies, and TV programs, were recognized as a "special kind of commodity." Not only were they regarded as tools to convey political ideology to the Chinese people, as they have been in the past, but they were also recognized as economic products that could be marketed for economic gains. There had been a discussion of making cultural products into commodities in the 1980s, but it was not until early 1990s that the idea gained official recognition from China's top leadership. During the National Conference on Culture and Thought Work held in 1994, then Chinese President Jiang Zemin said, "With the development of socialist market economy, the production and circulation of cultural products is increasingly tied to the basic law of market operation. Hence arises the issue of market profits. The increase of market profits will benefit the development of our cultural affairs. The discussion of that issue should no longer be forbidden."[40]

Second, cultural production units such as publishing houses, TV and radio stations, and movie studios were recognized as market entities. During the National Conference on Press and Publications held in 1992, Song Muwen, then general director of the Chinese GAPP, formally admitted that publishing houses should be recognized as enterprises. Song also urged the majority of Chinese publishing houses, except several central-level Party-run units, to transform into financially independent market entities by 1994.[41] This was the first time a senior Chinese official recognized the market nature of the country's publishing houses. When recalling the decision-making process, Song said,

> With the establishment of socialist market economy, the old way of "administrative units with enterprise management" (*shiyedanwei, qiyeguanli*) would no longer suit our needs. We should establish a full-fledged corporate governance system and turn our publishing houses into market entities. I am not trying to say that market reform is the elixir to deal with all the challenges, but further development of our country's publishing industry would be impossible without the introduction of market mechanism.[42]

In the following months, Chinese senior cultural officials made similar appeals to transform most other sectors of Chinese propaganda, such as movie studios, TV stations, and performing arts troupes, into market entities.[43] In 1995, several major publishing, TV, and movie industry units in Shanghai were merged into Shanghai TV and Movie Group, Inc. (*Shanghai Yingshijituan*) and New Century Publishing Group, Inc. (*Xinshiji Chubanjituan*). In 1999, the first newspaper group in Mainland China, Guangzhou Newspaper Group, Inc. (*Guangzhou Baoyejituan*), was established in southern China's Guangdong Province. In 2000, several leading performing arts troupes in Jiangsu Province were merged into Jiangsu Performing Arts Group, Inc. (*Jiangsu Yanyi Jituan*).[44]

The Chinese cultural industry benefited enormously from those reform measures and experienced dramatic growth in the 1990s. As of 1999, the Chinese publishing system produced 141,831 titles, an almost 100 percent increase compared with 1990 (80,224 titles).[45] The most rapid growth was in the TV/radio sector—by 2000, the Chinese TV/radio sector had produced 2,931,682 hours of radio programs and 526,483 hours of TV programs, an almost five times increase over the level of 1990 (647,762 hours of radio programs and 91,572 hours of TV programs).[46] The advertisement revenue of Chinese TV/radio stations reached 18.3 billion RMB (about $2.4 million) by 2000, more than thirty times what it was in 1990 (647 million RMB or $80 million).[47]

However, there was still plenty of room for further reform during this period. Although market mechanisms were introduced into the operation of the Chinese cultural industry, private and foreign capital was still kept out of the reforms discussed above until the late 1990s. In the Chinese publishing industry, for example, although private book merchants started to emerge in late 1980s,[48] they were not allowed to apply for publishing licenses from the GAPP. In fact, GAPP designed rigorous criteria for approving a license for a publishing company. Only the state-owned presses could meet those criteria. Therefore, a dilemma emerged: private copyright owners were much more responsive to market needs, but the government did not allow them to operate; state-sponsored copyright owners had permission from the government, but they remained docile accessories to the Chinese government and were very awkward in responding to market needs. At a conference on Chinese cultural reform held in 2000, then Chinese Vice Minister of Cultural Affairs Li Yuanchao admitted that similar problems existed in other areas of Chinese cultural affairs. According to him,

> Our cultural production units are mostly state-owned. That type of ownership is too monotonous. That would not bring about the incentive of further development and would not allow us to allocate market resources in a reasonable way. After we join the WTO [World Trade Organization], we have to diversify the ownership structure of our cultural enterprises to improve their competitiveness. Our cultural affairs should move from "government managed" (*zhengfu banwenhua*) to "society managed" (*shehui banwenhua*).[49]

But decision makers of Chinese cultural policy never agreed to loosen the government's grip over the production and distribution of cultural products. In the words of a Shanghai-based intellectual property rights (IPR) scholar, they just "wrapped the iron fist with a gentle layer of velvet."[50] While Song Muwen pioneered the introduction of a market mechanism in the operation of Chinese publishing houses, he also emphasized that "[as publishing enterprises], Chinese publishing houses should be managed as *state-owned* enterprises. Even after transforming into market entities, the selection of book subjects should be registered with related government branches. The appointment and dismissal of a publishing house's leadership should be determined by the Party and the government. That practice should not be changed."[51] Following these guidelines, the Chinese copyright bureaucracy established a more sophisticated censorship mechanism for the country's cultural products. Under that censorship mechanism, many movies or books containing politically controversial content were either banned or forced to make major revisions before being distributed to the audience despite Chinese viewers' and readers' positive feedback.[52] In 1996, the Chinese MOC and Ministry of Radio, Film, and TV (MORFT) jointly issued the Regulation on Examining the Content of Audiovisual Products.[53] In the same year, MORFT issued Regulations on Managing the Film Industry.[54] In 1997, the Chinese GAPP issued Regulations on Managing the Publishing Industry.[55] Those regulations further reinforced the already existent censorship system on copyright products. During the early twenty-first century, the restriction on private capital's access to the Chinese copyright industry was lifted with the introduction of the third phase of reform; the restriction on foreign capital's access continued to exist, except that it was exercised in a different way.

Phase III (2001–Present): Reforming Chinese Propaganda System Under the WTO Framework

China's accession to the WTO in 2001 marked both a deeper level of integration of the Chinese copyright industry into the world market and a new phase of domestic institutional reform. At the turn of the century, the Chinese propaganda system confronted dual challenges from both within and without. Domestically, the growth of the market mechanism in the Chinese cultural industry demanded a further loosening of the straitjacket designed by the government. Internationally, the flow of foreign copyright products forced the operation of the Chinese copyright industry to adjust to the need for international competition. By the early twenty-first century, Chinese leadership had foreseen these challenges.

A key step forward was to lift the restriction on private capital's involvement in Chinese cultural affairs. In China's economic and social development plan from 2001 to 2005, known as "the tenth five-year plan," it was clearly stated that "our cultural affairs policy should be improved to facilitate quicker development of our country's cultural industry."[56] Under that mandate, a series of reforms was introduced at the ministerial level to enhance the competitiveness of the Chinese cultural industry. In 2003, the Chinese MOC issued *Opinions on Supporting and Promoting the Development of Cultural Industry*.[57] In 2004, the Chinese MORFT issued Provisional Regulations on Movie Production, Distribution and Broadcasting and Regulations on China-Foreign Joint Movie Production.[58] For the first time, private capital was allowed to establish movie studios, and overseas capital was allowed to establish joint ventures with domestic movie studios.

In a similar vein, the Chinese State Council supported the reform measures at the ministerial level. In 2005, the State Council issued the Decision on Non-State Capital's Accession into Cultural Industry, further clarifying the scope and accession procedure for private and foreign capital to invest in the Chinese copyright industry.[59] In July 2009, the State Council issued the Promotion Plan for Cultural Industry,[60] known as the 2009 Plan, reiterating the necessity to "attract private and foreign capital to related cultural industries, [so that] they can participate in the building up of state-owned cultural enterprises." The 2009 Plan also represented a major step forward in China's cultural reform by expanding the scope of private and foreign capital to other sectors of the cultural industry such as TV, radio, and advertising.

The reform measures ignited another round of a quick development period for the Chinese cultural industry in the early twenty-first century. By the end of 2013, cultural outlets had expanded to 2,579 radio and TV stations broadcasting 2,634 radio programs and 3,370 TV programs, 573 publishing houses that produced 369,523 titles, and 38 movie studios that produced 824 movies. Compared with other countries in the world, China possessed the largest amount of radio and TV stations and published the largest amount of book titles. Moreover, China ranked third in movies produced, next to India and the United States.[61] By the end of 2013, there were 3.20 million websites registered in China, second only to the United States, and 564 million Internet users, highest around the globe.[62] Cultural industry institutions grew rapidly, and so did the total volume of their output. In 2012, the total output of the Chinese cultural industry reached over 4 hundred billion RMB (about $615 billion), recording an average annual growth rate of 23.6 percent since 2001.[63] This growth rate was the highest among the major economies in the world.[64]

All the more noticeable was the involvement of the previously banned private and foreign capital in the development of Chinese cultural industry. After lifting the access restriction on private capital, by 2012, private capital had participated in the production of 75 percent of Chinese domestic movies. These movies contributed over 80 percent of the country's box office income.[65] Foreign capital gained its first buckle of gold from the Chinese cultural industry as well. In 2005, the first China-foreign joint venture in book distribution, Liaoning-Bertelsmann Book Distribution, Inc., was established in northeast China's Liaoning Province.[66] In 2011, foreign capital participated in 108 of the 202 investment cases in Chinese cultural industry.[67]

The rapid growth of the Chinese copyright industry provided no reason for the Chinese leadership to loosen its grip on the country's cultural production. Shortly after a new round of reforms was introduced to the Chinese propaganda system in 2003, then Chinese president, Hu Jintao, delivered a speech to the politburo members, emphasizing that "[we should] hold high the banner of socialist culture and never imitate the Western model. Chinese cadres and masses should be on firm guard against the invasion of corrupt cultural notions from the Western countries and ensure the country's cultural security."[68] Ten years later, Hu's presidency was succeeded by Xi Jinping. The new president, however, made no concessions on the issue of safeguarding China's "cultural security." According to him, "[We are confronted] with unprecedented challenges and hardships during our struggle in the new historical period. Comrades on the front of propaganda and thought work should help our cadres and masses to clarify the boundary between right and wrong and maintain a firm stance on those issues concerning political principles."[69]

A Shanghai-based IPR scholar aptly summarized the reform of Chinese cultural policy in the early twenty-first century and the dilemma it faces:

> [In the early twenty-first century], there was no government-organized "antispiritual pollution campaign." In fact, the government would not be so stupid as to maintain ideological order in such a crude form as they did in the 1980s. We organized hundreds of rounds of crackdown on copyright piracy under the principle of "prospertize cultural market with one hand, stabilize the cultural market with the other hand" (*yishou zhua fanrong, yishou zhua wending*). But don't you think that at least some contradiction exists between those two goals? If a popular movie wins high box office income but contains some content offensive to the Chinese Communist Party, should the movie be on show to "prospertize the cultural market"? Or should it be cracked down to "stabilize the cultural market"? If crackdown happens, do the law enforcement people carry out the crackdown because the movie violated the author's copyright or because the movie's content offended the Communist Party? That contradiction cannot be resolved completely. Indeed, it is inherent with the Chinese political system.[70]

In sum, this section establishes that, when implementing copyright policy, the maintenance of ideological stability is the Chinese state's top priority. While it is important for observers of Chinese copyright policy to study the organizational history and institutional strengths of the country's copyright bureaucracies, they should not neglect the continuity and changes in the operational principles of these bureaucratic units. During the past three decades, market mechanisms have gradually gained the upper hand in the realm of Chinese propaganda and ideology policy. However, the Chinese government still maintains its grip over China's cultural affairs. The reform of the Chinese propaganda system, both its achievements and limitations, constitutes the policy environment for the development of the copyright industry in China and will inevitably inform the country's copyright protection practice.

A Distorted Chinese Cultural Market and Its Impact on the Chinese Copyright Industry

In his seminal study of the quality of copyright enforcement in China, Dimitrov argues that cases handled through judicial or quasi-judicial channels are more likely to be consistent and transparent and therefore bode well for the rise of rationalization in the future.[71] But a natural question arises: with the ideological factors put aside, what kind of copyright cases are more likely to be handled through judicial or quasi-judicial enforcement channels? A natural answer to this question is that the more economically powerful actors of the Chinese copyright industry are, the more likely they are to have their cases heard by the judicial or quasi-judicial enforcement agencies. But that answer still leaves unclear which part of the Chinese copyright industry tends to be more economically powerful. I argue that the incomplete reform of the Chinese propaganda policy creates an uneven impact on the Chinese domestic copyright industry. Certain parts of the Chinese copyright industry underwent more thorough market reform. Therefore, the copyright owners, like their foreign counterparts entering the Chinese market, are better financed and experienced in copyright protection and are more likely to reap satisfactory enforcement outcomes. Most Chinese copyright owners hate copyright piracy as much as their foreign counterparts, but they do not have enough financial resources to support expensive antipiracy investigations and lawsuits. Those factors render the Chinese domestic copyright industry into a constituency with an uneven level of support for the copyright norm, which in turn creates an uneven level of effectiveness in the enforcement cases.

According to a Beijing-based IPR scholar, the health of a country's cultural market relies on two core components: the production of high-quality copyrighted works and the efficient distribution of copyrighted works from producers to the consumers. He delineated what he deemed a benign circle under a healthy cultural market. Within the benign circle, high-quality copyrighted products can reach consumers through an efficient distribution system. The income earned from consumers of copyrighted products can provide financial resources to help produce more high-quality copyrighted products (see Figure 4).

According to the IPR scholar, the incomplete reform of China's propaganda policy distorted the benign circle. That is, the Chinese propaganda

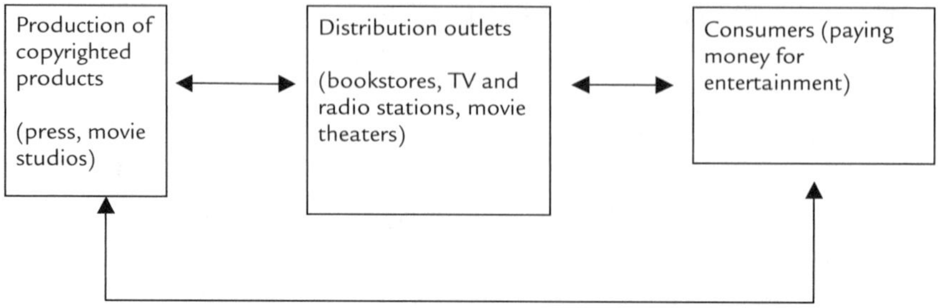

Figure 4. Benign circle for the development of the copyright industry.

system still maintains the power of final judgment over the content of copyrighted products. Moreover, the Chinese propaganda system cannot exercise direct control over Chinese consumers, but it can control, or at least attempt to control, the way in which copyrighted products can reach them. Due to the Chinese propaganda system's rigid control over the distribution channel of copyrighted works, copyright producers cannot directly distribute the copyrighted products to the distribution outlets. Therefore, a distorted circle comes into shape in China's cultural market (see Figure 5). In fact, the government's rigid control over the copyright industry at least partially contributes to the growth and survival of the illegal copyright market. (I will discuss that in greater detail in the third section of this chapter.)

Producing Copyrighted Products in China: Dancing with Shackles on the Feet

The first section of this chapter described the rapid growth in Chinese copyright industries sparked by market reforms in recent decades. Despite the astonishing growth of the copyright industries in recent years, the propaganda system's mission remains unchanged. That is, the Chinese propaganda system still maintains its restriction over producing copyrighted products and their content. That policy suppresses the creativity of most Chinese literature and artistic producers. According to a Nanjing-based copyright official, "[The] Chinese copyright industry is just like a kite, with its string held by the Chinese government. In the past, the latter held the string so tightly that the kite did not even fly. Now the kite can fly much higher, but the string holder worries that the kite would be out of his control and never gives up the string. But the point is, how can the kite fly high if the string is held so tightly?"[72]

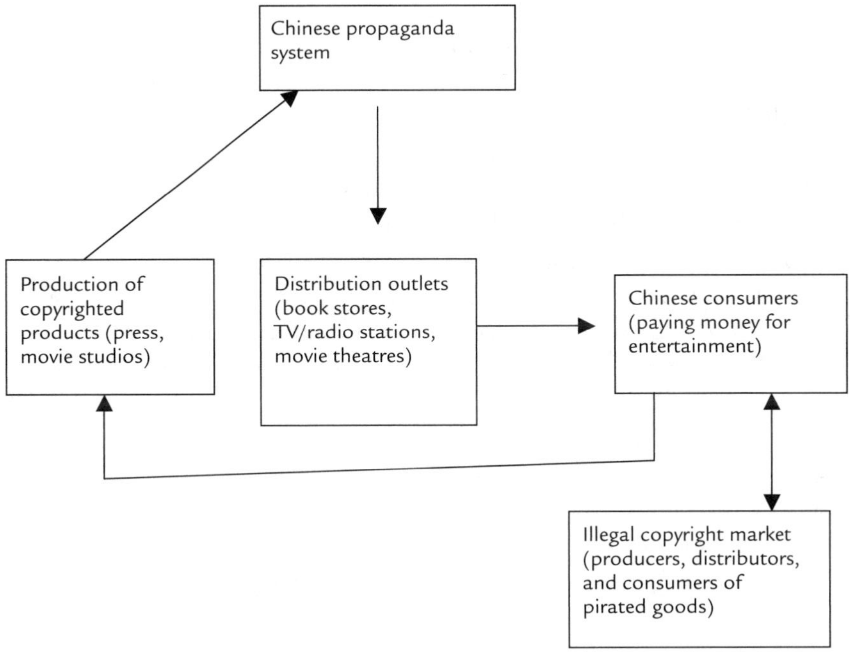

Figure 5. A distorted cultural market in China.

Evidence to support the official's comment is found in a full range of Chinese government regulations pertaining to the country's copyright industry. In the Chinese film industry, for example, foreign investors are permitted to establish joint ventures with state-owned movie studios, but their share cannot exceed 49 percent. Moreover, they are not permitted to establish their own studios. They are not allowed to set up joint ventures with the domestic privately owned studios either.[73] This policy was laid out by the Provisional Regulations on the Operational Eligibility of Movie Studios in 2004, and thus far, the Chinese government has showed no interest in revising it. According to a sarcastic comment by a Beijing-based IPR scholar, the only revision the Chinese government would make is to change the word "provisional" in the title of the regulations to "permanent."[74] In the publishing industry, there are similar restrictions on foreign capital's entry into the Chinese market. After joining the WTO in 2001, China allowed foreign capital to invest in China's press and publishing industry. However, according to the Provisions on Managing Press and Publication issued by GAPP in 2001 and revised in 2011, foreign companies were only allowed to operate in the distribution sector of the Chinese press and publication industry. The operation of the publishing and editing sector is still strictly limited to Chinese domestic capital.[75] Article 16 of the Regulations on the Management of Market for Press and Publication further provided that foreign capital cannot hold a dominant share in distribution companies composed of more than thirty chain stores.[76]

The Chinese propaganda system's control of the production of copyrighted works was not only directed against foreign capital. A censorship mechanism still exists in China, although the criteria are less rigid than before. During the new century, instead of exercising censorship power over certain cultural industry units as a whole, the focus of censorship has shifted to the content of specific cultural products. In the Chinese movie industry, private and foreign capital receive permission to access Chinese movie production, but they still have to acquire a production license before individual movies can be produced. According to the Regulations on Recording the Synopsis of Movie Script and Movie Management issued in 2006, Chinese movie studios are required to submit a 1,000-word synopsis of movie scripts to MORFT before the production process starts. For China-foreign jointly produced movies, the full text of the movie script is required.[77] In the revised edition of the regulation issued in 2011, the required length of the movie script synopsis was reduced to 300 words, but MORFT still maintained the power to censor movie scripts. In the publishing industry, similar restrictions also apply. According to Article 26 of the Provisions on Managing Press and Publication, the press and publications are forbidden to contain illegal content "that endangers state security and social stability, opposes the basic principles of Chinese constitution and other legal regulations, and damages state honor and national interests." GAPP maintains the final decision-making power over the interpretation of Article 26.[78]

The censorship policies have aroused much criticism from Chinese copyright professionals during the past decade. In 2003, for example, several leading Chinese directors headed by Jia Zhangke wrote an appeal letter to the MORFT, calling for the establishment of China's own rating system, drawing from the experience of developed countries, to replace the censorship mechanism.[79] Chinese government officials, however, replied by saying only that "we are actively investigating the possibility to set up such a system."[80] After seven years of "active investigation," Zhao Shi, vice director of MORFT, told the press that "China has already found an effective way to manage its movie industry. A movie-rating system does not fit the concrete condition of Chinese movie market."[81] The cold shoulder from the Chinese government enraged the country's movie professionals. Criticism against the movie censorship mechanism extended from the younger generation directors to their veteran counterparts and gained nationwide sympathy. In 2012, a veteran movie director, Xie Fei, wrote an open letter to the State Administration of Radio, Film, and Television, reiterating that the content examination system in China is outdated. Xie Fei also called upon the movies' subject content to be reviewed by a movie producers' organization instead of the government.[82] Xie Fei's father, Xie Juezai, was an old revolutionary guard who joined the Chinese Communist Party in 1925. With this family background, the call for a movie rating system moved from "outside the government system" (*tizhiwai*) to "within the government system" (*tizhinei*).

The Chinese government could no longer turn a deaf ear to these voices. In July 2013, the Chinese State Council issued the Notice to Distribute the Provisions on the Major Duties, Organizational Division, and Personnel Allocation of the SARFT, known as the 2013 Notice. Article 1 of the 2013 Notice provided that "content examination for movie scripts of 'general subjects' (*yiban ticai*) would be cancelled and replaced with the public notification of the movie synopsis."[83] According to the regulations, "general subjects" refers to all subjects other than "significant subjects" (*zhongda ticai*), such as China's ethnic relationships, religious affairs, military and diplomatic affairs, the police and judicial system, or major events in the history of the Chinese Communist Party (CCP). Soon after the SARFT made the regulations public on its website, criticism arose that the distinction between "general subjects" and "significant subjects" was too vague. Li Shaohong, president of the Chinese Movie Directors Association, expressed worry that the power to draw the distinction still rested with the Chinese government.[84] A Beijing-based copyright scholar stated the doubt plainly: "If a movie is about the love story between a Han Chinese young man and a Tibetan girl, is that a topic of 'general subject' or 'significant subject'? A love story is certainly about 'general subject,' but is it going to be turned into [a] 'significant subject' simply because the cast includes some actors or actresses from ethnic minority groups? Honestly I think that the SARFT only put the old wine into a new bottle."[85]

While a movie rating system has been in the United States since the late 1960s,[86] similar regulations are still in their infancy in China. Under the existing censorship system, it takes an average of forty-five to sixty days for a movie to get a production license. This system slows movie production and makes it harder for investors to get a return on their investment. Some outstanding movies have missed hitting a prime running schedule due to the inefficiency of the censorship mechanism. The pirated version of some movies already had circulated during the lengthy content examination period.[87] In 2013, China produced 638 movies, but only 305 of them made their way to the theater for public viewing.[88] The situation in 2014 was not any better. Only 329 of the 618 movies produced in that year were allowed to show in the movie theaters.[89] While the movies distributed in Chinese theaters are easier for copyright enforcement professionals to safeguard, movies that failed to pass content examination are not that lucky. They are either sold as cheap copyrighted goods or confiscated by the Chinese government. In both cases, the copyrights of those movies are easy prey for copyright infringers. As a movie producer commented, "Do I hate the copyright infringers? Of course. But at least they made my work known to the audience. Neither the government nor the copyright infringers respect my creativity. But they hurt me in different ways. The copyright infringers hurt my wallet. The government hurts my mind."[90]

Censorship mechanisms impact the Chinese publishing industry in similar ways. Due to the restrictions imposed by the Chinese press and publication, the first consideration for Chinese writers is meeting the requirements of the censorship bureaucracies rather than the demands of Chinese readers. Although the Chinese officials have claimed on various occasions that no censorship is practiced in the country,[91] journalists from international media found that the 580 publishing houses in China are required to employ in-house censors, most of whom are faithful CCP members. GAPP also possesses the mandate to order the removal of chapters or kill an entire book.[92] There are no accurate statistical data about how many authors and their books were banned in China in recent years, but books by prominent figures such as Hillary Clinton and Alan Greenspan were pulled from shelves due to their "sensitive content."[93] The comment by a manager of a Beijing-based publishing company vividly described the hardship confronting the Chinese authors: "Everybody keeps talking about protecting copyright, but before we talk about copyright, we should first talk about authors' right. In theory, we should respect the authors. But in reality, we are not respected because we have to worry if we are going to offend the Chinese government even before we publish books. Who is going to respect the copyright norm if the authors themselves are not respected by the government?"[94]

In the recent decade, China has invested heavily to develop its copyright industry, but money alone is not sufficient to produce high-quality copyrighted products. Equally important is a relatively free environment for creative expression. In this respect, the situation in China is still unsatisfactory for most copyright owners. In the words of a Beijing-based copyright owner, "Is the Chinese government sincere about copyright protection? Maybe. But it is more accurate to say that they protect what they want to protect. That is, those copyright owners should better understand that they cannot afford to offend the Chinese government."[95] This results in copyright owners having varying levels of strength when it comes to copyright protection.

Distribution of Copyrighted Products in China: Marketing Culture in a Fragmented Market

It is but the first step to produce high-quality copyrighted products for the purpose of developing the copyright industry. An equally important aspect is to distribute those products efficiently. However, as discussed in the following paragraphs, while the production of copyrighted goods is hindered by the Chinese propaganda system, the distribution of those goods is also under its grip.

For a long time, propaganda outlets in China were regarded as primary locales for the Chinese Communist Party to construct legitimacy. In 1949, when the communist forces took over China, the Communist Party ordered the troops to reserve a place in the downtown area for the Communist Party–run Xinhua Bookstore in any new city they took over to sell "revolutionary cultural works."[96] With the Communist Party in control in most provinces except Taiwan, a cultural product distribution system was established following the steps of the Chinese Communist troops. In 1956, all private bookstores nationwide were merged with the state-owned Xinhua Bookstore. Like other state-owned enterprises in China, Xinhua Bookstores operated as accessories to different levels of the Chinese government rather than as independent market entities. Instead of responding to the needs of readers and operating the cultural market as a market, Chinese cultural products were distributed at state order. In 1981, before the Chinese government initiated the reform of the country's book distribution system, there were only 8,709 state-owned and collectively owned Xinhua Bookstores nationwide, which was an average of about 100,000 people per bookstore. In the entire city of Beijing, there were only 101 Xinhua Bookstores as of the early 1980s.[97] This distribution system could hardly meet the demand of Chinese readers.

The Chinese movie industry, which had a similar distribution system as the bookstores, was initiated in the 1950s. In 1951, the China Film Company was established as the only company with the official mandate to distribute movies or movie-related products in China. Under the old distribution system known as "unified purchase and sale," the China Film Company purchased movies from various movie studios and distributed them to the cinemas at the local level. Regardless of the movies' quality or box office earnings, the purchase price settled by the China Film Company remained the same for decades. For example, in 1990, *Ju Dou*, an internationally known, award-winning movie about rural Chinese women in the 1930s, recorded 57 million RMB in box office earnings. However, the purchase price of *Ju Dou* by the China Film Company was only 700,000 RMB, as settled by the Chinese government, the same as another mediocre Chinese movie that only recorded 1 million RMB in box office earnings. Moreover, the majority of a movie's box office earnings went to the China Film Company rather than the movie studios. Obviously, such a distribution system did not increase the Chinese movie studios' incentives to improve their movie technology and produce high-quality movies. A vicious circle was thus formed. The monopolized distribution system could not provide sufficient economic resources for movie production, low-quality movies could not attract large audiences, and the dwindling audiences, in turn, could not generate enough box office earnings to upgrade China's theater system.[98]

The outdated distribution system of copyrighted products became the target of reform. In 1982, the National Conference on Book Distribution Work urged Xinhua Bookstores at different levels to transform themselves into corporate entities. More important, the Chinese government allowed the operation of privately owned bookstores. According to the conference, China should establish a book distribution system "with the State-owned Xinhua Bookstore as the main body, complemented by bookstores of multiple forms of economic ownership, multiple channels of books circulation, multiple means of purchase and sale, and reduced layers of circulation." Later, this reform orientation was summarized as "one main body, three multiples, and one reduced" (*yizhu sanduo yishao*).[99] The limited space of this chapter does not permit a detailed record of the various reform measures into the Chinese book distribution system following the 1982 Conference, but that conference laid the principle for the reform of the Chinese book distribution system for the next three decades. After more than thirty years of reform, private bookstores now constitute the majority of the distribution channel for books and published materials in China. As of 2013, there were 125,467 book distribution outlets in China, with 91.3 percent of them privately owned. It is also noteworthy that the first online bookstore in China—Modern Bookstore—was established in East China's Zhejiang Province in 1997. By 2013, there were 511 online bookstores in China, with 90 percent of them privately owned.[100]

In 1993, the MORFT issued *Opinions on Deepening the Reform of the Chinese Movie Industry*, known as the No. 3 Document. The No. 3 Document terminated the monopoly power of the China Film Company over the distribution of domestic films and entrusted movie studios with the power to directly negotiate the movies' sale prices with the theaters. Such reform measures transformed the formerly monopolized distribution channel into an open system.[101] In 2002, China established a theater-band system to further break down the barriers among different provincial movie markets. Under the theater-band system, movie theaters across different provinces were organized into different distribution coalitions, possessing the autonomy to determine which movies would be shown and on what schedule.[102] As of 2013, forty-six cross-regional theater bands have been established in twenty-five provinces and captured 90 percent of the country's box office income. In 2013, the Chinese theater band recorded a total of 5,077 newly built screens, or 13.9 screens per day.[103]

Despite the reforms, constraints still exist. In the publishing industry, although the first China-foreign joint distribution venture was established in 2005, under Article 5 of the Chinese State Council's Decision on Non-State Capital's Accession into Cultural Industry issued in the same year, foreign capital still cannot exceed 49 percent in joint-venture distributions.[104] More important, the state-owned Xinhua Bookstore is entrusted with the most profitable part of the book distribution business in China, the distribution of primary and high school textbooks. It is estimated that in 2013, 60 percent of the total profits of the Chinese publishing industry is associated with the textbook business. Coupled with the profits from distributing other published materials, the state-owned Xinhua Bookstore network accounted for 88.7 percent of the recorded profits in China's book distribution business.[105] Compared with the privately owned bookstores, Xinhua Bookstores enjoyed other important benefits such as tax deductions.[106] Those pressures greatly squeezed the breathing space for privately owned bookstores. Since 2008, a wave of bankruptcies has hit the once prosperous Chinese privately owned bookstores. It was estimated that over 10,000 privately owned entity bookstores went bankrupt between 2008 and 2012.[107] The pressure of subsistence forced the remaining privately owned bookstores to either move their businesses online or distribute pirated published materials to compensate for the operational costs. The Chinese government has not published accurate statistical data about how many privately owned bookstores are involved in distributing pirated materials. Chinese government officials have not singled out privately owned bookstores and accused them of distributing pirated books either. But Wu Shulin, vice director of GAPP, told the press in 2013 that the focus of the Chinese government's antipiracy efforts would be concentrated on "the piracy behavior by poorly regulated websites and marketing platforms."[108] That comment was largely interpreted as directed against the privately owned distribution outlets for copyright products because the state-owned Xinhua Bookstore network is under strict state regulation. Remarks by professionals in both the Xinhua Bookstore and privately owned bookstores confirmed that interpretation. When asked for the opinion on Wu Shulin's remarks, a branch manager of Xinhua Bookstore said, "A clean hand wants no washing. That old saying describes our situation very well. Why should we distribute pirated works if we can make profits through legitimate channels? We cannot afford to lose face like that."[109] But the opinion from the privately book distributors was less friendly. According to the manager of a privately owned bookstore, "[Wu Shulin's remark] was nothing more than 'scold the locust while pointing at the mulberry.' We know what he was talking about. But before they blame us, we should first find out who created all the problems. It is the Chinese government. We want to do business legally, but can we feed ourselves if we observe the government regulations? The government forced the young girls of good families to prostitute themselves (*biliang weichang*)!"[110]

Similar policy constraints impact the Chinese movie distribution network. Foreign investors are still forbidden to establish their own theaters and distribution companies. Under the Provisional Regulations on Foreign Investment in Movie Theater Construction issued in 2003, while foreign capital is allowed to establish joint ventures with Chinese movie distribution companies, their share cannot exceed 49 percent.[111] That regulation has remained unchanged for the past decade. The MORFT also stipulates that two-thirds of show times in Chinese movie theaters should be reserved for domestic films.[112] Moreover, China Film Company maintained the power to distribute imported foreign films. After China and the United States signed the Memorandum of Understanding Resolving the WTO Film-Related Issues and during then Chinese Vice President Xi Jinping's visit to the United States in 2012, Chinese private distribution companies were allowed to distribute imported films.[113] But foreign movie companies are still not allowed to distribute movies on their own, even though they have gained access to the Chinese market.

Due to those constraints, distribution channels at local levels have lost an important source of financial income to better reach their audience. In Chinese movie distribution channels, as of 2012, there were 3,293 movie theaters in China, compared to 6,200 U.S. movie theaters.[114] Given the vast population in China, that number of movie theaters at best inadequately meets the Chinese audience's demand for movie entertainment: the total number of screens in the United States reached 39,962 in 2012, an average of 8,000 people per screen. Despite the rapid increase in the number of movie screens in China during the past decade, there were only approximately 18,195 screens as of 2013, with 80,000 people per screen.[115]

Moreover, the geographical distribution of the theaters is disproportionally imbalanced. As of 2013, 70 percent of the renovated theaters have been concentrated in the eight major metro areas in China: Beijing, Shanghai, Shenzhen, Guangzhou, Chengdu, Wuhan, Hangzhou, and Chongqing. Statistical data show that the Chinese theater-band system only covers 35 percent of the county-level cities (*xianjishi*). That is, despite the hard work of the Chinese theater-band professionals in the past decade, most small and medium cities, not to mention the vast countryside, remain detached from the movie distribution channels. As a result, on average, one Chinese audience member went to a movie theater 0.47 times annually while one American audience member went to the movie theater 6 times annually in 2013.[116] This combination of an insufficient supply and an abundance of demand results in higher prices for movie tickets. Since official distribution channels cannot meet Chinese audiences' needs well, Chinese audiences prefer to purchase DVD players or home video projectors and turn to the unofficial cultural market to purchase illegal copyrighted products. It is unfair to say that all the DVDs purchased by Chinese customers are pirated, but it can be safely concluded that the gap between the insufficient supply and abundant demand for copyrighted products creates a space for pirated cultural products to grow.

Foreign Copyright Industry on Chinese Soil: Can the Chinese Sheep Dance with the Foreign Wolves?

Even though the Chinese government exercises many constraints on the development of the domestic copyright industry, the attitude of domestic copyright owners toward it cannot be described as complete hatred. As a Chinese copyright owner told me, "Our attitude towards the Chinese Propaganda Department is ambivalent: we hate it because it prevents us from further improving our competitiveness; we love it because it protects us from the greedy foreign copyright industry. Without it, Chinese copyright industry will be completely eaten up by foreign competitors."[117]

After closing its door to the foreign copyright industry for decades, in 1994, the Chinese government agreed to import ten foreign blockbusters annually.[118] In 1995, most of the ten were Hollywood movies.[119] The blockbusters reaped a total of $120 million in net box office income. When China entered the WTO, the Chinese government agreed to raise the quota to twenty foreign films.[120] In the 2012 China-U.S. movie memorandum of understanding (MOU), China added fourteen Hollywood blockbusters to the list. According to Tong Gang, former movie bureau chief of the MORFT, during the first decade of Hollywood blockbusters' presence in China (1994–2003), they contributed 60 percent of profits from the movie market in the country, followed by Mainland China–Hong Kong jointly made movies (30 percent) and mainland Chinese movies (10 percent). In 1998, *Titanic* recorded 360 million RMB in box office income, contributing more than 25 percent of the total box office earnings (1.4 billion RMB) in China that year. So far, that record has not been broken.[121]

As preceding scholarship rightly points out, the Chinese government did not import foreign films just on their merits. Instead, their original intention was to reestablish Chinese audience's interests in watching movies.[122] During its twenty years on Chinese soil, the foreign copyright industry reaped considerable benefits despite the restrictions imposed by the Chinese government. According to the MORFT, 303 movies were broadcast in China in 2012, with 226 of them domestic movies and 76 of them imported movies. Although Chinese domestic movies assumed 75 percent of the movies shown, they earned only 8 billion RMB in box office income, which accounted for 47.6 percent of China's total box office income in 2012. The quantity of foreign movies was much smaller, but they generated 52.4 percent of China's total box office income.[123] In 2013, Chinese domestic movies made a counterattack with the support of Chinese government. The SARFT unofficially allocated the time between June 10 and July 10 as the "month for protection of domestic movies." The running schedule around the Spring Festival and Christmas/New Year break was also reserved for Chinese domestic movies.[124] Under those protection measures, sixty imported foreign films were shown in China's theater band in 2013, accounting for about 20 percent of the total 305 films shown that year. Even so, the imported films still recorded 41.3 percent of the total box office earnings.[125] Shaking the Chinese domestic movie industry with their strong competitiveness, the foreign copyright industry brought forth cutting-edge business models and operational ideas.

The entrance of the foreign copyright industry forced the Chinese domestic copyright owners to adapt to the competition. In the words of a Beijing-based copyright scholar, "Everybody screamed that 'the wolves are coming' when foreign movies entered the Chinese market. But only some of them realized that the best way is to 'dance with the wolves' is to turn into wolves. Otherwise, they could only remain uncompetitive sheep and would be eaten by the wolves."[126] In 2002, Zhang Yimou's *Hero* marked the beginning of the "blockbuster era" for Chinese domestic movies. During the following decade, practitioners of the Chinese copyright industry improved their competitiveness through improving storytelling techniques to marketing strategies learned from their foreign counterparts. Certain parts of the Chinese copyright industry benefited greatly from the competition with their foreign counterparts. In 2013, for example, thirty-three Chinese domestic movies recorded a total of over 100 million RMB in box office income. *Journey to the West: Conquering the Demons* took first place on the box office income list (1.24 billion RMB), surpassing *Iron Man 3*, which took second place (748 million RMB).[127] Although criticized as overprotecting the country's domestic movies, China became one of a few countries whose domestic blockbusters were able to compete with Hollywood on their own soil.

Despite all these achievements, the Chinese copyright industry accounted for only 6.67 percent of Chinese gross domestic product (GDP) with its 4,000 billion RMB (about $120 million) total output.[128] Compared with the developed countries, the Chinese copyright industry was but an incipient player. According to the International Intellectual Property Alliance (IIPA), a U.S.-based organization of IPR holders, the total output of U.S. copyright industries in 2012 reached an estimated $1.77 trillion or 11.25 percent of U.S. GDP. As one of the major contributors to U.S. exports, in 2012, it was estimated that foreign sales and exports of the U.S. copyright industries increased to at least $142 billion, higher than quite a few other major industrial sectors. The sectors include the aerospace industry ($106 billion), agricultural exports ($70.1 billion), food ($64.7 billion), and pharmaceutical products ($50.9 billion).[129] By definition, a pillar industry should not only account for a significant percentage (normally 10 percent of a country's GDP) but also be able to promote the development of related industries.[130] Judged by that standard, the Chinese copyright industry is not yet a pillar industry for the Chinese economy.

This situation has a direct impact on the outcome of copyright protection: when faced with copyright infringement, foreign copyright owners are more likely to achieve satisfactory results because they are well financed and experienced in copyright protection. However, since they cannot act freely in China, in many cases, they obtain copyright protection by asking the foreign embassy or consulates in China to lobby or even pressure the Chinese government. The elite Chinese copyright owners have financial resources, experience, and the freedom to act in China, but they account for only a small part of the Chinese copyright industry. Most Chinese domestic copyright owners do not have enough financial resources to support an expensive antipiracy investigation and lawsuit. Therefore, even when infringement activities are detected, they could at best receive lukewarm help from the government enforcement bureaucracies. According to the complaint from the manager of a Beijing-based small publishing company, "We face enemies from all directions: above us, the Chinese government oversees our behavior; on our right, we face competition from foreign copyright industries; on our left, we have to fight with potential copyright infringers; below us, the level of Chinese mass consumers' sympathy for IPR is very low. We have little room to maneuver, if at all."[131] The above comment might only represent the situation of small and medium copyright enterprises in China. Yet, it is important to note that they constitute the bulk of Chinese copyright industry. While the elite Chinese copyright owners are more likely to reap satisfactory enforcement outcomes, most other copyright owners are not that lucky. It remains a challenging task for the majority of the Chinese domestic copyright industry to survive international competition and promote China's domestic culture.

Underground Cultural Market in China: Fighting a "People's War Against Piracy" Without the People's Support

This section analyzes the operation of the underground cultural market in China and focuses on the following questions: Who are the infringers? Who are the distributors and buyers of pirated goods? What is their attitude toward copyright? How does the underground cultural market work in China? What is its relationship with the legitimate market of Chinese copyright products? In answering those questions, I argue that the underground cultural market has an enormous competitive advantage compared with their legitimate counterparts. Although the exact size of that underground market remains unknown, it features cheap pirated goods and a flexible distribution system. Because of that, copyright infringement activities are able to survive rounds of antipiracy campaigns. The Chinese government has realized that, in addition to the crackdown on producing and distributing pirated goods, promoting Chinese public's sympathy toward the IPR norm is the best way to eliminate the root cause of copyright infringement. But this section suggests there is a low level of sympathy with IPR among most Chinese consumers, which further explains the rarity of effective copyright enforcement cases.

Cracking Down on the Production of Pirated Goods: Mission Impossible for the Chinese Government?

During the past three decades, the technology of producing pirated copyright products in China went through three stages: from pirated videotapes, to illegal production lines, to a rapidly growing online piracy. While the former two types of infringement were popular ways to infringe upon copyright in the 1980s and 1990s, respectively, copyrighted products have been increasingly uploaded to the Internet for unauthorized download during the early twenty-first century. While pirated videocassettes are technologically out of date, both illegal production lines and online piracy have persisted, creating double headaches for Chinese copyright owners.

Stage 1: Pirated Videotapes

According to a Shanghai-based former copyright official, the first videotapes were sold on the Chinese market around 1980, when the country opened its door to the outside world. Soon after, China was exposed to the outside world, and curiosity with foreign cultures, coupled with the huge profits associated with copyright infringements, gave birth to the growth of the pirated videotape industry. In 1984, the Shanghai police detected the first fourteen pirated videotapes in the city and probably in the country as well. After that, pirated videotapes grew exponentially. In 1987, the number of pirated videotapes detected in Shanghai rose to 1,447. In 1989, that number rose to 5,888. In 1994, that number rose to over 100,000.[132] The official could not find accurate statistical data about the number of pirated videotapes nationwide during that period, but the situation in Shanghai reflects the national trend.

From the mid-1980s to the mid-1990s, most underground replication factories for pirated videotapes were located in the suburban area and surrounding villages and were run by local peasants and township entrepreneurs. Each replication factory typically had around twenty replication machines and was able to produce several hundred pirated videotapes per day. Blank videotapes were purchased at the unit price of 8 to 12 RMB (a little above $1). Videotapes with content were sold at the price of 20 to 30 RMB (about $3) each. With an average price for legal videotapes at about 120 RMB (about $15), the pirated videotapes enjoyed an enormous price advantage.[133]

After the illegal videotapes were produced, they were distributed to the rest of the country through a wholesale channel known as "transshipment stations" (*lianyunzhan*). Mostly privately owned, the transshipment stations were run by the factory owners' friends or relatives. These transshipment stations labeled packages containing videotapes as clothing or toys to escape police inspection. Some of them even maintained an informal "security contract" with the railway and postal service to ensure the safe transportation of the pirated videotapes. Of course, the railway and postal service workers were paid with a certain amount of bribery, known as the "introduction fee" (*jieshaofei*). Typically, the fee was 2 to 2.5 RMB (about 40 cents) per videotape. If a package contained sixty illegal videotapes, the introduction fee was around 120 RMB. During the late 1980s, the fee made up almost one-third of the monthly salary of a county-level post office manager. The profits enticed the managers to turn a blind eye to the shipping of illegal videotapes, which in turn allowed the pirated goods to spread to other parts of the country.[134]

It is unfair to say that the Chinese government did nothing to stop the production and distribution of illegal videotapes, but the replication factories were easy to hide, and pirators had connections with their patrons in the Chinese government. Because the connections were so difficult to break, crackdown efforts never eliminated the production of illegal videotapes completely. In the words of a Guangdong-based former copyright official, "The pirated videotapes did not 'die' out because of our enforcement efforts. Instead, they phased out because a new way of producing pirated goods emerged. The new method to produce pirated goods only made piracy activities cheaper, easier, and more profitable."[135] This new way of producing pirated goods is the illegal production lines for pirated DVD/software.

Stage 2: Illegal Production Line for Pirated DVD/Software

Illegal production lines are mostly located in southern China's Guangdong and Fujian Provinces. According to the director of the Guangdong Provincial Copyright Administration, Huang Xiaoling, between 1996 and 2014, Guangdong Province detected 212 illegal production lines, accounting for 86 percent of the total detected illegal production lines in the country.[136] Soon after Guangdong Province detected the country's first illegal VCD/DVD production line in 1996, the Provincial Customs House found a transnational piracy supply chain operating both inside and outside of China. That is, parts of those illegal production lines assembled in China's coastal provinces were smuggled in and were shipped to other inland provinces in China along with pirated VCDs/DVDs.[137]

The profit margin of pirated videotapes was already huge. A Guangdong Customs House official told me in an interview in 2007 that the profit margin of the illegal pirated DVD/software production line was even more astonishing: the cost of the plastic material needed to make pirated DVDs was only 3,000 RMB (about $350) per *ton*; the cost of raw materials for making a single pirated DVD was only 0.35 RMB (about 4 cents). It takes only three seconds to burn one pirated DVD. Including the production cost of purchasing a DVD burning machine, workers' wages, and rent for the factory, the average cost of one pirated DVD is a little above 1 RMB (about 15 cents). If those pirated DVDs are sold at wholesale for 2 or 3

RMB (about 20 to 40 cents) to the lower-level vendors to be distributed to the other parts of the country, the profit rate for the factory owner is 100 percent or even higher. Considering that movie and software companies invest millions of dollars in producing a new movie or developing a new type of software, pirating these movies is almost too cheap to calculate.[138] During a follow-up phone interview with the official in January 2012, I was further told that one illegal production line might only require an average of 10 square meters (about 90 square feet) or less. In the 1990s, the copyright infringers typically hid the illegal production lines in underground factories. However, in recent years, the shrinking size of DVD burning machines has allowed the copyright infringers to move the illegal production line to mobile cargo trucks or even cargo ships sailing out at sea.[139] This has added to the difficulty of enforcement efforts.

As pirated DVDs reach Chinese consumers through several layers of the underground distribution system, the price can reach 10 RMB (about $1) per disc. At the same time, the average price of a legitimate DVD is between 20 and 30 RMB per disc. Legitimate DVDs are no match for pirated DVDs. The aforementioned customs official told me, "The pirators do not regard those machines just as DVD burning machines. They call them banknote printing machines. I agree with them. Producing pirated DVD/software is as profitable as trafficking drugs, but the punishment for producing pirated DVD/software is miniscule compared with drug trafficking."[140] The official's comment illustrates the difficulty of cracking down on the illegal production line. But the development of Internet technology in the recent decade would only compound the hardship of copyright protection.

Stage 3: Online Copyright Infringement

On May 31, 1999, Wang Meng and five other leading Chinese novelists sued a Beijing-based Internet company, Century Internet, Inc., for republishing their novels on the Internet without authorization. In December 1999, the IPR Tribunal of Haidian Intermediary People's Court ruled that the defendant should make a public apology to the six Chinese novelists, remove their novels from the website, and pay fines ranging from 720 RMB to 13,080 RMB to the six novelists respectively.[141] This case was widely regarded as the first Internet-related copyright infringement in China. Little did the Chinese copyright professionals know, with the development of the

Chinese Internet industry in the following decade, what a serious challenge online infringement would pose to their protection efforts.

In 2005, Wang Wei, a young man from China's Fujian Province, established the first video-sharing website in the country, Tudou.com, simulating the business model of YouTube. After Wang established Tudou, other video-sharing websites run by ambitious young Internet professionals took off. From 2009 to the first quarter of 2014, the total output of video-sharing websites multiplied more than ten times in only five years, from about 1.76 billion RMB to 22.5 billion RMB. The advertising income of Tudou.com almost reached the level of Zhejiang Satellite TV, a leading provincial-level TV station in China.[142] In 2006, 32 million Chinese Internet users regularly viewed domestic and foreign video-sharing websites. By December 2012, that number had reached 372 million, a more than ten times increase in less than six years.[143] Given the fact that China had 591 million Internet users by June 2013, which is the world's largest, the potential growth of video-sharing websites is astonishing.

While the rapid growth of video-sharing websites is good news for the Internet industry, it is by no means good news for the Chinese copyright industry. In fact, the Chinese copyright industry now has to fight on both fronts, not only against the illegal production factories for pirated goods but also against the rapidly growing Internet piracy. The China Alliance Against Internet Copyright Infringement estimated that online piracy cost the Chinese copyright industry about 10 billion RMB in 2013 and that the income of pirated online books was eight times the income of legal books.[144] The Haidian District in northwest Beijing houses 50 percent of the headquarters of China's video-sharing websites. In 2007, the IPR Special Tribunal of Haidian Intermediate People's Court received only 17 copyright cases related to video-sharing websites. In the first ten months of 2011, however, that number rose to 596.[145] Compared with the late 1990s, the stakes for those copyright cases are much higher. On May 20, 2014, the Shenzhen Municipal Market Supervision Administration (MSA) ordered a punishment of a total of 260 million RMB for the Shenzhen Qvod Technology Co. Ltd. (referred to as Qvod thereafter), a local Internet company sharing audiovisual content online. The former accused the latter of making 50 percent of its profits with pirated content on its website. Although Qvod refuted the accusation and used legal means to reduce the financial punishment, Chinese copyright professionals widely agreed that that litigation involved the highest value of objects in the history of the country's copyright enforcement.[146]

Not everybody welcomed that enforcement move. Shortly after the financial punishment was ordered, the Shenzhen MSA received negative feedback from the Chinese consumers. Specifically, many consumers criticized them as "indifferent to the interests of mass public." Some loyal supporters proposed online that each Qvod user should donate 1 RMB to help Qvod survive the financial punishment and, more important, show their support for Qvod's infringement activities.[147] While the final result of Qvod's copyright case is still unknown, the supporters' attitudes remind Chinese IPR observers of a previously neglected aspect of the country's IPR enforcement: the low sympathy toward the IPR norm among the majority of the Chinese mass public. That problem, as discussed in the following two sections, is a key factor that supports the selling and buying of pirated goods.

Selling Pirated Goods: A Case Study of Mr. Wang and His Fellow Peddlers in Beijing

The cost of producing pirated goods is minuscule. Despite years of reform, the distribution system of pirated goods is much more flexible than the system for legal copyright products. In this section, I offer an in-depth case study of groups of Chinese street peddlers, yielding some insights into the distribution system of pirated goods that is mysterious to outsiders. Because of the vast number of street peddlers in China and the underground nature of their network, there have not been any reliable statistical data about them. This case study demonstrates that in addition to cheap prices, the flexibility in distributing pirated goods makes them even more competitive compared with legal copyrighted products.

Selling pirated goods on the street does not require any sophisticated training. This relatively low threshold for entering the business makes selling pirated goods an attractive way to make a living for lower-income people in China. Indeed, street peddlers are the most salient part of the underground distribution system of pirated goods. The exact number of street peddlers in China is unknown, but the influence of street peddlers on the implementation of Chinese copyright policy is evident in their "business activities."

During my fieldwork in Beijing, I made friends with Mr. Wang,[148] one of the thousands of street peddlers making a living by selling pirated goods in Beijing. A migrant worker from Anhui Province, Mr. Wang came to Beijing in 2005 after the township factory that he worked for went bankrupt. With the accumulation of more experience and personal connections in this business, his monthly income rose to 3,000 RMB, and Mr. Wang started to enjoy a reputation among his fellow pirated DVD peddlers for being capable and friendly. Moreover, compared with the working staff in the state-owned audiovisual stores, Mr. Wang is very familiar with the development of the movie market. Every day after 6:00 p.m., Mr. Wang starts his business at the gate of the nearby subway station. Most of the twenty-odd peddlers on Mr. Wang's personal network are migrant workers from Anhui Province and its neighboring Henan Province. Their business activities are located in border areas between southwestern Beijing's Fengtai and Haidian Districts.

The pirated DVDs Mr. Wang and his fellow peddlers sell are distributed by an "upper-line" guy based in Beijing's neighboring Hebei Province. The source of the pirated goods is from China's coastal provinces such as Guangdong and Fujian. Exactly how they are produced in southern China and shipped to Beijing remains a mystery to Mr. Wang and many other people. Indeed, curiosity over these matters risks Mr. Wang's business but also possibly his personal security. This upper-line guy promised to Mr. Wang that he would compensate him for his economic fines if Mr. Wang's pirated DVDs were confiscated by the police as long as Mr. Wang never tells the police the whereabouts of the upper-line guy. The upper-line guy always keeps his promise.

The pirated DVDs sold by Mr. Wang and his fellow peddlers range from classic movies by Chinese domestic filmmakers in the 1960s to recent ones by filmmakers in Hong Kong, Taiwan, Japan, Korea, and the United States. In Mr. Wang's words, they can "meet the taste of people at every walk of life in Beijing." Mr. Wang and his fellow peddlers are welcomed by residents in surrounding neighborhoods, some of whom are Westerners working or studying in Beijing.

Mr. Wang and his fellow peddlers are not free from trouble. The biggest source of trouble comes from the law enforcement squad from the local cultural market management office. However, street peddlers have developed increasingly sophisticated skills over rounds of cat-and-mouse games with law enforcement officials. A female peddler, Ms. Yin,[149] often carries a baby in her arms as a shield to protect her from police searches. This tactic has proved to be very effective. Like many female peddlers, she rents the baby from another female migrant worker in Beijing, who comes from the same village.[150] Both Mr. Wang and Ms. Yin urged me not to probe further because otherwise, they could not guarantee my safety.

When asked about their attitude toward copyright, Mr. Wang and his fellow peddlers' first response was "What is copyright?" After I explained to them in as easy language as I could, they made the following reply:

> I do not care about copyright at all. I only care about making a living. Do not blame us as thieves. We are not. At least selling pirated DVD[s] is better than robbery or burglary because it does no harm to common people. Our monthly income is only the cost of a banquet for those movie stars or even less. Do they know anything about our terrible living conditions? Do they care? Did the Americans urge the Chinese government to put us in prison? That is a wonderful idea. In prison, at least the government will feed us and we do not have to work so hard. Besides, does the Chinese government have so much room for so many of us in the prison? Be it Americans, Japanese, or those disgusting guys in the Chinese government, they will never be able to annihilate us.[151]

The trade of street peddlers is highly fluid and constantly changing. When I returned to China and tried to contact the old friends in January 2013, Mr. Wang and his fellow peddlers were no longer in that business. Instead, he was running his own restaurant. The funds to start his restaurant came in no small part from the money he had raised through selling pirated DVDs. Mr. Wang's business was replaced by a group of new migrant workers from Anhui and Henan. Many of them learned how to play the "cat-and-mouse game" with law enforcement. Proud of his "achievements," Mr. Wang told me, "Do you remember what I said before? Our revolutionary cause will never be annihilated. The back waves can always supersede the old ones! Those stupid people in the government should not waste time cracking down upon people like us. They should help us to improve our life. After all, who is going to sell pirated goods if we have a better way to feed ourselves?"[152] Compared with the well-educated Internet professionals and the owners of illegal pirated goods factories, street peddlers occupy a much lower social standing. But their lower social standing does not make them trivial players on the stage. The sheer number of them makes them the foundation of the pyramid of the piracy chain in China.

When discussing the operation of the underground distribution system in China, a Beijing-based former copyright official told me, "For us, those street peddlers are pirators. For the street peddlers, however, selling pirated DVDs is no different from selling any kind of small articles of daily use such as clothes and shoes. They even regard themselves as heroes challenging the dominance of traditional copyright industry. If we do not have any better means to eliminate the production and distribution of pirated goods from the supply side, the most effective means to protect copyright is to enhance Chinese mass public' sympathy with the copyright norm."[153] That official certainly made a point, but a careful examination of Chinese consumers' attitudes toward copyright indicates that the point is easier said than done. Except for those with higher income and education levels, most Chinese consumers have low levels of sympathy for IPR, which is an even more of a nightmarish hurdle for Chinese copyright owners to jump over to defend their rights.

Buying Pirated Goods: Copyright? Who Cares?

Unlike patents, whose primary consumers are industrial enterprises, the primary consumers of copyrighted products are China's public. Combining my own interview data and survey data gathered by Chinese IPR scholars, I argue that the primary factor influencing the behavior of the consumers is economic. The popularity of pirated goods among Chinese consumers also reflects the weaknesses of the legal copyright market in China. Due to government constraints, even high-quality copyrighted products cannot reach consumers in an efficient manner, creating room for pirated goods to grow and survive rounds of antipiracy campaigns. This section also suggests that consumers with higher education/income levels have higher levels of respect for the IPR norm. Unfortunately, they are not the majority of Chinese consumers, which further explains the rarity of effective enforcement outcomes.

The main reason that Chinese consumers buy pirated copyright goods is their cheap price. Additionally, diversified content and a more efficient distribution system make the pirated goods all the more competitive. When I asked why they bought pirated goods, one consumer answered,

> If you want to enjoy the picture and sound of a movie, going to the theater is certainly a better choice than watching DVD at home.

> Only movie theaters have that kind of equipment. But the point is, how many people have the privilege to enjoy that leisure? For the majority of people, who would spend 50 RMB to view a movie in the theater if they can obtain the same movie for less than 10 RMB on the street? Who would be so patient as to wait several days if pirated movies can appear on the market before the legal ones get a chance to show in the theaters? We only need to get the story. Only the well-off petty bourgeoisie (*xiaozi*) would indulge themselves with that kind of stupid emotional appeal created by the surroundings of movie theaters.[154]

The comment is mirrored in the results from a nationwide survey conducted by central China's Wuhan University. According to the survey, 79.24 percent of Chinese consumers admitted that they have purchased pirated books, DVDs, or software, with 67.39 percent of them admitting that the top reason for buying pirated goods is "cheap price," and the second reason is "more interesting content." Only 14.20 percent of the consumers would report to the government enforcement agency after they realized they bought pirated copyright products.[155]

The survey also indicates a positive relationship between consumers' education and income level and their sympathy with the copyright norm. When asked about whether they are aware of IPR law, 65.08 percent of respondents with a college education or higher answered "yes." Among them, 74.81 percent have a monthly salary of 10,000 RMB (about $1,500) or higher, which is the level of an upper middle-class income in China. When asked about their attitudes related to piracy, 53 percent of respondents with a college education answered that "piracy constitutes copyright infringement." For those respondents without college education, only 10 percent chose that answer. When asked, "What factors contribute to the respect for copyright norm?" 60 percent chose "education level," 45 percent chose "family income," and only 23 percent chose "moral consideration."[156]

The survey data pose both hope and challenges for China's copyright enforcement endeavor. On one hand, respect for copyright has taken root in the minds of the well-educated Chinese middle class. On the other hand, most Chinese consumers remain indifferent to the copyright norm. To some extent, due to their low sympathy for IPR, Chinese consumers with lower incomes and education levels involuntarily help the copyright infringers dispose of stolen goods. To solve that issue, the government should engage in consistent efforts to raid against piracy activities, but it also should fix the deeper-level institutional problems with both the production and the distribution of copyright goods in China to better meet the Chinese people's demand for a better cultural life.

In sum, in fighting a "people's war against piracy," the government cannot win the war without the people's support. As mentioned in the Introduction, as of 2007, China has employed 330,000 IPR enforcement staff. Although the country has not published recent statistical data about the number of enforcement staff since then, researchers can safely conclude that the total number of enforcement staff in China must be among the highest in the world. Even if Chinese IPR enforcement staff worked seven days a week, twenty-four hours a day, they would not be able to completely monitor the selling behavior of tens of thousands of street peddlers or the consumption behavior of the country's 1.3 billion people. Interestingly, if not ironically, the rampancy of pirated copyrighted goods at least partially stems from the Chinese government's rigid control over the country's cultural life. That is, incomplete market reform has only benefited a limited number of copyright owners; the inefficient distribution system further hinders the circulation of high-quality copyrighted products even after they are produced. Both factors contribute to the unsatisfactory development of the Chinese copyright industry, which, in turn, contributes to Chinese copyright owners' uneven level of capabilities to safeguard their economic and moral rights. Not surprisingly, those sectors that experience more thorough market reforms tend to be more competitive and thus more capable to defend their copyright. The promotion of IPR sympathy among Chinese consumers so far has only succeeded among those with higher levels of income and education. Promoting respect for the copyright norm among the majority of Chinese consumers is a more daunting but probably a more important task for the Chinese government than raiding the piracy chains. In promoting the effectiveness of copyright enforcement, the government should first examine the problems within its own propaganda and cultural affairs policy.

Conclusion

This chapter focuses on the implementation of copyright policy in China. Picking up from the analysis on China's adoption of copyright norm, I demonstrate the importance of the political and economic environment in which Chinese copyright policy is implemented. Without the improvement of that macroenvironment, Chinese copyright constituency will not get the chance to grow strong, acquire enough resources, and induce an effective enforcement outcome. If certain sectors of the Chinese copyright industry undergo a more thorough market reform, copyright holders in those sectors are more likely to possess a higher level of market competitiveness and thus more likely to attract the government's support when copyright infringement happens. Unfortunately, those copyright holders are limited in numbers. Chinese government's constraints on the country's cultural affairs hinder the efforts by the majority of Chinese domestic holders to promote their competitiveness. To a significant extent, in fighting against the rampancy of copyright infringement in China, the Chinese government is engaged in a protracted war with a self-created enemy. That is, the government-imposed constraints on the Chinese copyright industry prevent the latter from realizing its development potential, which in turn prevents Chinese mass consumers' needs for entertainment from being met. That further has contributed to the growth of an underground cultural market, which has been difficult to eliminate by government-organized antipiracy raids.

The Chinese government would have to remove the unnecessary constraints on the country's cultural industry if it wants to see the prevalence of effective copyright enforcement in the future. The development of Chinese cultural industry in the past decades indicates a positive relationship between the thoroughness of market reform and the competitiveness of China's domestic copyright holders. After all, the real motivation for effective copyright enforcement should originate from the expansion of China's own copyright constituency. The removal of the unnecessary constraints on Chinese cultural affairs will erode the Chinese Communist Party's hard grip on ideological and propaganda affairs, a realm that has already witnessed profound reform since the late 1970s. Researchers should not be surprised to witness how the Chinese Communist Party itself will be changed as that process further unfolds.

A Beijing-based copyright scholar's comment aptly described the challenge in promoting the effectiveness of copyright enforcement in China: "People keep asking about how to improve the effectiveness of IPR enforcement. In essence, that is a pseudo-question. How can we improve the effectiveness of enforcement if the overall political and economic environment remains unchanged? It is just like treating patients. An experienced doctor should not only focus on getting rid of the symptoms but also enhance the overall physical well-being of the patient."[157] In that vein, the Chinese copyright official's comment on the Chinese Communist Party's Central Propaganda Department, the Chinese copyright owners' complaints about government's restraint, and even the Chinese street peddlers and most consumers' indifference to the copyright issue discussed earlier in the chapter all point to the greater political and economic contexts, both domestic and international, in which the Chinese copyright policy operates. Notwithstanding decades of reform, China remains an authoritarian country governed by the Communist Party. Like the issue of patents, China's struggle over copyright is also part of the country's painful transition to an unknown future, something for decision makers and researchers alike to keep in mind to achieve a better understanding of the most populous country in the world. The study of copyright protection in China should be situated in the greater scenario of China's institutional reform in political and economic realms, all of which are parts of the country's endeavor to build a full-fledged market economy and, probably, a higher level of political democracy.

To echo the metaphor made by the IPR scholar earlier in this section, raiding piracy activity is just like getting rid of a patient's symptoms. There is much more to be done to improve the patient's health. Those measures should at least include international cooperation against the transnational piracy network, consistent education campaigns to promote the public's sympathy for IPR, more policy measures to build the competitiveness of the Chinese copyright industry, and more thorough institutional reforms related to the Chinese propaganda system, one of the cornerstones of Chinese communist system.

CHAPTER 5

Chinese Trademark Legislation

Introduction: The Rise, Fall, and Revival of the Tong Ren Tang Chinese Medical Clinic

In 1629, Yue Xianyang was born in Beijing, the capital of the Chinese empire. Inheriting a complete set of medical skills from his father, Yue Xianyang, in his thirties, established his fame across Beijing as an accomplished doctor. While healing patients, Yue also produced medicine with medicinal herbs collected from various sources. In 1669, Yue established his own Chinese traditional medicine clinic and named it "Tong Ren Tang." The name of the clinic has a deep meaning. In the Chinese language, "tong" means "shared" while "ren" means "benevolence." "Tang" is a respectful term for "medical clinic." By naming his medical clinic "Tong Ren Tang," Yue Xianyang identified his hope to share his benevolence as a doctor, a value held highly by Chinese traditional culture, with the common people. Yue Xianyang lived up to this lofty ideal with his accomplishments in Chinese traditional medicine. In 1684, Yue Xiangyang was selected as a member of the Royal Medical Academy (*taiyiyuan*). In 1702, the Tong Ren Tang clinic was awarded a plaque bearing the work of a royal calligrapher. In 1723, Tong Ren Tang became the sole supplier of medicinal herbs/herbal medicines to the royal court.[1] This represented political honor, professional recognition, and economic benefits for the Yue family and their clinic. For almost two centuries, Tong Ren Tang remained one of the most respected brands in the Chinese traditional medical industry.

Tong Ren Tang did not stay detached from the impact of the profound political transformation that China experienced in the early twentieth century. During the first half of the twentieth century, the operation of Tong

Ren Tang was undergoing serious disruption from the decades of foreign invasion and civil war. The success of the Chinese Communist Revolution in 1949 brought hope for Yue Songsheng, then general manager of Tong Ren Tang. As part of the general scheme to build a socialist public economy, the Chinese Communist Party called upon private enterprises to follow the principle of "state-private joint management" (*gongsi heying*). Yue Songsheng enthusiastically responded to the call. On August 27, 1954, Yue Songsheng held the first state-private joint conference with the Chinese government, transforming Tong Ren Tang from a private enterprise to an enterprise jointly owned by the state and private shareholders.[2] The Chinese Communist Party was also allowed to establish a branch of Tong Reng Tang. The backup from the Chinese government lent Tong Ren Tang much-needed support in terms of technological equipment, merchandise, and financial resources. On January 15, 1956, Yue Songsheng was selected as the representative of private business in Beijing to present a "report of success" to then Chinese top leader Mao Zedong on the Tiananmen Rostrum. As part of the "great socialist transformation" in China, Tong Ren Tang turned into a de facto state-owned enterprise.

Tong Ren Tang's status as a state-owned enterprise did not save the brand from the political disaster imposed by the Cultural Revolution in 1966. On August 20, 1966, a group of radical "young revolutionaries" removed the 264-year-old plaque designed by the royal calligrapher, the symbol of the Tong Ren Tang brand, from the front of the clinic; cut it into pieces; and set it on fire. The medical professionals of the Tong Ren Tang clinic were persecuted and publicly humiliated as "capitalistic parasites." Two years later, Yue Songsheng committed suicide after he and his wife were forced to confess their "crimes as exploitative class" in public. Finally, the very name of "Tong Ren Tang" was accused of carrying the "residual influence of the imperial dynasty" and was forced to change to the generic name of "Beijing Traditional Medicine Shop" (*Beijing Zhongyaodian*).[3]

The end of the Cultural Revolution in 1976 created an opportunity for Teng Ren Tang to reemerge from the debris of the decade-long political disaster. In 1979, the Beijing Municipal Government decided to reinstall the name of "Tong Ren Tang."[4] One year later, Yue Songsheng was exonerated. On February 9, 1985, Tong Ren Tang celebrated the 315th anniversary of its birth. In 1989, the State Administration for Industry and Commerce (SAIC) recognized Tong Ren Tang as the first "well-known trademark" (*chiming shangbiao*) in China. As of the early twenty-first century, Tong

Ren Tang had been extended from Beijing to over one hundred overseas locations, including London, Toronto, Sydney, San Francisco, and Dubai. The decision makers of Tong Ren Tang established a goal of becoming the leading brand of the international natural medicine industry.[5] In the words of a senior staff of Tong Ren Tang, "We are fully aware of the gap between Tong Ren Tang and the world's pharmaceutical giants such as Pfizer and Novartis. But our aim was not to compete for the position of No. 1. Instead, our aim is to be the unique 'Only One.' For us, the brand of Tong Ren Tang is just like our own child. We took so much pain to cultivate and protect the brand. We will never tolerate anything that is likely to smirch it."[6]

The rise, fall, and revival of Tong Ren Tang provides a window to examine the development of the Chinese trademark regime. While quite a few preceding scholars devote their attention to the analysis of Chinese trademark codes,[7] the above story indicates the close relationship between the evolution of the Chinese trademark regime and China's gradual acceptance of the legitimacy of the market economy. Beginning with the example of Tong Ren Tang, this chapter teases out the often neglected logic between the two. While conventional wisdom holds that trademark legislation is primarily determined by the Chinese central government, I argue that the strength of the country's trademark holders at the societal level should not be downplayed. Although they do business in an authoritarian country, Chinese trademark holders still manage to have their voice heard by the Chinese government and advance their agenda. Based on interviews with recently accessed intellectual property rights (IPR) professionals in China and newly detected archival material, I also identify the once neglected impact of China's bilateral and multilateral negotiation on the decision making of revising Chinese trademark legislation in the 1990s. That is, although the trademark issue was not a salient one on the negotiation agenda with the developed countries—mainly the United States—Chinese trademark professionals derived insights about IPR protection from the U.S.-China IPR negotiation in the early 1990s and China's World Trade Organization (WTO) entry negotiation in the late 1990s. This ideational change informed the revision of Chinese trademark law even *without* direct foreign pressure.

This chapter is organized as follows. The first section provides a definition of trademark and trademark infringement. The following several sections analyze the evolution of the Chinese trademark regime during different phases of the People's Republic of China: the planned economy era (1949–1978), the early reform era (1978–1992), the pre-WTO era (1992–2001), and the post-WTO era (2002–present). The last section summarizes how the evolution of the Chinese trademark legislation reflects changes in the policymaking process in China.

Trademark and Trademark Infringement

Trademark is a distinctive sign that indicates that a specific good or service is produced or provided by a specific person, group, or business. Usually, trademark consists of one or more distinctive words, letters, numbers, drawings or pictures, emblems, or other graphic representations. According to the Trade-Related Aspects of Intellectual Property Rights (TRIPS) Agreement, "Any sign, or any combination of signs, capable of distinguishing the goods or services of one undertaking from those of other undertakings, shall be capable of constituting a trademark."[8] Trademark protects the legal rights of its owner by conveying information about the character and reputation of the good or service to the consumers. Once reputation and goodwill have been established, the trademark itself may acquire commercial value.

Chinese Trademark Regime Under the Planned Economy, 1950–1976

Trademarks provide an important means to measure the business reputation of a certain product and/or service. The history of trademark can be traced back as early as when human society first engaged in handicraft production and business transactions. During the Qin dynasty (221–206 BC), the first imperial dynasty in ancient China, bronzers were ordered to engrave their names on the dagger-ax they made as a means to hold accountability for the quality of the products. With the gradual growth of business exchange in ancient China, the prototype of trademarks emerged. In 1127, a needle shop in North China's Jinan City, Shandong Province, designed its own trademark, known as "White Rabbit," which is widely believed to be the earliest trademark in China.[9] The copper plate used to print the trademark is now in the collection of the Chinese National History Museum.

During China's imperial times, a number of well-respected trademarks emerged in such industries as ceramics, textile, Chinese traditional medicine, and food and beverage. Some of them, such as the aforementioned Tong Ren Tang, survived the test of centuries of storm and wind, in both political and economic realms, and last until today. The development of trademark activities in ancient China called for some primitive types of trademark protection by the Chinese government. In 1659, the magistrate in East China's Songjiang County protected Jin Sanyang, a draper owning the business mark of Sanyang, against the infringement activities of Shen Qingcheng, another draper in neighboring Suzhou City. That was the first government order to crack down on counterfeit trademark activities recorded in ancient Chinese history.[10]

From the late nineteenth century to the early twentieth century, Western powers forced imperial China to open its once closed economy to international trade. Under that scenario, Chinese business elites started to learn from their Western counterparts and developed the notion of Western-style trademark protection. In 1890, Xiechang Match Co. Ltd. in Shanghai registered the trademark of "Weishui" for its match-related products. That was the first officially registered trademark in imperial China known to the researchers so far.[11] In 1903, North China's Tianjin Customs House recorded about 200 trademark registrations from foreign companies. That number reached 14,000 in South China's Shanghai Customs House in the same year.[12] With the expansion of foreign trade, in 1904, the Manchurian royal court promulgated the Experimental Regulations on Chinese and Foreign Trademark Registration (*Zhongwai Shangbiao Zhuce Shiban Zhangcheng*), known as the 1904 Experimental Regulations, drafted by Robert E. Bredon, a retired British military medical officer who then served as the deputy inspector general of Chinese Imperial Customs.[13]

Despite those developments, the toppling of the imperial dynasty in 1911 prevented the growth of a full-fledged legal regime governing trademark practice in China. In 1923, China promulgated its first rudimentary trademark law. But the ensuing civil strife between warlords prevented the meaningful implementation of the Chinese trademark law. From 1923 to 1927, the Chinese Trademark Administration changed general directors seven times. From 1923 to 1940, the entire country registered only 50,000 trademarks.[14] The success of the Chinese Communist Revolution in 1949 eventually brought an end to decades of political mayhem in China. During the revolutionary war, the Chinese Communist Party (CCP) received precious support from some Chinese private entrepreneurs, known as the "petty bourgeoisie." Before the establishment of the People's Republic in October 1949, the CCP Vice Chairman, Liu Shaoqi, told the private entrepreneurs in a policy speech that "[private enterprises] play a significant role in Chinese economy. . . . It is not a wise policy to eliminate private ownership immediately. Our policy is to allow state-owned enterprises and private enterprises to develop in a parallel manner."[15] That policy speech served as a primary guideline for the Chinese government to design its policy toward the country's private enterprises. As a part of that general policy framework, China provided a transient period of trademark protection in the country's early trademark legislation.

The key trademark legislation in the early period of the People's Republic was the Provisional Regulations on Trademark Registration promulgated in 1950, known as the 1950 Trademark Regulations.[16] As of 1950, private enterprises were still allowed to operate in China. A trademark under the 1950 Trademark Regulations was still viewed as the means for a business enterprise to distinguish and market its products. One of the major purposes of the 1950 Trademark Regulations was "to assure the right of exclusive use of . . . trademarks of industry and commerce."[17] Under the 1950 Trademark Regulations, trademark registration remained largely voluntary.[18] The 1950 Trademark Regulations provided further provisions on trademark registration (Articles 7–12), trademark examination (Articles 13–16), and trademark opposition (Articles 24–28). The 1950 Trademark Regulations also entrusted the Central Administration for Private Enterprises as the primary governing body of Chinese trademark affairs.

Two years after the 1950 Trademark Regulations were adopted, the Central Administration for Private Enterprises (CAPE) and the Central Administration for Foreign Enterprises (CAFE) were merged into the Central Administration of Industry and Commerce (CAIC) to govern Chinese trademark affairs. Xu Dixin, a leading economist, was appointed as the general director of CAIC and served on that position for fourteen years.[19] Another important position held by Xu Dixin was vice director of the Chinese Communist Party's United Front Department, in charge of the relationship between the CCP and private entrepreneurs. That appointment was an important signal of the CCP's tolerance of private entrepreneurs during the early years of the People's Republic. Although the 1950 Trademark Regulations and the ensuing establishment of the CAIC was a promising start for the establishment of the Chinese trade regime, the prevailing political trend in China during the 1950s did not provide a chance for the further development of the Chinese trademark regime. In 1953, the Chinese Communist Party initiated the "great socialist transformation," aimed at establishing the dominance of socialist public ownership. Chinese private enterprises became a major target of the transformation. Three years later, China accomplished the "great socialist transformation" of private enterprises, transforming them into state-owned or collectively owned enterprises and establishing an all-encompassing planned economy.[20]

The Chinese government celebrated the establishment of the planned economy as "the advent of the age of socialism," but the underlying principle of the planned economy was diametrically opposite to the notion of trademark. First, throughout the years of the planned economy, enterprises were nothing more than accessories of the Chinese government branches at different levels. Their top priority was to fulfill the quota set by the government rather than meet the demands of mass consumers. There was no need to market their products with trademarks. Second, the supply of many commodities constantly fell short of meeting demand under the planned economy. When commodities were in short supply, consumers did not have the luxury to choose between commodities bearing different brands. Therefore, trademarks were of trivial importance in the marketplace. Chinese enterprises possessed no interest in designing and promoting their trademarks. In fact, few enterprises saw any reason to register because registration created little advantage for them. In 1957, for example, there were only forty-eight cases of trademark registration in East China's Nanjing City, an industry and commerce center in affluent East China.[21] Researchers have not found accurate statistical data about trademark registration across China in 1957, but statistics show that there were only 40,000 valid registered trademarks between 1949 and 1961.[22]

In 1963, the 1950 Trademark Regulations were superseded by the Regulations on Trademark Control, known as the 1963 Trademark Regulations. As the title of the new Trademark Regulations suggests, the 1963 Trademark Regulations emphasized control over rather than rights to trademarks. Compared with the already brief 1950 Trademark Regulations, the 1963 Trademark Regulations were reduced to fourteen articles. The parts on trademark review and objection were reduced to only five articles. The content of the 1963 Trademark Regulations mirrored the further centralization of Chinese economic activities and suppression of private business and commercial competition.

The 1963 Trademark Regulations completely eliminated any reference to the "exclusive right" of a trademark registrant to trademarks. It emphasized much more the recognition of quality and the defense of the consumer from low-quality goods rather than the protection of enterprises' commercial advantage. Article 1 of the 1963 Trademark Regulations provided that the purpose of 1963 Trademark Regulations was to "strengthen trademark control and encourage enterprises to ensure and improve the quality of their products."[23] Defining trademark as "a mark representing certain quality of a commodity," Article 3 of the 1963 Trademark Regulations further states that "industrial and commercial administrative authorities should . . . exercise supervision and control of the quality of the commodity."[24] In line with the stated purpose of the regulation and their definition of trademark, Article 11 provided that a registration should be canceled by the Central Administration of Industry and Commerce if "the quality of a commodity deteriorates as a result of rough work."[25] The 1963 Trademark Regulations contained no provision regarding the protection against trademark infringement.

With the market mechanism suppressed by the government, the 1963 Trademark Regulations were largely unsuccessful. Between 1963 and 1966, the number of registered trademarks increased by only about 20,000. When the decade-long Cultural Revolution broke out in 1966, there were only 50,000 valid, registered trademarks in China.[26] Even the 50,000 remaining trademarks were criticized as "representing capitalistic values" during the Cultural Revolution and fell into disuse. In November 1966, CAIC, the primary organ in charge of Chinese trademark affairs, was ordered to be dismantled, and its long-time general director, Xu Dixin, was arrested and put in jail for five years.[27]

Despite the heavy blow, the Chinese trademark regime was not completely annihilated. During the Cultural Revolution, China maintained its trade relationship with foreign countries to a limited extent. The function of trademark registration for exported goods was entrusted to the China Council for the Promotion of International Trade (CCPIT). Many exiled or jailed CAIC officials lost their physical freedom, but they never stopped thinking. When CAIC General Director Xu Dixin was in prison, the only book he was allowed to access was Karl Marx's *Capital.* Drawing from his years of experience as both a scholar and a government official, Xu wrote down his reflections about the operation of Chinese economy in the margins of *Capital.*[28] The recollection of a former CAIC official aptly described the feelings of the other Chinese trademark professionals during the difficult time:

> I would never forget the first winter I spent in the countryside after I was exiled from Beijing and forced to do physical labor for the purpose of "thoughts rectification." I got a terrible fever and could not access any medical treatment. When I laid on the bed, I kept asking myself: Am I going to die? Can I return to my position and continue my work? Is the trademark cause a complete abandonment of socialist principles, as the criticism goes? Would our country remain like that forever? I was in despair for a while. But later I realized that hope was vital to my survival. I would not die. I cannot die! I should return to my work alive and healthy. In fact, as I look back, I should probably express gratitude to that difficult experience since I was blessed with plenty of time to think, not only about trademark issues, but also the broader question on the relationship between trademark and socialist economy. While in Beijing, I never had that chance to study that kind of question. We should wait, wait for the opportunity of revival—not only the revival of ourselves, but also the country's being redirected to the right course.[29]

Chinese Trademark Law in the Early Reform Era, 1978–1990

The opportunity for revival eventually came when China introduced economic reform policies in 1978. As part of the scheme of economic reform, the once dismantled SAIC was reinstalled in September 1978, with Wei Jinfei as the general director. One of the top priorities of the SAIC was to rearrange the disorderly situation in the country's trademark affairs. During the Cultural Revolution, the Chinese CAIC at the level of central government was dismantled and the task of trademark registration was delegated to various provinces. That change broke the once unified Chinese market into different geographical areas by provinces and produced numerous "trademarks in confusion." Specifically, if a company found another company in a different province using identical or similar trademarks on the same kind of goods, it could not oppose this use because the trademark enforcement mandate stopped at the provincial border. As of October 1979, the total number of valid registered trademarks in China was only 32,500, a 40 percent decrease from 50,000 at the eve of the Cultural Revolution in 1966.[30] That level was only one-third of the total registered trademarks in Japan in 1979 (107,042).[31] Of the 32,500 valid trademarks, about one-third (10,692) were "trademarks in confusion." According to Ou Wanxiong, a founding member of the trademark bureau of the Chinese SAIC, when he started to work as a trademark examiner at the SAIC in 1979, there were at least five different Chinese companies producing clothing with the brand Friendship, twelve different companies producing cigarettes with the brand Front Gate, and six different companies producing cosmetics with the brand Peony Flowers.[32] The policy makers working on Chinese trademark reforms believed that eliminating the root cause for that embarrassing phenomenon required more than reinstalling the 1963 Trademark Regulations. For them, a full-fledged trademark law was needed.

Policy Environment for the Adoption of Chinese Trademark Law

The first full-fledged Chinese trademark law was adopted in 1982 and came into effect in 1983. Different from its counterparts in patent and copyright, available archival data did not indicate that the adoption of the Chinese trademark law encountered heavy opposition during the legislative process. But the lack of opposition does not mean that the birth process of the trademark regime in China during the 1980s was smooth.

It is generally agreed that the market mechanism constitutes the foundation of a country's trademark regime. During the early period of Chinese economic reform, it took many debates among Chinese policy makers to recognize the legitimacy of the market mechanism. In 1978, China's then top leader Deng Xiaoping announced the beginning of market reform. On March 23, 1979, the SAIC held a conference and submitted a report to the Chinese State Council. For the first time, the report raised the issue of developing a private economy. According to the report, "[Government at different levels] can allow some idle labor to engage in such private forms of economy as reparation, maintenance, and social service." At the same time, the Chinese government was still worried that the revival of a private economy would challenge the dominance of the planned economy. Therefore, the report added that the practitioners of the private economy were not allowed to hire more than eight workers and that the local government still aimed to steer private business to the road of collectivization.[33]

Many newly rehabilitated Chinese scholars turned out to be strong advocates for Chinese economic reform as well. Among them was Xu Dixin, the former general director of the CAIC. Xu was appointed the vice president of the Chinese Academy of Social Sciences (CASS) in 1977 after he regained freedom. In 1979, he compiled the notes made on the margin of *Capital* during his term in prison into a book titled *On Socialist Production, Circulation and Distribution.* In that book, Xu questioned the planned economy model that he had tightly adhered to for years and advocated for the introduction of the market mechanism into the Chinese economy. Xu's book was published by the People's Press, the publishing organ directly managed by the CCP Central Propaganda Department. The People's Press, which was supposed to serve as the CCP mouthpiece, published a book criticizing the long-held orthodox economic belief of the CCP. This action represented a promising change in the Chinese political climate.

With permission from the Chinese government and the advocacy of Chinese academia, the Chinese private economy reemerged after decades of suppression. During a short period of time, the Chinese private economy developed rapidly and exceeded the expectations of the Chinese leadership. In 1980, Zhang Huamei, a private storekeeper in East China's Zhejiang Province, received her business certificate and became the first individual entrepreneur in China.[34] In 1981, Nian Guangjiu, a private entrepreneur selling melon seeds in East China's Anhui Province, became one of the first generation of millionaires in China.[35] At the same time, the total number of individual- and private-owned enterprises jumped to 1.83 million in 1981, more than ten times the level in 1977.[36] The growth of the private economy challenged the practice of "unified production, unified sale" under the planned economy model. As the cracks in the old planned economy widened, consumers had more choice over various goods on the market and increasingly relied on the brands of the goods to make consumption decisions. In 1980 alone, the SAIC received 26,000 trademark applications, almost half the total trademark applications received in the past three decades.[37] The 1963 Trademark Regulations again were no longer sufficient to serve as the legal foundation of Chinese enterprises' trademark activities.

Another important development during the early reform period was the expansion of Chinese foreign trade. China started opening its door to foreign exchange in the late 1970s. By 1978, the country's total trade volume had reached $20.6 billion, with $9.74 billion in exports and $10.87 billion in imports.[38] China's total trade volume was ranked only thirty-second in the world at that time, but the country's growing foreign trade had already brought the trademark issue to salience. In 1979, twenty-one countries and regions filed 5,130 trademark applications in China. Foreign investors naturally demanded protection for their trademarks from the potential Chinese infringers. On the other hand, owners of the trademarks of Chinese exported goods reported over thirty malicious rush registrations by foreign companies in 1979. The appeals by both foreign investors in China and Chinese exporters to foreign countries also propelled the country's decision makers to draft a new trademark law.

The recognition of the legitimacy of the market mechanism and the "opening to the outside" policy met resistance from hardliners adhering to the old-style Communist ideology. When it came to the adoption of a trademark law, however, Chinese business and government actors alike shared an interest in institutionalizing a trademark registration and protection system. That is, regardless of whether a factory was privately owned or government operated, it was necessary to protect Chinese consumers against shoddy products and to distinguish higher-quality goods from lower-quality ones. In that sense, although the notion of trademark has a capitalistic origin, the adoption of a trademark law was not completely against the principle of the socialist economy in China.

The First Trademark Law in China

In 1982, the Standing Committee of the National People's Congress (NPC) in China promulgated the new Trademark Law, which went into effect in 1983. A set of Detailed Implementing Rules went into effect in 1983 to supersede the 1963 Trademark Regulations. The 1983 Trademark Law departed substantially from the 1963 Trademark Regulations in many ways. First and foremost was the reinstallation of exclusive rights to trademarks. As Ren Zhonglin, then director of the SAIC, stated,

> After the Third Plenum of the 11th Communist Party's National Congress in 1978, many enterprises attach increasing importance to exclusive rights of registered trademark with the expansion of enterprise autonomy. However, since the 1963 Trademark Regulations did not provide protection of exclusive rights to trademark, we do not have any legal instrument to rely upon for the purpose of protecting it. This is harmful to the interests of manufacturers

> and consumers. This is also harmful to safeguard our social economic order.[39]

Under those guidelines, the 1983 Trademark Law provided in Article 1 that "this law is specially formulated to strengthen the supervision of trademark, protect the right to use a specific trademark."[40] Under Article 3, "the person who registers the trademark is entitled to the right to use the specific trademark and is protected by law."[41] The inclusion of these protection measures indicated that the country's new policy intended to encourage brand competition and put an end to the 1963 Trademark Regulations that left a trademark virtually unprotected against infringement.

Moreover, the 1983 Trademark Law also reflected the revival, albeit limited, of private enterprises, a significant change in the country's economic policy. Under Article 4, the types of economic entities eligible to register trademarks were expanded from enterprises to institutions and individual industrialists or merchants.[42] By doing so, the Chinese government expanded the protection against trademark infringement from government-run enterprises to private and individualist enterprises alike.

The 1963 Trademark Regulations only emphasized the function of quality control. The 1983 Trademark Law, however, added a series of concrete measures to protect the exclusive rights of trademark holders. As Ren Zhonglin stated, to protect the trademark holder's exclusive rights,

> [the 1983 Trademark Law] clarified the scope of infringement activity and specified punishment measure against it. The new trademark law also delineated the responsibility of administrative enforcement organ and legislative organ. [The new trademark law provides] that trademark owner can resort to county-level Industry and Commerce Administrations for protection against trademark infringement. Responsible state organs are authorized to order the trademark infringer to stop illegal activity, eliminate negative influence, and compensate for the economic losses.[43]

Under Articles 37, 38, 39, and 40, a whole set of protection measures was specified to protect the registered trademarks against infringement.[44]

Another key difference between the 1983 Trademark Law and the 1963 Trademark Regulations was the treatment of foreign trademarks. Under the 1963 Trademark Regulations, foreign words could not be used in registered trademarks.[45] However, this prohibition was eliminated in the 1983 Trademark Law. Legal professionals interpreted the decision as adding considerable flexibility to the marketing of commodities produced by foreign-Chinese joint ventures and bearing foreign trademarks.

Moreover, under the 1963 Trademark Regulations, foreign trademarks must meet two requirements to be registered in China: the home country of the applicant should have a signed trademark reciprocity treaty with China, and the applicant from abroad should have registered the trademark in his or her home country and be able to present a certificate of registration.[46] In contrast, under the 1983 Trademark Law, "A foreigner or foreign enterprises applying for the registration of a trademark in China should follow the procedures in accordance with the agreement signed between his own country and the PRC, an international treaty signed by both countries, or reciprocal principles."[47] This move was again interpreted as following international practice to promote foreign trade.

After the adoption of the 1983 Trademark Law, China joined the Paris Convention for the Protection of Industrial Property (also known as the Paris Convention) in 1985 and the Madrid Agreement for International Registration of Trademarks (also known as the Madrid Agreement) in 1989. Those moves marked the establishment of a full-fledged trademark regime in China and the country's participation in the international trademark regime. The Chinese enterprises increasingly recognized the importance of trademark in their business competition. In 1982, there were 84,047 valid trademarks in China, including 70,899 domestic trademarks and 13,148 foreign trademarks. In 1991, that number increased to 318,915, a growth of almost four times, including 271,056 domestic trademarks and 53,523 foreign trademarks.[48] In the 1990s, with the deepening of China's domestic reform and its further integration into the international trademark regime, significant changes were introduced to the 1983 Trademark Law. However, the 1983 Trademark Law set a solid foundation for the further buildup of the Chinese trademark regime during the reform era.

Chinese Trademark Regime During the Pre-WTO Era, 1990–2001

The 1990s witnessed China's deeper integration into the global economy. The U.S.-China bilateral IPR negotiations in the early 1990s and China's

WTO entry had a tangible influence on the Chinese trademark regime, although the U.S. side did not pressure China on the issue of trademark as harshly as it did on patents and copyright. Shortly after the U.S.-China bilateral negotiations, however, China introduced a major revision to the 1983 trademark law in 1992 and adopted its first Anti-Unfair Competition Law in 1993 and the Provisional Regulations on the Recognition and Management of Well-Known Trademarks in 1996. This section explores the mechanism for those amendments. Based on interviews with Chinese trademark professionals, I found that the U.S.-China IPR negotiations impacted the Chinese trademark regime in the sense that Chinese trademark professionals derived much-needed insights from the IPR negotiations, which in turn contributed to the further growth of the Chinese trademark regime.

Chinese Trademark Affairs on the Eve of U.S.-China IPR Negotiations

Chinese enterprises recorded an impressive improvement in their trademark practice in the 1980s after the adoption of the first Chinese trademark law, but certain trademark regulations were exposed to critique with the development of the Chinese economy by the late 1980s. First, the rapid development of China's service industry in the 1980s called for the protection of the service trademark. In the 1980s, the Chinese service industry recorded an annual growth of 10.9 percent. In 1978, the Chinese service industry accounted for 21.4 percent of the country's total gross domestic product (GDP). In 1988, that number increased to 30.5 percent.[49] The service industry's percentage of the GDP of developed countries was 65 percent on average. Although the Chinese service industry accounted for a lower proportion compared with developed countries, it constituted an important part of the country's economy. China acceded to the Paris Convention and Madrid Agreement in the late 1980s. Over 100 member states of the Paris Convention and Madrid Agreement provided protection for the service trademark, with a significant number investing in China. Both the domestic call for trademark protection and the international legal obligation propelled Chinese trademark law to add provisions on the registration and protection of service trademark.

Second, with the adoption of the 1982 Chinese trademark law, a considerable number of Chinese trademarks established their fame. In 1991, China conducted the first round of selection of "well-known trademarks," with 124 trademarks winning the honor.[50] At the same time, with the growth of foreign investment in China, a number of leading foreign companies also registered trademarks in China, with many of them becoming well-known trademarks. Among those foreign countries, the United States registered only 122 trademarks in China as of 1979. By the end of 1990, the United States registered 12,528 trademarks in China, an increase of 100 times in eleven years.[51] Foreign companies brought investment and technological knowhow to China, and the appeal for trademark protection also increased. In 1987, the Chinese SAIC trademark office handled the first opposition case concerning a well-known trademark. The SAIC trademark office ruled that "PIZZA HUT," as well as its logo of a roof from U.S. Pizza Hut International, Co., was a well-known trademark. Therefore, the SAIC rejected the application of New Vision Global, an Australian company, to register the same trademark on identical services.[52] The SAIC trademark bureau ruled that the "Pizza Hut" trademark deserved protection as a well-known trademark. In 1989, China's Tong Ren Tang encountered a rush registration in Japan. This was the first rush registration of a Chinese well-known trademark overseas. In solving the dispute, the SAIC trademark office decided that Tong Ren Tang was a well-known trademark and that it deserved protection even as an unregistered trademark in Japan.[53] The internationally accepted norm was to provide an equal level of protection to both well-known trademarks and registered trademarks, even if the well-known trademarks have not fulfilled the registration process. But the 1982 Trademark Law did not have any explicit provision about the protection of well-known trademarks and thus lagged behind in its business practice. That loophole in Chinese trademark law potentially harmed the business interests of the holders of well-known trademarks, both domestic and foreign. Further amendments were needed.

In light of those new developments, the Chinese government started to collect advice from the country's business and legal professionals in late 1989 in preparation for the new round of trademark law revisions.[54] The U.S.-China IPR negotiations in the early 1990s provided a good opportunity for China to accelerate its trademark legislation.

U.S.-China IPR Negotiations in the Early 1990s and Their Impact on the Chinese Trademark Regime

The United States and China went through three rounds of IPR negotiations in the early 1990s, reaching three agreements in the form of a memorandum of understanding (MOU) signed in 1992, Exchange of Letters and

Action Plan in 1995, and IPR Enforce Agreement in 1996. As Mertha rightly pointed out, the U.S. demands were overwhelmingly driven by domestic U.S. industries, favoring some IPR subfields (patent and copyright) over others (trademarks).[55] As a result, key parts of the 1992 MOU were on patents and copyrights, without any trademark-specific provisions apart from trade secrets, as outlined in Article 4. The 1995 Exchange of Letters and Action Plan and the 1996 Agreement focused overwhelmingly on copyright-related issues, with less than three pages of the 1995 Action Plan covering the issue of "well-known trademark" protection.[56] The Chinese legislative record, however, suggests that China introduced a series of revisions to its trademark laws in the 1990s, including the revision of Chinese trademark law in 1992, the adoption of the Chinese Anti-Unfair Competition Law in 1993, and the Provisional Regulations on the Recognition and Management of Well-Known Trademarks in 1996. A natural question thus arises: why did China revise its trademark laws despite the absence of obvious foreign pressure? I argue that the U.S.-China IPR negotiations impacted the Chinese trademark regime in a more sophisticated way than the Chinese patent and copyright regime. In particular, the U.S.-China IPR negotiations played a catalytic role in pushing forward Chinese trademark legislation, although trademark was not a salient topic on the negotiation table. While the development of Chinese trademark works constituted the internal driving force for further progress of the Chinese trademark regime, negotiations with the United States provided a window of opportunity for Chinese trademark professionals to "lock in" their legislative agenda.

Chapters 1 and 3, respectively, analyzed how the 1992 U.S.-China MOU on IPR impacted the Chinese patent and copyright regime. As China revised the country's patent law and copyright law to meet its international obligations, the country also revised its trademark law in 1993. Article 4 of the Chinese trademark law expanded protection to the service trademark. Articles 38, 39, and 40 strengthened efforts to crack down on trademark infringement behavior. On the same day that the Chinese NPC adopted the revised trademark law, the articles concerning trademark infringement in the Chinese criminal law were also revised. The maximum prison term for a trademark counterfeit crime was increased from three to seven years. Public servants who support, connive, and shield counterfeit activities were also subject to criminal prosecution.[57] In September 1993, China adopted the first Anti-Unfair Competition Law.[58]

When asked why China revised its trademark law without obvious external pressure, a former SAIC official answered,

> When I heard that the U.S. tried to pressure China on the negotiation table on IPR issues, I immediately knew that the U.S. kissed the baby for the nurse's sake. Their real intention was not just IPR protection, but access to the Chinese market in the name of IPR protection. It is not a pleasant thing to argue with the U.S. on the negotiation table, but isn't it also a good opportunity to push ahead our own trademark legislations? Why should we wait until the other countries point their fingers at us? We should take the initiative by ourselves.[59]

The 1992 U.S.-China MOU on IPR and the ensuing revisions of Chinese IPR legislation quieted developments on the IPR front for a short period of time. However, on June 30, 1994, the United States placed China on the Special 301 list again, criticizing the latter for not enforcing the existing IPR laws effectively. The rampancy of copyright piracy and trademark infringement was signaled out in the Special 301 report.[60] In July 1994, China and the United States started another round of IPR negotiations. Dong Baolin, chief of the Treaty and Law Section, SAIC Trademark Office, joined the Chinese negotiation team. Although a major focus of the negotiations was on the issue of copyright protection and market access of copyright products, trademark protection was also an important issue on the agenda. The main requests by the U.S. side concerning the issue of trademark were twofold. First, China should cancel the restriction on the qualification of trademark agents related to foreign trademarks. Second, China should provide explicit protection of well-known trademarks. China should protect all U.S. trademarks that are and are not registered. The United States also requested that China report on the progress of IPR enforcement every ninety days. The Chinese side rejected that request on the grounds that it encroached upon China's judicial sovereignty, but the Chinese counterparts eventually accepted the U.S. requests for the national treatment of foreign trademarks and the protection of well-known trademarks.

After nine rounds of negotiations, China and the United States reached a second IPR agreement on February 26, 1995. The 1995 Agreement incorporated the requests on the issue of trademark by the U.S. side. According to the 1995 Agreement,

> Any trademark agent permitted to act on behalf of Chinese individuals and entities will now also be permitted to act on behalf of foreign individuals and entities. For the purposes of obtaining enforcement actions by the AIC and Customs, wholly-owned subsidiaries of foreign companies, joint ventures involving foreigners in China, and any licensee in China will be permitted to act on behalf of the foreign owner of the mark.
>
> Trademarks that the Trademark Office of AIC determines are well known, but are not registered in China, will be protected against infringement, including providing the right to oppose or cancel the registration of a duplicate or confusingly similar mark. The owner of an unregistered well-known mark will be able to enforce his rights against infringement and counterfeiting to the same extent a registered trademark owner can enforce rights.[61]

In 1996, the Chinese SAIC adopted the Provisional Regulations on the Recognition and Management of Well-Known Trademarks, the first special legal regulation regarding the protection of well-known trademarks. Two years later, that Provisional Regulations were replaced by the Regulations on the Recognition and Protection of Well-Known Trademarks.[62] It is generally agreed that the protection offered in the 1998 Regulations reached the level set forth by the TRIPS Agreement and the Paris Convention.

After the signing of the 1995 U.S.-China IPR agreement, other developed countries, such as those from the European Union and Japan, also requested that a similar standard of IPR protection be extended to them. China accepted their request. Since many companies from developed countries investing in China were holders of well-known trademarks and their commercial values surpassed that of their Chinese counterparts, this decision by the Chinese government was criticized as protecting foreign interests. More than one decade later, Duan Ruichun, then director of the Office of the Chinese State Council IPR Working Conference, explained the rationale behind those concessions. According to him,

> A natural question for us during the negotiation was what kind of IPR protection standard we should take. . . . The answer is that it was neither the standard that the U.S. imposed upon us, nor was it the "bottom line" as proposed by some of our comrades. The reasonable standard should be the multilateral rules reached during the

> Uruguay round negotiation, accepted by the majority of signatory parties, including the developed and the developing countries. . . . Providing special protection for well-known trademarks was an international norm outlined in Paris Convention. As a signatory of Paris Convention, our trademark law did not have an explicit provision on that issue for a long time. That is against international norm. We made quite some concessions on that issue. That may seem a concession on the negotiation table, but that represented a big step forward in terms of improving our legal regime and merging into the commonly accepted international norm. It is better to take that step earlier rather than later.[63]

After the 1995 U.S.-China IPR negotiations, the two countries engaged in another round of bilateral negotiations in 1996. The 1996 negotiations were even more focused on the issue of copyright.[64] After 1996, the United States ceased to pressure China on the IPR issue with Special 301. But the legacy of those negotiations went beyond the realm of IPR. According to a former Chinese IPR official,

> If you ask me who are the winners and who are the losers in those negotiations, I should say that both the U.S. and China gained from the IPR negotiations. Some comrades kept telling me that China is a powerful country and that launching a trade war against the U.S. was the easy answer to their pressure on IPR. In fact, the easy thing is to reject the U.S. request completely, but is that a sign of China's power? Probably not. Instead, the best way is to reject those unreasonable parts of the demands from the U.S. and choose those that may benefit us. Remember this: negotiation is not only about the use of power; it is also about the use of wisdom.[65]

Chinese Trademark Regime and the Country's WTO Entry

U.S.-China IPR negotiations in the 1990s played a "push-behind" role in the development of the Chinese trademark regime. By the end of 2000, China had accumulated over 1 million registered trademarks. At the turn of the new century, China trademark registration was growing by 150,000 every year. Before China started the second round of amendments of the trademark law, the country was already ranked as one of the top in the world for the number of registered trademarks.[66] On October 27, 2001, about one month before China's WTO entry, the Chinese NPC amended the Chinese trademark law.[67]

There are no systematic data about the policy debate surrounding the second amendment of the Chinese trademark law. Compared with the 1993 amendment, which introduced nine major changes to the Chinese trademark law, the 2001 amendment introduced a total of forty-seven major revisions. With those revisions, then Chinese SAIC General Director Wang Zhongfu claimed that the Chinese trademark law was now fully aligned with the TRIPS Agreement standard.[68] The amendments concentrated on the following areas.

Article 8 of the amended Chinese trademark law expanded the scope of trademarks from two-dimensional trademarks to three-dimensional trademarks and marks of color combinations. The amended Chinese trademark law also rendered protection to geographical indications in Article 16. Before the 2001 amendment of the Chinese trademark law, Chinese individuals were not allowed to file trademark applications in China. The amended Chinese trademark law removed that barrier. Under Articles 4 and 5, Chinese individuals are able to enjoy the same right of trademark application as domestic and foreign enterprises.

Another key aspect of the 2002 amendment was lifting the protection of well-known trademarks from the level of regulations (*tiaoli*), as discussed in the aforementioned 1996 Provisional Regulations of Recognition and Management of Well-Known Trademarks, to being in law (*falu*). Article 13 of the amended Chinese trademark law echoed Article 16 of the TRIPS Agreement and explicitly provided that any trademark that constitutes a reproduction, imitation, or translation that is liable to create confusion with a well-known trademark should be denied registration and prohibited from use. Article 14 further established the criteria for the recognition of well-known trademarks for the trademark examiners and IPR judges.

The 2001 Chinese trademark law extended the period of dispute action from one year to five years. That is, before the amendment of the trademark law, if a trademark registrant identified a later-registered trademark as confusingly similar or filed in bad faith, he or she could only file the dispute petition to the Trademark Review and Adjudication Board of the SAIC within a year of the later-registered trademark's registration date. Under Article 41 of the amended trademark law, that period was extended to five years. This decision was welcomed by the trademark owners because they were given a better chance to file a dispute if they only learned that their rights were infringed upon by an inappropriate registration after the first year.

Finally, the amended Chinese trademark law improved the relief for trademark owners against infringement. Under Article 53 of the amended law, the authorities in charge of administrative enforcement—namely, the local Administration for Industry and Commerce (AIC)—could order the infringer to immediately stop the infringing act, forfeit and destroy the infringing goods and tools of offense, and impose a fine. The amended law also added that economic remedies could be available only through civil litigation through the People's Court. That revision was praised as not only rendering more effective measures to the administrative authorities but also further clarifying the division of labor between administrative authorities and the People's Court.

The amendments to the Chinese trademark law in 2001 contain many more details, and the introduction above demonstrates that the amended Chinese trademark law makes it easier for trademark owners to obtain trademark registrations and defend their trademarks from infringement through administrative and legal means. These changes represent significant progress in trademark protection.

Chinese Trademark Regime During the Post-WTO Era

China's WTO entry offered the country's trademark regime another opportunity for further development. One year after China amended its trademark law in 2001, the country's total volume of trademark applications reached over 300,000. As of 2012, China has recorded 6.09 million valid registered trademarks.[69] That record outnumbered the United States and consolidated China's position as the owner of the largest number of registered trademarks in the world. Despite those achievements, the drawback of the 2001 trademark law necessitated another round of revision during the first decade of its practice. The specific drawbacks included the following. First, the procedure as outlined in the 2001 trademark law proved to be too lengthy. It took twelve months for a trademark to receive a registration certificate from the first round of review by the SAIC and twenty months if that trademark encountered a dispute from another trademark and needed a second round of review. As of 2007, 1.8 million trademark applications have been backlogged at the SAIC Trademark Office. The review process created a dilemma for the Chinese enterprises: on one hand, market competition required them to acquire a trademark for their products; on the other hand, the lengthy process impeded their market competition. Both domestic and foreign trademark applicants called for a shortening of the review process.

Second, the 2001 trademark law highlighted the protection of well-known trademarks, which was a much-welcomed move for the Chinese business community. In practice, however, the recognition of well-known trademarks became an "image project" for government branches at the local level. Instead of enhancing the competitiveness of their products and service, different companies invested heavily in advertisement to promote their reputation. Some companies even intentionally filed trademark lawsuits to attract attention from the media. That move was tolerated and even encouraged by the local government. As the result, the number of "well-known trademarks" has rocketed over the past ten years. For example, in 2001, the Chinese courts recognized only two well-known trademarks: Safeguard and DuPont. Only four years later, the Chinese court recognized 106 well-known trademarks. As of 2009, the cumulative number of well-known trademarks recognized by the Chinese court has reached over 400. Together with the 1,624 well-known trademarks recognized by the SAIC, the total number of well-known trademarks has reached over 2,000.[70] Although the quantity of well-known trademarks has grown dramatically in the past years, the quality of those trademarks has not kept pace with the increase. That discrepancy not only wasted economic resources but also misled mass consumers. Chinese trademark professionals and legal scholars thus called for additional revisions to the well-known trademark provisions so that the recognition of well-known trademarks could be steered in the right direction.

Finally, the rapid growth of the Chinese economy made the standard for economic relief against trademark infringement set by the 2001 trademark law obsolete. The 2001 Trademark Law set 500,000 RMB as the maximum amount of economic compensation for trademark infringements. The trademark infringement activities after 2001 increased in terms of both sheer numbers and the scale of individual cases. Therefore, the original standard for economic compensation was no longer a deterrent. A higher level of economic compensation for trademark infringement was needed.

The above aspects drew attention from the Chinese trademark policy makers as China marked the tenth anniversary of the country's WTO entry.

Starting in November 2009, the SAIC proposed to revise the 2001 trademark law and submitted the proposal to the Chinese State Council Legal Affairs Office. The Chinese State Council Legal Affairs Office distributed the proposal to government officials, judges, business professionals, and legal scholars across the country for their feedback. On December 24, 2012, Zhou Bohua, then SAIC general director, reported to the NPC the draft of the third amendment of Chinese trademark law based on the feedback.[71] In his report, Zhou addressed the issues related to the above three aspects. Four days later, the draft amendment was posted on the website of the Chinese NPC for the final round of feedback collection, featuring forty revisions to the 2001 Trademark Law.[72] In August 2013, the Standing Committee of the Chinese NPC approved the revision of the 2001 Chinese trademark law. The new trademark law would take effect on May 1, 2014.[73]

According to the amended trademark law, "a producer or operator shall not use the words 'well known trademark' on its goods, packaging, or container, or in its advertising, exhibitions, or other commercial activities."[74] That provision helped to steer the recognition of well-known trademarks in the right direction. That is, the recognition of "well-known trademarks" was originally intended to protect certain trademarks rather than for advertisement purposes. It was not meant to be used as a means of market competition or to influence consumers' purchase decisions.

The amended trademark law also provides that "where a trademark application complies with the relevant provisions of this law, the Trademark Office shall complete its examination within nine months from the time of its acceptance of the application, and shall publish its preliminarily examination."[75] That revision helps to alleviate the backlogging phenomenon of trademark registration and reduce the lengthy waiting time for the trademark applicants.

The 2014 Trademark Law increased the level of maximum financial punishment for trademark infringement activities. "Where the actual losses suffered by the right owner, the profits earned by the infringer, or the licensing royalties of trademark infringement cannot be determined, a People's Court shall award damages up to RMB 3,000,000, depending on the facts of the case."[76] The increased level of maximum financial punishment becomes more of a deterrent to the trademark infringers and provides a better economic remedy for the trademark holders.

There is still room for further improvements in Chinese trademark law despite the aforementioned revisions. In the future, Chinese trademark law is likely to face the demands from Chinese trademark holders to further clarify the nature of trademark as a type of *private* right. Before the third revision of the Chinese trademark law, various Chinese trademark holders and scholars had called for eliminating the provision of "improving the administration of trademarks, . . . and encouraging producers and operators to guarantee the quality of their goods and services" in Article 1 of the current version of the trademark law. They argued that emphasizing the function of trademark administration (*shangbiao guanli*) bears the legacy of the planned economy and that the emphasis of Chinese trademark law should be shifted to "protecting the interests of consumers, producers and operators and promoting the development of the socialist market economy" as outlined in the latter part of Article 1 of the law.[77] Had the Chinese NPC, the primary trademark law revision body, followed those opinions, the power of the trademark office of the Chinese SAIC, the country's primary trademark administration organ, would have been significantly trimmed. Eventually, those opinions did not win the upper hand during the tug-of-war with the Chinese SAIC since the latter possessed a stronger lobbying power than Chinese trademark holders and their sympathizers in Chinese academia. Despite the setback, a number of Chinese IPR scholars expect those demands to be raised again in the future amendment of Chinese trademark law with the deepening of Chinese market reform.[78] Researchers thus far do not know whether those demands will prevail in the next round of policy debates. However, it can be safely predicted that the voices of Chinese trademark holders are getting stronger in formulating the country's trademark legislation in the future.

Conclusion

Extant evidence indicates that the adoption of China's trademark law was not as controversial as the adoption of patent and copyright laws. However, that does not mean that the practice of China's trademark legislation is free from tensions among different political and economic factors. After all, the adoption of a trademark law is part of China's abandonment of the planned economy model and acceptance of the legitimacy of the market mechanism, a process full of controversies, debates, and struggles. Domestically, the different provisions of China's trademark law reflect the interests of different sociopolitical and economic groups. Not only was their influence present before a certain law was adopted, but they also chose specific parts of the trademark norm to reflect their needs. Internationally, China's involvement in bilateral and multilateral IPR negotiations provided the country's trademark professionals necessary insights to revise the country's trademark legislation, even though trademark was not a salient issue on the negotiation table. Like Chinese patent and copyright legislations, Chinese government actors are not the sole decision makers in the process of the country's de jure compliance with the international trademark norms. Societal factors, such as domestic and foreign business groups, also played a growing role in affecting the government's legislation choices.

Behind the evolution of Chinese trademark law was the country's gradual political and economic liberalization. Suppressed by the planned economy for almost three decades, Chinese trademark activities became active again during the economic reform era. Realizing that or not, Chinese trademark professionals' incremental push for the improvement of the country's trademark law also eroded the once dominant planned economy model. While a sound market provides the supporting infrastructure for Chinese trademark law, a full-fledged trademark law serves to back-feed the operation of a sound market. That mutually reinforcing relationship constitutes an important part of China's overall reform and opening scheme. The ongoing debates over recognizing the nature of trademark as a type of private right are also a manifestation of the competition between the Chinese state and market forces in the country's economic reform.

While various political and economic groups, both domestic and foreign, shaped China's adoption of trademark norm through competition, collaboration, and compromise, their interaction did not cease during the implementation stage. In fact, there was more interest competition among them when Chinese trademark law reached the ground. The discussion of those issues will be the focus of next chapter.

CHAPTER 6

The Implementation of Trademark Policy in China

In spring 2008, Company B,[1] a U.S. company with its China headquarters located in South China's Guangdong Province, noticed that its sale of shampoo and detergent powder in East China's Jiangsu Province was strangely lower than expected, even though there had not been any significant changes to its marketing strategy in that region. Moreover, its peer producers of shampoo and detergent did not report an increase in the volume of their sales in the same region either. They concluded that some counterfeit goods likely had been circulated in the market. Along with hiring an investigation firm located in Shanghai, they also urged H County's local trademark enforcement squad to carry out a raid in this region against possible counterfeiters. Mr. Kang, an employee with the investigation firm, allowed me to observe the raid. In mid-July, I met two representatives with the investigation firm, Mr. Tan and Mr. Mao, and stayed in a local hotel to wait for the raid.

To ensure the confidentiality of the raid, I was instructed not to ask questions of those working for the investigation firm and the local enforcement squad officials during the waiting period, a nerve-racking time indeed. The only clue I heard about the raid was that the counterfeit shampoo and detergent powder was produced in Guangdong and shipped to northern Jiangsu. After waiting about five days, I was told that the raid was about to be carried out.

Getting up before dawn, the trademark enforcement squad of H County's Quality and Technology Supervision Bureau (QTSB), Mr. Tan, Mr. Mao, and I drove in a van to a house located at the western part of the H

County. In the basement of the house, we found a room full of counterfeit shampoo. After raiding the place, we drove to two other warehouses based on an anonymous tip. Altogether, raids to those three locations resulted in the confiscation of 289 bags of counterfeit detergent powder and 110 bags of detergent shampoo. For the sake of preserving confidentiality, I was only allowed to observe a small fraction of the raid. The enforcement official asked me to return to the office before they finished their anticounterfeit raid. Later I was told that those counterfeit goods included not only the brand of Company B but also the brands of Company L, a China-U.K. joint venture, and Company J, a Shanghai-based domestic company.

When the enforcement official called Company B, Company L, and Company J respectively, the three companies responded in different ways. As the original initiator of the raid, Company B, not surprisingly, regarded the counterfeit goods as a serious issue and promised to send a representative right away. Company L thanked the enforcement squad, promised to send a representative to the spot, and hinted that there would possibly be some financial reward. However, the first thing Company J asked was how many bags of counterfeit goods covered their brand. When the enforcement official told them that it was 89 bags, Company J told the official that it did not consider it to be a full-fledged case when the counterfeit goods amounted to fewer than 100 bags. The enforcement officials were very disappointed by Company J's indifference. One official on the spot said, "Why should we work so hard to protect trademark holders' interests while they do not really care? We should probably tell the counterfeiter that they should infringe upon Company J's brand to their hearts' content." After the raid was over, the enforcement officials asked me to leave H County. Therefore, I did not find out whether the case was passed along to the local Public Security Bureau (PSB) or People's Court as a criminal offense.

As a small example of trademark enforcement efforts in China, the above anticounterfeit raid was only partially successful. Nevertheless, the raid yielded the following findings: first, the effectiveness of trademark protection is dependent not only on the enforcement capacity of the Chinese state but also on how well the Chinese business cooperates with the Chinese state. In his 2009 study of the quality of Chinese intellectual property rights (IPR) enforcement, Martin Dimitrov convincingly argued that multiple trademark enforcers in China prevented high-quality trademark enforcement from happening.[2] In the above real-world example, however, there was only one enforcer (H County QTSB). Therefore, problems such as duplicative enforcement and responsibility shirking did not exist. Given this, an important dimension—the Chinese business community (including both the country's domestic companies and foreign businesses investing in China)—should be included in the equation. In fact, although it was the IPR enforcement bureaucracy that initiated the raid, it had to rely on the clues provided by the trademark holder (Company B) whose business interests were being hurt by the counterfeit goods. There were only twelve members of the enforcement squad of H County while the population in the region was half a million. It was therefore impossible for the enforcement squad to keep an eye on the consumption behavior of the city's populace even if they worked seven days a week, twenty-four hours a day, even if they were completely well coordinated, completely uncorrupt, and entrusted with completely clear bureaucratic mandates. Because it is the business community's interests that are most directly affected, the IPR enforcement bureaucracy mainly relies on businesses to provide clues to organize anticounterfeit raids. According to an IPR official, without the clues provided by the business actors, the IPR enforcement bureaucracy is both "deaf and blind."

Second, while trademark holders provide important clues for anticounterfeit activities, not all the trademark holders are enthusiastic about protecting their trademarks. The above real-world example demonstrates that attitudes vary among the trademark holders: the response of the foreign companies (Company B and Company L) was serious and prompt. The domestic companies (Company J) are also serious about trademark protection but not as serious as their foreign counterparts. Domestic companies certainly want to protect their trademarks, but they may tolerate counterfeit activity unless their business interests are being badly harmed. Statistical data released by the Chinese media in recent years reveal a similar tendency. For example, of the 2,317 anticounterfeit cases in Guangdong, China's most affluent province, in 2013, only 7.9 percent of the cases were started with the clues provided by domestic trademark holders, even though domestic companies accounted for 90 percent of all companies.[3] The attitudes of trademark holders in turn determine the effectiveness of enforcement efforts. That is, the more supportive the business actors are, the more effective the enforcement outcome. The question is, why are only a small handful of Chinese domestic companies enthusiastic about protecting their trademarks while trademark is supposedly an important part of their competitive edge? While foreign investors in China are serious players in trademark protection, why aren't their Chinese counterparts equally serious? This chapter seeks to explain the mechanism that creates these different attitudes.

Finally, the above fieldwork example illustrates different attitudes among corporate actors, but the case does not reveal Chinese consumers' attitudes toward the trademark issue. While corporate actors are important players on the stage, Chinese consumers play a significant role in the implementation of Chinese trademark policy as well. My findings suggest a more nuanced pattern of Chinese consumers' attitudes toward trademark and counterfeiting. They are interested in the authenticity of certain products but not others. When do they prefer counterfeit goods and when do they not prefer such goods? More important, how do their attitudes impact the effectiveness of implementing Chinese trademark policy? I also address these issues in this chapter.

The central argument advanced in this chapter is as follows: while it is important to study how the anticounterfeit raids are organized by government agencies, such as the Chinese QTSB and Administration for Industry and Commerce (AIC), scholars should also examine the political and economic environment from which the Chinese trademark policy originates and operates. Specifically, the legacy of China's planned economy and the immaturity of the country's market mechanism prevent the efforts by the QTSB and AIC to forge a healthy policy environment in the country to produce high-quality goods/services and market them in a fully competitive market. Therefore, despite impressive achievements since the introduction of reform and opening, China has cultivated only a limited number of its own valued brands. Trademark is not yet the key aspect of many Chinese domestic companies' marketing strategies; except for some elite Chinese private companies and foreign companies investing in China, most Chinese domestic companies still rely on nonmarket forces, such as state intervention or unfair competition techniques, to reap market benefits. Therefore, these companies are not as dependent on trademark as their foreign counterparts. The uneven level of trademark values affects the Chinese business community's differentiated attitudes toward trademark, which in turn explains the uneven level of effectiveness of trademark enforcement efforts.

This chapter contains the following parts. The first section analyzes the operation of the QTSB and AIC. These two government agencies are respectively entrusted with the responsibility to maintain high product quality and establish a healthy market order, two fundamental aspects of the policy environment that shape the value of trademarks in China. The second section examines how the policy environment created and maintained by the Chinese state impacts the country's trademark holders, particularly the values of Chinese brands. This shapes the Chinese business community's attitudes toward trademark and the effectiveness of trademark enforcement. The third section discusses how the attitudes of Chinese consumers impact the distribution and consumption of counterfeit goods. I conclude the chapter by placing the implementation of Chinese trademark policy in the general political and economic setting in a transitional China.

The Operation of the QTSB and AIC: Shaping the Policy Environment for Brand Building in China

There are various means to measure the value of a brand. It is generally agreed that the fundamental aspects of a brand's value are determined by two factors: the high quality of goods/services and the long-term consumer recognition for the goods/services. To that end, it is important to institutionalize a rigorous system that oversees the production of goods/services and a healthy market environment for those goods/services to reach the consumers and win over their loyalty. In China, the QTSB and AIC are respectively entrusted with overseeing the issue areas of production and circulation.

In his 2005 study of Chinese IPR policy, Andrew Mertha thoroughly traced the organizational history of the two bureaucracies in China.[4] Detailed as his study was, Mertha's analysis can be improved in the following ways: first, Mertha was right that the QTSB and AIC are the two primary anticounterfeit bureaucracies in the country, but cracking down on counterfeit goods was not their only responsibility. In fact, those two bureaucratic organizations are also entrusted with other important responsibilities that can shape the production and circulation of Chinese goods and services, which in a significant way shapes the value of Chinese trademarks. Second, it is important for researchers to study the evolution of the institutional structure of the QTSB and AIC, but equally important, if not more important, is to comprehend how the evolution of their institutional culture over years of economic reform informs their behavior in formulating and implementing Chinese trademark policy. While the institutional structure of a government organization provides the physical strength, its institutional culture shapes its preferences in making policy decisions. The study of the bureaucratic structure of those two organizations alone neglects some important aspects of the policy environment that shapes Chinese trademark policy.

In this section, I demonstrate how China's transition to a market economy impacted the operation of the QTSB and AIC and how the operation of the QTSB and AIC significantly impacted the production and circulation of Chinese goods and services. I argue that although the QTSB and AIC have made impressive achievements in adjusting to the needs of Chinese market reform, the immaturity of the country's market economy constitutes serious weaknesses that hinder the emergence of high-quality goods/services and the rise of a healthy market environment. That, in turn, hinders the growth of world-renowned Chinese domestic brands and contributes to many Chinese domestic companies' weak sympathy for the IPR norm.

The Operation of the QTSB: The Not So Solid Foundation for Chinese Trademarks

As Mertha pointed out, the QTSB at different levels in China went through several institutional forerunners before the State Quality and Technology Supervision Bureau was formally established in 1988. The institutional forerunners included the State Bureau of Measurements (1954–1958), the State Bureau of Standards and Measurements (1972–1978), and the State Standards Bureau (1978–1982).[5] A natural question arises: while Mertha was right that the Chinese QTSB is primarily responsible for maintaining product quality and overall standardization in China, how successful (or unsuccessful) was the QTSB in fulfilling its mission, particularly during China's market transition? The following section demonstrates that although Chinese quality management professionals earnestly tried to improve the overall level of the country's quality work, deep-rooted social, political, and economic problems in China's immature market economy hindered the promotion of Chinese product quality. Although China is well known as the world's leading manufacturing power, the quality of many Chinese products has raised complaints and suspicions among both domestic and international consumers. While quality is the foundation of a trademark's reputation, only a handful of Chinese companies can claim that their trademarks have a solid quality base.

The predecessor of the QTSB, the State Bureau of Measurements (SBM), was established in 1954. According to the recollection of a first-generation SBM staff member, the top priority of the SBM during the early years was to promote the quality of Chinese products by establishing nationwide standards for Chinese industrial enterprises to follow.[6] The specific goals of the SBM can be summarized as "standardization, serialization, and universalization" (*biaozhunhua, xiliehua, tongyonghua*). Specifically, standardization refers to the formulation of quality and technological standards for industrial enterprises to follow. The products should reach the standards of being eligible to sell on the market. Serialization means categorizing products of the same industry according to their different sizes and weights to simplify the process of industrial production. Universalization means the main components of machines of the same category, even when produced by different factories, can be interchanged nationwide. This helps to reduce the complexity of repairing machines and other industrial products when technological problems arise.

The SBM's staff worked diligently to fulfill their mission. By 1963, the SBM and other ministries designed over 7,300 national-level or ministerial-level technological standards that were applied in major industrial sectors, such as food, iron and steel, chemical engineering, architecture, textiles, and electrical engineering.[7] The technological standards significantly helped promote Chinese industrial production.

During the planned economy era, the SBM institutionalized a Soviet-style practice to oversee the quality of Chinese products. This practice focused on the supervision of product quality *after* the production process. That is, after certain products were produced, the quality control personnel eliminated lower-quality products during the examination process and only allowed products that met the standard to be sold to the consumers.[8] While the system sounds reasonable at first, the rationale of that system was producer oriented rather than consumer oriented. That is, consumers had little choice as to what kind of goods to purchase. Instead, they bought the products as they were produced and sold. Like other communist countries that suffered from a "shortage economy," Chinese consumers had little choice over what products to purchase. Compared with a mature market economy, such a quality control system did not meet the material and cultural demands of the Chinese populace, even though the Chinese populace's demands remained quite limited.

The gap between Chinese consumers' demands and the meager supply of Chinese products and services has been vividly represented in the government-issued tickets as a purchasing tool since the 1950s. In 1955, the Chinese State Council ordered that grains must be purchased using tickets. By 1961, the coverage of tickets had expanded to 161 other basic products such as oil, meat, sugar, bar soap, cloth, bicycles, radios, and sewing machines. During the height of the shortage economy in the early 1960s, even a member of a division head–level official's family (*siji ganbu*) could only get two *jin* of lean meat (about 2.2 pounds), two *jin* of fresh eggs, and one *jin* of refined oil (about 1.1 pounds) per month, not to mention "luxury goods" such as radios and bicycles.[9] Existing evidence indicates there were very few complaints about the quality of Chinese products during that period. But it is likely because the meager supply of goods did not allow Chinese consumers room to complain. When I visited the home of an ordinary Beijing resident in 2008, he showed a thermos flask purchased in the 1970s. The Beijing resident had changed the corks for the thermos flask more than a dozen times, but the inner shell has remained intact over the past three decades. When I marveled at the quality of the thermos flask, he said,

> You young people did not know our difficult situation. Do you know how this thermos flask was purchased? I waited in long line outside the shop for hours. When it was eventually my turn, the stocked goods already ran out. It was winter time. Do you know how cold it was? Eventually I bought the flask through an internal connection with the marketing cooperative (*gongxiaoshe*) with a ticket. A fed person never knows the suffering of the hungry. Brand? That was used to distinguish one type of thermos flasks from others. It was a luxury for us at that time. We had no room to pick and choose.[10]

The difficulty in purchasing a thermos flask is certainly one example of the Chinese shortage economy during the prereform era. But recollections of the shortage economy by average consumers who went through that period clearly illustrate the gap between Chinese consumers' demands and the limited producing capacity of the Chinese economy during the prereform era. As a symbol of a product/service's quality, brand had little, if any, place on the priority list of Chinese industrial enterprises.

Even the above out-of-date Soviet-style quality control practices were suspended during the Cultural Revolution. The Cultural Revolution witnessed the paralysis of the State Science and Technology Commission, the direct higher authority of the SBM. The technical standards overseeing Chinese industrial production were condemned as part of "dominance by vertical authority" (*tiaotiao zhuanzheng*) from the "bourgeoisie technocrats."[11] The ten-year-long internal strife caused a series of quality downslides. Even in the strictly regulated military aviation industry, for example, the quality examination system was completely abolished in 1966. F-6 fighters, then the mainstay of the Chinese Air Force, reported at least six quality problems in just the one month of December 1969. The problems must seem ridiculous to those with experience in the aviation industry: some F-6 fighters could not put down the undercarriage, some buffers of F-6 fighters experienced gas leaks, and some other F-6 fighters could not turn on their fire switches. Typically, a country's military aviation industry practices the strictest technical standards. Given all those quality problems, however, one can imagine the quality situation of Chinese civilian products. Reports about those quality problems, together with reports from other industries, reached Zhou Enlai, then Chinese premier.[12] With deep worries about those quality problems, Zhou Enlai organized a National Economic Planning Conference in early 1972. During the conference, Zhou used the aviation industry as the breach and called on industrial enterprises across the country to reestablish and improve the once abolished quality control system. He also urged Chinese industrial enterprises to reemphasize the once neglected important issues of energy efficiency, productivity, and production cost. Under Zhou's initiation, the once disbanded SBM was reinstitutionalized as the State Standard and Measurement Bureau in November 1972.[13]

But the Chinese leadership's efforts to improve the country's quality work were at best partially successful given the dominance of the extreme leftist ideology during the Cultural Revolution. When China opened trade with foreign countries after the Cultural Revolution was over in 1976, quality problems started to be exposed to the outside world. In 1978, for example, the Chinese State Commodity Inspection Bureau held an exhibition in Beijing on the quality inspection of imported and exported goods. Although it was an exhibition held by the Chinese government, visitors were shocked to find the quality problems of some Chinese exported goods: electric fans blowing backward; high-heel shoes with broken heels, causing consumers to fall down; and frozen dumplings contaminated by *Escherichia coli*. Visitors were also shocked to learn that the frozen chickens exported to the former Yugoslavia in 1977 were detected to contain excessive quantities of pesticide residue and therefore had been driven out of the latter's market.[14]

In light of quality problems on both the domestic and foreign trade fronts, China launched a "quality month" (*zhiliangyue*) movement in September 1978. In the video conference to launch the movement, then Chinese Vice Premier Kang Shi'en called upon the country's industrial production units to "mobilize the masses to expose quality problems nationwide and educate cadres about the harmful effects of poor quality products."[15] When the "quality month" movement was over, *People's Daily*, the mouthpiece of the Chinese Communist Party, praised the rise of "a considerable number of model enterprises with high quality products and a record high of product acceptance rate." After the first "quality month movement" in 1978, the Chinese government decided to hold a "quality month movement" in September each year.[16] Little did they realize that such campaign-style quality promotion movement would at best yield superficial outcomes.

During the late 1970s, a market mechanism was introduced into the Chinese economy. At that point, Chinese consumers' demand for more diversified goods and services began erupting after decades of suppression. The old quality control system could no longer be strictly observed because that system slowed down the speed at which industrial products reached consumers. Meanwhile, the loosening of the old quality control system was not superseded by a well-developed new quality control system. The old quality control system was reduced to a name, but an effective new system had not yet started to fully function. Without fixing the root cause of the quality problems in China, the aforementioned campaign-style quality promotion activities could at best temporarily promote Chinese industrial enterprises' awareness of the importance of the quality issue. Shortly after the "quality month" movement was over, the Chinese Communist Party's mouthpiece, *People's Daily*, reported the first case of large-scale adulterated wine in central China's Henan Province.[17] Thus, a satirical remark became very popular among Chinese industrial enterprises: the "quality month movement has no official residence: we chilled in September due to its presence and celebrate in October during its absence" (*zhiliangyue, meihukou, jiuyuelaile shiyuezou*).[18] According to a report to the Chinese State Council by the State Economic Commission, the acceptance rate of Chinese industrial products declined by 11.3 percent during the first several years of the 1980s. The report also admitted that less than 10 percent of Chinese industrial products' quality reached international standards. A ten- to twenty-year gap existed between most Chinese industrial products and those of the developed countries.[19]

In light of these problems, China introduced a total quality management (TQM) system to comprehensively monitor quality operations in the country. The TQM system originated in the United States in the 1950s. The initiator of that system was a Romanian American engineer named Joseph Juran. In the early 1960s, American engineer Armand Feigenbaum further developed Juran's idea into a more comprehensive scheme.[20] TQM is a complicated quality management system. In it, the achievement of high quality in certain products is not just regarded as the result of rigorous supervision after production; instead, quality control is conducted in a complete manner. TQM advocates the combination of design, production, and postsale service, based on thorough market research prior to production. Moreover, instead of regarding quality work as the sole responsibility of only the quality control personnel, TQM advocates that all employees of a company, including the company's leader, mid-level manager, research and development staff, workers, and logistic staff alike, should be involved, organized by a complete set of production regulations. Instead of attempting to eliminate low-quality products *after* they are produced, TQM attempts to get rid of problems that may cause quality problems *during* the production process.

For example, the production of a sweater in a typical Chinese sweater factory consists of more than thirty different procedures, from selecting the appropriate wool to knitting the wool into a sweater ready for sale in an apparel shop. Under the old quality management system, the quality of the sweater would be examined only at the very end of the production process, after the sweater was finished and before it was shipped to the apparel shop. Under TQM, however, quality examination is conducted across all thirty different procedures. Although it seems that the quality management personnel's task is lighter under TQM, the entire standard for the quality control process gets higher, as the quality examination duties are distributed to the production personnel, who were not previously responsible for quality inspection. Obviously, TQM requires a thorough overhaul of the corporate governance structure of an enterprise.

As early as 1977, Liu Yuanzhang, a research fellow with the Mathematics Institute, Chinese Academy of Science, organized a series of seminars in suburban Beijing's Qinghe Woolen Textile Factory to introduce TQM practices for experimental purposes. Liu's experiments soon gained popularity in other leading Chinese enterprises such as the Beijing Internal Combustion Factory, Second Automobile Factory, and Taiyuan Iron and Steel Company. In less than two years, Liu and his colleagues held over 200 TQM seminars nationwide. In collaboration with the Ministry of Machinery and the Ministry of Electronic Industry, the seminars trained about 30,000 quality management staff.[21] After China formally embarked on market reform, the spirit of TQM was represented in a series of government regulations adopted in the early 1980s. Thanks to his pioneering contribution in advocating for TQM, Liu was invited to advise the Chinese government and won praise as the "Father of Chinese Quality Management."[22]

As a key member of the advisory board, Liu participated in the drafting of the Provisional Guideline on Total Quality Management in Industrial Enterprises in 1980, known as the 1980 Provisional Guideline. Adopted by the State Economic Commission, the 1980 Provisional Guideline was one of the first Chinese government regulations on quality work during the economic reform era. According to the 1980 Provisional Guideline, the task of quality management was distributed to design, production, use, and human resource training.[23] In 1986, the Chinese State Council approved the Regulations on the Quality Responsibility of Industrial Products, further clarifying the responsibilities of government units, industrial production enterprises, and storage and circulation enterprises in maintaining a high level of quality work.[24] In 1988, the State Technology Supervision Bureau (STSB) was established to manage the country's standardization, measurement, and quality work. The STSB adopted the working principle to "hold product quality as the core and standardization as the foundation" (*yi zhiliang wei zhongxin, yi biaozhunhua wei jicu*). Under the STSB's initiation, the Chinese National People's Congress adopted the Standardization Law and Product Quality Law in 1988 and 1993, respectively. Together with the Measurement Law adopted earlier, the laws marked the establishment of a complete legal framework to regulate Chinese quality work.

The Chinese government's ambition to improve the country's quality work did not stop at strengthening the bureaucratic institutions. In 1993, then STSB General Director Xu Penghang proposed to the Chinese State Council that China should adopt a mid- to long-term quality rejuvenation plan to guide the country's quality work. Xu's proposal received warm support from then Vice Premier Li Lanqing. Although still a vice ministerial–

level unit, the STSB managed to coordinate forty-five ministerial units of the Chinese State Council to participate in drafting the quality rejuvenation plan. After eleven major revisions, the Chinese State Council promulgated the Guideline for Quality Rejuvenation (1996–2010), known as the 1996 Guideline, in December 1996.[25] The 1996 Guideline set up the following goal for China's quality work: by 2010, more than 85 percent of Chinese major industrial products should be produced according to the international standard, with the acceptance rate of key products reaching over 95 percent. By 2010, the reliability of major durable consumer goods should approach or reach the level of advanced industrial countries, and the quality and safety index of major consumer goods should reach the international standard.[26]

Before quality promotion became a national strategy, Chinese quality management professionals at different levels had already been working hard to advance the country's quality work. In 1979, the China Quality Control Association (CQCA) was established in Beijing, with Yue Zhijian, then director of the State Standardization Bureau, as the first president. During the past thirty-five years, branches of the CQCA reached from ministerial/provincial levels all the way down to local levels, supervising quality management work under their official duties. By 2014, the CQCA recorded over 240,000 members nationwide, with 3,749 corporate members. Those corporate members covered a wide range of industries, from manufacturing to the service industry.[27] Under the leadership of the CQCA, employees of Chinese enterprises organized quality control (QC) groups. By 2014, 1.62 million QC groups operated in 68.6 million Chinese enterprises. In 2014 alone, the activities of QC groups contributed a total of 47.8 billion RMB in profits to Chinese industrial production.[28] Another contribution by the CQCA was training registered quality management engineers. In 2001, the Chinese QTSB established a national-level examination for registered quality management engineers under the CQCA's initiation. The exam attracted almost 100,000 participants in 2001. By 2003, China had recorded a total of 25,239 registered quality management engineers. Ten years later, that number rose to 123,000.[29]

The National Product Quality Supervision and Spot-Check Report serves as the indicator of the overall level of Chinese quality work. In 1985, the State Economic Commission conducted the first nationwide spot check of the quality of thirty-three types of industrial products. The result of that spot check was compiled as the first National Product Quality Supervision and Spot-Check Report.[30] Since 1986, the National Product Quality Supervision and Spot-Check Reports have been regularly published on a three-month basis.[31] After 1988, the function of quality supervision and spot check was transferred to the STSB and its successor, the QTSB. In addition to the regular supervision and spot checks, China also started to conduct special spot checks on those products with "special social impacts" at irregular intervals in 1994. By 2012, the National Product Quality Supervision and Spot-Check Reports had covered over 356,000 products by 309,000 enterprises.[32] According to the first National Product Quality Supervision and Spot-Check Report published in 1985, the average acceptance rate of the industrial products was only 66.5 percent.[33] By 2013, that number had risen to 88.9 percent.[34]

After the Guideline for Quality Rejuvenation (1996–2010) fulfilled its mission, the Chinese government formally issued the Guideline for Quality Development (2011–2020) in 2012. The 2012 Guideline delineated a more ambitious goal for Chinese quality work: by 2015, the acceptance rate of major agricultural products should reach 96 percent while the acceptance rate of major industrial products should reach 90 percent. The 2012 Guideline also explicitly provided that enterprises should be the main actors in the country's quality work.[35] On various occasions, Chinese top leadership emphasized the importance of quality work. For example, on May 10, 2014, Chinese President Xi Jinping urged Chinese industrial enterprises to "transform 'made in China' to 'made by China,' transform 'Chinese speed' to 'Chinese quality,' transform 'Chinese products' to 'Chinese brands.' "[36] On September 15, 2014, Chinese Premier Li Keqiang told the participants of the China Quality Conference that quality is the key to the country's industrial upgrading and concerns the well-being of billions of Chinese people. He also urged that Chinese industrial enterprises should firmly establish the notion that "quality is life and quality determines economic profits."[37]

It is unfair to say that Chinese leadership attaches little importance to the country's quality work. But they have to face the fact that the country's economy still operates under an immature market mechanism. On one hand, the market economy did not gain full recognition in China until the early 1990s. Many Chinese companies still adhere to the mind-set developed during the planned economy era. For them, the notion of TQM remains a foreign concept. According to a nationwide survey conducted in 2013 by the Quality Development Studies Institute of Wuhan University, 79.8 percent of corporate respondents still believe that quality management is only the business of the quality control personnel and is irrelevant to the other divisions of their companies.[38]

On the other hand, many Chinese companies only operate according to the "bad aspect" of the market economy by focusing on short-term benefits, ignoring the internationally accepted moral norms. Leaders of those companies only pay lip service to quality management. As long as their products can be marketed at a low cost and they can make profits, quality work is only of secondary importance. It is not until serious quality problems arise that quality management can be given some temporary importance. Under that mechanism, it comes as no surprise that respect for quality is only internalized in a handful of Chinese enterprises.

During various internally held seminars, Chinese quality professionals have sharply criticized the seriousness of the country's quality problems based on their firsthand experience. In 2011, one year before the 2012 Guideline was adopted, Liu Yuanzhang, the veteran advocate of TQM in China, published his memoir, *A Record of Gratitude: My Career in Chinese Quality Work.* The memoir recorded a seminar convened by the state QTSB to discuss Chinese quality work. Instead of praising Chinese quality work's achievements according to the officially set tone, the seminar participants voiced strong concerns. According to Liu, Sun Bo, head of the QTSB's Quality Management Division, asserted that the Chinese economy did not achieve a "coordinated development of growth, quality, and economic benefits." Zhang Peng, head of the Quality and Safety Division of Chinese Construction Ministry, admitted that "deeper level quality problems still plague the field of construction and urban development." Yang Xuetong, vice chair of the Association of Chinese Machinery Industry, pointed out that "Chinese machinery and electronic products fell far short of the goals established by the 1996 Guideline and lag significantly behind the international level." When summarizing the comments by the above quality professionals, Liu Yuanzhang lamented, "All in all, Chinese quality work did not fulfill its mission ideally. What is the reason for that? Nobody asked that question (on the seminar); nobody attempted to answer that question, either."[39]

In recent years, a series of quality problems, both internationally and domestically, with Chinese products provided vivid evidence for the aforementioned criticisms. In 2013, for example, the U.S. Consumer Product Safety Commission (CPSC) reported 290 recalls of unsafe products, with 198 of them produced in Mainland China.[40] According to a report released by the EU Customs House, in 2013, of the more than 760 million euros' worth of intercepted fake and knockoff products, 66 percent were produced in China.[41] These problems seriously damaged China's image as a major export power.

The quality problems with Chinese products were not limited to those in the export sector only. Although the Chinese government was reluctant to publish any systematic reports on quality problems, numerous media reports, including some government-run sources, revealed a serious deficiency in Chinese quality work. On April 15, 2012, for example, a report by the state-run Chinese Central Television (CCTV) shocked the country's pharmaceutical industry and mass consumers at large. Unscrupulous enterprises in northern China's Hebei Province processed leather waste into edible gelatin and sold this product to their accomplices in Xinchang County, southeast China's Zhejiang Province, who in turn made capsules with the poisonous edible gelatin. Further investigation by the Chinese State Food and Drug Administration (SFDA) indicated that the clients of the poisonous capsules included 254 Chinese pharmaceutical companies, accounting for 12.4 percent of the country's total pharmaceutical enterprises. Most notable among them was Xiuzheng Pharmacy, the second largest company in the Chinese pharmaceutical industry. With the fifty-three criminal suspects arrested, ten edible gelatin and capsule factories closed, and 230 tons of edible gelatin confiscated, it was expected that the poisonous capsule incident was over.[42] However, the shock wave was felt again in September 2014. Poisonous capsules were again detected in Xinchang County's neighbor, Ninghai County. This time, the result was even more shocking: an estimated 90 million poisonous capsules were produced and sold on the market by the criminal suspects.[43] The poisonous capsules incident was only the tip of the iceberg of rampant quality problems in China. Although the complete inside story of China's quality problems was not disclosed to the public, during the past several years, incidents such as poisonous milk powder in 2008,[44] swill-cooked edible oil in 2013,[45] and problematic meat in 2014[46] have revealed a harsh reality: despite the impressive achievements that Chinese quality work had made in the past decades, the majority of Chinese enterprises still put profits ahead of quality in their operations.

The comment by Guo Ruoxu, vice president of the Chinese Quality Control Association, sharply described that situation:

> [After three decades of painstaking efforts], we can speak with confidence that our quality awareness has been promoted greatly. But

> honestly, this kind of improvement is in many ways represented in the fact that we no longer feel strange about the concept of "quality." In our society, only a handful of enterprises and their managers actively pursue the production of high quality products and services. For most of the others, quality work is only a supporting actor. When problems arise, quality work may receive some importance. In "normal" times, quality remains a "soft task."[47]

In sum, the Chinese QTSB at various levels, together with Chinese quality management professionals, has made commendable efforts to promote the quality of products and services in the country. But those efforts have yielded success in only some Chinese enterprises. While cracking down on fake and knockoff goods is an important part of the QTSB's duty, it is even a bigger headache for the QTSB to get the majority of Chinese enterprises to observe the norm of quality management. Given that situation, the implementation of the Chinese quality control policy is only partially effective. It provides at best a shaky foundation for Chinese trademark protection.

The Operation of the Chinese AIC: The Not So Friendly Environment for Chinese Brands

The production of high-quality products is the first step in building the value of a brand. An equally important, if not more important, next step is to market the products efficiently and to establish long-term consumer loyalty. A healthy and fair market is therefore essential for the growth of a brand. With the QTSB primarily responsible for overseeing the production aspects, the AIC is primarily responsible for the circulation aspects. The previous section establishes that the Chinese QTSB has been partially successful in fulfilling its mission, but has the AIC also been partially successful in fulfilling its mission? If yes, how does that impact implementation of the Chinese trademark policy?

As Mertha rightly pointed out in his 2005 study, the primary responsibilities of the State Administration for Industry and Commerce (SAIC) include "supervising the economic activities of industrial and commercial enterprises, protecting legitimate enterprises and clamping down on illegal enterprises, safeguarding the socialist economic path."[48] But here are some questions that Mertha's account did not answer: Does the AIC supervise the economic activities of different types of aforementioned "industrial and commercial enterprises" (state owned, foreign invested, and privately owned) differently? If yes, how does that difference impact different enterprises' behavior in market competition? While trademark is a key aspect of a company's marketing strategy, how do the differences in market competition behavior impact the different enterprises' attitudes toward trademark?

Moreover, Andrew Mertha documented the internal structure within the Chinese AIC at different levels. With some variation, an AIC typically includes a general office, personnel department, fair trade department, enterprise registration and management department, market supervision and management department, foreign enterprises department, trademark and advertisement department, economic contracts department, and a property auditing department.[49] Some key questions remain to be explored: How are those departments related to one another? How does the interaction among those departments shape the environment in which Chinese enterprises operate their trademark policy?

This section adopts a more comprehensive approach to examine the operation of AIC and its impact on Chinese trademark policy. I argue that the Chinese AIC's impact on the country's trademark policy is represented in not only protecting trademark and cracking down on counterfeit goods but also cultivating a healthy market order for various enterprises to compete and for their trademarks to grow. I also demonstrate that, despite decades of hard efforts by the AIC personnel, a fully competitive market has yet to emerge in China. The market mechanism has gained full recognition by policy makers and business practitioners in China, but only some Chinese companies benefit from market competition and operate their business according to the market principle. State intervention frequently distorts market operations, which in turn breeds unfair competition in China. This hinders the growth of world-renowned Chinese brands.

Like the QTSB, the AIC also went through several institutional forerunners before its current incarnation. The predecessor of the SAIC, the Central Administration of Industry and Commerce (CAIC), was established in the early 1950s to oversee the "socialist transformation of private enterprises." After the central planning model gained full control over the Chinese economy, the primary task for the AIC at different levels was to maintain the state's economic plan and serve as "the tool for class struggle on the economic front."[50] After China embarked on market reform in the late 1970s, the AIC was reestablished after the decade-long Cultural Revolution. The primary functions of the reestablished AIC were summarized as "four 'management' and one 'crackdown'" (*siguan yida*), namely, the management of marketplace, the management of enterprise registration, the management of private economy, the management of trademark affairs, and the crackdown of speculation and profiteering.[51] Since then, the Chinese State Council has passed five schemes to determine the AIC's bureaucratic mandate, internal departments, and personnel allocation, known as the "three determination" schemes (*sanding fang'an*), in 1983, 1987, 1994, 1998, 2001, and 2008. In 1983, the AIC's primary function was updated to "six management, one crackdown, and one prevention" (*liuguan yida yifang*). That is, in addition to the previous "four management, and one crackdown," the AIC was also entrusted with the management of an individual-owned economy, the management of advertisement affairs, and the prevention of an unhealthy tendency in the realm of commodity circulation.[52] In 1994, the task of antiunfair competition was added to the AIC's bureaucratic mandate.[53] In 1998, the AIC formally started to shoulder the responsibility of protecting consumer rights.[54] In 2001, the crackdown on pyramid selling was added to the AIC's bureaucratic mandate.[55] In the most recent "three determination schemes" adopted in 2008, the thirteen main functions of the AIC were classified under five major categories: the registration and supervision of various market entities, the maintenance of free market transactions and fair competition, the protection of consumers' rights, the crackdown on trademark infringement, and the supervision of advertisement affairs.[56]

Since the early 1990s, policy speeches by the leaders of the SAIC have further clarified that the major role of the AIC in Chinese economic reform was to establish and safeguard a sound market order in the country. In 1992, the Fourteenth Chinese Communist Party National Congress formally established the legitimacy of the market mechanism. Steering the overall orientation for Chinese economic reform, that Party Congress also shaped the AIC's working goal in the next two decades to come. When addressing the Third Conference of the All-China Industry and Commerce Society, then SAIC General Director Liu Minxue said,

> [Since the introduction of reform and opening policy], comrades of AIC at different levels have done a lot of work to implement the Party's general line of reform and opening, but the management style, working regulations, and way of thinking still kept a lot of legacy from the planned economy era. That does not suit the

> requirement for market economy. Now that China has established the general orientation of building a socialist market economy, our comrades across AIC's different branches should adjust themselves to that sea change. We should transform our function from serving planned economy to serving socialist market economy. That is the new task facing us during the new era.[57]

From then on, the cultivation of a market environment featured with free and fair competition became the main task of the Chinese AIC. After Liu finished his tenure in 1994, the SAIC successively changed three general directors: Wang Zhongfu (1994–2006), Zhou Bohua (2006–2013), and Zhang Mao (2013–present). All three SAIC general directors consistently emphasized the importance of maintaining a fair market order upon their appointment. For example, Wang Zhongfu stated in 1995 that "the fairness of market trade order is the key standard to measure the effectiveness of our work. That should be given primary importance among all priorities. The prevention of unfair competition and the protection of producers' and consumers' rights are the foundations of a socialist market economy."[58] In 2007, Zhou Bohua told the National Working Conference on the Administration of Industry and Commerce that "as the country's market supervision and administrative enforcement organ, the AIC should build and maintain a fully competitive market. That is not only the basic function of AIC's at different levels, but also the ultimate purpose of our work."[59] In 2013, Zhang Mao stated in an article that "[AICs at different levels] should adhere to the goal of maintaining an equal competitive order for various market entities and create a sound environment for their development."[60]

None of the above policy statements explicitly refer to the trademark issue, but a careful examination identifies an intrinsic connection between a free and fair market order and the effective implementation of a country's trademark policy. That is, the efficacy of a country's trademark policy should not only be measured by such tangible indicators as the number of trademark enforcement cases, the economic worth of the confiscated counterfeit goods, and the amount of financial punishments imposed on the counterfeiters. Under a mature market economy, a country's trademark policy is a branch growing out of the root of that country's market operations. For the trademark norm to be truly observed, a sound policy and legislative framework should first be established to define the market mechanism. If companies cannot survive and thrive through fair competition, they are both unable and unwilling to make investments to promote the values of their trademarks. With Chinese SAIC leaders' repeated emphasis on establishing a fair market order and the painstaking efforts by AIC professionals at different levels, China has made great steps toward that direction. But serious limitations still exist. The achievements in China's market-building efforts present Chinese brand holders many wanted opportunities, but the limitations prevent them from bringing their potential into full play.

Chapter 5 establishes that Chinese trademark legislation has reached the international standard for trademark norms. Supposedly, the most ideal environment for a country's trademark law to operate is a full-fledged market economy, but Chinese trademark holders frequently face market distortion forces. The most important source of those forces is the Chinese state and its representatives in the economic realm, Chinese state-owned enterprises (SOEs). Despite repeated calls to break the monopoly status of Chinese SOEs, the Chinese government remains unwilling to change the economic foundation of the country's communist political system. Chapter 2 analyzes how the dominant status of Chinese SOEs contributes to their lukewarm attitude toward the implementation of patent policy. I find that a similar problem exists with Chinese SOEs when it comes to the implementation of trademark policy. Because of this, the efforts by the Chinese AIC to build a fully competitive market are only partially successful.

Since the late 1980s, the AIC has initiated a series of laws to regulate Chinese market order with the support of the Chinese National People's Congress, including the Provisional Regulations Against Illicit Trading in 1987, Anti-Unfair Competition Law and Consumer Rights Protection Law in 1993, and Advertisement Law in 1994. In the early twenty-first century, the AIC played a significant role in the adoption of the Anti-Trust Law, known as China's "economic constitution," in 2007. In 2008, the Anti-Trust Law came into effect. According to Ning Wanglu, then director of the AIC Anti-Unfair Competition and Anti-Trust Division, the adoption of the Anti-Trust Law marked the establishment of a complete set of market competition legislative regimes in China.[61] Under the State Council Anti-Trust Commission, the Anti-Unfair Competition and Anti-Trust Division of the AIC, together with the Anti-Trust Division of Ministry of Commerce (MOFCOM) and the Price Supervision Division of State Development and Reform Commission (SDRC), constitutes the troika of antitrust operation in China. The labor is divided among the three divisions as follows: the AIC investigates the abuse of market manipulation power, the MOFCOM investigates the concentration of undertakings, and the SDRC investigates the manipulation of market prices. Although still criticized as scattering the enforcement capacity of the antitrust operation, entrusting the antitrust mandate to the above agencies represents a further concrete step to regulate market order by the Chinese government. The practice of Chinese antitrust operation since 2008, however, suggests that there is still much work ahead to fulfill the mission of the "economic constitution."

Before the adoption of the Anti-Trust Law in 2007, the Chinese public held high hopes for curbing the monopolistic behavior of the SOEs and thus a fair market order. According to an online survey conducted by sina.com, the country's largest Internet company, 54.5 percent of respondents believed that the SOEs should be the first target of the antitrust operation.[62] However, the seventh article of the Chinese Anti-Trust Law provides that "with respect to the industries controlled by the state-owned economy and concerning the lifeline of national economy and national security or the industries lawfully enjoying exclusive production and sales, the State shall protect these lawful business operations conducted by the business operators therein."[63] That article provides a great excuse for central-level SOEs to defend themselves. Between 2008 and 2012, the antitrust organs of the MOFCOM, AIC, and SDRC altogether conducted 642 antitrust investigations. Only one investigation was targeted at the central-level SOEs. On November 10, 2011, the SDRC launched an antitrust investigation of the state-owned China Telecom and China Unicom.[64] The day after the investigation was reported by the Chinese Central Television, the *People's Post and Telecommunication News* published an editorial entitled "Distorted Information Misleads the Mass Public" (*Hunxiao Shiting, Wudao Gongzhong*). The editorial defended China Telecom and China Unicom, arguing that the charge of monopoly against the two telecommunications giants was unfair.[65] Observers with basic knowledge of the Chinese telecommunication industry were aware of the background of that editorial: the *People's Post and Telecommunication News* is the mouthpiece of the Ministry of Industry and Information Technology, the patron ministry of China Telecom and China Unicom. On December 3, 2011, China Telecom and China Unicom filed an application to the SDRC and urged that the antitrust investigation be stopped.[66] The investigation lasted for more than two years. In February 2014, the SDRC published a lukewarm decision and claimed that "a lawful decision will be made at a proper time." The result was interpreted as representing that the investigation ended up without findings. According to

Southern Weekend, an outspoken newspaper based in South China's Guangdong Province, Chinese antitrust organizations had been planning to investigate such sectors as insurance, banking, and energy supplies since 2008, but those plans were aborted due to the intervention of their patron ministries. The reason is clear: all three antitrust organs were division-level units (*sijuji danwei*), but most of the central-level SOEs were ministerial-level units (*buji*). Once the antitrust operations were targeted at those business giants backed by the Chinese government, the results would hardly be satisfactory.[67]

In 2013 and 2014, Chinese antitrust law showed its teeth with a series of heavy-handed probes. In January 2013, a total of 350 million RMB in tickets were issued to six leading TV panel producers investing in Mainland China, including Samsung and LG from Korea and Chi Mei, Optoelectronics, AU Optronics, CPT, and Hann Star from Taiwan. It was the largest number of antitrust tickets issued to foreign business investing in China since the adoption of the Chinese Anti-Trust Law.[68] In February 2013, the Sichuan Provincial Development and Reform Commission (DRC) issued a total of 202 million RMB in tickets to Wuliangye Co. Ltd., a leading Chinese liquor company, for price manipulation. This was the first mass-scale antitrust ticket issued to a Chinese domestic business actor.[69] Since then, a constantly increasing number of antitrust tickets have been issued by the Chinese antitrust apparatus. The targets of the antitrust probe have included a number of world-renowned companies investing in China, such as Mitsubishi, Microsoft, Nestle, Daimler-Benz, and Audi. By the end of 2014, the three antitrust organs in China had issued a total of 2.94 billion RMB in tickets.[70] The advent of 2015 did not slow the wielding of China's antitrust fist. On February 10, 2015, Qualcomm, an American company specializing in wireless telecommunication products and services, was issued a ticket of 6.088 billion RMB (about $975 million) for its alleged monopolistic behavior. That amount was the largest in Chinese corporate history.[71] In light of the heavy-handed operations, Huang Yong, vice director of the Advisory Board for the State Council Anti-Trust Commission, told the press that the enforcement of antitrust law will become a "normal happening" (*changtai*) in China.[72]

However, China's frequent antitrust operations in recent years did not mean that the country's "economic constitution" would fulfill its mission to establish a fair market order in the country. Empirical evidence suggests that very few, if any, of the main targets of antitrust operations were monopolistic SOEs during the past two years. Such selective enforcement was ridiculed by some Chinese scholars as "anti-trust operation with Chinese characteristics" (*zhongguoshi fanlongduan*).[73]

In fact, the selective enforcement of antitrust law aroused complaints by foreign investors in China that they were unfairly being singled out.[74] When those worries were raised to Chinese Premier Li Keqiang at the 2014 World Economic Forum held in Tianjin, Li replied with the following: "The only criteria for our enforcement are whether or not the companies' business behavior constitutes monopoly and distort market order. The targets of our anti-trust probe include both domestic companies and foreign companies. . . . As far as I know, foreign companies only accounted for 10 percent of the total amount of anti-trust probes. Therefore, such critique as 'selective enforcement' is groundless."[75]

Li's reply contains a grain of truth. During the early stage of China's opening and reform, the Chinese government granted foreign investors a de facto super-national treatment, which allowed them to reap considerable benefits from the Chinese market. With the growing maturity of Chinese market reform, it is justified to provide fair treatment to Chinese domestic companies and foreign companies alike. However, the doubts about the selective enforcement of antitrust laws cannot be completely soothed if the monopolistic status of the Chinese central-level SOEs remains unchallenged. Shortly before Li Keqiang discussed Chinese antitrust practice at the World Economic Forum, *IT Times Weekly*, a leading magazine representing China's high-tech sector, published an editorial that completely voiced the concerns of Chinese private entrepreneurs.

> Compared with the market distortion behavior of multinational corporations investing in China, more disgruntling is the monopolistic behavior of some central level Chinese SOEs. After all, the products and services provided by foreign investors are only complemental to the products and services that already exist in China. But the products and services by the central level SOEs are in rigid demand in China and are closely bound up with Chinese people's daily life. That is, Chinese people's daily life cannot function smoothly without them. . . . While it is a welcomed move for Chinese anti-trust operations to become a "normal happening," an all the more welcomed move would be to put the state-owned monopolistic enterprises on the anti-trust operating table.[76]

The idea of breaking the monopolistic status of Chinese central-level SOEs was easier said than done. A Beijing-based trademark attorney expressed his suspicion in a blunt way:

> In making the reply to the participants of World Economic Forum, Li was careful to use the term "domestic companies" (*guonei qiye*) rather than "state-owned companies" (*guoyou qiye*). Observers with common sense of Chinese economy should be aware of the difference between those two terms. Li Keqiang, together with other Chinese top leaders, keeps talking about introducing "deeper-level reform" (*shengaige*) and establish a fair market order recently. They also claimed that various vested interest groups should be prevented from distorting Chinese market. But they forget one thing, or maybe they intentionally avoid talking about that: the most important vested interest group, Chinese Communist Party, remains untouched. Would any Chinese leader be so courageous enough to change the economic foundation of the country's communist political system? I doubt it.[77]

In a nutshell, although cracking down on counterfeit goods is an important function of the Chinese QTSB and AIC at different levels, a more thorough understanding of Chinese trademark policy requires the examination of the deeper-level elements in the policy environment shaping the values of Chinese trademarks. The weaknesses in Chinese quality management practice and the not so sound market order, as analyzed above, mirror the problems inherent in the country's political and economic institutions: despite its rocketing gross domestic product (GDP) and spectacular manufacturing ability, China has not developed a sound market infrastructure to support the growth of a sufficient amount of real-world renowned trademarks in the country's goods and services. China's embarrassing role as a "big but weak" (*da'erbuqiang*) player in global trademark affairs has pushed some of the country's producers to sell their products bearing counterfeit trademarks so that they can take advantage of other trademarks' good reputation. Trademark may first appear as an economic and legal issue, but the mechanism causing the problems in the implementation of Chinese trademark policy is heavily political in nature. In that regard, both the QTSB and AIC have a long way to go to fulfill their missions. Indeed, the challenges facing the QTSB and AIC are only a small part of the daunting challenges posed by further political and economic reform in China.

Chinese Business Community's Operation of Trademark Strategy

This section analyzes the achievements and limitations of the Chinese business community's brand-building efforts under the policy environment delineated in the previous section. I argue that although the Chinese business community made impressive achievements in building their brands in the past three decades, significant weaknesses still remain. Specifically, while some Chinese brands have achieved international fame as a result of China's rapid economic development since the late 1970s, they are heavily concentrated in the state-owned sector. Moreover, most of the leading Chinese brands belong to the service sector rather than the consumer products sector, which is at odds with China's status as a major manufacturing power in the world. Those achievements and weaknesses constitute the foundation of the Chinese business community's differentiated attitudes toward trademark, which in turn explains the different levels of effectiveness of trademark enforcement.

I also argue that, after decades of market reform, most of the Chinese business community already has been aware of the importance of trademark as a key component of their competitiveness. However, due to the constraints imposed by the policy environment analyzed in the previous section, ambitious Chinese trademark holders encounter a dilemma: establishing the reputation of a trademark requires long-term investment, but those private enterprises with the sincerity to promote their trademarks' value do not possess the financial resources to pursue their trademark strategy, except for a small number of elite private enterprises. State-owned enterprises possess the financial resources to promote well-known trademarks, but they have limited enthusiasm to do so since their profits are guaranteed by the state.

Chinese Business Community's Brand-Building Efforts Since Reform and Opening: Achievements and Limitations

The Chinese business community did not realize the importance of trademark strategy in the very beginning. They learned the importance of trademark through the combination of market reform and foreign competition.

After the Chinese Communist Party came into power in 1949, a Soviet-style planned economy model was established in China. During the three decades of the prereform era, Chinese enterprises were more production units than corporate entities. Their major business function was to meet the production quota set by the Chinese state. Unlike their Western counterparts, they were not responsible for marketing their products. When the market mechanism was introduced in the late 1970s, China had accumulated only about 32,500 valid trademarks.[78] During the planned economy era, the Chinese business community and Chinese consumers developed some incipient trademark awareness. In some consumer goods sectors such as bicycles, food, and cosmetics, the Chinese business community cultivated some popular brands with considerable appeal among the country's consumers. However, the reputation of those brands was not established from market competition. As will be discussed later, when the waves of market reform surged after the late 1970s and early 1980s in China, the majority of them did not survive the test.

Scholars have summarized the history of Chinese trademark development in the 1980s with two key words: awakening (*qimeng*) and initialization (*chuchuang*). That is, the reform and opening policy introduced in the late 1970s, particularly the advent of foreign investors, awakened the long-suppressed trademark awareness of Chinese domestic companies. Some Chinese trademark holders who gained a prominent position in the arena of business competition later also started the initial stage of their brand-building efforts. In 1981, Coca-Cola established its first joint venture with Chinese domestic companies in South China's Guangdong Province and became one of the first foreign consumer product companies to begin its adventure in China.[79] Following Coca-Cola, foreign enterprises swarmed into the Chinese market. Chinese consumers became increasingly familiar with foreign brands that were not known to them before. At the same time, some sharp-minded Chinese entrepreneurs became the first movers to adopt a market mechanism in building their brands. In the mid-1980s, two major business events marked the awakening of Chinese domestic companies' trademark awareness. In 1984, Jianlibao, a beverage company in South China's Guangdong Province, became the first company to promote consumer recognition by sponsoring Chinese sports teams in international competition. In three years, Jianlibao's total volume of sales rocketed from 3.45 million RMB to 130 million RMB. Jianlibao thus won the praise of "Chinese magic water."[80] In 1985, Zhang Ruimin, then head of Qingdao

Refrigerator Co., ordered his employees to sledgehammer seventy-six faulty refrigerators they had made into pieces in public. That widely reported event showed Zhang's determination to produce high-quality consumer electronics and home appliances for Chinese consumers. In 1991, the Qingdao Refrigerator Co. adopted the name of Haier and eventually transformed it into the top brand in the Chinese home appliance industry. Zhang Ruimin's bold move was praised as setting the foundation for Haier's vibrant growth. One of the sledgehammers was displayed in Haier's headquarters to commemorate that event.[81] Jianlibao and Haier are two of the most prominent examples of brand builders among the Chinese business community. The rapid growth of the Chinese advertisement industry also provided a favorable environment for Chinese companies' brand-building endeavors. On January 4, North China's *Tianjin Daily* published a commercial advertisement for Bluesky Toothpaste. This was the first newspaper commercial advertisement in postreform China. On January 28, 1979, a Shanghai TV station broadcast the first TV commercial advertisement in postreform China.[82] From then on, the Chinese advertisement industry grew at an exponential scale. By 1988, over 1,500 Chinese newspapers had regularly published commercial advertisements. Over 200 TV stations and 400 radio stations had broadcast advertisement programs, covering more than 85 percent of the country. By 1989, the total investment that Chinese companies made on advertisements had reached 1.99 billion RMB, more than nine times that of the level of 1983.[83] For sure, not all companies attached an equal level of importance to trademark as Jianlibao and Haier. However, it could be safely concluded that an increasing number of Chinese business actors in the 1980s reached the consensus that brand building is a key component of a company's marketing competitiveness. Those efforts merged into an irreversible trend with the deepening of Chinese market reform in the 1990s.

In the 1990s, trademark fully demonstrated its might in market competition, which in turn led to the formation of a steadfast constituency of the trademark norm among Chinese business actors. Meanwhile, more than ten years of economic reform cultivated Chinese consumers' increasingly sophisticated tastes for trademark. According to a survey conducted by the government-run *People's Daily* in 1994, 84 percent of respondents relied on trademark as the primary guidance for their consumption behavior.[84] Between 1992 and 1994, the average growth rate of the total sales volume of the top 100 Chinese well-known trademarks (*chiming shangbiao*) was

11.21 percent higher than the country's average level, reaching 40.49 percent.[85] Chinese consumers' demands and the benefits reaped from trademarks further convinced the country's business community of the importance of trademarks. As the beneficiaries of their consistent brand-building efforts, 130 leading Chinese companies held a three-day conference in southeast China's Fuzhou city in 1993, adopting a declaration entitled *We Should Be the Trailblazer for Brand Building in China.*[86] That declaration, later known as Fuzhou Declaration, represented the shaping of a solid community of domestic corporate advocates for trademark protection in China.

The rapid expansion of foreign brands in China in the 1990s also provided precious, sometimes painful, educational experiences for Chinese trademark holders. With their rich experiences in market competition, multinational corporations expanded the influence of their brands in China through various ways. In 1997, for example, China attracted a total foreign direct investment of $45.25 billion, more than ten times that of 1992.[87] On one hand, foreign companies heavily invested in advertising their own brands. On the other hand, during the process of establishing joint ventures with Chinese domestic companies, they purchased the brands of their Chinese counterparts and turned them into subsidiary brands of the parent companies. Behind the aggressive expansion of foreign companies in China was the phasing out of some once popular Chinese brands. According to a study conducted by the Chinese Academy of Social Sciences (CASS) in 1995, 90 percent of the China foreign joint ventures used the trademarks of the foreign side. Foreign brands took over 55 percent of China's bicycle market, 65 percent of the cosmetics market, 90 percent of the camera film market, and 98 percent of the soft drinks market.[88] Some other Chinese brands, however, weathered the fierce competition, consolidated their positions, and began their overseas expansion. In 1998, for example, the aforementioned Haier Group began to export its products to developed countries such as Australia, Germany, and France. During the negotiation with the distributors, Haier insisted that they should use their own brands when sold on the overseas market.[89] When recalling the survival experience of his company in the 1990s, a Shanghai-based apparel businessman told me,

> There are two different kinds of brand owners in China. Some brand owners treat their brands like their own children. No matter how frail the children look like in the first place, the parents always

> devote all their efforts to raise the children and never abandon them. Some other brand owners treat their brands like pigs. Their only goal is to feed the pigs so that they are fat enough to sell at a good price to the butchers. It was no surprise that some Chinese brands died out during the 1990s. No matter how frail a child is, it has a chance to grow up. No matter how fat a pig is, the ultimate destination for a pig is the slaughterhouse.[90]

After China joined the WTO in 2001, the country's deeper integration into the world economy vividly exposed the difference between "children" and "pigs." The reality of market competition forced the Chinese business community to emphasize the establishment of their independent brands (*zizhu pinpai*). In February 2004, *Economic Daily*, China's most influential newspaper in economics and finance, organized a roundtable discussion participated by the country's leading trademark officials, scholars, and business practitioners. This event triggered what was known as the "Great Discussion of Chinese Home Grown Brands" (*zuzhu pinpai dataolun*).[91] In looking back, *China Quality and Brand*, the leading journal in the study of Chinese brand building, regarded 2004 as the year marking "the great awakening of home grown brand consciousness."[92]

The early twenty-first century was a happy time for some Chinese brand owners but a stressful time for others. After China's WTO entry, the brands of some Chinese companies not only survived domestic competition but also managed to expand their influence overseas. For example, Legend Co. Ltd., a Chinese personal computer (PC) producer, purchased the PC sector of IBM in 2005. Bearing the new brand of Lenovo, that company became the largest PC producer in the world in 2013.[93] For other Chinese companies that lacked independent brands, however, the international market put them at a competitive disadvantage. In 2014, Hon Hai/Foxconn Technology, a Taiwanese multinational electronics contract manufacturing company with its production base located in Mainland China, produced 80 percent of the Apple iPhone 6s that were circulated on the global market. However, most of the profits from these sales were earned by brand owners and retailers. While the average price of an iPhone 6 on the international market was about $600 to $700, the profits shared with Foxconn totaled only $4.[94]

After the introduction of the reform and opening policy, particularly after China's entry into the WTO in 2001, Chinese brands left a deep footprint in the arena of global trademark affairs. According to a report released

Table 3. Distribution of the Top 500 Most Influential Brands by Major Countries in the World (2012–2014)

Ranking	*Country*	*Number of Brands (2012)*	*Number of Brands (2013)*	*Number of Brands (2014)*
1	United States	231	232	227
2	France	44	47	44
3	Japan	40	39	42
4	United Kingdom	43	41	39
5	China	23	25	29
6	Germany	23	23	23
7	Switzerland	21	21	21
8	Italy	21	18	18
9	Netherlands	9	9	8
10	Sweden	8	7	7

Source: World Brand Lab Report (2014), available online at http://www.worldbrandlab.com/world/2014/nation.htm (last accessed July 20, 2015).

by the Chinese Ministry of Industry and Information Technology (MIIT), of the 550 major industrial products, China was ranked number 1 in the world in terms of the total output volume. In 2013, the total output of the Chinese manufacturing sector accounted for 20.8 percent of the entire world and has maintained the position of the world's number 1 manufacturing power since 2010. With that achievement, China has earned the title of being the "world factory."[95] By 2014, the total number of valid trademark registrations in China had reached 8.39 million, the highest in the world.[96]

Chinese trademark practitioners can also find a reason to be proud of their achievements through international comparison. According to a report published by the World Brand Lab, a specialized research institute headed by the Nobel Economics Prize winner Robert Mundell, while the United States was still ranked number 1 on the report, assuming almost 50 percent of the top 500 world's most influential brands in 2014, China was the only developing country ranked as one of the top ten countries in the 2014 annual report (see Table 3). Equally impressive was the progress that

Chinese brands made during the past decade. In 2004, only one Chinese brand (Haier) was included in the "Top 500 Most Influential Brands" in the world.[97] In 2014, the number of Chinese brands making the list rose to twenty-nine (see Table 4).

Despite these impressive achievements, weaknesses still exist. Indeed, those weaknesses affect the configuration of Chinese trademark policy greatly. First, among the twenty-nine Chinese domestic brands that made the list of the top 500 world's most influential brands, most belong to SOEs. As shown in Table 4, only seven are private enterprises (Lenovo, Haier, Tencent, Huawei, Baidu, Alibaba, and Tsingtao Beer).[98] Moreover, most of the top Chinese brands are concentrated in the service sector, such as telecommunication, energy, and finance, rather than consumer goods. This is at odds with China's position as one of the world's leading manufacturing powers. There is a significant lag between the brands of Chinese consumer products and the foreign brands on the Chinese market. The following part of this section will further analyze the mechanism that contributes to the above situation.

Chinese Business Community's Trademark Strategy: What Went Right? What Went Wrong?

In the twenty-first century, very few, if any, Chinese companies would openly denounce trademark as a trivial issue, but they have pursued their trademark strategy in different ways due to their different positions in the country's economic map. Moreover, not all of them have been successful in promoting their trademarks. The success and setback in Chinese business actors' trademark strategy shape their attitudes toward trademark. Specifically, I identify three types of business actors: foreign companies investing in China, Chinese SOEs, and Chinese private companies.

The attitudes toward trademark by the first two types of business actors are pretty straightforward. With most of them originating from advanced industrialized countries, foreign companies investing in China are fully aware of the importance of trademark. With a series of mature brand expansion models, they reaped considerable profits on the Chinese market. With rich experiences in trademark protection, foreign trademark holders are generally successful in reaching the Chinese enforcement agencies for effective protection when trademark infringement happens. Between 2006 and 2010, foreign trademark holders (as plaintiffs) won more than 55.2

Table 4. Twenty-Nine Chinese Brands Included in the World's Top 500 Most Influential Brands Report (2014)

Ranking	*Brand Name*	*Ownership Type*	*History of Brands (Years)*	*Industry*
57	China Central Television (CCTV)	State owned	55	Media
60	China State Grid	State owned	11	Electricity
65	Industry and Commerce Banking Corporation (ICBC)	State owned	29	Banking
81	China Mobile	State owned	13	Telecommunication
86	Lenovo	Private	29	Computer
172	Haier	Private	29	Electronics
183	Tencent	Private	16	Internet
213	Huawei	Private	27	Electronics
221	Bank of China	State owned	101	Banking
232	China Construction Bank	State owned	59	Banking
233	China Life Insurance	State owned	64	Insurance
252	PetroChina	State owned	25	Energy
278	Baidu	Private	25	Internet
296	Sinopec	State owned	13	Energy
317	Chang Hong	Private	55	Electronics
322	Air China	State owned	25	Aviation
324	Alibaba	Private	15	Internet
327	China Unicom	State owned	20	Telecommunication
333	CITIC Group	State owned	35	Finance
341	China Telecom	State owned	12	Telecommunication
350	Tsingtao Beer	Private	111	Food and beverage

369	*People's Daily*	State owned	66	Media
371	Xinhua News Agency	State owned	83	Media
378	SINOCHEM	State owned	64	Energy
392	China Agricultural Bank	State owned	63	Finance
396	CEFC China Energy Company	State owned	25	Energy
409	China State Construction	State owned	32	Construction
441	China Railway Construction Corporation (CRCC)	State-owned	66	Construction

Source: World Brand Lab Report (2014), available online at http://www.worldbrandlab.com/world/2014/china.htm (last accessed July 20, 2015).

percent of the trademark disputes in Beijing.[99] In East China's Zhejiang Province, that rate reached 95 percent in 2014.[100]

As the economic foundation of China's communist political system, the profits of Chinese SOEs stem more from their monopoly over certain industries rather than market competition. Although the majority of state-owned enterprises turned into market entities after market reform started in the late 1970s, it remained the Chinese government's policy that SOEs should control the lifeline of the Chinese economy.[101] For those state-owned companies, once they acquire government support, they can maximize their profits in the realms where there are no credible competitors. Therefore, the values of their brands grow more out of support from the Chinese state rather than from brand-building efforts by themselves. It is not surprising that the top brands in China are concentrated in the state-owned sector. As one Jiangsu-based trademark official told me in 2008,

> Market competition is somewhat similar to a soccer game, with consumer loyalty as its prize. Different companies are just like the players in that soccer game while the government is just like the referee of the game. However, some players do not obey the rules. They can still avoid being punished because of their closer connection with the referee. To make it worse, at some critical points the referee jumps into the soccer field and takes the role of soccer player. At that point, it is unnecessary for the players to compete for the prize

> of the game because the result of the game is already determined. That is, the consumers have no other choice.[102]

In a follow-up interview in 2013, that official further critiqued the puffiness of the brands of Chinese SOEs. According to him,

> Do you remember that, in the 1990s, many once popular Chinese brands phased out in the face of competition from foreign brands? I would not feel surprised if any brands of Chinese state-owned enterprises phase out if they are really pushed to a full-fledged market competition. Like those old brands that disappeared in the 1990s, they are the remnants of planned economy. Is there any possibility that they would continue to exist? Maybe. The brands of state-owned enterprises will remain alive as long as the Communist Party is alive.[103]

Chinese domestic private companies have ambivalent attitudes toward trademark. On one hand, years of market reform already educated them about the importance of trademark. As previously suggested, the values of some elite Chinese private enterprises' trademarks have caught up with their international counterparts. On the other hand, however, the elite Chinese private enterprises account for only a small number of the country's business community. Even for those private companies with the sincerity to build the values of their trademarks, they would have to face the reality that they operate their businesses under a policy environment heavily distorted by the Chinese state. As a result, due to the Chinese state's heavy intervention into the economic activities, Chinese companies often resort to government power to compete against the other companies. Instead of relying on the reputation of their brands as regulated by legal norms, many Chinese companies rely on various unfair means to compete against other companies. State distortion of the Chinese market prevents the majority of the country's private companies from promoting their trademarks' reputation through legal and economic means. Instead, their first priority is to curry the favor of the government branches in charge of market regulation.

On average, it takes a brand twelve to fifteen years to establish itself on the market in the developed countries. For that brand to grow into a world-renowned brand, an average of thirty to fifty years of nurturing is required. Under a distorted market in China, however, half of the companies' life span is five to seven years.[104] Thus, ambitious Chinese trademark holders face a dilemma: establishing the reputation of a trademark requires long-term investments, but those private enterprises with the sincerity to promote their trademarks' value do not possess the financial resources to pursue their trademark strategy, except for a small number of elite private enterprises. State-owned enterprises possess the financial resources to promote well-known trademarks, but they do not feel the necessity to do so since their profits are guaranteed by the state. The comment by a trademark attorney aptly describes that dilemma: "[In pursuing their trademark strategy], those who have the willingness do not have the ability; those who possess the ability do not have the willingness."[105]

Due to the weaknesses in the policy environment for brand building and the problems with their own trademark strategies, the majority of Chinese companies still lack the means to add value to manufactured goods through an effective marketing strategy. This constitutes the major reason for the lack of a real world–renowned trademark in China, which in turn explains some Chinese companies' weak sympathy for trademark protection. This situation pushed some of the country's producers to sell their products bearing counterfeit trademarks so that they can take advantage of other trademarks' good reputations. Although quickly growing, the still weak constituency for the trademark norm is the major reason for the lack of effective trademark enforcement in China.

Producing and Consuming Counterfeit Goods: How Do Illegal Goods Gain de Facto Legitimacy?

This section studies the illegal side of Chinese trademark affairs (i.e., the production and consumption of counterfeit goods). I demonstrate a more sophisticated picture of producing counterfeit goods in China. That is, with the improvement of Chinese manufacturing ability, the quality of some counterfeit goods has been improved so that a type of "fake, but not shoddy goods" (*jiamao buweilie*) has emerged since the 1990s. This situation further added to the difficulty for effective trademark enforcement to emerge in China. Citing both survey and interview data, I also demonstrate that, in many cases, Chinese consumers care more about the quality of the purchased goods rather than the authenticity of the trademark. This allows room for the growth of a market for counterfeit goods. They stop to tolerate trademark infringement activities only when their vital interests are threatened. The emergence of "fake, but not shoddy goods," combined with Chinese consumers' insufficient sympathy for a trademark norm in most cases, gains de facto legitimacy for counterfeit goods. When the Chinese state, business community, and consumers reach a consensus on certain trademark cases, effective enforcement of trademark law is possible. That scenario, unfortunately, is rare.

Producing Counterfeit Goods: From "Fake and Shoddy Goods" (*Jiamao Weilie*) to "Fake and Not Shoddy Goods" (*Jiamao Buweilie*)

Conventional wisdom equates "fake goods" with "shoddy goods," but there exists an important difference between the two types of goods. According to the Chinese Product Quality Law, "shoddy goods" refers to products that have "unreasonable dangers threatening the safety of human life and property, and (fail to) conform to the national standards or trade standards safeguarding the health or safety of human life and property where there are such standards."[106] According to Implementation Regulation of Chinese Trademark Law, however, "counterfeit goods" refer to goods "using words or designs that are identical with or similar to another person's registered trademark on the same kind of goods or similar goods as the name or decoration of the goods to an extent that is sufficient to cause misidentification."[107] In other words, some counterfeit goods both bear fake trademarks and are low quality; some other counterfeit goods bear fake trademarks but are not necessarily low quality. In fact, with the improvement of Chinese companies' manufacturing ability, the second type of counterfeit goods becomes increasingly popular in the country's market. That is, the quality of the counterfeiters' goods is similar to or even higher than that of the legitimate producers, even though they bear fake brands on their products.

When the first round of fake goods emerged on the Chinese market in the late 1970s and early 1980s,[108] they were considered "low-quality goods" since their producers did not have the same level of design and producing ability as their legitimate counterparts. By the early 1990s, however, the technology of producing counterfeit goods was so improved that some counterfeit goods achieved a similar or even higher level of the quality of legitimate products. This issue was first raised at the National Trademark Conference held in 1990. In a speech delivered to conference participants, then head of the SAIC Trademark Bureau, Li Jizhong, acknowledged that "some counterfeit goods are not necessarily of low quality." That was the first official recognition of "fake, but not shoddy goods."[109] Several years later, the discussion of "fake but not shoddy products" gained a place in the report by the country's top legislative body, the National People's Congress (NPC). In a report by then vice chair of the NPC Standing Committee, Ni Zhifu, in 1994, it was admitted that "some comrades develop a wrong idea that the emergence of counterfeit products is inevitable in the stage of market reform. They believe that the problem is not so serious as long as the fake goods are of decent quality."[110]

The exact size of the market for "fake and not so shoddy products" remains unknown to the outside world due to the illegal nature of the business, but concrete examples abound to remind people of its existence. For example, an official from the Guangdong Customs House told me that they confiscated a large number of counterfeit Italian leather shoes in the spring of 2007. But when the Italian trademark holder came to the site, they found out that the handmade counterfeit shoes were of higher quality than the real machine-made ones. Therefore, the Italian trademark holders asked the government not to impose financial punishments and allowed the counterfeiters to sell their handmade shoes bearing the real Italian trademark, under the condition that the latter agree to be the contractor for the legitimate trademark holders.[111] This example is not unique. In North China's Yuncheng City, Shandong Province, the city QTSB detected an underground wine-producing factory in 2010. When the sample counterfeit wine was brought to a lab to test, it turned out to meet the quality standards. After tasting the wine, the taster from the legitimate wine producer was surprised that the counterfeit wine tasted better than the real one. Further investigation indicated that the producer of the counterfeit wine hired an enologist who had retired from the legal wine factory. The current enologist of the legal factory was in fact his student before his retirement.[112]

If the counterfeiters can do such a good job in manufacturing, why do they not produce legitimate goods and market them through legitimate channels to build their own brands? The reason is obvious: the most important proportion of a brand's value is not in the production cost but in the research and development (R&D) cost during the brand-building process and the marketing network forged through long-term investments. Many Chinese small and medium-sized companies do not have the financial resources to invest in advertising their products on TV, radio, or other media outlets like their more mature business competitors. They often target low- or medium-income people as their target consumers when they start to earn their first bucket of gold. For many of them, the top priority was not to create their own brands because their own brands were no match for the more mature competitors on the market. Instead, the strategy that they used was to take advantage of the reputation of the established brands, produce goods bearing those brands, and sell them at a much cheaper price to the local customers.

Consumption of Counterfeit Goods

The production aspect of counterfeit goods is just one side of the story. Equally important are the attitudes of Chinese consumers. When would they prefer counterfeit goods and when they would not? This section provides a more sophisticated perspective to study Chinese consumers' attitudes toward trademark. On one hand, survey data conducted at different stages of Chinese economic development show that in the majority of cases, Chinese consumers, as victims of counterfeit activities, have little leverage against infringement upon their interests. On the other hand, in many cases, Chinese consumers can tolerate trademark infringement to the extent that the counterfeit goods do not hurt their fundamental interests, such as health and safety. I also show that consumers' income/education level is positively correlated with their willingness/ability to defend their rights. The promotion of effective trademark protection is thus dependent on them.

Before China started its market reform in the late 1970s, Chinese consumers only passively purchased consumers goods supplied by Chinese producers. The notion of consumer rights did not come into full shape during the early stage of market reform. In a survey conducted by the Chinese Consumer Association in 1991, after the respondents realized that they had purchased counterfeit goods, only 37.5 percent chose to return the goods to the sellers and ask for a refund; if the counterfeit goods were worth less than 100 RMB (about $15), 66 percent of respondents chose not to bother to argue with the seller and keep the counterfeit goods.[113] With years of consumer rights advocacy in the past two decades, consumers have become increasingly aware of their legitimate rights and increasingly picky about the products' quality. Such was particularly the case with consumers with higher income/education levels.

According to a survey conducted by central China's Wuhan University in 2012, when the purchase of fake products occurred, among respondents with a graduate education, 65.8 percent would raise the issue to the producers and retailers of the fake products to defend their rights. Among respondents with an undergraduate education, that number was 58.36 percent. When the respondents are grouped according to their income level, 74.81 percent of respondents with a monthly income of 10,000 RMB (about $1,500) would raise the issue to the producers and retailers of the fake products. Among respondents with a monthly income between 5,000 and 10,000 RMB, that number was 70.59 percent. For respondents with an income level of 3,000 RMB, however, that number dropped to 47.73 percent.[114] The survey data indicated a positive correlation between the consumers' education/income level and their willingness to defend their rights.

The data present hope for trademark owners to mobilize consumers as a supportive wing to defend their trademarks. However, survey data also show that the aforementioned middle- or high-income consumers accounted for only 18.25 percent of the total respondent pool.[115] For 64.45 percent of the respondents, they still admitted that they have purchased counterfeit goods even if they know they were fake.[116] The only exceptions are in the fields that are likely to pose threats to consumers' health and safety. Among the respondents across all income/education levels, 69.5 percent, 63.38 percent, and 63.33 percent never made any purchase of home appliances, food, and drugs if they have any doubt about the authenticity of the trademarks.[117]

For the other products that are not directly related to consumers' health and safety, the authenticity of trademarks is not that important. Under some circumstances, the consumers even knowingly choose to buy counterfeit products if counterfeit goods can help to uphold their sense of vanity. According to a 2008 survey conducted by the Chinese Quality Association in Beijing, Tianjin, and Shenyang, 30 percent of the respondents hold that opinion.[118] On the thirtieth anniversary of the establishment of the Chinese Consumer Rights Protection Association, Ai Feng, vice chair of the Chinese Well-Known Trademark Promotion Committee, delivered a speech that vividly analyzes how the mass consumers' attitudes influence Chinese business community's brand-building endeavor. According to him,

> A popular notion is that consumers should be regarded as "God" in business activities. However, as far as I know, this "God" is a muddle

> minded God with little, if any, knowledge about the products they purchase. This "God" is also a weak God with little, if any, bargaining power to defend their interests. Sometimes this "God" is short sighted and even become accomplices of counterfeiters by consuming counterfeit products. . . . The promotion of Chinese trademarks is ultimately dependent on the promotion of mass consumers' own quality. Without effective supervision from the Chinese consumers, our callings for trademark promotion can hardly be carried out on the ground.[119]

Due to the Chinese consumers' weak sympathy for trademark under most circumstances, law enforcement agencies mainly rely on corporate actors to provide clues for counterfeit activities. However, as analyzed in the second section of this chapter, many Chinese small and medium-sized private companies do not have as much stake in brand protection as their foreign counterparts. That situation makes it all the more difficult for the enforcement efforts by Chinese trademark protection units to be supported by the country's societal actors. Small wonder only a small percentage of enforcement outcomes can be counted as effective.

Conclusion

Is there any possibility for higher quality enforcement in the realm of trademark even though the quality of Chinese trademark enforcement is generally low? My study shows that effective trademark enforcement is possible, but it depends on whether a consensus can be reached among the enforcement apparatus, business community, and Chinese consumers. That is, not only should the enforcement apparatus possess sufficient capabilities, but the trademark owners themselves should also possess the strength and the willingness to protect their legal rights. The enforcement outcome could be further improved if Chinese consumers were mobilized to support trademark protection efforts. When the three parties are able to reach consensus on certain issues, it is reasonable to expect effective trademark enforcement outcomes. Unfortunately, under the majority of circumstances, either the Chinese trademark holders did not possess enough resources or willingness, or the Chinese consumers only halfheartedly support trademark protection.

My study also teases out the subtle but important connection between the implementation of Chinese trademark policy and the country's institutional reform. That is, the lack of effectiveness in trademark enforcement should contribute to the weaknesses at both the micro level and the macro level in the Chinese political and economic structure. Those weaknesses are signs of China's incomplete reform in both economic and political realms. At the micro level, Chinese domestic companies still lack an effective quality management mechanism based on a sound corporate governance system, which creates problems for the improvement of the overall level of Chinese products' quality. At the macro level, the market competition in China remains vulnerable to state interference, powered by the monopoly of SOEs. In fact, it is reasonable to expect a thorough reform into the means in which the Chinese state governs the country's economic activities as China develops its own world-renowned trademarks on the international economic stage. Without that, the Chinese business community and mass consumers are not able to benefit from the implementation of the country's trademark policy. In many cases, trademark infringement activities will still be tolerated or even welcomed by China's societal actors, and effective trademark protection will remain rare. Consequently, China will still be blamed for not fully complying with the international trademark norm.

In the future, the practice of Chinese trademark policy will further prove that the primary driving force for effective trademark protection should originate from Chinese business and mass consumers' support for the trademark norm rather than administrative orders imposed by the Chinese state. Toward that end, Chinese enterprises, particularly private companies, should become the major players of brand building while Chinese government branches at various levels should be transformed from market supervisors to service providers. As a warning signal, the slowdown of Chinese economic growth in recent years again demonstrates the imperativeness of shifting the country's economic expansion mode from state led to market driven. An open, fair, and fully competitive market order is the necessary condition to generate and maintain a sound state-business relationship, which will eventually lay the foundation for a robust civil society to emerge in China. The effectiveness of trademark protection will be largely determined by how successfully (or unsuccessfully) China can accomplish that transformation.

The handling of all those issues goes beyond the realm of Chinese trademark policy. While the production and consumption of counterfeit goods in China are partially the result of the country's ongoing market reform and opening to the outside, it can be safely concluded that the problem cannot be resolved without the introduction of further reform measures. Those measures should include the establishment of a healthier policy environment through more thorough reforms of China's quality management and market competition policies so that trademark can be truly held as a key aspect of Chinese domestic companies' market competitiveness. They should also include consistent education campaigns to promote the public's sympathy for IPR and cooperative efforts between the Chinese state and societal actors such as the foreign and domestic business community and consumers to crack down on trademark infringement activities. All are part of the political and economic reforms that China will inevitably experience in its efforts to bid a farewell to the legacy of its authoritarian past and build the country into a credible world power.

Conclusion

During the research for this book, I befriended Mr. Zhu,[1] a senior research fellow with the IPR Studies Center of the prestigious Chinese Academy of Social Sciences (CASS). Since the late 1980s, he has been actively involved in advising the Chinese government and business community on intellectual property rights (IPR) issues and educating the new generation of Chinese IPR professionals. When recalling his involvement in China's IPR negotiation with Western countries in the 1990s, particularly when listening to their accusation of the rampancy of piracy and counterfeiting activities in China, he felt those words cut to his heart. Throughout the years, he kept asking himself the following thought-provoking, if not painful, questions:

> In the past, China used to contribute so many great inventions that impacted the trajectory of human history, but how come the home country of so many great inventions turned out to be blamed as the thieves of intellectual property? Before we blame the Western countries for being so domineering, should we blame ourselves first? Had the Chinese government been supported by a well-functioning IP industry, wouldn't it have possessed a much less disadvantageous position on the negotiation table? After all, copying others is not a sign of strength but weakness. It is just like a class. Typically, a straight-A student would not plagiarize the homework of a C student.[2]

What explains the rampancy of IPR infringement and the rarity of effective IPR protection in China? Or to follow the aforesaid metaphor, why does China score "A" only under some circumstances and "C" under most others in IPR protection? How can China move from being a "C student" to being a "straight-A student" in IPR enforcement? Those questions have been the primary considerations driving the research of this book. Findings in this book suggest that some IPR enforcement cases in China can overcome political barriers and yield successful outcomes while many more others cannot. In studying the contrast, this book identifies the tension between two different attitudes toward the IPR norms held by Chinese state and society actors: the first is to reap short-term benefits of IPR infringement; the second is to achieve long-term benefits by embracing the IPR norms and promoting intellectual creation. The effectiveness of IPR enforcement outcomes depends on which consideration takes the upper hand in fighting against IPR infringement.

The conclusion of this book consists of three parts. The first part will summarize the book's theoretical argument. The second part will situate Chinese IPR policy under the greater historical backdrop and provide a forecast of Chinese IPR policy's future development, based on the dynamics identified in my study so far. The third part will provide several policy recommendations for both China and its trading partners such as the United States to facilitate effective IPR protection. Echoing the analysis in the preceding chapter, I argue that focusing on IPR per se is insufficient to bring about a high-quality enforcement outcome. In combating IPR infringement, China will have to further pluralize its political system and further free up its market potential. All those require a fundamental transformation in the way in which China is governed. Realizing that or not, policy makers, the business community, and academia both at home and abroad are making a small but substantive contribution to that transformation process in their efforts to fight against IPR infringement and promote IPR protection in the Central Kingdom.

Summary of the Theoretical Argument: State-Society Interaction in IPR Enforcement in China

Preceding scholarship has approached the issue of Chinese IPR enforcement through the entry point of the Chinese state. Certainly, China deserves criticism for its vague and overlapping bureaucratic mandate of an IPR enforcement apparatus and protectionist measures favoring IPR infringers by the local government. As discussed in previous chapters, however, focusing only on the Chinese state yields an insufficient understanding of the problems arising during the implementation, not to mention the internalization, of Chinese IPR laws.

In enforcing IPR laws, the real problem is that under many circumstances, the Chinese government has been *unwilling* but not *unable to* protect IPR. To understand why the Chinese state has taken effective IPR protection measures under some circumstances but not others, the impact of Chinese societal actors on the Chinese state should be considered. In that sense, the theoretical argument advanced in this book hinges on the important role of Chinese societal actors and their interaction with the state. As demonstrated in the preceding chapters, during the adoption stage, the country's societal actors were still able to exert their impact on the legislative process through professional opinions and lobbying efforts, even though the conventional wisdom is that the adoption stage was primarily happening at the level of the Chinese central government. The role of Chinese societal actors, defined as the Chinese domestic business community, foreign business investing in China, and Chinese consumers, became even more salient when the IPR laws adopted at the central government level began to be implemented on the ground. Without the support of pro-IPR groups, it would be very hard for the Chinese IPR enforcement organs to acquire useful clues about infringement activities, not to mention carry out effective protection measures. Without the nurturing of a robust constituency for IPR norms, effective IPR protection measures are not consistent, which makes internalizing the IPR norm into the Chinese society more difficult.

Although the adoption, implementation, and internalization of IPR norms in China have been difficult, the advocates for the IPR norms in China have managed to exert influence on the Chinese state. China's progress in enforcing the IPR norms has been an important part of the country's steady steps toward an innovation-oriented economy. During the country's integration with the global economy, China witnessed an expanding interest in foreign trade and investment as well as international cultural and technological exchange. China's market reform cultivated an increasingly strong IPR community that has interests in scientific and technological innovation, literature and artistic creation, and brand building. With China's rapid economic growth, those people who enjoy growing affluence have become more sympathetic to IPR protection. Together with the newly rising business groups that advocate IPR protection, they constitute the reliable forces for IPR norms to be effectively enforced. If the Chinese state and societal actors are able to reach a consensus, as they have on some occasions, effective IPR enforcement is more likely to happen. Due to the incomplete political and economic reform in China, however, many business actors and mass consumers are indifferent or even hostile to the IPR norms. As the primary actor to carry out IPR enforcement, the Chinese state is sandwiched between those different appeals on IPR. Despite China's consistent enforcement and legislative efforts, the effectiveness of many IPR enforcement cases leaves much room for improvement.

Last but not least, this book urges researchers to extend their insights beyond the realm of Chinese IPR policy and examine the broader environment of Chinese political and economic development. That is, in all the three subfields of Chinese IPR policy under study, the adoption, implementation, and internalization of the IPR norm awakened the IPR holders' awareness of their individual economic and moral rights, which opened up the otherwise closed parts of Chinese society. In the establishment of legal regimes in all the three aforementioned issue areas, the reform-minded pre-IPR camps managed to overcome the opposition of anti-IPR camps that still adhere to the mind-set of socialist public ownership. In the implementation stage and internalization stage, Chinese state-owned enterprises' lukewarm attitudes toward IPR have become an important barrier for the IPR norm to be truly respected by the Chinese business community. In the case of Chinese copyright policy, the Chinese propaganda system adheres to the dominance of Communist ideology and remains reluctant to offer further free room to the country's literary and artistic creators. In that regard, while the promotion of effective IPR enforcement requires successful coordination between the Chinese state and the country's societal actors, a more thorough reform of China's economic and probably political system is required for the country to eradicate the negative association with counterfeited and pirated goods.

Highlighting the importance of Chinese societal actors in IPR enforcement is not meant to deny the validity of scholarly arguments that focus on the Chinese state. Indeed, throughout the book, the evolution of the policy discourses on Chinese patent, copyright, and trademark bureaucracies at different stages has been considered a crucial component in the implementation of those policies. However important those state actors are, an explanation that brings in the societal actors can aid our understanding of Chinese IPR policy. Instead of rejecting the previous analysis as wrong, my project is complementary to the state-focused explanations.

Protecting IPR in a Transitional China: The Past, the Present, and the Future

According to a Beijing-based IPR scholar, "We have to keep in mind that the IPR norm operates in a transitional and rising China. The country is transitional in the sense [that] it is moving from an authoritarian society to an open society, from a planned economy to a market economy. The country is a rising one in the sense that its economic and political might is bound to bring profound changes to the existing world order. We cannot afford to ignore the bigger picture."[3] With the greater picture in mind, it comes as little surprise that IPR protection efforts received bitter reproach in China during the initial phase of the country's interaction with the global IPR system. As a result of China's autarkic economic policies during the planned economy era, the first generation of the country's leadership was unwilling to participate in an international regime that would open some important parts of the Chinese economy to foreign competition. Although there existed a pro-IPR camp during the prereform era, they could hardly exert any meaningful influence to establish a full-fledged IPR regime meeting the international standard. Driven by the combined forces of the growing influence of the Chinese IPR community and the country's expanding interests in foreign trade and economic exchange, the Chinese government eventually realized the importance of protecting intellectual creation as private property. With the IPR laws in place, the influence of China's IPR constituency is a key determinant for the result of IPR enforcement, particularly when the government apparatus makes a decision about whether to stand with the IPR holders or the IPR infringers.

Through the study of the IPR development experiences of other once-developing economies, such as Japan, Singapore, South Korea, Taiwan, and even the nineteenth-century United States, scholars found interesting similarities among China and those major players in the global IPR arena.[4] The United States champions IPR protection around the globe in contemporary times. As a sharp criticizer of China's rampant IPR infringement activities, the United States has also developed a set of IPR strategies that many Chinese IPR professionals wish to learn from. However, in the nineteenth century, the country was not a "straight-A student" in IPR protection. Studies show that almost half of the bestsellers in the United States were pirated mostly from English novels between 1800 and 1860.[5] World-renowned novelists such as Charles Dickens and Anthony Trollope were frustrated to see their books published in the United States without permission and without any royalties being paid.[6] While British authors complained about the lack of copyright protection in the United States, works by such American authors as James Cooper, Ralph Emerson, Herman Melville, Walt Whitman, and Edgar Allen Poe were not granted due copyright protection in Britain and other European countries as well. In the mid-nineteenth century, persistent advocacy and pressure from American authors and publishers eventually resulted in the enactment of the International Copyright Act by the U.S. Congress in 1891. That act in turn heralded more than a century of gradual changes in the practice of America's copyright protection.[7] That is, the United States adopted a "singular and . . . [even] cavalier attitude," in the words of William Alford,[8] toward the intellectual property of foreigners when it was a less developed country. Today it has been turned into a leading advocate for strong IPR protection in the world. Drawing from the experience of the United States and probably other IPR powers, it can be soundly predicted that effective IPR enforcement will become more prevalent in China if the country's technological and economic development has reached a stage at which observing IPR norms will serve the interests of the majority of the Chinese business community and mass consumers.

With China's rapid development and its increasingly active participation in the World Trade Organization (WTO) and World Intellectual Property Organization (WIPO) during the new millennium, some senior Chinese officials have stated that "[in the IPR realm] China took about thirty years to accomplish what the Western countries took more than a century to achieve."[9] Having said that, Chinese IPR policy is deeply embedded in the country's unique political, social, economic, and cultural context. While the United States and other major IPR powers emphasized political pluralism and market economy as the key to economic prosperity, China took a different path. On one hand, China's "socialist market economy" model dazzled the world with its efficiency to modernize a once backward country. On the other hand, however, it is also associated with controlling the free flow of ideas, the deprivation of underprivileged social groups, the distortion of market order by state-owned enterprises, and even rampant corruption problems. All that hurt the innovation incentives of the Chinese business community and mass public, particularly the younger generation. China's economic slowdown in recent years has further exposed the exigency to reform the country's governance model and turn its economic growth model into innovation-oriented one. In that vein, whether China can realize its IPR ambition depends on how far the country can move along on the road to reform its governance model, both economically and politically.

Policy Implications: IPR and China's Rise in the Twenty-First Century

Although this study is focused on the effective enforcement of Chinese IPR policy, it has broader implications for both Chinese international relations and domestic politics. That is, will a rising China destabilize the current political and economic world order? Or can a rising China achieve a harmonious coexistence with the outside world? If so, what policy adjustments should be made by both the international community and China? This book does not answer those ambitious overarching questions. However, the policy implications flowing from the above discussed theoretical argument and empirical findings can shed light on the general theme of this study.

First, given the importance of societal actors in China's compliance with IPR norms, the policy focus should be shifted from external coercion of IPR norms to domestic promotion. In fact, although most scholars have resorted to the bureaucratic/institutional argument to explain Chinese IPR policy, some have already realized that it is inadequate to solely rely on bureaucratic and legal procedures to protect IPR. For those scholars, the task of IPR protection cannot be accomplished without a normative shift by Chinese society at large.[10] That is, the Chinese public should be more sophisticated and lower their tolerance for pirated and counterfeit goods, which could possibly trigger a fundamental conceptual change in local government's understanding of the role of intellectual property rights. Scholars, therefore, have suggested that it is crucial for domestic players in the Chinese economy to develop their own intellectual property and become sufficiently powerful in the political system so that they can move the system toward more effective IPR protection.[11] It is also recommended that, to win the acceptance of the local leaders and the Chinese public, American business should invest part of their profits back into educating the local community about IPR.[12] If successfully implemented, these initiatives will help alleviate the public's skepticism, if not hostility, toward Western IPR norms. The transformation of China from an IPR infringer to an IPR enforcer is the essential means to solving the problem of IPR infringement in the world's biggest developing country.

While the above policy initiative focuses on the international side of the IPR issue, China should make an effort to promote individual rights and civil liberties to really reap the benefits of IPR. There is a close link between the respect for individual rights and the promotion of creative activities and the successful functioning of an effective IPR system. So far, China has come to recognize IPR as an essential mechanism to promote the country from an early development stage relying on a heavy input of cheap labor and natural resources to an upgraded development model relying on innovation. The Communist Party remains reluctant to accommodate the necessary political transformation brought forth by the above economic process. As the Chinese economy continues to change, it is reasonable to expect IPR holders to play a more important role or even demand further policy changes. Certainly, upholding individual rights in a country with more than 2,000 years of imperial history is a painful task. However, as an ancient Chinese teaching goes, wise political leaders should "dig a well before drought hits and strengthen a roof before heavy rain pours down." When the Chinese Communist Party engages in upgrading the country's economic development with IPR, the further promotion of individual rights is inevitable. Understanding that not only helps researchers to develop a more comprehensive knowledge of Chinese IPR policy but also helps decision makers to adopt a forward-looking strategy to introduce further economic and political reform in China.

In 2013, Mr. Zhu retired after almost three decades of dedicated service in the Chinese IPR circle. He and other fellow Chinese IPR practitioners should feel gratified that China has moved quickly to catch up with the existing intellectual property powers. In light of China's achievements in IPR during the first decade of the twenty-first century, as already documented in the previous chapters of this book, some observers of Chinese IPR policy have already recognized that "the oft-repeated story about China as a major pirating nation is too simple and too outdated. Although that story fits well within the fifteen second sound bites usually found in media reports, it does not fully capture the reality."[13] Despite the optimistic forecasts by his academic counterparts, Mr. Zhu still learned of unhappy news when he started to enjoy his retirement. Among the news was that Chinese movie producers found a large number of pirated Chinese movies in the market in Vietnam.[14] However, rather than feeling cut to his heart, as in

China's IPR negotiations with the developed countries in the 1990s, Mr. Zhu was, in his own words, "pleasantly annoyed" by the news. He was annoyed because Chinese IPR holders lost benefits from trading with foreign countries. But he also felt grudgingly pleased because the creativity of Chinese IPR holders eventually gained recognition from foreign consumers, although in an unpleasant manner. According to him, "Being copied by other countries is a solid evidence that China is moving from a C student to an A student in global IPR affairs."[15] Of course, Mr. Zhu's experience was only a single case of the numerous stories, bitter and sweet, of Chinese IPR professionals. However, appreciation of the political and economic logic behind their stories will inspire us to achieve a deeper understanding of a largely omitted part of the picture of Chinese IPR policy, a continuously changing China and its relationship with the rest of the world.

APPENDIX

Interviews Cited

Place	*Date*	*Interviewee's Occupation*	*Interviewee's Affiliation*
Hong Kong	May 20, 2007	Customs official	Guangdong Customs House (phone interview)
N Province[1]	March 5, 2008	Legal representative	Branch of The China No. 1 Pencil Company in N Province
Anhui	August 31, 2007	Intellectual property rights (IPR) representative	An Anhui-based state-owned enterprise (SOE)
	May 14, 2013	IPR representative (follow-up interview via Skype)	An Anhui-based SOE
	December 27, 2013	Manager	Anhui branch of a Xinhua bookstore
	December 28, 2013	Manager	A privately owned bookstore in Hefei, Anhui
Beijing	October 7, 2007	A Beijing-based consumer	
	October 10, 2007	IPR attorney	A Beijing-based law firm
	October 15, 2007	Former staff	Xinhua bookstore

Place	*Date*	*Interviewee's Occupation*	*Interviewee's Affiliation*
	October 17, 2007	Former IPR official	China Patent Association
	October 17, 2007	Former IPR official	State Intellectual Property Office (SIPO)
	October 22, 2007	IPR official	Ministry of Commerce
	October 30, 2007	Copyright holder	Beijing-based publishing company
	November 1, 2007	IPR judge	Beijing Intermediate People's Court
	November 3, 2007	Former IPR official	State Copyright Administration
	November 3, 2007	A street peddler from H Province	
	November 4, 2007	IPR scholar	Chinese Academy of Social Sciences (CASS)
	November 5, 2007	IPR scholar	CASS
	November 10, 2007	A female street peddler	
	November 28, 2007	Copyright official	Beijing Municipal Copyright Administration
	November 9, 2007	A former electrical engineer	China Patent Association
	October 30, 2007, to November 15, 2007	A number of street peddlers selling pirated goods in Beijing	
	November 9, 2007	Former electrical engineer	A Beijing-based patent law firm
	November 20, 2007	IPR attorney	A Beijing-based law firm

Place	*Date*	*Interviewee's Occupation*	*Interviewee's Affiliation*
	November 22, 2007	Official	Chinese National People's Congress
	November 28, 2007	Former IPR official	State Copyright Administration
	December 1, 2007	IPR scholar	Chinese Academy of Social Sciences
	December 6, 2007	Copyright official	Ministry of Culture
	December 7, 2007	IPR Scholar	CASS
	December 8, 2007	IPR scholar	Ministry of Science and Technology (MOST)
	December 30, 2009	Former IPR official	Ministry of Commerce (phone interview from Hefei, Anhui)
	January 8, 2010	IPR attorney	A Beijing-based law firm (phone interview from Hefei, Anhui)
	January 10, 2010	IPR scholar	CASS (phone interview from Hefei, Anhui)
	January 12, 2010	Senior staff in charge of trademark affairs	Tong Ren Tang Inc. (phone interview from Hefei, Anhui)
	January 14, 2010	IPR scholar	CASS (phone interview from Hefei, Anhui)
	January 22, 2010	Former official	Central Administration for Industry and Commerce (phone interview from Hefei, Anhui)
	December 29, 2010	IPR judge	IPR Special Tribunal, People's Supreme Court (phone interview from Hefei, Anhui)

Place	*Date*	*Interviewee's Occupation*	*Interviewee's Affiliation*
	July 4, 2011	IPR official	State Copyright Administration (phone interview from Hefei, Anhui)
	June 18, 2012	IPR scholar	Chinese University of Politics and Law (phone interview from Hefei, Anhui)
	December 29, 2012	Manager	A Beijing-based publishing company (phone interview from Hefei, Anhui)
	December 29, 2012	Copyright owner	A Beijing-based media company (phone interview from Hefei, Anhui)
	December 30, 2012	IPR scholar	CASS (phone interview from Hefei, Anhui)
	January 5, 2013	Official (follow-up interview)	Chinese National People's Congress
	January 12, 2013	Former IPR official	Ministry of Commerce (phone interview from Hefei, Anhui)
	January 13, 2013	IPR scholar	CASS (phone interview from Hefei, Anhui)
	May 23, 2013	IPR scholar	CASS (phone interview from Hefei, Anhui)
	May 24, 2013	IPR scholar	Beijing Film Academy (phone interview from Hefei, Anhui)
	December 19, 2013	Former copyright official	State Copyright Administration (phone interview from Hefei, Anhui)
	December 21, 2013	Copyright scholar	Beijing Film Academy (phone interview from Hefei, Anhui)

Place	*Date*	*Interviewee's Occupation*	*Interviewee's Affiliation*
	December 27, 2013	Movie producer	A Beijing-based film studio (phone interview from Hefei, Anhui)
	January 3, 2014	IPR scholar	CASS
	January 9, 2014	Former copyright official	Beijing Copyright Administration
	May 24, 2014	IPR scholar	CASS (phone interview from the United States)
	March 3, 2015	Trademark attorney	A Beijing-based law firm (phone interview from the United States)
H Province[2]	January 11, 2013	Two patent officials	Intellectual property office (IPO) of H Province
Jiangsu	April 4, 2008	Trademark official	Jiangsu Provincial Administration of Industry and Commerce (AIC)
	April 29, 2008	Trademark official based in Nanjing, Jiangsu	Jiangsu Provincial AIC
	March 13, 2008	IPR judge	Nanjing City Intermediate People's Court
	March 14, 2008	Copyright owner	A Nanjing-based motion picture studio
	March 31, 2008	IPR scholar	Policy Analysis Department, Jiangsu Provincial Intellectual Property Office
	April 30, 2008	Former IPR official studying at Nanjing University	
	August 3, 2008	IPR official	Huai'an City, Jiangsu Province

Place	*Date*	*Interviewee's Occupation*	*Interviewee's Affiliation*
	January 4, 2010	Patent official	Jiangsu Provincial Intellectual Property Office
	January 7, 2013	IPR official (follow-up interview)	Jiangsu Provincial Intellectual Property Office
Shanghai	July 9, 2008	IPR official	Shanghai Municipal Intellectual Property Office
	July 25, 2008	IPR scholar	Fudan University
	August 9, 2008	IPR attorney	Shanghai branch of a Western law firm
	January 9, 2010	IPR official (follow-up of the July 9, 2008, interview)	Shanghai Municipal Intellectual Property Office
	December 19, 2012	IPR scholar	Policy Research Department, Shanghai Municipal Government
	December 28, 2012	IPR official (follow-up interview)	Shanghai Municipal Intellectual Property Office
	January 5, 2013	IPR official	Shanghai Municipal AIC
	January 8, 2013	IPR scholar	Fudan University
	January 9, 2013	A Shanghai-based consumer	
	December 30, 2013	Former quality supervision official	Shanghai Municipal Quality and Technology Supervision Bureau (QTSB)
Guangdong	September 1, 2012	IPR official	Guangdong Customs House (phone interview from Hefei, Anhui)
	January 7, 2013	Copyright official	Guangdong Customs House (phone interview from Hefei, Anhui)

1. The interviewee asked that a pseudonym be used for the name of the province here.
2. A pseudonym is used here at the request of the interviewee.

NOTES

Introduction

1. At the request of my interviewees, I use pseudonyms in this book unless otherwise noted.

2. Interview with the legal representative of an IPR holder, Bilin City, March 5, 2008.

3. Jiang Liqin, the general director of the Anti-Counterfeit Office of The China No. 1 Pencil Company, made this point during an interview with the Chinese media. For further information about the interview, see Li Peng, "Counterfeit Double Black Pencils: The Curse for Chinese Exam Takers" (Jiaqianbi Fanlan: Kaofen Zhihuo), *Beijing Science and Technology Daily* (Beijing Kejibao), March 30, 2009.

4. Again, I use pseudonyms here.

5. Interview with a legal adviser of an IPR holder, Bilin, March 5, 2008.

6. Full names of the city and the companies involved are concealed at the request of my interviewees.

7. Participant observation, Anhui Province, August 8–18, 2007.

8. *People's Daily*, November 10, 2011, 1.

9. See, for example, Michael P. Ryan, *Playing by the Rules: American Trade Power and Diplomacy in the Pacific* (Washington, D.C.: Georgetown University Press, 1995); Michael P. Ryan, *Knowledge Diplomacy: Global Competition and the Politics of Intellectual Property* (Washington, D.C.: Brookings Institution Press, 1998).

10. For an analysis on how multilateral pressure pushes different countries to adopt IPR protection measures, see Kenneth Shadlen, Andrew Schrank, and Marcus Kurtz, "The Political Economy of Intellectual Property Protection: The Case of Software," *International Studies Quarterly* 49 (2005): 45–71.

11. Andrew Mertha, *The Politics of Piracy: Intellectual Property in Contemporary China* (Ithaca, N.Y.: Cornell University Press, 2005); Martin K. Dimitrov, *Piracy and the State: The Politics of Intellectual Property Rights in China* (New York: Cambridge University Press, 2009).

12. Interview with a Beijing-based IPR official, October 22, 2007.

13. Interview with a Jiangsu-based IPR official, August 3, 2008.

14. For example, Mertha finds interbureaucratic competition between two trademark enforcement bureaucracies, the State Administration for Industry and Commerce (SAIC) and the General Administration of Quality and Supervision, Inspection, and Quarantine (AQSIQ). Consequently, the volume of trademark cases has increased, and enforcement has become more effective than the other issue areas. Dimitrov argues that the quality of IPR enforcement,

measured by consistency, transparency, and procedural fairness, is more important than the volume of enforcement. He also finds that rationalized enforcement is more likely to emerge in new regulatory areas, such as patents, because the Chinese central government entrusts the State Intellectual Property Office (SIPO) with clearly specified enforcement mandates. Mertha, *The Politics of Piracy*; Dimitrov, *Piracy and the State.*

15. Phone interview with a Beijing-based IPR official, January 9, 2010.

16. William Alford, *To Steal a Book Is an Elegant Offense: Intellectual Property Law in Chinese Civilization* (Stanford, Calif.: Stanford University Press, 1995).

17. Gordon C. K. Cheung, *Intellectual Property Rights in China: Politics of Piracy, Trade, and Protection* (London: Routledge, 2009), 60–61.

18. Yang Fan, *Faked in China: National Branding, Counterfeit Culture, and Globalization* (Bloomington: Indiana University Press, 2016).

19. Interview with a Beijing-based IPR scholar, November 4, 2007.

20. Phone interview with a Beijing-based IPR scholar from Hefei, Anhui, January 10, 2010.

21. John Gerring, "What Is a Case Study and What Is It Good For?" *American Political Science Review* 98, no. 2 (2004): 342. Also see Dietrich Rueschemeyer, "Can One or a Few Cases Yield Theoretical Gains?" in *Comparative Historical Analysis in the Social Sciences*, ed. James Mahoney and Dietrich Rueschmeyer (Cambridge: Cambridge University Press, 2003).

22. After the publications by Alford, Mertha, and Dimitrov, a large number of studies of Chinese IPR policy in the new century have focused on the legal codes of the country's IPR laws. Alford, *To Steal a Book Is an Elegant Offense*; Mertha, *The Politics of Piracy*; Dimitrov, *Piracy and the State.* The most recent book-length analysis of Chinese IPR policy is by Yang, but as I argued earlier, more efforts should be made to explore how different state and societal groups in China perceive the IPR issue. Yang, *Faked in China.*

23. Andrew Cortell and James Davis, "How Do International Institutions Matter? The Domestic Impact of International Norms Rules and Norms," *International Studies Quarterly* 40, no. 4 (1996).

24. Thomas Risse, Stephen Ropp, and Kathryn Sikkink, eds., *The Power of Human Rights: International Norms and Domestic Change* (Cambridge: Cambridge University Press, 1999).

25. There were too many interviewees raising those issues on various occasions to name. On the following occasions, the discussion of those questions dominated the conversation between the author and the interviewees: interview with a Beijing-based copyright official, November 28, 2007; interview with a Beijing-based IPR scholar associated with the Chinese Academy of Social Sciences, December 7, 2007; interview with a Jiangsu-based trademark official, Nanjing, Jiangsu, April 4, 2008; follow-up interviews with two Jiangsu-based IPR officials, Nanjing, Jiangsu, January 6, 2010; interview with a Shanghai-based IPR official, Shanghai, January 5, 2013; phone interview with a Beijing-based IPR scholar, May 20, 2013.

26. Related statistical data can be accessed at the website of the government-run Chinese Central Television (CCTV), http://english.cntv.cn/program/bizasia/20120118/114671.shtm (accessed February 14, 2013).

27. For a press briefing of those three salient issues, see http://news.sina.com.cn/z/zmmyqjl/index.shtml (accessed February 14, 2013).

28. For information on China-U.S. strategic economic dialogue, see http://www.ustreas.gov/initiatives/us-china/ (accessed February 14, 2013).

29. Interview with a Beijing-based IPR scholar, Beijing, November 5, 2007.

30. For a discussion of strategic ratification of international law, see Beth Simmons, *Mobilizing for Human Rights: International Law in Domestic Politics* (Cambridge: Cambridge University Press, 2009), 57–111. For a discussion focused on China, see Ann Kent, *Beyond Compliance: China, International Organizations, and Global Security* (Stanford, Calif.: Stanford University Press, 2007).

31. That will be further elaborated in Chapter 6, where I will discuss an only partially successful trademark enforcement case in the affluent Jiangsu Province in East China.

32. That will be further elaborated in Chapter 2, where I will discuss my research experience with two patent officials from the less affluent H Province in Central China.

33. I will discuss my experience with that interviewee in Chapter 2.

34. I have described the meetings earlier in the introduction chapter.

Chapter 1

1. The full text of the Agreement on China's Entry into the WTO is available in *People's Daily*, January 26, 2002, 5.

2. Interview with an IPR attorney in Beijing, October 10, 2007. I use a pseudonym here at the request of my interviewee.

3. Phone interview with a retired IPR attorney in Beijing from Hefei, Anhui, January 8, 2010.

4. Many legal scholars have published monographs on Chinese patent law since the late 1990s. A representative example of a comprehensive discussion of Chinese IPR legal provisions is Peter Feng, *Intellectual Property Right in China* (Hong Kong: Sweet and Maxwell Asia, 1997). One of the most recent scholarly works on Chinese patent law is Stefen Luginbuefl and Peter Ganea, eds., *Patent Law in Greater China* (Cheltenham: Edward Elgar, 2014).

5. TRIPS Section 5, Article 27.

6. For a discussion of the history of the IPR norm, see, for example, Christopher May and Susan Sell, *Intellectual Property Rights: A Critical History* (Boulder, Colo.: Lynne Rienner, 2006).

7. For a summary of the scholarly literature recording these debates, see Jerome Reichman, "Compliance with the TRIPS Agreement: A Scholarly Debate," *Vanderbilt Journal of Transnational Law* 29, no. 3 (1996).

8. See, for example, Fang Linlin, "Duan Ruichun on IPR Protection," *Science and Technology Daily*, June 10, 2007, 5.

9. There are numerous scholarly works that critique the role of patent in the economic development of developing countries. For a representative example, see Donald G. Richards, *Intellectual Property Rights and Global Capitalism: The Political Economy of the TRIPS Agreement* (Armonk, N.Y.: M. E. Sharpe, 2004).

10. The full text of the Decision on Recruiting Intellectuals at Mass Scale is available in the *Selected Works of Mao Zedong*, vol. 2 (Beijing: People's Press), 618–619.

11. For example, on May 7, 1948, the CCP-controlled Harbin City government issued the Provisional Regulations on Rewarding Technological Professionals. See Zhao Yuanguo, *The Conceiving and Birth of Chinese Patent Law* (Zhongguo Zhuanli Fa De Yunyu Yu Dansheng) (Beijing: Intellectual Property Rights Press, 2003), 9.

12. Part of Mao Zedong's speech is available online at https://www.wxyjs.org.cn/mzdsxyj_568/201801/t20180105_236357.htm (accessed June 15, 2012).

13. For further information about the First National Conference on the Issue of Intellectuals, see http://www.gov.cn/test/2009-09/27/content_1427683.htm (accessed June 15, 2012).

14. Chen Jianxin et al., eds., *Contemporary Development of Chinese Science and Technology* (Dangdai Zhongguo Kexue Jishu Fazhan) (Wuhan: Hubei Education Press, 1994).

15. Interview with a scholar on Chinese science and technology policy, December 8, 2007.

16. Interview with a former electrical engineer, Beijing, November 9, 2007.

17. Interview with a retired IPR official, Beijing, October 17, 2007.

18. Full text of the 1950 Provisional Regulations can be found in *People's Daily*, August 17, 1950, 2.

19. Full text of the 1954 Regulations can be found in *People's Daily*, August 28, 1954, 2.

20. Zhao, *The Conceiving and Birth of Chinese Patent Law* (Zhongguo Zhuanli Fa De Yunyu Yu Dansheng), 10.

21. Full text of these two regulations is available in *People's Daily*, December 2, 1963, 2.

22. Wu Heng, *Five Decades on the Front of Science and Technology* (Keji Zhanxian Wushi Nian) (Beijing: Science and Technology Documentation Press, 1992), 252–253.

23. Interview with a Beijing-based former IPR official, October 17, 2007.

24. The full text of Deng Xiaoping's speech can be accessed online at http://www.lzkj.gov.cn/2008/3-7/News_16058.htm (accessed May 25, 2012).

25. Guo Moruo's speech can be found in *People's Daily*, April 1, 1978, 3.

26. Excerpts of Deng Xiaoping's speech can be accessed online at http://opinion.people.com.cn/n/2014/1130/c1003-26118983.html (accessed May 26, 2012).

27. Interview with a Beijing-based electrical engineer, November 9, 2007.

28. See http://mnc.people.com.cn/GB/7748890.html (accessed April 1, 2012).

29. The statistical data come from the website of UN Conference of Trade and Development (UNCTAD), available online at http://unctad.org/en/Pages/Statistics.aspx/fdi/ReportFolders/ReportFolders.aspx (accessed April 15, 2012).

30. Article 5, Law Concerning Enterprises Operated Exclusively with Foreign Capital, full text available online at http://www.danmex.org/html-en/china-laws-details.php?news_id=18 (accessed April 7, 2012).

31. *People's Daily*, November 12, 1973, 4.

32. A colleague of Ren Jianxin recollected Ren's contribution to the establishment of the Chinese IPR system in an article in 2014; see Qixue Wei, "Ren Jianxin: Trailblazer of the Cause of Chinese Intellectual Property Rights" (Ren Jianxin: Woguo Zhishi Chanquan Shiye De Kaituozhe), *Chinese Trademark* (Zhonghua Shangbiao) 19, no. 2 (2014).

33. *People's Daily*, July 12, 1980, 4.

34. Wu, *Five Decades on the Front of Science and Technology* (Keji Zhanxian Wushi Nian), 517–527.

35. The major points of the letter are on file with Zhao, *The Conceiving and Birth of Chinese Patent Law* (Zhongguo Zhuanli Fa De Yunyu Yu Dansheng), 56–64.

36. Mertha summarized the major points of the debate in greater detail. See Mertha, *The Politics of Piracy*, 82–87.

37. The major points of this report are on file with Zhao, *The Conceiving and Birth of Chinese Patent Law* (Zhongguo Zhuanli Fa De Yunyu Yu Dansheng), 165–167.

38. Ibid., 171.

39. The major points of Wu Heng's report are on file with Zhao, *The Conceiving and Birth of Chinese Patent Law* (Zhongguo Zhuanli Fa De Yunyu Yu Dansheng), 172–175.

40. The original report of that internal document cannot be found. However, the key points of the reports were recast in Zhao, *The Conceiving and Birth of Chinese Patent Law* (Zhongguo Zhuanli Fa De Yunyu Yu Dansheng), 186.

41. Huang Kunyi's main points were recorded in Mertha, *The Politics of Piracy*, 86.

42. The full text of Zhao's report can be found in *People's Daily*, December 14, 1982, 1.

43. The full text of Bo Yibo's speech can be found in *People's Daily*, January 7, 1983, 4.

44. Zhao, *The Conceiving and Birth of Chinese Patent Law* (Zhongguo Zhuanli Fa De Yunyu Yu Dansheng), 206.

45. The full text of the 1984 Patent Law is available online at http://www.chinabaike.com/law/zy/xf/cw/1331110.html (accessed April 15, 2012).

46. Gao Lulin, then director of the State Patent Bureau (SPB), recorded that in an article published in the mid-1990s. See Gao Lulin, "Ten Years of Achievements and Experience: Celebrating the First Decade of Chinese Patent Law" (Zhongguo Zhuanlifa Shishi Shinianlai Qude De Xianzhu Chengjiu Yu Jiben Jingyan), *Chinese Patents and Trademarks* (Zhongguo Zhuanli yu Shangbiao) 2, no. 2 (1995).

47. The data are taken from an article by Jiang Ying, former director of the State Intellectual Property Office (SIPO). Jiang Ying, "Ten Years of China's Patent Review System" (Zhongguo Zhuanli Shencha Zhidu Jianli De Shinian), *Intellectual Property Rights* (Zhishi Chanquan) 2, no. 2 (1995).

48. Zhao, *The Conceiving and Birth of Chinese Patent Law* (Zhongguo Zhuanli Fa De Yunyu Yu Dansheng), 206.

49. Article 45, 1984 Chinese Patent Law.

50. For a summary of the key differences between the 1984 Chinese Patent Law and that of the developed countries, see Zheng Chengsi, "On Several Features of Chinese Patent Law" (Lun Woguo Zhuanlifa De Jige Tedian), *Journal of Graduate School of Chinese Academy of Social Sciences* (Zhongguo Shehui Kexueyuan Yanjiushengyuan Xuebao) 2, no. 6 (1984).

51. Full text of the Implementation Accord is available online at http://china.findlaw.cn/fagui/guojifa/gj/23/24213.html (accessed June 15, 2012).

52. Full text of the agreement is available online at http://tcc.export.gov/Trade_Agreements/All_Trade_Agreements/People_China.asp (accessed May 31, 2012).

53. See, for example, Eric McDowell, "Lack of Copyright Disturbs US Authors," *New York Times*, January 10, 1984.

54. See, for example, Li Mingde, *Special 301 and China-US IPR Dispute* (Tebie 301 Tiaokuan Yu Zhongmei Zhishi Chanquan Zhengduan) (Beijing: Social Science Publishers, 2000), 176.

55. I discuss the issue of copyright legislation in Chapter 3.

56. For the disputes over the 1989 China-U.S. IPR negotiation, see Wu Haimin, *The Contest Between Great Powers* (Daguo De Jiaoliang) (Wuhan: Changjiang Wenyi Press, 2009), 14–15.

57. USTR: Report to Congress on Section 301 Developments, 1991. Available online at http://keionline.org/sites/default/files/ustr_special301_1991.pdf (accessed April 14, 2012).

58. Full text of the 1992 MOU is available online at http://www.copyrightnote.org/statute/cn0052.html (accessed April 17, 2012).

59. Gao's address is available online at http://www.legalinfo.gov.cn/zt/2005-01/19/content_180186.htm (accessed April 4, 2012).

60. Full text of these two regulations is available online at http://www.people.com.cn/zixun/flfgk/item/dwjjf/falv/7/7-5-01.htm l (accessed January 5, 2012).

61. Full text of the TRIPS Agreement is available online at http://www.wto.org/english/docs_e/legal_e/27-trips_01_e.htm (accessed March 5, 2012).

62. There is enormous literature on the evolution of the international IPR regime. For one of the most comprehensive analysis, see May and Sell, *Intellectual Property Rights.*

63. For related information on these revisions, see *People's Daily*, August 25, 2000, and October 27, 2001.

64. *People's Daily*, August 28, 2000, 5.

65. Full text of the Doha Declaration can be accessed online at http://www.wto.org/english/thewto_e/minist_e/min01_e/mindecl_e.htm#trips (accessed June 20, 2012).

66. For example, the U.S.-China Bilateral Protocol on China's entry into the WTO remains confidential almost ten years after it was signed in 1999, partially for fear of Chinese domestic critique of too many concessions made by the Chinese side.

67. Interview with a Beijing-based IPR official, November 28, 2007.

68. Interview with an IPR official in Beijing, October 22, 2007.

69. See, for example, Zhao Ping, "Enormous Stake Is Tied to the Result of Cisco vs. Huawei: If Huawei Loses, the Consequence Can Be Serious," *China Business News*, March 3, 2003.

70. See, for example, Alysha Webb, "GM Probes Alleged Case of Car Theft; Local Maker Chery Says Its QQ Is Not Chevrolet Spark," *Automotive News*, July 14, 2003, 4.

71. Interview with an IPR scholar in Anhui, August 30, 2007.

72. For the result of GM vs. Chery, see, for example, Xinhua News Agency, "GM and Chery Reached Reconciliation over Their IPR Dispute," November 19, 2005; for the result of Cisco vs. Huawei, see, for example, Wu Hui, "Leading Case on IPR Between China and the US Ended Up in Reconciliation," *China Intellectual Property News*, July 31, 2004.

73. These materials were published in the *Internal Reference Material on Economic Reform* (Gaige Neican). Representative among these views are *Foreign Monopoly Comes Near* (Jianxing Jianjin De Yanglongduan), from vol. 31, 2004, and *Four Major Problems in China's Foreign Investment Policy*, from vol. 36, 2004.

74. State Intellectual Property Office Working Group, *Investigation Report on IPR Disputes Between GM and Chery*, 2004 (unpublished internal material).

75. State Intellectual Property Office, *Guidelines for the Third Revision of Patent Law and Its Implementation Regulations*, March 2005 (unpublished manuscript).

76. A chronology of major events during the third revision of Chinese patent law is available online at http://www.sipo.gov.cn/tfs/dtxx/gndt/201312/t20131231_894096.html (accessed March 3, 2013).

77. Interview with an IPR judge in Beijing, November 1, 2007.

78. Full text of the revised Chinese patent law, December 28, 2008, is available on p. 3. A comparison between the third revision and the second revision of the Chinese patent law is available online at http://www.chinaiprlaw.cn/file/2009010514281.html (accessed January 14, 2009).

79. Interview with the representative of a foreign business association, Shanghai, July 21, 2008; interview with an American lawyer, Shanghai, August 5, 2008.

80. That was criticized by a report by the State Council Development Center as using patent application as an "image project" (*zhengji gongcheng*). See State Council Development Studies Center, "Our Country's Patent Regime Should Make Timely Adjustment" (Woguo Zhuanli Zhidu Xuyao Jishi Tiaozheng), *China Economy Times* (Zhongguo Jingji Shibao), September 5, 2013.

81. For a comprehensive analysis of those problems, see Shunde Li, "Concrete Problems Confronting Chinese Patent Regime" (Zhongguo Zhuanli Zhidu Mianlin De Xianshi Wenti), *Intellectual Property Rights* (Zhishi Chanquan) 31, no. 4 (2015).

82. The details of those revisions are recorded in State Intellectual Property Office, "Explanation About the Revision of Chinese Patent Law" (Guanyu Zhonghua Renmin Gonghe Guo Zhuanli Fa Xiugai Cao'an De Shuoming), available online at http://www.sipo.gov.cn/tz/gz/201504/t20150401_1095939.html (accessed August 1, 2015).

83. Part of that report is available at *Democracy and Law Times* (Mingzhu Yu Fazhi Shibao), April 7, 2014, 3.

84. For an interview with the SIPO Law and Regulation Division on the fourth revision of the Chinese patent law, see Zhao Jianguo, "The Fourth Revision of Chinese Patent Law Attracts Great Attention" (Zhuanlifa Disici Xiugai Beishou Guanzhu), *China Intellectual Property News* (Zhongguo Zhishi Chanquan Bao), April 10, 2015, 1.

85. *Legal Daily*, April 5, 2016, 11.

86. Phone interview with a Beijing-based retired IPR attorney, January 8, 2010.

Chapter 2

1. I use a pseudonym here at the request of my interviewees.

2. Informal interview with a street peddler from H Province, Beijing, November 3, 2007.

3. At the request of my interviewees, I used a pseudonym for the city cited as the example.

4. Participant observation, Changxi City, H Province, January 11, 2013.

5. Informal interview with two patent officials from H Province, January 11, 2013.

6. Phone interview with a Beijing-based IPR scholar, January 13, 2013.

7. For a discussion of the organizational evolution, see Mertha, *The Politics of Piracy*, 87–90. Dimitrov discusses the relationship between the Chinese patent administrative apparatus and IPR courts. See Dimitrov, *Piracy and the State*, 95–108.

8. Article 29, Chinese Patent Law, 2008.

9. Article 60, Chinese Patent Law, 2008.

10. Ibid.

11. Dimitrov, *Piracy and the State*, 101–108.

12. Interview with two IPR judges, Anhui, August 30, 2007; interview with an IPR judge, Nanjing, Jiangsu, March 20, 2008. These decisions can be accessed online at http://ipr.chinaourt.org.

13. *China Intellectual Property Yearbook*, 2002–2010.

14. "Chronicle of Major Events of SIPO's Development," in *Historical Choice, Great Practice: Commemorative Volume of 30th Anniversary of SIPO's Establishment*, ed. Lipu Tian (Beijing: Intellectual Property Press, 2010), 751.

15. Cheng Yongshun, "Recollection of the Birth of the First Intellectual Property Rights Tribunal in China," *China Intellectual Property Rights News*, March 5, 2003.

16. Wang Shengjun, "Report by the People's Supreme Court to the National People's Congress on the Judicial Protection of IPR," *Gazette of Chinese National People's Congress* 1 (2013): 97.

17. Xiao Yang's speech is available in *People's Court Daily*, November 17, 2004.

18. For a summary of Wang Shenjun's speech, see Policy Research Department of Chinese Supreme People's Court, "The Historical Repositioning of Mediation Work by People's Court," *People's Adjudication* 41, no. 17 (2009): 65–69.

19. For a detailed elaboration of Kong's idea, see Xiangjun Kong, "Law, Policy, and Politics in IPR Legal Trial," *People's Adjudication* 40, no. 13 (2008): 24–27.

20. Interview with an IPR judge in Nanjing, March 13, 2008.

21. *China Intellectual Property Yearbook*, 2004, 95.

22. *China Intellectual Property Yearbook*, 2011, 25.

23. Phone interview with a Beijing-based IPR judge, December 29, 2010.

24. Zhang Zhijiang, Liu Junlin, and Wu Jiang, eds., *Fifty Years of Chinese Government Organization (1949–1999)* (Beijing: Party-Buildling Literature Press, 2000), 156–157.

25. For the recollection of a former seminar participant, see Wang Zhengfa, "The People Who Opened the Gate of Chinese Patent System," *China Invention and Patent* 5, no. 3 (2009).

26. Ibid.

27. The full text of the Chinese State Council's reply about the initiative to establish the SPB is available at http://cpc.people.com.cn/GB/64184/64186/66700/4495284.html (accessed July 30, 2013).

28. A representative document on Chinese science and technology reform in the mid-1980s is the 1985 Decision on the Reform of Science and Technology System, known as the 1985 Decision. The full text of the 1985 Decision is available at *People's Daily*, March 20, 1985, 1.

29. Song Jian, "Science and Technology Reform and China's Economic Modernization," *Today's China* 33, no. 1 (1985).

30. Kunyi Huang, "The Implementation of Patent Law Will Push Forward China's Science and Technology Reform," *Chinese Science and Technology Forum* 2, no. 3 (1986).

31. The full text of Jiang Ying's article is available in *People's Daily*, November 14, 1998, 7.

32. See Chinese State Council, Regulation on Functional Departments, Personnel and Budgetary Allocation of SIPO, June 17, 1998. The full text of the regulation is available at http://www.sipo.gov.cn/tz/gz/200807/t20080721_412089.html (accessed July 31, 2013).

33. *People's Daily*, December 29, 2004, 1.

34. The full text of the 2008 Guideline is available at http://www.chinanews.com/gn/news/2008/06-10/1277555.shtml (accessed July 30, 2013).

35. Ma Weiye, "A New Chapter of Chinese Patent Protection," in *Historical Decision, Great Choice: Commemorative Volume of the 30th Anniversary of the Establishment of SIPO*, ed. Lipu Tian (Beijing: Intellectual Property Press, 2010).

36. *Gazette of Henan Province* (Henan Zhengbao) 11 (2000): 30–31.

37. *Gazette of Beijing Municipality* (Beijing Zhengbao) 7 (2002): 36–38.

38. Mertha, *The Politics of Piracy*, 93–97.

39. For a representative case of the functions of regional IPOs, see the Regulations on the Functions, Personnel and Budgetary Allocation of Guangzhou City IPO, available in *Gazette of Guangzhou City* 74 (2010): 36–39.

40. Interview with two patent officials based in H Province, January 11, 2013.

41. Ibid.

42. Interview with an IPR scholar, Nanjing, Jiangsu, March 31, 2008.

43. The full text of the 2012 Opinion is available online at http://news.xinhuanet.com/tech/2012-09/23/c_113176891.htm (accessed July 30, 2013).

44. Interview with a Jiangsu-based patent official, January 4, 2010.

45. For the details of Zuo Ye's report, see Jinna Wu, "Do Not Turn Patent Work into a New 'Face Project,'" *Science and Technology News*, March 7, 2013.

46. Interview with an IPR official in Shanghai, July 9, 2008. The official reiterated his view in several follow-up interviews with the author on January 9, 2010, and December 28, 2012.

47. Ibid.

48. National Statistics Bureau, *Statistical Bulletin on Science and Technology Investment*, available online at http://www.stats.gov.cn/tjgb/rdpcgb/qgrdpcgb/t20121025_402845404.htm (accessed July 30, 2013).

49. *People's Daily*, November 14, 2012, 4.

50. The full text of the World Economic Forum (WEF) *Global Competitiveness Yearbook*, 2001–2002, can be accessed online at http://www.nectec.or.th/pld/indicators/documents/WEF-%20Global%20Competitiveness%20Report%202001.pdf (accessed July 15, 2013).

51. The full text of the *Global Competitiveness Yearbook*, 2012–2013, can be accessed online at http://www3.weforum.org/docs/WEF_GlobalCompetitivenessReport_2012-13.pdf (accessed July 15, 2013). China's country profiles are available on pp. 138–139.

52. See Wang Shengjun, "Report by the Supreme People's Court on the Work of IPR Trials to the Standing Committee of National People's Congress," 94–95.

53. The full text of Hu Jintao's speech is available online at http://news.xinhuanet.com/18cpcnc/2012-11/17/c_113711665.htm (accessed July 28, 2013).

54. Xinhua News Agency, interview with Li Rongrong, December 18, 2006. Full text of the interview can be accessed online at http://www.gov.cn/ztzl/2006-12/18/content_472256.htm (accessed July 30, 2013).

55. Jiang Jiemin made the speech at a meeting with retired officials of the State Asset Management Commission on April 11, 2013. For a report about Jiang's speech, see *China Enterprises News*, April 23, 2013, G01. Six months later, Jiang Jiemin was arrested for corruption.

56. *China Daily*, July 14, 2015, 13.

57. Li Wei, ed., *Report on Independent Innovation of Central State-Owned Enterprises* (Beijing: China Economic Publishing House, 2012), 18.

58. Ibid., 19.

59. Tian Lipu's speech on the 2006 Working Conference of Directors of Provincial Intellectual Property Offices, March 22, 2006. Full text available online at http://www.sipo.gov.cn/sipo2008/ztzl/ndcs/qgjzh/2006/200804/t20080411_373058.html (accessed August 20, 2009).

60. See the speech by Huang Shuhe, vice director of the SASAC, on the First IPR Working Conference of Central Level State-Owned Enterprises in 2007. Available in *Gazette of State-Owned Assets Supervision and Administration Commission of the State Council* 8 (2007).

61. Interview with a state-owned enterprise employee, Anhui, August 31, 2007.

62. Luo Jianhua, "Shanghai SOE's Lost Nearly 90 Percent of IPR Disputes," *Shanghai Morning News*, April 27, 2013.

63. Skype interview with an Anhui-based state-owned enterprise employee, May 14, 2013.

64. *China Venture Capital Yearbook*, 2011, 20.

65. General Office of Ministry of Science and Technology, *Report of China's Experimental Innovative Enterprises* (Beijing: Economic Management Press, 2011).

66. For a most recent discussion on how the research funds are wasted under the Chinese science and technology system, see Shi Yigong and Yi Rao, "China's Research Culture," *Science* 329, no. 5996 (September 2010).

67. Cheng Siwei made the speech at the 2009 China Venture Capital Forum. The full text of Cheng's speech is available in *China Venture Capital Yearbook*, 2010, 19–23.

68. Zhou Yubo, "The Development Process and Future Perspective of Chinese Enterprises' Intellectual Property Rights Work," in *Intellectual Property Rights and the "Reform and Opening to the Outside" Policy*, ed. Lipu Tian (Beijing: Intellectual Property Press, 2010).

69. Wang, "Report by the People's Supreme Court to the National People's Congress on the Judicial Protection of IPR."

70. There are too many cases in which Chinese private companies lose their business opportunities because of their weak position in patent lawsuits. For a recent discussion of that issue, see "Patent: The Pain for Chinese Companies," *China Invention and Patent* 8, no. 4 (2012).

71. Interview with an IPR official, Nanjing, Jiangsu, April 29, 2008. According to a follow-up interview with him conducted on January 7, 2013, the problem has persisted during the past several years.

72. Interview with an IPR attorney, Beijing, September 27, 2007.

73. Phone interview with a Chinese IPR holder, December 30, 2010.

74. The official made the point during my first interview with him on November 22, 2007. He reiterated his view during a follow-up phone interview on January 5, 2013.

75. Numerous government and corporate reports pointed out that issue. One of the most authoritative accounts of the challenges facing the Chinese economy can be found in Premier Li Keqiang's Report on Government Work, delivered to the annual National People's Congress on March 5, 2016. The full text of Li Keqiang's report can be found online at http://news.xinhuanet.com/finance/2016-03/05/c_128775704.htm (accessed November 29, 2016).

76. Chinese President Xi Jinping first used that term during his visit to central China's Henan Province in May 2014. After Xi's visit, the mouthpiece of the Chinese Communist Party, *People's Daily*, further elaborated on that issue in three editorials consecutively published from August 5 to August 7, 2014. See *People's Daily*, August 5 to August 7, 2014, 1.

77. See Chinese State Council, "Opinion on the Development of Mixed Ownership Economy" (Guowuyuan Guanyu Fazhan Hunhe Suoyouzhi Jingji de Yijian), *Chinese State Council Gazette* 29 (2015): 13–18.

Chapter 3

1. *People's Daily*, June 17, 1961, 4.

2. Over 500 people attended Shi Guangnan's funeral. Among them was Li Ruihuan, then a standing member of the Chinese Communist Party politburo. For more information, see *People's Daily*, April 15, 1990, 3.

3. For further information about how Wang Liping reported Shi Guangnan's case to the Standing Committee of the Chinese National People's Congress, see *People's Daily*, September 8, 1990, 3.

4. TRIPS Agreement, Article 9 (2).

5. TRIPS Agreement, Article 10 (1).

6. See Neil W. Netanel, "Copyright and a Democratic Civil Society," *Yale Law Journal* 106 (1996): 347.

7. In 1910, the government of the Qing Dynasty adopted the Copyright Law of Qing Dynasty. For a scholarly analysis of the Copyright Law of Qing Dynasty, see Yang Ming, "Institutions and Texts: A Historical Examination of Copyright Law of Qing Dynasty" (Zhidu Yu Wenben: Daqing Zhuzuo Quanlu De Lishi Shengshi), *Journal of Huazhong University of Science and Technology* (Huazhong Keji Daxue Xuebao) 19, no. 5 (2013).

8. See Zhou Lin and Mingshan Li, eds., *Documents on the History of Chinese Copyright* (Zhongguo Banquanshi Yanjiu Wenxian) (Beijing: Zhongguo Fangzheng Press, 1999), 206–207.

9. See Li Mingshan, *Modern History of Chinese Copyright* (Zhongguo Jindai Banquan Shi) (Zhengzhou: Henan University Press, 2003), 241.

10. Lu Dingyi, "Speech on the Closing Ceremony of the National Publishing Conference" (Lu Dingyi Zai Quanguo Chuban Gongzuo Huiyi Bimushi Shang De Jianghua), *People's Daily*, October 21, 1949.

11. Hu Yuzhi, "On People's Publishing Work and Its Future Orientation" (Lun Renmin De Chuban Shiye Jiqi Fazhan Fangxiang), *People's Daily*, September 28, 1950.

12. The full text of the 1950 Resolution is available in *People's Daily*, November 1, 1950, 3. The full text of the 1952 Provisional Regulations is available in *People's Daily*, August 19, 1952, 3.

13. For the full text of the 1957 Regulations and the Implementation Regulations, see Zhou and Li, eds., *Documents on the History of Chinese Copyright* (Zhongguo Banquanshi Yanjiu Wenxian), 300–307.

14. During the seminar commemorating the 100th anniversary of Hu Yuzhi's birth, his contribution to China's copyright legislation in the 1950s was highlighted in a speech delivered by then vice chair of the Chinese National People's Congress, Wang Hanbin. See *People's Daily*, September 4, 1997, 4.

15. Article 7, 1950 Publishing Resolution.

16. Article 7, 1952 Provisional Regulations.

17. Article 4, 1957 Provisional Regulations.

18. Article 12, 1950 Publishing Resolution.

19. Article 10, 1950 Publishing Resolution.

20. Article 11, 1952 Provisional Regulations.

21. For a sample publishing contract by People's Press, see Zhou and Li, eds., *Documents on the History of Chinese Copyright* (Zhongguo Banquanshi Yanjiu Wenxian), 267–273.

22. Zhang Xi, *Several Words: Recollecting My Experience at the China Authors Association* (Zhiyan Pianyu: Zai Zhongguo Zuoxie Gongzuo De Huiyi) (Beijing: Shiyue Wenyi Press, 2002). The online version of Zhang's memoir can be found at http://www.edubridge.com/erxiantang/l2/zhangxi.htm (accessed July 23, 2012).

23. There are numerous scholarly works on the 1957 Anti-Rightist Movement in China. For an overview of the Anti-Rightist Movement, see Zhu Zheng, *Summer 1957: From the*

Debates Among One Hundred Schools to the Debates Between Two Schools (1957nianxia: Cong Baijia Zhenming Dao Liangjia Zhenming) (Zhengzhou: Henan People's Press, 1998).

24. "How Should We Treat Royalty?" (Zenyang Kandai Gaofei), *People's Daily*, October 5, 1958.

25. The full text of the 1958 Provisional Regulations is available online at http://www.cpll.cn/law3085.html (accessed April 12, 2013).

26. The 1961 Royalty Directive was based on the Report on the Abolition of the Royalty System and Thorough Reform of the Remuneration System, drafted by the Ministry of Culture in 1960. The full text of the 1961 Royalty Directive is available online at http://www.cpll.cn/law3147.html (accessed April 12, 2012).

27. That was recorded in the biography of Wang Kuang, former director of the State Publication Administration. See Ye Haiying, "Three Footprints in Wang Kuang's Life" (Wang Kuang Rensheng Zhong De Sange Jiaoying), *Wind of South Guangdong Sea* 10, no. 6 (2007). Full text is available online at http://www.yuehaifeng.com.cn/YHF2007/yhf2007-05-11.htm (accessed July 30, 2012).

28. The full text of the 1977 Directive is available in Zhou and Li, eds., *Documents on the History of Chinese Copyright* (Zhongguo Banquanshi Yanjiu Wenxian), 332–333.

29. Shen Rengan, "Some Recollections About the Drafting of Chinese Copyright Law" (Youguan Zhongguo Zhuzuoquanfa Zhiding De Huigu), in *Chinese IPR System in the Past Two Decades* (Zhongguo Zhishi Chanquan Ershinian), ed. Chuntian Liu (Beijing: Patent Documentation Press, 1998).

30. Song Muwen, *My Three Decades' Experience with Chinese Publication Cause* (Qinli Chuban Sanshinian) (Beijing: Commercial Press, 2007), 414–415.

31. Full text of the China-U.S. Trade Agreement is available online at http://tcc.export.gov/Trade_Agreements/All_Trade_Agreements/People_China.asp (accessed May 31, 2012).

32. Song, *My Three Decades' Experience with Chinese Publication Cause* (Qinli Chuban Sanshinian), 417.

33. Ibid., 422.

34. Ibid., 423.

35. The main points of the report submitted on November 2, 1988, are on file with Song, *My Three Decades' Experience with Chinese Publication Cause* (Qinli Chuban Sanshinian), 424–425.

36. The main points of Huang Shuhai's report are on file with Song, *My Three Decades' Experience with Chinese Publication Cause* (Qinli Chuban Sanshinian), 428–429.

37. Song, *My Three Decades' Experience with Chinese Publication Cause* (Qinli Chuban Sanshinian), 430.

38. For a discussion of these disputes, see Zhang Naigeng, "Intellectual Property Law in China: Basic Policy and New Development," *Annual Survey of International and Comparative Law* 4, no. 1 (1997). Also see Shen, "Some Recollections About the Drafting of Chinese Copyright Law" (Youguan Zhongguo Zhuzuoquanfa Zhiding De Huigu).

39. Interview with a Beijing-based IPR official, November 3, 2007. Later this anecdote was confirmed in Song Muwen's memoir published in 2007. For more information on this debate, see Song, *My Three Decades' Experience with Chinese Publication Cause* (Qinli Chuban Sanshinian), 443.

40. The full text of the 1990 copyright law is available online at http://www.chinaconsulatesf.org/eng/kj/wjfg/t43948.htm (accessed August 9, 2012).

41. Mertha, *The Politics of Piracy*, 130–132.

42. For an analysis of China-U.S. bilateral IPR negotiations in the 1990s, see ibid., 68–76.

43. The full text of the 1992 MOU is available in *People's Daily*, October 26, 1994, 3.

44. *People's Daily*, October 15, 1992, 4.

45. *People's Daily*, July 30, 1992, 1.

46. See the website of the UN Treaty Collection at https://treaties.un.org/pages/ViewDetails.aspx?src=TREATY&mtdsg_no=XIV-4&chapter=14&lang=en (accessed July 19, 2012).

47. The full text of the Regulations on Implementing Universal Copyright Convention is available online at http://news.xinhuanet.com/newmedia/2003-05/27/content_889110.htm (accessed August 25, 2012).

48. For a discussion of the criticism, see Wu, *The Contest Between Great Powers* (Daguo De Jiaoliang), 98–99.

49. Ibid., 101.

50. Then vice director of the Publishing Bureau, Chinese Communist Party Central Propaganda Department, Yuan Liang, recalled the details of the meeting between Hu Yaobang and Toyoko Yamasaki. He later recounted the meeting with Shen Rengan, former director of the National Copyright Administration. See Shen Rengan, "The Unforgettable Past: Comrade Hu Yaobang and Chinese Copyright Work" (Buneng Wangque De Guanhuai: Ji Hu Yaobang Tongzhi Dui Banquan Gongzuo De Guanhuai), *China Publishing Journal* 27, no. 12 (2005).

51. Details of the small group meeting are recorded in Wu, *The Contest Between Great Powers* (Daguo De Jiaoliang), 100–101.

52. Report about the visits by the Chinese delegation to Geneva and Paris was published in *People's Daily*, October 7, 1991, 4.

53. Liu Gao, "China's Accession to the International Copyright Conventions: Before and After" (Woguo Jiaru Guoji Banquan Gongyue De Qianqian Houhou), in *China Copyright Yearbook* (Beijing: China National People's Congress Press, 2009).

54. Wu, *The Contest Between Great Powers* (Daguo De Jiaoliang), 88.

55. Details of the discussion can be found in ibid., 102.

56. Liu Gao, "China's Accession to the International Copyright Conventions: Before and After" (Zhongguo Jiaru Guoji Banquan Gongyue De Qianqian Houhou), in *Two Decades of Chinese Intellectual Property Rights* (Zhongguo Zhishi Chanquan Ershi Nian), ed. Chuntian Liu (Beijing: Patent Literature Press, 1999), 61.

57. Ibid., 62.

58. Phone interview with a Beijing-based IPR scholar, January 14, 2010.

59. For an exhaustive summary of those areas in which foreign copyright was accorded more protection than Chinese domestic copyright, see Mertha, *The Politics of Piracy*, 131–132.

60. The full text of the 1990 Copyright Law (with English translation) is available online at http://www.law-lib.com/law/law_view.asp?id=6938 (accessed August 6, 2012).

61. Mertha, *The Politics of Piracy*, 131.

62. For further information about the Wuhan Joint Seminar, see Gao Quan, "Joint Seminar Held in Wuhan to Discuss Copyright Law Revision," *Publishing Reference Materials* (Chuban Caokao), August 8, 1996.

63. Song, *My Three Decades' Experience with Chinese Publication Cause* (Qinli Chuban Sanshinian), 466–468.

64. Ibid., 470.

65. Phone interview with a Beijing-based IPR official, July 4, 2011.

66. The correspondence between the Ministry of Radio, Film, and Television and the NPC Standing Committee over the revision of Chinese copyright law before China's WTO entry has not been declassified yet. The major points of their opposition opinions were summarized from interviews with various IPR professionals involved in the revision of Chinese copyright law in the late 1990s. These include the following: interview with a former IPR official in Beijing, November 27, 2007; interview with a Beijing-based IPR scholar, January 8, 2008; phone interview with a Beijing-based IPR scholar, January 9, 2010; and phone interview with a Beijing-based IPR official, November 15, 2010.

67. For the recollection of one of the initiators, see Song Muwen, "The Hard Earned Progress: Some Reflections on the Revision of Copyright Law" (Laizhi Buyi De Zhongyao Jinzhan), *Study of Press and Publication* 16, no. 12 (2001): 6.

68. Song, *My Three Decades' Experience with Chinese Publication Cause* (Qinli Chuban Sanshinian), 481.

69. Ibid., 483.

70. Part of Gu Jianfen's speech is available in Ji A, "The Influence of Public Opinion Rapidly Increases in China's Legislation Process" (Minyi Lifa Wendu Biaosheng), November 18, 2005, available online at http://www.xinhuanet.com/report/media/mzfz.htm (accessed November 7, 2012).

71. Song, *My Three Decades' Experience with Chinese Publication Cause* (Qinli Chuban Sanshinian), 484.

72. The full text of Shi Zongyuan's speech can be found in *China Copyright Yearbook*, 89–92.

73. Xu Jialu, "The Importance of Revising Copyright Law" (Xiugai Zhuzuoquan Fa Yiyi Zhongda), *Democracy* (Minzhu) 9, no. 8 (1998): 6.

74. Details of the meeting between Peng Peiyun and the Ministry of Radio, Film, and TV are not disclosed yet. In a personal interview with Peng Peiyun on November 29, 2007, I learned about Peng Peiyun's position during the meeting with the Ministry of Radio, Film, and TV.

75. The full text of the 2001 Chinese copyright law is available online at http://www.wipo.int/clea/docs_new/pdf/en/cn/cn019en.pdf (accessed August 25, 2012).

76. Song, *My Three Decades' Experience with Chinese Publication Cause* (Qinli Chuban Sanshinian), 485.

77. *People's Daily*, February 27, 2010, 4. The revision partially resulted from the WTO resolution on a dispute between China and the United States from 2007 to 2009. For a comprehensive discussion of the WTO resolution, see Peter Yu, "The U.S.-China Dispute over TRIPS Enforcement," http://www.law.drake.edu/academics/ip/docs/ipResearch-op5.pdf (accessed January 3, 2012) and http://www.law.drake.edu/academics/ip/docs/ipResearch-op5.pdf (accessed July 31, 2012).

78. Zhang Kangkang's letter is on file with *People's Political Consultation News* (Renmin Zhengxie Bao), March 5, 2011, 2. For a detailed discussion of how Zhang Kangkang interacted with Wen Jiabao, see Wu Lisi, "Behind the Third Revision of Chinese Copyright Law" (Zhuzuoquanfa Xiugai Muhou), *Xinmin Journal* 13, no. 6 (2012).

79. *China Press and Publication News*, July 14, 2011.

80. The full text of the draft is available at http://news.xinhuanet.com/legal/2012-04/01/c_122918269.htm (accessed August 23, 2012).

81. Part of Liu Huan's speech is available in Wang Xinrong, "I Should Be in Charge of My Own Copyright" (Wode Zhuzuoquan Wo Zuozhu), *China Art News* (Zhongguo Yishu Bao), April 13, 2012, 1.

82. For an interview with Wang Feng, see Wang Jun, "The Proposed Revision of Copyright Law Aroused Strong Doubts Among Chinese Musicians" (Zhuzuoquanfa Xiugai Cao'an Yinfa Yinyuejie Qianglie Zhiyi), *Shenzhen Special Economic Zone Daily* (Shenzhen Tequ Bao), April 16, 2012, B05.

83. Interview with Yan Xiaohong by *No. 1 Finance and Economic News* (Diyi Caijing Ribao), April 25, 2012, 4.

84. Phone interview with a Beijing-based scholar from Hefei, Anhui, December 30, 2012.

85. The details of those appeals are recorded in Chen Xiang, "The Story of the Third Major Revision of Chinese Copyright Law" (Zhuzuoquanfa Disanci Xiugai Shimo), *China Reading* (Zhongguo Dushu Bao), March 6, 2013, 6.

86. The report by *Legal News* (Fazhi Ribao) on that issue is available online at http://www.iprchn.com/Index_NewsContent.aspx?NewsId=82126 (accessed February 26, 2015).

87. For a representative analysis of those two issues, see an interview with Wang Ziqiang, head of the Copyright Division of the Chinese National Copyright Administration (NCA) by *Legal Daily*, June 28, 2013, 6.

Chapter 4

1. In this chapter, copyright industry is defined as industry whose core competitiveness relies on the substantive rights of authors and other creative artists. Due to limited space, I will not elaborate on other sectors of copyright industry such as museum exhibition, performing arts, architecture and fashion design, and software in this chapter.

2. Interview with a copyright official, Beijing, December 6, 2007.

3. Jiang Jianguo, "Grasp the Main Spirit of Comrade Xi Jinping's Speech, Practise Socialist Core Values" (Shenke Bawo Xi Jinping Tongzhi Jianghua Jingsheng, Jianxing Shehui Zhuyi Hexin Jiazhiguan), *China Press and Publication News*, April 21, 2014.

4. See "Notice by the State Council on the Establishment of Leading Group on Intellectual Property Rights Strategy" (Guowuyuan bangongting guanyu Cengli Guojia Zhishi Chanquan Zhanlue Zhiding Gongzuo Lingdao Xiaozu De Tongzhi), *Gazette of the State Council of the People's Republic of China* 8 (2005): 14. It is also important to note that the SARFT and GAPP were merged in March 2013.

5. Mertha, *The Politics of Piracy*, 133–145.

6. Dimitrov, *Piracy and the State*, 231–232.

7. Mertha, *The Politics of Piracy*, 145–152.

8. For a recent elaboration of Chinese leadership's thinking on propaganda work, see the speech by Xi Jinping, the current Chinese president, *2013 National Propaganda and Thought Work Conference*, August 19, 2014, available online at http://cpc.people.com.cn/n/2013/0821/c64094-22636876.html (accessed August 30, 2014).

9. For a discussion of the Soviet propaganda system, see Peter Kenez, *The Birth of the Propaganda State: Soviet Methods of Mass Mobilization, 1917–1929* (Cambridge: Cambridge University Press, 1985).

10. For a collection of Jiang Qing's speeches on ideological work, see *Comrade Jiang Qing on Literature and Artistic Work*, reprinted by the Center for Chinese Research Materials, Association of Research Libraries, 1975. For a narrative of Communist ideology's influence on prereform Chinese literature and artistic works production by a Mainland China–based scholar, see Chen Tushou, *Does the Heaven Known Human Beings' Sicknesses: Narrative of Post-1949 Chinese Literature and Artistic Circle* (Renyoubing, Tianzhifou: 1949 Nian Yilai Zhongguowenyijie Jishi) (Beijing: People's Literature Press, 2003).

11. Interview with a Shanghai-based IPR scholar, January 8, 2013.

12. The data are drawn from *China Statistical Yearbook*, 1989; *China Radio and TV Yearbook*, 1984; and the website of Chinese State Bureau of Statistics.

13. There are a significant number of books and academic articles on China's media reform since the 1980s. For a representative example, see Daniel Lynch, *After the Propaganda State: Media, Politics, and "Thought Work" in Reformed China* (Stanford, Calif.: Stanford University Press, 1999).

14. Interview with an IPR scholar, Beijing, December 1, 2007.

15. Hao Jing, "Chinese Cultural Industries in the Past 60 Years" (Wenhua Chanye 60 Nian: Huiwang Jueqi Zhilu), *Xinhua News Agency*, September 28, 2009.

16. Zhao Dan's article can be accessed online at http://www.ilf.cn/Mate/3932.html (accessed October 10, 2013).

17. The six movie studios were Beijing, Shanghai, Changchun, Xi'an, Zhujiang, and Emei. For further information about the reform of Chinese movie production system in 1980, see Ding Yaping, *History of Contemporary Chinese Movies*, vol. 2 (Beijing: Chinese Film Press, 2011), 594.

18. See Rao Shuguang, *History of the Development of Movie Market in China* (Zhongguo Dianying Shichang Fazhanshi) (Beijing: China Movie Press, 2009), 387.

19. See Yu Youxian, ed., *China's Publishing Industry in 50 Years* (Xinzhongguo Chuban 50 Nian) (Beijing: People's Fine Arts Press, 1999), 24.

20. See Song, *My Three Decades' Experience with Chinese Publication Cause* (Qinli Chuban Sanshinian), 84–87.

21. The full text of this report can be accessed in *Publication Work* (Chuban Gongzuo), June 29, 1980, 33–35.

22. Chen Hanbo, "Speech on the National Conference on Publishing Work," *Publishing Work* 2, no. 6 (1980): 41.

23. *People's Daily*, April 18, 1982, 4.

24. *People's Daily*, September 25, 1983, 1.

25. Deng Xiaoping, *Selected Works of Deng Xiaoping*, vol. 2 (Beijing: People's Press, 1994), 255–256.

26. The move received strong critique from the Chinese media, including the government-run *People's Daily.* See, for example, Gu Tu, "Closing Down Dancing Ballrooms and Closing Cultural Life" (Fengbi Wuting Yu Fengbi Wenhua), *People's Daily*, January 25, 1988.

27. "Wang Meng on Culture and Artistic Work in the New Year," *People's Daily*, January 1, 1988, 2.

28. Full text of this notice can be accessed online at http://www.law-lib.com/law/law_view.asp?id=48020 (accessed October 17, 2013).

29. Liao Wang Journal Reporting Team, "A Comprehensive Discussion on Managing the Cultural Market" (Wenhua Shichang Lilun Yanjiu Zongshu), *Liao Wang Journal* (Liaowang Zhoukan) 38 (1988): 21–23.

30. Gao's article was published in two parts on the November 2 and November 6 issues of *China Cultural News.*

31. *Chinese Statistical Yearbook*, 1989, 873–874.

32. Ibid., 878.

33. Ibid., 788.

34. *People's Daily*, September 5, 1989, 1.

35. For part of He Jingzhi's speech, see, for example, Xinhua News Agency, "Symposium on Deng Xiaoping's Thoughts on Literature and Artistic Work," *People's Daily*, December 23, 1989, 1.

36. Phone interview with a former Chinese copyright official, December 19, 2013.

37. See, for example, Chen Xitian, "When East Wind Breezes, Spring Comes—Comrade Deng Xiaoping's Visit to Shenzhen" (Dongfang Fenglai Manyanchun: Deng Xiaoping Tongzhi Zai Shenzhen Jishi), full text available online at http://news.xinhuanet.com/newscenter/2003-08/19/content_1033952.htm (accessed October 19, 2013).

38. Full text of this decision is available in *People's Daily*, June 30, 1992, 1.

39. Luo Gan, *A Significant Strategic Move* (Zhongda De Zhanlue Juece) (Beijing: Chinese Politics and Law University Press, 1992), 360–370.

40. The full text of Jiang Zemin's speech can be accessed online at http://news.xinhuanet.com/ziliao/2005-03/17/content_2709294.htm (accessed October 26, 2014).

41. Details of the conference can be found in Song Muwen, "Promote the Reform and Development of Chinese Publishing Industry in the Spirit of the 14th CCP National Congress" (Anzhao Shisida Jingsheng Jiakuai Chubanye De Gaige Yu Fazhan), in *My Thirty Years in Chinese Publishing Cause* (Qinli Chuban Sanshinian), ed. Song Muwen (Beijing: Commercial Press, 1992).

42. See Song, *My Three Decades' Experience with Chinese Publication Cause* (Qinli Chuban Sanshinian), 579.

43. For speeches by related Chinese senior officials, see Liu Zhongde, "Quicken the Step of Reform, Make Our Movie Industry Prosper" (Jiakuai Gaige Bufa, Fanrong Dianying Shiye), *Chinese Movie* 35, no. 2 (1993); Liu Zhongde, "The Emphasis of Cultural Reform in 1994 Will Be Laid on the Management of Performing Arts Troupes" (Jinnian Wenhua Tizhi Gaige Jiangzuo Zhongda Gaige, Yishu Biaoyan Tuanti Shi Gaige De Zhongzhong Zhizhong), *China Theatre* 1, no. 2 (1994); Zhong Chengxiang, "A Philosophical Thinking on Certain Trends in TV and Movie Production" (Dui Dangqian Yinshi Chuangzuo Yizhong Sichao De Zhexue Sikao, Xuexi Dangde Shisida Zhengzhi Baogao De Tihui), *China Television* (Zhongguo Dianshi) 11, no. 1 (1993).

44. Details of these reforms can be found in Fu Caiwu and Danna Song, "Origin and Evolution of Chinese Cultural System Reform" (Woguo Wenhua Tizhi De Yuanqi, Yanjin, He Gaige Duice), *Journal of Jianghan University* 21, no. 2 (2004).

45. *China Statistical Yearbook*, 2000, 714.

46. Ibid., 712.

47. *China Advertisement Yearbook*, 2002.

48. The rise of private book merchants in the 1990s was recorded in Wu Haimin, *The Magic Cube of Book License: Incremental Suicide of Chinese Publishing Houses* (Shuhao Mofang: Chuban Yezhe De Manxing Zisha) (Beijing: Huayi Press, 1995).

49. Li Yuanchao, "Three Priorities on Our Policy Agenda: What Can We Do to Develop Our Cultural Industry" (Zuohao Sanjianshi: Women Nengwei Fazhan Wenhua Chanye Zuoshengme), *Chinese Reform* (Zhongguo Gaige) 14, no. 5 (2000).

50. Interview with a Shanghai-based IPR scholar, July 25, 2008.

51. Song, *My Three Decades' Experience with Chinese Publication Cause* (Qinli Chuban Sanshinian), 579.

52. Representative among those movies/books were Chen Kaige's *Farewell My Concubine* (movie), Zhang Yimou's *To Live* (movie), Tian Zhuangzhuang's *Blue Kite* (movie), and Yu Qiuyu's *Painful Cultural Journey* (book). For further information, see Yu Qiuyu, "Yu Qiuyu on Piracy" (Yu Qiuyu Shuo Daoban), *Shandong Library Journal* 5, no. 1 (1999).

53. Full text of those regulations can be accessed in *Gazette of the State Council of the People's Republic of China* (Zhonghua Renmin Gongheguo Guowuyuan Gongbao) 31, no. 3 (1996): 91–96.

54. *Gazette of the State Council of the People's Republic of China* (Zhonghua Renmin Gongheguo Guowuyuan Gongbao) 19 (1996): 6–14.

55. *Gazette of the State Council of the People's Republic of China* (Zhonghua Renmin Gongheguo Guowuyuan Gongbao) 2 (1996): 7–15.

56. Full text of the tenth five-year plan can be accessed at http://www1.peopledaily.com.cn/GB/shizheng/16/20010318/419582.html (accessed November 2, 2014).

57. Full text can be accessed online at http://www.gzcm.gov.cn/show.aspx?id=489&cid=56 (accessed October 20, 2014).

58. Full text can be accessed online respectively at http://review.jcrb.com/zyw/n79/ca169684.htm and http://www.jincao.com/fa/23/law23.33.htm (accessed October 20, 2014).

59. Full text of this decision is available online at http://news.xinhuanet.com/newscenter/2005-08/08/content_3325946.htm (accessed October 20, 2014).

60. Full text of this plan can be accessed in *People's Daily*, September 27, 2009, 3.

61. *China Statistical Yearbook*, 2013, 804.

62. China Internet Information Center (CNNIC), "2012 Statistical Report on the Development of Internet in China," available online at http://www.cnnic.cn/hlwfzyj/hlwxzbg/hlwtjbg/201301/P020130801546406723463.pdf (accessed November 2, 2014).

63. *People's Daily*, January 7, 2013, available online at http://expo.people.com.cn/n/2013/0107/c57922-20116244.html (accessed November 3, 2014).

64. For example, from 2007 to 2010, the U.S. copyright industry recorded an annual growth rate of 3 percent. See International Intellectual Property Alliance (IIPA), "Copyright Industry in American Economy: 2011 Report," available online at http://www.iipa.com/pdf/2011CopyrightIndustriesReport.PDF (accessed November 2, 2014).

65. Ding Chenxin, "Private Capital Plays a Major Role in Chinese Movie Industry" (Minying Ziben Yi Chengwei Yinshiye Zhujiao), *China News Week* (Zhongguo Xinwen Zhoukan) 12, no. 41 (2012).

66. *China Press and Publication News*, May 27, 2005, 1.

67. *Shenzhen Jinbao Daily*, February 21, 2012, 3.

68. *People's Daily*, August 13, 2003, 1.

69. *People's Daily*, August 20, 2013, 1.

70. Interview with an IPR scholar, Shanghai, December 19, 2013.

71. Dimitrov, *Piracy and the State*, 221–248.

72. Interview with a Nanjing-based copyright official, April 30, 2008.

73. See Article 6 of Provisional Regulations on Operational Eligibility of Movie Studios; full text available online at http://www.gov.cn/gongbao/content/2005/content_64252.htm (accessed February 12, 2014).

74. Phone interview with a Beijing-based IPR scholar, May 23, 2013.

75. See *China Publishing Yearbook*, 2012, 373.

76. For the full text of the Regulations on the Management of Market for Press and Publication, see *China Publishing Yearbook*, 2012, 375–378.

77. For the details of Chinese movie censorship mechanism, see Ministry of Radio, Film, and TV, "Regulations on Recording the Synopsis of Movie Script and Movie Management," May 22, 2006. Full text available online at http://www.sarft.gov.cn/articles/2006/06/22/20070924091945340310.html (accessed February 16, 2014).

78. Full text of the Provisions on Managing Press and Publication is available in *People's Daily*, January 15, 2002. 11. The revised version of the Provisions on Managing Press and Publication is available in *China Publishing Yearbook*, 2012, 373.

79. See Jia Zhangke, "Jiang Zhangke et al.'s Letter to the MORFT" (Jiazhangke Deng Shangshu Dianyingju), *Remote Corner of the Earth* (Tianya) (January 2004): 189–190.

80. For the reply of MORFT, see Dianying Dazhong, "Moves of the Movie Market" (Dianying Shichang Dongtai), *Popular Film* (Dazhong Dianying) 24, no. 7 (2003).

81. *People's Daily*, August 19, 2010, available online at http://culture.people.com.cn/GB/22226/57597/57599/12486047.html (accessed May 31, 2014).

82. The open letter was posted on Xie's microblog. The full text of the open letter is available online at http://news.mtime.com/2012/12/16/1503251.html (accessed May 31, 2014).

83. The full text of the 2013 Notice is available online at http://www.gov.cn/zwgk/2013-07/17/content_2449645.htm (accessed February 16, 2014).

84. Interview with Li Shaohong by *Jinghua Times*, April 10, 2013, available online at http://news.mtime.com/2013/04/10/1509949.html (accessed May 31, 2014).

85. Phone interview with a Beijing-based copyright scholar, December 21, 2013.

86. A movie rating system was established in the United States in 1968; see *Ginsberg v. New York*, 390 U.S. 629 (1968).

87. A representative case is Jia Zhangke's award-winning movie, *A Touch of Sin* (Tianzhuding). When Jia Zhangke was lobbying the SARFT for a license to show the movie in Mainland China, the pirated version of his movie could already be downloaded online.

88. That data are taken from the China Film Makers Association, "Chinese Film Industry Report 2014–2015" (Zhongguo Dianying Chanye Yanjiu Baogao 2014–2015), 2015, p. 11, available online at https://www.supplyfinder.com/downloads/pdfs/3003.pdf (accessed November 15, 2013).

89. Ibid.

90. Phone interview with a movie producer in Beijing, December 27, 2012.

91. For example, Chinese Foreign Ministry Spokeswoman Hua Chunying made that statement at a press conference on January 4, 2013. The full text of Hua Chunying's statement is available online at http://www.mfa.gov.cn/mfa_chn/fyrbt_602243/jzhsl_602247/t1002817.shtml (accessed May 31, 2014). Earlier, Tie Ning, chairwoman of the Chinese Writers' Association, told the press at the 2009 Frankfurt Book Fair that China did not have a censorship system. A full report about Tie Ning's comment is available online at http://www.spiegel.de/international/world/china-the-unwelcome-guest-controversy-as-frankfurt-book-fair-fetes-beijing-a-654713.html (accessed May 31, 2014).

92. Jacobs Andrew, "Authors Accept Censors' Rules to Sell in China," *New York Times*, October 20, 2013.

93. Ibid.

94. Phone interview with the manager of a publishing company, Beijing, December 29, 2012.

95. Phone interview with a Beijing-based copyright owner, December 29, 2012.

96. See, for example, an interview with Zhang Yashan, chief office manager of Xinhua Bookstore, by *Beijing Youth Daily*, October 7, 2004. Full text of the interview is available online at http://www.people.com.cn/GB/shizheng/1026/2900940.html (accessed October 15, 2014).

97. See, for example, Jiang Dunxiong and Yingjiang Zeng, "There Are Too Few Bookstores in the Cities: What Should We Do?" *People's Daily*, January 4, 1981.

98. Xiang Bing, "Pull Through Troublesome Situation, Re-Create the Glory: The First Anniversary of China's Movie Distribution Reform," *People's Daily*, May 5, 1994.

99. For a recollection of the 1982 conference, see Huang Qinnan, "Brief Analysis of the Protection of Trademark Rights" (Luelun Dui Shangbiao Zhuanyongquan De Baohu), *Journal of Beijing College of Politics and Law* 2, no. 3 (1981).

100. See *China Press and Publication News*, February 17, 2014, 7.

101. The full text of the *Opinions on Deepening the Reform of Chinese Movie Industry* is available at *Movie Reports* (Dianying Tongxun) 1 (1993): 2–3.

102. See interview with Zhang Peimin, then vice director of MORFT Movie Bureau. *Movie Art* (Dianying Yishu) 3 (2002): 14–16.

103. Sun Hui, Hanwen Liu, and Jiawei Song, "Analysis Report of China Film Industry in 2013" (2013nian Zhongguo Dianying Chanye Fenxi Baogao), *Contemporary Cinema* (Dangdai Dianying) 29, no. 3 (2014).

104. Full text of the decision is available in *People's Daily*, August 9, 2005, 2.

105. China Press and Publishing Studies Institute, "2013 Development Report of Chinese Press and Publishing Distribution Industry" (2013nian Zhongguo Chubanwu Faxing Chanye Fazhan Baogao), *China Press and Publication News*, February 17, 2014.

106. Ibid.

107. Zheng Huang and Guo Chenyang, "Chinese Private Bookstores Face Shuffling" (Minying Shudian Mianlian Xipai), *China Business and Trade* 20, no. 7 (2012).

108. Interview with Wu Shulin by *Legal Daily*, April 26, 2013, 6.

109. Interview with a branch manager of Xinhua Bookstore, Hefei, Anhui, December 27, 2013.

110. Interview with the manager of a privately owned bookstore, Hefei, Anhui, December 28, 2013.

111. Full text of the regulation can be accessed at *Laws and Regulations* (Sifa Yewu Wenxuan) 6 (2004): 23–25.

112. For the full text of those regulations, see "State Council's Guideline Opinion on Revitalizing the Movie Industry" (Guowuyuan Guanyu Fanrong Dianying Chanye De Zhidao Yijian), *China Film News* (Zhongguo Dianying Bao), February 4, 2010, 1.

113. Jonathan Landreth, "Xi Jinping's Film Deals: Search for a Walt Disney of China?" *Christian Science Monitor*, February 18, 2012.

114. Liu Hanwen and Linming Zhang, "Analysis Report of China Film Industry in 2012" (2012 Nian Zhngguo Dianying Chanye Baogao), *Contemporary Cinema* (Dangdai Dianying) 29, no. 3 (2013).

115. Sun, Liu, and Song, "Analysis Report of China Film Industry in 2013" (2013nian Zhongguo Dianying Chanye Fenxi Baogao).

116. Ibid.

117. Interview with a copyright owner, Nanjing, Jiangsu, March 14, 2008.

118. *China Movie Yearbook*, 1995, 168–169.

119. The Hollywood movies include *Lion King, True Lies, Fugitive, Speed, Bad Boys, Die Hard 4.0*, and so on.

120. Interview with Liu Jianzhong, then director of the Movie Division of the Chinese Ministry of Radio, Film, and TV, by a journalist from *China Film News* (Zhongguo Dianying Bao), January 21, 2002.

121. Ding, *History of Contemporary Chinese Movie*, 264.

122. For a representative analysis by an American scholar, see Stanley Rosen, "The Wolf at the Door: Hollywood and the Film Market in China," in *Southern California and the World*, ed. Eric J. Heikkila and Rafael Pizarro (Westport, Conn.: Praeger, 2002).

123. Liu and Zhang, "Analysis Report of China Film Industry in 2012" (2012 Nian Zhngguo Dianying Chanye Baogao).

124. The author has not found any official government document about the "month for protection of domestic movies," but that practice is evident in the operation of Chinese domestic movie theater bands. Evidence is provided in the interview with theater band professionals in Hefei, Anhui, December 29, 2013.

125. Yin Xiao, "Chinese Movies in 2013: Domestic Challenges and External Threats" (2013nian Zhongguo Dianying De Neiyou Waihuan), *Literature and Artistic News*, January 18, 2014.

126. Phone interview with a Beijing-based copyright scholar, May 24, 2013.

127. Sun, Liu, and Song, "Analysis Report of China Film Industry in 2013" (2013nian Zhongguo Dianying Chanye Fenxi Baogao).

128. The vice director of the Chinese State Copyright Administration, Yan Xiaohong, made that statement at the 2014 International Copyright Forum. The full text of the report is available online at http://news.ifeng.com/a/20140916/41993223_0.shtml (accessed October 20, 2014).

129. International Intellectual Property Alliances, *Copyright Industries in the U.S. Economy: The 2013 Report*, available online at http://www.ifpi.org/content/library/20070130-highlights.pdf (accessed October 6, 2013).

130. There has been enormous literature on the role of the pillar industry in a country's economic development. A classic definition for "pillar industry" is provided in Walt Rostow, *The Economics of Take-Off into Sustained Growth* (New York: St. Martin's, 1964).

131. Interview with a publishing company's manager, Beijing, October 30, 2007.

132. The official relied on a report by Wu Haimin, senior correspondent of *Chinese Press and Publication News*, for statistical data of the underground cultural market in Shanghai from 1984 to 1995. For the full text of Wu's report, see Wu Haimin, "Investigation Report of Chinese Underground Cultural Market" (Zhongguo Wenhua Shichang Anfang Baogao), *Beijing Literature* (Beijing Wenxue) 25, no. 1 (1996).

133. Ibid.

134. Interview with a Shanghai-based former copyright official, December 29, 2013.

135. Phone interview with a Guangdong-based former copyright official, January 7, 2013.

136. Interview with Huang Xiaoling by *Nanfang Metropolitan News*, April 16, 2014, available online at http://epaper.oeeee.com/A/html/2014-04/16/content_2055409.htm (accessed May 6, 2014). Also available online at http://wen.oeeee.com/a/20140416/1091474.html (accessed July 7, 2015).

137. See, for example, Fang Min, "Dirty Story Behind the Illegal V.C.D. Production Line" (Feifa Guangpan Shngchan: Jiekai Heimu), *Enterprise Marketing* (Qiye Xiaoshou) 3, no. 7 (1997).

138. Interview with a Guangdong customs official, May 20, 2007.

139. Phone interview with a Guangdong customs official, September 1, 2012.

140. Ibid.

141. For an analysis by the IPR judges making legal decisions on this case, see Wuhan University Institute of Quality Supervision, *2012 Observation Report on Quality Development in China* (2012nian Zhongguo Zhiliang Guance Baogao) (Beijing: China Standard Press, 2013).

142. Cao Di, "Key Statistical Data About Chinese Video-Sharing Websites 2009–2014," *I-Research Consulting Group, Inc.* (2014), available online at http://report.iresearch.cn/report/201106/1554.shtml (accessed February 21, 2014).

143. Ibid.

144. Wei Wei, "The Biggest Lawsuit Concerning Online Piracy Was Born" (Wangluo Shipin Zuida Suopei an Dansheng), *Beijing Business Daily* (Beijing Shangbao), November 14, 2013, 3.

145. Interview with Wu Yuanmei, a judge of the Haidian Intermediate People's Court, *Legal Daily* (Fazhi Ribao), December 15, 2011, 5.

146. Yang Yang, "Making Profits Through Online Piracy Is No Longer Tolerated" (Daoban Zhifu Buzai Beiyunxu), *Economic Observation News* (Jingji Guancha Bao), May 26, 2014, 4.

147. Xi Wang, "Grey Area of Video-Sharing Websites Remains Alive" (Shipin Wangzhan De Huise Jianghu Haizai), *IT Times* (IT Shibao), June 9, 2014, available online at http://tech.163.com/14/0609/09/9U9PDVKP000915BF.html (accessed June 24, 2014).

148. At the request of my interviewees, I have replaced their real names with pseudonyms.

149. Again, I use a pseudonym rather than the real name here.

150. Interview with a female street peddler, Beijing, November 10, 2007.

151. Interview with street peddlers in Beijing, October 30, 2007, to November 15, 2007.

152. Phone interview with a former street peddler in Beijing, January 13, 2013.

153. Phone interview with a Beijing-based former copyright official, January 9, 2014.

154. Informal interview with a consumer of a pirated DVD in Shanghai, January 9, 2013.

155. Wuhan University Institute of Quality Supervision, *2012 Observation Report on Quality Development in China* (2012nian Zhongguo Zhiliang Guance Baogao), 17.

156. Ibid., 150–151.

157. Phone interview with a Beijing-based IPR scholar, June 18, 2012.

Chapter 5

1. For a comprehensive chronology of Tong Ren Tang, see Bian Dongzi, *Tong Ren Tang: The National Treasure* (Guobao Tongren Tang) (Beijing: People's Press, 2010).

2. The report about the conference is available in *People's Daily*, August 29, 1954, 2.

3. For Tong Ren Tang's experience in the Cultural Revolution, see Huibao Wen, "History of Tong Ren Tang," *Weihui Daily*, January 19, 2015, T07.

4. *People's Daily*, September 3, 1979.

5. By 2015, Tong Ren Tang had 110 overseas retail stores. See *Beijing Daily* (Beijing Ribao), April 7, 2015, 1.

6. Phone interview with an employee of Tong Ren Tang, January 12, 2010.

7. See, for example, Khoon Tan Loke and Clifford Borg-Marks, *Trademark Law in the People's Republic of China* (Hong Kong: Oxford University Press, 1998); Khoon Tan Loke, *Pirates in the Middle Kingdom: The Art of Trademark War* (Hong Kong: Sweet & Maxwell Asia, 2004).

8. Article 15, Section 2, TRIPS Agreement.

9. For a comprehensive analysis of Chinese trademarks in ancient times, see Cao Wanjun, "An Analysis of the Evolution of Trademarks in Ancient China" (Qianxi Zhongguo Gudai Shangbiao Biaoshi Yange), *China Collective Economy* 21, no. 30 (2009): 84–85.

10. The historical record can be found in *Selection of Historical Inscriptions on Stone Tablet in Shanghai* (Shanghai Lishi Beike Ziliao Xuanji) (Shanghai: Shanghai People's Press, 1980), 77.

11. Information about the registration of the "Weishui" trademark can be found on the website of the Shanghai Municipal Office of Local Records and Gazette at http://www.shtong.gov.cn/node2/node2245/node66046/node66051/node66085/node66114/userobject1ai61681.html (accessed May 21, 2016).

12. *Patent and Trademark Review*, published by Richard and Co., vol. 11, March 1913, 262. During her dissertation research, Wang Liming from Soochow University confirmed the validity of the aforementioned statistical data. See Wang Liming, "Research on the First Intellectual Property Negotiation Between China and Foreign Countries in Late Qing Dynasty" (Wanqing Zhongwai Shouci Zhishi Chanquan Tanpan Yanjiu) (Ph.D. diss., Soochow University, 2008), 21.

13. For one of the most recent studies of the promulgation of the 1904 Experimental Regulations, see Qu Chunhai, "The Evaluation of Some Historical Facts About the Experimental Regulations on Chinese and Foreign Trademark Registrations During the Late Qing Dynasty" (Qingmo Guanyu Zhongwai Shangbiao Zhuce Shiban Zhangcheng Jiaoshe Shishi Kaoping), *Historical Records* (Lishi Dang'an) 31, no. 4 (2012). The full text of that article is available online at http://www.cssn.cn/ddzg/ddzg_ldjs/ddzg_zz/201310/t20131030_786173.shtml (accessed May 21, 2016).

14. For the history of Chinese trademark affairs during the era of the Republic of China (1911–1949), see Zuo Xuchu, "Chinese Trademark Management in the Era of the Republic of China" (Minguo Shiqi Zhongguo Shangbiao Guanli Gaikuang), *China Trademark* 17, no. 1 (2012).

15. The full text of Liu's policy speech is available online at http://www.marxists.org/chinese/liushaoqi/marxist.org-chinese-lsq-19490428.htm (accessed March 20, 2013).

16. The full text of the 1950 Trademark Regulations is available in *People's Daily*, August 30, 1950, 2.

17. Article 1, 1950 Trademark Regulations.

18. Articles 2 and 33, 1950 Trademark Regulations.

19. Xu Dixin, "The United Front Work with the Private Entrepreneurs Under the Leadership of Comrade Zhou Enlai," in *Endless Remembrance: Zhou Enlai, the People's Leader*, ed. Central Documentation Research Office (Beijing: People's Press, 1988).

20. Numerous literature exists on the "Great Socialist Transformation." The first person to raise that issue was Mao Zedong. According to Bo Yibo, then Chinese finance minister, Mao Zedong initiated that policy on a meeting with the other members of the CCP Central Secretariat on July 29, 1952. See Bo Yibo, *Recollection of Some Major Historical Decisions and Events*, vol. 1 (Beijing: People's Press, 1997), 21.

21. See *Gazette of Nanjing*. The section on the management of trademark in the 1950s is available online at http://njdfz.nje.cn/UpLoadFile/html/%E5%B8%82%E5%BF%975-7/html/7Noname001.html (accessed March 20, 2013).

22. Ibid.

23. The full text of the 1963 Trademark Regulations can be found online at http://www.lawon.cn/law/viewDetail.jsp?id=129953 (accessed August 21, 2012).

24. Article 3, 1963 Trademark Regulations.

25. Article 11, 1963 Trademark Regulations.

26. Li Jizhong, "Improve Trademark Work to Adapt to the Request of Economic Reform" (Shiying Gaige Yuyao Wanshan Shangbiao Gongzuo Tixi), *Industrial Property Rights* (Gongye Chanquan) 2, no. 1 (1989): 80.

27. See the memoir of Xu Dixin's wife, Fang Zhuofen: Fang Zhuofen and Fang Wu, *In Memory of Xu Dixin* (Shenzhen: Haitian Press, 2002).

28. Ibid.

29. Phone interview with a former CAIC official in Beijing, January 22, 2010.

30. Liu Peizhi, "The Vibrant Development of Chinese Trademark Affairs During the Reform and Opening Era" (Zai Gaige Kaifang Zhong Pengbo Fazhan De Shangbiao Shiye), in *Chinese Intellectual Property Work in the Past Two Decades*, ed. Chuntian Liu (Beijing: Patent Documentation Press, 1998), 133.

31. For the statistical data on trademark registration by office, see the website of the World Intellectual Property Organization (WIPO) at http://www.wipo.int/ipstats/en/statistics/marks/ (accessed March 15, 2013).

32. Ou Wanxiong, "A Recollection by a Veteran Trademark Examiner," in *Intellectual Property Rights and the 30th Anniversary of Opening and Reform*, ed. Editorial Board (Beijing: Intellectual Property Rights Press, 2008).

33. For a detailed report about the SAIC conference, see *People's Daily*, March 28, 1979, 1.

34. See Zhang Lin, "Chinese Individual Ownership Economy: Those People, Those Events," *Glory* 17, no. 6 (2011).

35. Ibid., 37.

36. See the webpage run by the Chinese State Council Information Office at http://www.china.com.cn/chinese/OP-c/265281.htm (accessed March 30, 2013).

37. For a discussion of the Chinese trademark application in the early 1980s, see An Qinghu, "The Development of Chinese Trademark Affairs" (Zhongguo Shangbiao Shiye De Fazhan), *Observation of Chinese Development* 1, no. 6 (2005): 38.

38. The statistical data about China foreign trade in the late 1970s can be accessed online at http://www.china.com.cn/aboutchina/data/txt/2006-11/09/content_7335919.htm (accessed March 30, 2013).

39. Ren Zhonglin, "Explanation of the PRC Trademark Law (Draft): Address Before the Standing Committee of the National People's Congress," August 19, 1982. The full text of Ren's speech is available online at http://www.legalinfo.gov.cn/zt/2005-01/19/content_183660.htm (accessed April 13, 2012).

40. The full text of the 1983 Trademark Law is available in *People's Daily*, August 27, 1982, 2.

41. Article 3, 1983 Trademark Law.

42. Article 4, 1983 Trademark Law.

43. Ren, "Explanation of the PRC Trademark Law (Draft)."

44. Articles 37, 38, 39, and 40, 1983 Trademark Law.

45. Article 5, 1963 Trademark Regulations.

46. Article 12, 1963 Trademark Regulations.

47. Article 9, 1983 Trademark Law.

48. Dong Baolin, "Chinese Trademark in the Past Ten Years," in *Chinese Intellectual Property Yearbook*, ed. Chinese Intellectual Property Office (Beijing: Intellectual Property Press, 2000).

49. Han Yujun, "The Development of Chinese Service Industry: An International Comparison," *Economic Review* 26, no. 4 (2011).

50. *People's Daily*, September 20, 1991, 2.

51. See Ou Wanxiong, "Protect Foreign Registered Trademarks in China According to Chinese Law: Some Notes by a Trademark Examiner" (Yifa Baohu Waiguo Zai Woguo De Zhuce Shangbiao: Yiwei Shangbiao Shenchayuan De Zhaji), *Law Science Magazine* 11, no. 4 (1991): 38.

52. For the recollection by the lawyer who handled the dispute, see Zheng Xiaojun, "A Recollection of Pizza Hut vs. New Vision Global," *China Trademark* 21, no. 10 (2006).

53. For details of this case, see An Qinghu, "Well-Known Trademark and China's Well-Known Trademark System," *China Industry and Commerce News*, March 4, 2004.

54. Liu Jiyang, "Working Report of Chinese Industrial Property Studies Association" (Zhongguo Gongye Chanquan Yanjiuhui Gongzuo Baogao), *Industrial Property Rights* (Gongye Chanquan) 3, no. 1 (1989).

55. Mertha, *The Politics of Piracy*, 35–76.

56. The full text of the 1995 Exchange of Letters and Action Plan can be accessed online at http://tcc.export.gov/Trade_Agreements/All_Trade_Agreements/exp_005363.asp (accessed March 21, 2013).

57. The full text of the Chinese National People's Congress on the revision of the 1993 Chinese Trademark Law can be accessed in *People's Daily*, February 25, 1993, 5.

58. The full text of the Chinese Anti-Unfair Competition Law is available in *People's Daily*, September 4, 1993, 5.

59. Phone interview with a Beijing-based former IPR official, January 12, 2013.

60. The full text of the U.S. Special 301 report in 1994 can be accessed online at http://keionline.org/sites/default/files/ustr_special301_1994.pdf (accessed March 20, 2013).

61. Article D 4(b) and Article I 1(d) of the 1995 Action Plan.

62. The full text of the 1998 Regulations on the Recognition and Protection of Well-known Trademarks can be accessed online at http://www.gyygsj.gov.cn/baweb/show/shiju/bawebFile/3530.html (accessed March 31, 2013).

63. Duan Ruichun, "Cooperation, Conflict, and Interests Game: A Look Back at the China-U.S. IPR Negotiations," in *Intellectual Property Rights and the 30th Anniversary of Opening and Reform*, ed. China State Intellectual Property Office (Beijing: Intellectual Property Rights Press, 2008), 509.

64. The full text of the 1996 Enforcement Agreement is available online at http://tcc.export.gov/Trade_Agreements/All_Trade_Agreements/exp_005361.asp (accessed April 1, 2013).

65. Phone interview with a Beijing-based former IPR official, December 30, 2009.

66. For a discussion of Chinese trademark application and registration, see Liu Ren, "Chinese Trademark Application and Registration Ranked as the World's No. 1 for Six Consecutive Years" (Zhongguo Shangbiao Zhuce Shenqing Liang Lianxu Liunian Ju Shijie Diyi), *Chinese Intellectual Property News* (Zhongguo Zhishi Chanquan Bao), December 5, 2008, 2.

67. The full text of the 2001 Chinese Trademark Law is available in *People's Daily*, November 5, 2001, 5.

68. See Wang Zhongfu's interview with journalists from Xinhua News Agency, available online at http://www.china.com.cn/chinese/kuaixun/82528.htm (accessed April 2, 2013).

69. Report by Xinhua News Agency, August 23, 2012, available online at http://www.gov.cn/jrzg/2012-09/03/content_2216127.htm (accessed April 5, 2013).

70. Tao Xinliang, "Analysis of the Current Situation of the Recognition and Protection of Well-Known Trademarks in China and Policy Recommendations," in *Several Issues in the Third Amendment of Chinese Trademark Law*, ed. Chinese Academy of Social Sciences IPR Center (Beijing: Intellectual Property Rights Press, 2009), 190.

71. *People's Daily*, December 25, 2012, 2.

72. The full text of the amendments is available online at http://www.npc.gov.cn/npc/xinwen/lfgz/flca/2012-12/28/content_1749326.htm (accessed April 2, 2013).

73. The Chinese National People's Congress published the amended Chinese trademark law online at http://sbj.saic.gov.cn/flfg1/flfg/201309/t20130903_137807.html (accessed July 7, 2014).

74. Article 14, 2014 Trademark Law.

75. Article 28, 2014 Trademark Law.

76. Article 63, 2014 Trademark Law.

77. Many legal scholars expressed those opinions in their academic publications. For some representative examples, see Wu Handong and Chaozheng Wang, "Revision of Trademark Law Under the Greater Scenario of Chinese Economic Development" (Zhongguo Jingji Fazhan Daju Zhongde Shaobiaofa Xiugai), *Chinese Studies of Administration for Industry and Commerce* (Zhongguo Gongshang Guanli Yanjiu) 21, no. 2 (2013); Zhang Huibin, "Achievements, Limitations, and Future Trends of Chinese Trademark Legislation" (Zhongguo Shangbiao Lifa De Chengji Wenti Yu Zouxiang), *Hubei Social Science* (Hubei Shehui Kexue) 25, no. 12 (2012); Deng Hongguang and Yuan Zhou, "Future Development of Chinese Trademark Law" (Shangbiaofa De Weilai Fazhan), *Journal of South China Normal University: Social Science Edition* (Huanan Shifan Daxue Xuebao: Shehui Kexue Ban) 28, no. 4 (2011).

78. Several Chinese IPR professionals raised that point during my phone interview with them. During the following conversations, the discussion of that point was particularly emphasized: phone interview with a Beijing-based IPR scholar, May 12, 2014; phone interview

with a Shanghai-based IPR scholar, May 14, 2014; follow-up phone interview with a Beijing-based IPR scholar, May 15, 2014.

Chapter 6

1. At the request of my interviewees, I have replaced their real names with pseudonyms.

2. See Dimitrov, *Piracy and the State*, 185–220.

3. *Guangdong Science and Technology News* (Guangdong Keji Bao), April 18, 2014, 6.

4. Mertha, *The Politics of Piracy*, 173–194.

5. Ibid., 180–181.

6. Cai Zhengping, "My Experience at the State Bureau of Measurement During the 1950s" (Wosuo Jingli De Caochuang Shiqide Guojia Jiliangju), *China Measurement* (Zhongguo Jiliang) 18, no. 8 (2013).

7. *People's Daily*, May 5, 1963, 2.

8. For a discussion of Soviet quality control policy, see V. V. Boitsov, *Standardization in the USSR, 1925–1975* (New Delhi: Oxonian Press, 1980).

9. See, for example, Li Heping, "From 'Ticket Economy' to 'Credit Card Life'" (Cong Piaozheng Jingji Dao Shuaka Shenghuo), *Beijing Archives* (Beijing Dang'an) 28, no. 3 (2012).

10. Interview with an elderly Beijing resident, October 7, 2008.

11. For an analysis about how the dismantling of those technical standards harmed Chinese industrial production, see Guoliang Zhao and Guo Yuanxi, "On the Relationship Between 'Horizontal Authority' and 'Vertical Authority' in the Management of Chinese Industry" (Lun Woguo Gongye Guanli Zhong De Tiaokuai Guanxi), *Journal of Sichuan University* 10, no. 3 (1984).

12. For the recollection of how the Chinese State Council identified those quality problems, see Ye Xiao, "How Zhou Enlai Saved Chinese Aviation Industry During the Cultural Revolution" (Wenge Zhong Zhou Enlai Zhenjiu Zhongguo Hangkong Gongye Jishi), *History of the Chinese Communist Party* (Dangshi) 22, no. 1 (2006).

13. For details of Zhou Enlai's opinion on Chinese quality work, see Yongqin Wang, "How Zhou Enlai Resisted the Ultra Leftist Trend During the Cultural Revolution" (Zhou Enlai Zai Wengezhong Shi Zenyang Pi Jizuo De), *Science of Leadership* (Lingdao Kexue) 26, no. 12 (2001).

14. Ren, "Explanation of the PRC Trademark Law (Draft)."

15. *People's Daily*, September 1, 1978, 1.

16. *People's Daily*, October 11, 1978, 2.

17. *People's Daily*, May 25, 1979, 3.

18. Interview with a Shanghai-based former quality supervision official, December 30, 2013.

19. Chinese State Council, "Notice on Circulating the Report on the Decline of Quality of Industrial Products by the State Economic Commission" (Guowuyua Pizhuan Guojia Jingwei Guanyu Gongye Chanpin Zhiliang Xiajiang De Baogao Tongzhi), *State Council Gazette* (Guowuyuan Gongbao) 18, no. 7 (1985).

20. See, for example, Joseph Juran, *Quality Control Handbook* (New York: McGraw-Hill, 1962). Also see A. V. Feigenbaum, *Total Quality Control* (New York: McGraw-Hill, 1991).

21. *People's Daily*, January 17, 1980, 2.

22. For Liu's role in advocating total quality management in China, see Liu Ming, "In Memory of Liu Yuanzhang, My Dear Father" (Zhuiyi Wode Fuqin Liu Yuanzhang), *China Quality* (Zhongguo Zhiliang) 20, no. 7 (2014).

23. The full text of the 1980 Provisional Guideline on Total Quality Management in Industrial Enterprises is available at *Gazette of Chinese State Council* 13, no. 6 (1980): 1–5.

24. The full text of the 1986 Regulations on the Quality Responsibility of Industrial Products is available at *Gazette of the State Council of the People's Republic of China* 19, no. 12 (1986): 418–423.

25. For details about how the 1996 Guideline was adopted, see Guo Ruoxu, "The Process of Drafting Guideline for Quality Rejuvenation (1996–2010)" (Zhiliang Zhenxing Gangyao Chutai Shimo), *China Brand and Anti-Counterfeiting* (Zhongguo Pingpai Yu Fangwei) 9, no. 8 (2008).

26. The full text of the Guideline for Quality Rejuvenation (1996–2010) is available at *Quality Management of Chinese Public Health* 1 (1997): 6–9.

27. *China Quality News*, January 21, 2015.

28. *China Quality News*, September 22, 2014, 2.

29. *China Quality News*, April 25, 2014, 2.

30. Part of that report is available online at http://www.cqn.com.cn/news/zjpd/zjbk/zjyw/mcsy/386880.html (accessed November 30, 2014).

31. The full text of the Regulations on National Product Quality Supervision and Spot Check is available online at http://www.scjyzb.net/newsli21_396.htm (accessed November 30, 2014).

32. State QTSB Quality Supervision Division, "Promote Product Supervision Work to a New Level According to the Product Quality Law" (Yifa Tuidong Chanpin Zhiliang Jiandu Gongzuo Yueshang Xin Taijie), *China Quality News*, September 23, 2013.

33. Ibid.

34. Xie Peng, "State Q.T.S.B. Publishes the Result of National Quality Supervision and Spot-Check in 2013" (Zhijian Zongju Fabu 2013 Nian Chanpin Zhiliang Guojia Jiandu Choucha Qingkuang), *China Quality News*, March 3, 2014.

35. The full text of the Guideline for Quality Development (2011–2020) is available online at http://politics.people.com.cn/GB/17074710.html (accessed November 25, 2014).

36. *People's Daily*, May 11, 2014, 1.

37. Full text of Li Keqiang's speech is available in *People's Daily*, September 16, 2014, 3.

38. Wuhan University Institute of Quality Supervision, *2012 Observation Report on Quality Development in China* (2012nian Zhongguo Zhiliang Guance Baogao), 15.

39. Yuanzhang Liu, *A Record of Gratitude: My Career in Chinese Quality Work* (Gan'enlu: Wode Zhiliang Shengya) (Beijing: Science Press, 2011), 254–255.

40. *China Quality and Technology Supervision* (Zhongguo Zhiliang Jishu Jiandu) (December 2014): 81.

41. European Union Customs House, "Report of E.U. Customs Enforcement on Intellectual Property Rights Results at the E.U. Border in 2013," 2014, 18. The full text is available online at https://ec.europa.eu/taxation_customs/sites/taxation/files/resources/documents/customs/customs_controls/counterfeit_piracy/statistics/2014_ipr_statistics_en.pdf (accessed November 19, 2014).

42. The report about the Xinchang poisonous capsules in 2012 was first made by the CCTV *Weekly Quality Report* on April 15, 2012. After that, major Chinese media such as

People's Daily and *Jiefang Daily* also reported the incident. See Chen Xihan, Linjun Kong, and Jiangang Liang, "After the Poisonous Capsules" (Zhuizong Dujiaonang), *Jiefang Daily* (Jiefang Ribao), April 17, 2012. Also see Zimei Fu, "Three Questions About the Poisonous Capsules Incident" (Sanwen Dujiangnang Shijian), *People's Daily*, May 7, 2012.

43. Luo Ruiming, "The Direction of 90 Million Poisonous Capsules Cannot Afford to Remain Unknown" (9000 Wanli Dujiaonang Quxiang Buneng Chengmi), *China Business News* (Zhongguo Shangbao), September 12, 2014.

44. The reports on the poisonous milk powder incidents can be found in *People's Daily*, September 14, 2008, 2; *People's Daily*, September 20, 2008, 5.

45. See Hui Zhi, "The Craziness Behind the Swill-Cooked Edible Oil" (Digouyou Beihou De Fengkuang), *Prosecutional Review* 19, no. 12 (2013).

46. See *Nanfang Daily*, July 23, 2014, 18.

47. Guo Ruoxu, "My Opinions on Promoting Quality Work" (Tuijin Zhilaing Gonguo De Qianjian), *China Brand and Anti-Counterfeiting* (Zhongguo Pingpai Yu Fangwei) 9, no. 11 (2008): 26.

48. Mertha, *The Politics of Piracy*, 175.

49. Ibid., 176.

50. A key document illustrating that idea was *Chinese State Council's Directive on Further Replacing the Role of Private Economy*, issued on April 13, 1964. The full text of that document was reprinted in Economic Research Institute of State Planning Commission, "Important Economic Events in P.R.C. History" (Zhonghua Renmin Gongheguo Jingji Dashiji), *Study of Planned Economy* (Jihua Jingji Yanjiu) 26 (1983): 82.

51. Numerous scholarly articles analyzed the AIC's functions during the early reform era. For a most recent one, see Li Wentao, "Some Thoughts on Deepening Reform and Transforming the A.I.C.'s Functions" (Dui Dangqian Gongshang Bumen Shenhua Gaige He Zhuanhua Zhineng De Sikao), *China Study of Administration of Industry and Commerce* (Zhongguo Gongshang Guanli Yanjiu) 11, no. 7 (2014).

52. Ibid.

53. Chinese State Council, "Notice on the Determination of S.A.I.C.'s Major Mandate, Internal Department, and Personnel Allocation" (Guanyu Guojia Gongshang Xingzheng Guanli Zongju Zhuyao Zhize, Neibu Jigoue Renyuan Bianzhi De Tongzhi), *Administration on Industry and Commerce* (Gongshang Guanli) 4, no. 4 (1994).

54. Chinese State Council, "Notice on the Determination of S.A.I.C.'s Major Mandate, Internal Department, and Personnel Allocation" (Guanyu Guojia Gongshang Xingzheng Guanli Zongju Zhuyao Zhize, Neibu Jigoue Renyuan Bianzhi De Tongzhi), *Gazette of Chinese State Council* 30, no. 5 (1998).

55. Chinese State Council, "Notice on the Determination of S.A.I.C.'s Major Mandate, Internal Department, and Personnel Allocation" (Guanyu Guojia Gongshang Xingzheng Guanli Zongju Zhuyao Zhize, Neibu Jigoue Renyuan Bianzhi De Tongzhi), *Gazette of Chinese State Council* 33, no. 9 (2001), available online at https://www.jetro.go.jp/ext_images/world/asia/cn/ip/law/pdf/origin/2007081034900594.pdf (accessed November 17, 2014).

56. Chinese State Council, "Notice on the Determination of S.A.I.C.'s Major Mandate, Internal Department, and Personnel Allocation" (Guanyu Guojia Gongshang Xingzheng Guanli Zongju Zhuyao Zhize, Neibu Jigoue Renyuan Bianzhi De Tongzhi), *Gazette of Chinese State Council* 40, no. 16 (2008), available online at http://gkml.saic.gov.cn/auto3743/200809/t20080901_112597.html (accessed November 17, 2014).

57. Liu Minxue, "Speech on the Third Conference of the All-China Industry and Commerce Society" (Zai Disanci Quanguo Gongshang Xuehui Huiyishang De Jianghua), *China Study of Administration of Industry and Commerce* (Zhongguo Gongshang Guanli Yanjiu) 1, no. 2 (1992): 59.

58. Wang Zhongfu, "Strengthen Law Enforcement, Safeguard Market Order: Speech on the National Conference of A.I.C. Directors" (Jiaqiang Zhifa Lidu, Weihu Shichang Zhixu: Zai Quanguo Gongshang Juzhang Huiyi Shang De Jianghua), *China Study of Administration of Industry and Commerce* (Zhongguo Gongshang Guanli Yanjiu) 3, no. 2 (1995): 5.

59. Bohua Zhou, "Speech on the National Conference of A.I.C. Directors" (Zai Quanguo Gongshang Xingzheng Guanli Juzhang Huiyi De Jianghua), *China Study of Administration of Industry and Commerce* (Zhongguo Gongshang Guanli Yanjiu) 7, no. 7 (2007): 9.

60. Zhang Mao, "Steadily Push Forward Reform on Administration of Industry and Commerce, Vitalize Various Market Entities" (Wenbu Tuijing Gongshang Guanli Gaige, Jifa Shichang Zhuti Huoli), *China Market* (Zhongguo Shichang) 19, no. 43 (2013): 4.

61. Liu Anwei, "Three Milestones of Fair Trade and Market Competition Legislation in China: Interview with Ning Wanglu, Head of A.I.C. Anti-Trust and Fair Trade Division" (Gongping Jiaoyi Zhifa De Sange Lichengbei: Fang Guojia Gongshang Zongju Gongping Zhifa He Fanlong Duan Zhifasi Sizhang Ning Wanglu), *Administration on Industry and Commerce* (Gongshang Guanli) 24, no. 9 (2008).

62. Finance Channel of Sina.com, Survey on Anti-Trust Law (Fan Longduanfa Diaocha Wenjuan), August 15, 2007.

63. The English translation of the Chinese Anti-Trust Law is available online at http://www.lawinfochina.com/display.aspx?lib = law&id = 0&CGid = 96789 (accessed June 3, 2015).

64. *Legal Daily*, November 10, 2011, 6.

65. The full text of the editorial is available online at http://www.cnii.com.cn/index/content/2011-11/11/content_932892_3.htm (accessed February 1, 2015).

66. *Worker's Daily*, December 3, 2011, 1.

67. The full text of the report by *Southern Weekend* is available online at http://www.infzm.com/content/94649http://www.infzm.com/content/94649 (accessed February 12, 2015).

68. *Securities Times* (Zhengquan Ribao), January 5, 2015, A02.

69. *China Trade News* (Zhongguo Maoyi Bao), February 28, 2015, 5.

70. *Xinhua Daily Report* (Xinhua Meiri Dianxun), December 24, 2013, 6.

71. *Science and Technology Daily* (Keji Ribao), February 11, 2015.

72. An interview with Huang Yong by *Legal Daily*, January 5, 2015, 6.

73. Zhao Wei, "Anti-Trust Operations with Chinese Characteristics" (Zhongguo Shi Fanlongduan), *Zhejiang Economy* (Zhejiang Jingji) 26, no. 3 (2011). Also see Hu Bo, "Anti-Trust Operation with Chinese Characteristics Originate from a Set of Market Principles with Chinese Characteristics" (Zhongguoshi Fanlongduan Yuanyu Shichang Guizhi De Zhonguohua), *Chinese Auto* 20, no. 9 (2014).

74. Victoria Ruan, "Americans Echo Gripes on China's Business Climate," *South China Morning Post*, September 3, 2014.

75. The full text of Li's dialogue with the World Economic Forum participants is available in *People's Daily*, September 12, 2014, 3.

76. "Please Prove with Concrete Facts That Chinese Anti-Trust Law Is Not Selectively Enforced" (Yong Shiji Xingdong Zhengming Zhongguo Fanlongduan Bushi Neiwai Youbie), *IT Times Weekly* 13, no. 17 (2014).

77. Phone interview with a Beijing-based trademark attorney, March 3, 2015.

78. Liu, "The Vibrant Development of Chinese Trademark Affairs During the Reform and Opening Era" (Zai Gaige Kaifang Zhong Pengbo Fazhan De Shangbiao Shiye), 133.

79. See, for example, Wu Chuanzheng, "Coca-Cola's 25 Years in China" (Kekou Kele Zai Zhongguo de 25nian), *Nanfang Weekend* (Nanfang Zhoumo), November 18, 2004.

80. During its thirty years of development, Jianlibao experienced many ups and downs. For the history of Jianlibao's brand-building and corporate development, see Wu Hua and Zheng Wenjie, "Jianlibao's Road of Development" (Jianlibao De Fazhanzhilu), *People's Daily*, August 28, 1987.

81. Interview with Zhang Ruimin by *China Entrepreneur* (Zhongguo Qiyejia) 10 (1994): 50.

82. Fan Lubin, "Notes on the 30 Years of Development of Chinese Advertisement Industry" (Zhongguo Guanggaoye 30 Nian Zhaji), *Chinese Advertisement* (Zhongguo Guanggao) 16, no. 5 (2010): 116.

83. Ibid., 119.

84. *People's Daily*, August 16, 1994, 9.

85. Beijing Well-Known Trademarks Evaluation Institute, "Research Report on the Most Valued Chinese Brands in 1995" (95 Zhongguo Zuiyong Jiazhi De Pinpai Yanjiu Baogao), *China Quality: 10000 Miles of Journey* (Zhongguo Zhiliang Wanlixing) 2, no. 5 (1996): 10.

86. Shuo Qin, "Declaration of China's Intangible Assets" (Zhongguo Wuxing Zichan De Xuanyan), *Window of South Wind* (Nanfengchuang) 8, no. 9 (1993). Also see Yongfeng Gao, "Running the Tide of Hearts" (Xinchao Zhulang), *China Quality: 10000 Miles of Journey* (Zhongguo Zhiliang Wanlixing) 1, no. 1 (1995).

87. Na Lei and Liao Hui, "A Study of FDI in China During the Past Three Decades: Influence and Development" (Gaige Kaifang 30nian Woguo Yingjing Waizi De Yinxiang Yu Fazhan Yanjiu), *Modern Business, Trade, and Industry* (Xiandai Gongmao Shangye) 14, no. 2 (2008): 134–135.

88. Taihong Lu et al., "The Progress and Prospect of Chinese Home Grown Brands" (Woguo Zizhu Pinpai De Jinbu Yu Zhanwang), *Journal of Dr. Sun Yat-sen University* (Zhongshan Daxue Xuebao) 34, no. 3 (1996): 7.

89. See, for example, Xuan Zhang, "Haier Group: Build Famous Brands Overseas" (Hai'er Jituan: Guomen Zhiwai Chuang Mingpai), *Chinese Foreign Trade* (Zhongguo Duiwai Maoyi) 7, no. 7 (1998).

90. Phone interview with a Shanghai-based entrepreneur, January 7, 2014.

91. The details of the Great Discussion of Chinese Home Grown Brands are recorded in Guo Fengbing, "The Great Discussion on Home Grown Brands: Before and After" (Zizhu Pinpai Dataolun De Qianqian Houhou), *China Quality and Brands* (Zhongguo Zhiliang Yu Pinpai) 1, no. 5 (2004).

92. "2004: The Year of the Great Awakening of Home Grown Brand Consciousness" (2004: Zizhu Pinpai Yishi Da Juexing De Yinian), *China Quality and Brands* (Zhongguo Zhiliang Yu Pinpai) 1, no. 12 (2004).

93. See, for example, Eric Pfanner, "King of PCs, Lenovo Sets Smartphone Ambitions," *New York Times*, December 27, 2013.

94. See the report on Foxconn by *Guangzhou Evening News* (Yangcheng Wanbao), October 27, 2014. The full text is available online at http://finance.people.com.cn/stock/n/2014/1027/c67815-25912764.html (accessed June 6, 2015).

95. The full text of the report is available on MIIT's website at http://www.miit.gov.cn/n11293472/n11293832/n11294042/n11481465/16595200.html (accessed June 6, 2015).

96. For information on Chinese trademark registration in 2014, see the website of the Chinese State Administration of Industry and Commerce (SAIC) at http://sbj.saic.gov.cn/ztbd/xsbfsxyzn/gzgl/201504/t20150422_155392.html (accessed June 7, 2015).

97. The 2004 Report of the World's Most Influential Brands is available online at http://www.worldbrandlab.com/brand_01.jsp (accessed June 7, 2015).

98. Even Haier and Tsingtao Beer are not private enterprises in a complete sense. Haier is regarded as under partial public ownership while a significant portion of Tsingtao Beer's holdings belongs to the Qingdao City State-Assets Supervision and Management Commission. A discussion of Haier's ownership structure is available online at http://finance.people.com.cn/GB/43429/125491/125503/125550/7472951.htmlhttp://finance.people.com.cn/GB/43429/125491/125503/125550/7472951.html (accessed July 12, 2015). An interview with Jin Zhiguo, CEO of Tsingtao Beer, is available online at http://cq.cnfood.cn/n/2013/1212/5445.html (accessed July 12, 2015).

99. Part of the report by the Beijing First Intermediate People's Court is available online at http://www.fdi-law.com/view.php?id=99658 (accessed July 14, 2015).

100. The report about foreign-related IPR disputes in Zhejiang Province is available online at http://news.wenweipo.com/2014/04/17/NN1404170010.htm (accessed July 14, 2015).

101. For a recent discussion of that policy, see State-Owned Assets Supervision and Administration Commission, "SASAC Leadership Studied the Important Spirits of Comrade Xi Jinping's Important Speeches on SOE Reform" (Guoziwei Dangwei Xuexi Xi Jinping Tongzhi Guanyu Guoqi Gaige Zhongyao Jianghua Jingsheng), *Bulletin of Propaganda Department of SASAC* 12, no. 1 (2015).

102. Interview with a trademark official, Nanjing, Jiangsu, April 29, 2008.

103. Follow-up interview with a trademark official, Nanjing, Jiangsu, December 27, 2013.

104. The number is taken from an article by SAIC General Director Zhang Mao. See Zhang Mao, "Deepen Industry and Commerce Reform, Vitalize Chinese Economy" (Shenhua Shangshi Zhidu Gaige, Jifa Jingji Huoli), *Administration Reform* (Xingzheng Gaige) 6, no. 5 (2015).

105. Interview with a Beijing-based trademark attorney, November 20, 2007.

106. Article 14, Chinese Quality Product Law.

107. Article 41, Implementation Regulation of Chinese Trademark Law.

108. For one of the earliest scholarly analyses about the emergence of fake goods in China, see Huang, "Brief Analysis of the Protection of Trademark Rights" (Luelun Dui Shangbiao Zhuanyongquan De Baohu).

109. Li Jizhong, "Speech on the National Trademark Work Conference" (Zai Quanguo Shangbiao Gongzuo Huiyi Shang De Jianghua), *Industrial Property Rights* (Gongye Chanquan) 3, no. 2 (1990).

110. Ni Zhifu, "Report to the Standing Committee of National People's Congress on the Implementation of Anti Unfair Competition Law, Consumers Rights Law, Product Quality Law, and the Decision on Punishing the Production and Retailing of Counterfeit Goods" (Quanguo Renda Changweihui Guanyu Zhixing Sanfa Yijueding Qingkuang De Jiancha Baogao), *Gazette of Chinese National People's Congress* 35, no. 8 (1994).

111. Interview with a Guangdong-based IPR official, Guangdong Zhuhai, May 20, 2007.

112. That example was reported in Wang Ruiju, "Two Issues That I Encountered During the Quality Supervision Work" (Wozai Zhiliang Jiandu Gongzuo Zhong Yudao De Liangge Wenti), *Science Forum* (Keji Luntan) 25, no. 4 (2010).

113. *People's Daily*, February 5, 1991, 2.

114. Wuhan University Institute of Quality Supervision, *2012 Observation Report on Quality Development in China* (2012nian Zhongguo Zhiliang Guance Baogao), 152.

115. Ibid.

116. Ibid., 186.

117. Ibid., 68–69.

118. The result of that survey was published in *China Quality: A 10,000 Mile Journey* (Zhongguo Zhiliang Wanli Xing) 4 (2008): 16–18.

119. The full text of Ai Feng's speech is available online at http://www.cca.org.cn/ztbd/detail/21359.html (accessed July 20, 2015).

Conclusion

1. At the request of my interviewee, I use a pseudonym here.

2. Phone interview with a Beijing-based IPR scholar, January 3, 2014.

3. Phone interview with a Beijing-based IPR scholar, May 24, 2014.

4. For a comparative examination of the IPR experiences of China and other important world economic powers, see Peter Yu, "The Global Intellectual Property Order and Its Undetermined Future," *WIPO Journal* 1, no. 1 (2009).

5. For a recent discussion of book piracy in nineteenth-century America, see Peter Yu, "The Copyright Divide," *Cardozo Law Review* 25, no. 1 (2003): 336–353.

6. For a discussion of how Charles Dickens struggled with copyright problems in nineteenth-century United States, see, for example, Edward Hudon, "Literary Piracy, Charles Dickens and the American Copyright Law," *American Bar Association Journal* 50, no. 12 (1964). For a discussion of Anthony Trollope's copyright problems in the United States, see Michael Sadleir and Frederick Page, eds., *An Autobiography of Anthony Trollope* (New York: Oxford University Press, 1980), 308.

7. Numerous scholars discussed the enactment of the International Copyright Act in the United States in the late nineteenth century. For a representative discussion in this regard, see Barbara Ringer, "The Role of the United States in International Copyright: Past, Present, and Future," *Georgetown Law Journal* 56, no. 6 (1968).

8. William Alford, "Making the World Safe for What: Intellectual Property Rights, Human Rights and Foreign Economic Policy in the Post-European Cold War World," *New York University Journal of International Law and Politics* 29, nos. 1–2 (1996–1997): 146.

9. One of the most recent comments of its kind was made by Song Xiaoming, head of the IPR Special Tribunal of the Chinese People's Supreme Court. Song made this comment during a press conference in Beijing on April 24, 2017. The full text of Song's comment is available online at http://china.cnr.cn/gdgg/20170424/t20170424_523722769.shtml (accessed April 26, 2017).

10. This argument was briefly alluded to in Andrew Mertha, "Pirates, Politics, and Trade Policy: Structuring the Negotiations and Enforcing the Outcomes of the Sino-US Intellectual Property Dialogue, 1991–1999" (Ph.D. diss., University of Michigan, 2001), 189–190.

11. A leading China expert, Kenneth Lieberthal, made that argument in his recent book. See Lieberthal, *Managing the China Challenge.*

12. See, for example, Peter K. Yu, "From Pirates to Partners: Protecting Intellectual Property in China in the Twenty-First Century," *American University Law Review* 50 (2000).

13. Peter Yu, "Rise and Decline of the Intellectual Property Powers," *Campbell Law Review* 34, no. 3 (2012): 580.

14. Phone interview with a Beijing-based IPR scholar, May 24, 2014.

15. Ibid.

BIBLIOGRAPHY

"2004: The Year of the Great Awakening of Home Grown Brand Consciousness" (2004: Zizhu Pinpai Yishi Da Juexing De Yinian). *China Quality and Brands* (Zhongguo Zhiliang Yu Pinpai) no. 12 (2004): 14–20.

Alford, William. "Making the World Safe for What: Intellectual Property Rights, Human Rights and Foreign Economic Policy in the Post-European Cold War World." *New York University Journal of International Law and Politics* 29, nos. 1–2 (1996–1997): 135–152.

Alford, William. *To Steal a Book Is an Elegant Offense: Intellectual Property Law in Chinese Civilization.* Stanford, Calif.: Stanford University Press, 1995.

An Qinghu. "The Development of Chinese Trademark Affairs" (Zhongguo Shangbiao Shiye De Fazhan). *Observation of Chinese Development* 1, no. 6 (2005): 38–40.

An Qinghu. "Well-Known Trademark and China's Well-Known Trademark System." *China Industry and Commerce News*, March 4, 2004.

Andrew, Jacobs. "Authors Accept Censors' Rules to Sell in China." *New York Times*, October 20, 2013, 1.

Beijing Well-Known Trademarks Evaluation Institute. "Research Report on the Most Valued Chinese Brands in 1995" (95 Zhongguo Zuiyong Jiazhi De Pinpai Yanjiu Baogao). *China Quality: 10000 Miles of Journey* (Zhongguo Zhiliang Wwanlixing) no. 5 (1996): 7–12.

Bian Dongzi. *Tong Ren Tang: The National Treasure* (Guobao Tongren Tang). Beijing: People's Press, 2010.

Bo Yibo. *Recollection of Some Major Historical Decisions and Events.* Vol. 1. Beijing: People's Press, 1997.

Bohua Zhou. "Speech on the National Conference of A.I.C. Directors" (Zai Quanguo Gongshang Xingzheng Guanli Juzhang Huiyi De Jianghua). *China Study of Administration of Industry and Commerce* (Zhongguo Gongshang Guanli Yanjiu) 7, no. 7 (2007): 4–13.

Boitsov, V. V. *Standardization in the USSR, 1925–1975.* New Delhi: Oxonian Press, 1980.

Cai Zhengping. "My Experience at the State Bureau of Measurement During the 1950s" (Wosuo Jingli De Caochuang Shiqide Guojia Jiliangju). *China Measurement* (Zhongguo Jiliang), 18, 8 (2013): 60–61.

Cao Di. *Key Statistical Data About Chinese Video-Sharing Websites 2009–2014.* Shengzhen: I-Research Consulting Group, 2014.

Cao Wanjun. "An Analysis of the Evolution of Trademarks in Ancient China" (Qianxi Zhongguo Gudai Shangbiao Biaoshi Yange). *China Collective Economy* 21, no. 20 (2009): 84–85.

Chen Hanbo. "Speech on the National Conference on Publishing Work." *Publishing Work* no. 6 (1980): 23–43.

Chen Jianxin et al., eds. *Contemporary Development of Chinese Science and Technology* (Dangdai Zhongguo Kexue Jishu Fazhan). Wuhan: Hubei Education Press, 1994.

Chen Tushou. *Does the Heaven Known Human Beings' Sicknesses: Narrative of Post 1949 Chinese Literature and Artistic Circle* (Renyoubing, Tianzhifou: 1949 Nian Yilai Zhongguowenyijie Jishi). Beijing: People's Literature Press, 2003.

Chen Xiang. "The Story of the Third Major Revision of Chinese Copyright Law" (Zhuzuoquanfa Disanci Xiugai Shimo). *China Reading* (Zhongguo Dushu Bao), March 6, 2013, 6.

Chen Xihan, Kong Linjun, and Liang Jiangang. "After the 'Poisonous Capsules'" (Zhuizong Dujiaonang). *Jiefang Daily* (Jiefang Ribao), April 17, 2012.

Chen Xitian. "When East Wind Breezes, Spring Comes—Comrade Deng Xiaoping's Visit to Shenzhen" (Dongfang Fenglai Manyanchun: Deng Xiaoping Tongzhi Zai Shenzhen Jishi). 1992. http://news.xinhuanet.com/newscenter/2003–08/19/content_1033952.htm.

Cheng Yongshun. "Recollection of the Birth of the First Intellectual Property Rights Tribunal in China." *China Intellectual Property Rights News*, March 5, 2003.

Cheung, Gordon C. K. *Intellectual Property Rights in China: Politics of Piracy, Trade, and Protection*. London: Routledge, 2009.

China Film Makers Association. *Chinese Film Industry Report 2014–2015* (Zhongguo Dianying Chanye Yanjiu Baogao 2014–2015). 2015. Available online at https://www.supplyfinder.com/downloads/pdfs/3003.pdf (accessed November 15, 2013).

China Internet Information Center. *2012 Statistical Report on the Development of Internet in China*. 2013. Available online at http://www.cnnic.cn/hlwfzyj/hlwxzbg/hlwtjbg/201301/P020130801546406723463.pdf (accessed November 2, 2014).

China Press and Publishing Studies Institute. "2013 Development Report of Chinese Press and Publishing Distribution Industry" (2013nian Zhongguo Chubanwu Faxing Chanye Fazhan Baogao). *China Press and Publication News*, February 17, 2014.

"Chronicle of Major Events of SIPO's Development." In *Historical Choice, Great Practice: Commemorative Volume of 30th Anniversary of SIPO's Establishment*, ed. Lipu Tian. Beijing: Intellectual Property Press, 2010.

Cortell, Andrew, and James Davis. "How Do International Institutions Matter? The Domestic Impact of International Norms Rules and Norms." *International Studies Quarterly* 40, no. 4 (1996): 451–478.

Cortell, Andrew, and James Davis. "Understanding the Domestic Impact of International Norms: A Research Agenda." *International Studies Review* 2, no. 1 (2000): 65–88.

China Press and Publishing Studies Institute. "2013 Development Report of Chinese Press and Publishing DistributionIndustry" (2013nian Zhongguo Chubanwu Faxing Chanye Fazhan Baogao). *China Press and Publication News*, February 17, 2014.

Chinese State Council. "Notice on Circulating the Report on the Decline of Quality of Industrial Products by the State Economic Commission" (Guowuyua Pizhuan Guojia Jingwei Guanyu Gongye Chanpin Zhiliang Xiajiang De Baogao Tongzhi). *State Council Gazette* (Guowuyuan Gongbao) 18, no. 7 (1985): 853–857.

Chinese State Council. "Notice on the Determination of S.A.I.C.'s Major Mandate, Internal Department, and Personnel Allocation" (Guanyu Guojia Gongshang Xingzheng Guanli Zongju Zhuyao Zhize, Neibu Jigoue Renyuan Bianzhi De Tongzhi). *Administration on Industry and Commerce* (Gongshang Guanli) 4, no. 4 (1994): 6–8.

Chinese State Council. "Notice on the Determination of S.A.I.C.'s Major Mandate, Internal Department, and Personnel Allocation (Guanyu Guojia Gongshang Xingzheng Guanli

Zongju Zhuyao Zhize, Neibu Jigoue Renyuan Bianzhi De Tongzhi)." *Gazette of Chinese State Council* 30, no. 5 (1998): 26–28.

Chinese State Council. "Notice on the Determination of S.A.I.C.'s Major Mandate, Internal Department, and Personnel Allocation" (Guanyu Guojia Gongshang Xingzheng Guanli Zongju Zhuyao Zhize, Neibu Jigou he Renyuan Bianzhi De Tongzhi). *Gazette of Chinese State Council* 40, no. 16 (2008). Available online at http://gkml.saic.gov.cn/auto3743/200809/t20080901_112597.html (accessed November 17, 2014).

Chinese State Council. "Notice on the Determination of S.A.I.C.'s Major Mandate, Internal Department, and Personnel Allocation" (Guanyu Guojia Gongshang Xingzheng Guanli Zongju Zhuyao Zhize, Neibu Jigoue Renyuan Bianzhi De Tongzhi). *Gazette of Chinese State Council* 33, no. 9 (2001). Available online at https://www.jetro.go.jp/ext_images/world/asia/cn/ip/law/pdf/origin/20070810349005 94.pdf (accessed November 17, 2014).

Chinese State Council. "Opinion on the Development of Mixed Ownership Economy" (Guowuyuan Guanyu Fazhan Hunhe Suoyouzhi Jingji de Yijian). *Chinese State Council Gazette* 29 (2015): 13–18.

Curtis, Cook. *Patents, Profits and Power: How Intellectual Property Rules the Global Economy.* London; Sterling, Va.: Kogan Page Press, 2002.

Deng Hongguang and Yuan Zhou. "Future Development of Chinese Trademark Law" (Shangbiaofa De Weilai Fazhan). *Journal of South China Normal University: Social Science Edition* (Huanan Shifan Daxue Xuebao: Shehui Kexue Ban) no. 4 (2011): 114–119.

Dianying Dazhong. "Moves of the Movie Market" (Dianying Shichang Dongtai). *Popular Film* (Dazhong Dianying) no. 7 (2003): 4.

Dimitrov, Martin K. *Piracy and the State: The Politics of Intellectual Property Rights in China.* New York: Cambridge University Press, 2009.

Ding Chenxin. "Private Capital Plays a Major Role in Chinese Movie Industry" (Minying Ziben Yi Chengwei Yinshiye Zhujiao). *China News Week* (Zhongguo Xinwen Zhoukan) no. 41 (2012): 76–78.

Ding Yaping. *History of Contemporary Chinese Movies.* Vol. 2. Beijing: Chinese Film Press, 2011.

Dong Baolin. "Chinese Trademark in the Past Ten Years." In *Chinese Intellectual Property Yearbook*, ed. Chinese Intellectual Property Office, 46–48. Beijing: Intellectual Property Press, 2000.

Duan Ruichun. "Cooperation, Conflict, and Interests Game: A Look Back at the China-U.S. IPR Negotiations." In *Intellectual Property Rights and the 30th Anniversary of Opening and Reform*, ed. China State Intellectual Property Office. Beijing: Intellectual Property Rights Press, 2008.

Economic Research Institute of State Planning Commission. "Important Economic Events in P.R.C. History" (Zhonghua Renmin Gongheguo Jingji Dashiji). *Study of Planned Economy* (Jihua Jingji Yanjiu) 26 (1983): 82.

European Union Customs House. *Report of E.U. Customs Enforcement on Intellectual Property Rights Results at the E.U. Border in 2013.* 2014. Full text available online at https://ec.europa.eu/taxation_customs/sites/taxation/files/resources/documents/customs/customs_controls/counterfeit_piracy/statistics/2014_ipr_statistics_en.pdf (accessed November 19, 2014).

Fan Lubin. "Notes on the 30 Years of Development of Chinese Advertisement Industry" (Zhongguo Guanggaoye 30 Nian Zhaji). *Chinese Advertisement* (Zhongguo Guanggao) 16, no. 5 (2010): 115–121.

Fan Yang. *Faked in China: National Branding, Counterfeit Culture, and Globalization*. Bloomington: Indiana University Press, 2016.

Fang Min. "Dirty Story Behind the Illegal V.C.D. Production Line" (Feifa Guangpan Shngchan: Jiekai Heimu). *Enterprise Marketing* (Qiye Xiaoshou) no. 7 (1997): 26–30.

Fang Zhuofen and Wu Fang. *In Memory of Xu Dixin*. Shenzhen: Haitian Press, 2002.

Feigenbaum, A. V. *Total Quality Control*. New York: McGraw-Hill, 1991.

Feng, Peter. *Intellectual Property Right in China*. Hong Kong: Sweet and Maxwell Asia, 1997.

Fu Caiwu and Danna Song. "Origin and Evolution of Chinese Cultural System Reform" (Woguo Wenhua Tizhi De Yuanqi, Yanjin, He Gaige Duice). *Journal of Jianghan University* 21, no. 2 (2004): 83–89.

Gao Lulin. "Ten Years of Achievements and Experience: Celebrating the First Decade of Chinese Patent Law" (Zhongguo Zhuanlifa Shishi Shinianlai Qude De Xianzhu Chengjiu Yu Jiben Jingyan). *Chinese Patents and Trademarks* (Zhongguo Zhuanli Yu Shangbiao) no. 2 (1995): 3–11.

Gao Quan. "Joint Seminar Held in Wuhan to Discuss Copyright Law Revision." *Publishing Reference Materials* (Chuban Caokao), August 8, 1996, 6.

Gerring, John. "What Is a Case Study and What Is It Good For?" *American Political Science Review* 98, no. 2 (2004): 341–354.

Gu Tu. "Closing Down Dancing Ballrooms and Closing Cultural Life" (Fengbi Wuting Yu Fengbi Wenhua). *People's Daily*, January 25, 1988, 8.

Guo Fengbing. "The Great Discussion on Home Grown Brands: Before and After" (Zizhu Pinpai Dataolun De Qianqian Houhou). *China Quality and Brands* (Zhongguo Zhiliang Yu Pinpai) no. 5 (2004): 17–21.

Guo Ruoxu. "My Opinions on Promoting Quality Work" (Tuijin Zhilaing Gonguo De Qianjian). *China Brand and Anti-Counterfeiting* (Zhongguo Pingpai Yu Fangwei) 9, no. 11 (2008): 34–36.

Guo Ruoxu. "The Process of Drafting Guideline for Quality Rejuvenation (1996–2010)" (Zhiliang Zhenxing Gangyao Chutai Shimo). *China Brand and Anti-Counterfeiting* (Zhongguo Pingpai Yu Fangwei) 9, no. 8 (2008): 14–20.

Guoliang Zhao and Guo Yuanxi. "On the Relationship Between 'Horizontal Authority' and 'Vertical Authority' in the Management of Chinese Industry" (Lun Woguo Gongye Guanli Zhong De Tiaokuai Guanxi). *Journal of Sichuan University* no. 3 (1984): 11–16.

Han Yujun. "The Development of Chinese Service Industry: An International Comparison." *Economic Review* no. 4 (2011): 98–100.

Hao Jing. "Chinese Cultural Industries in the Past 60 Years" (Wenhua Chanye 60 Nian: Huiwang Jueqi Zhilu). *Xinhua News Agency*, September 28, 2009.

"How Should We Treat Royalty?" (Zenyang Kandai Gaofei). *People's Daily*, October 5, 1958, 2.

Hu Bo. "Anti-Trust Operation with Chinese Characteristics Originate from a Set of Market Principles with Chinese Characteristics" (Zhongguoshi Fanlongduan Yuanyu Shichang Guizhi De Zhonguohua). *Chinese Auto* 20, no. 9 (2014): 12–14.

Hu Yuzhi. "On People's Publishing Work and Its Future Orientation" (Lun Renmin De Chuban Shiye Jiqi Fazhan Fangxiang). *People's Daily*, September 28, 1950.

Huang Kunyi. "The Implementation of Patent Law Will Push Forward China's Science and Technology Reform." *Chinese Science and Technology Forum*, March (1986): 34–36.

Huang Qinnan. "Brief Analysis of the Protection of Trademark Rights" (Luelun Dui Shangbiao Zhuanyongquan De Baohu). *Journal of Beijing College of Politics and Law* no. 3 (1981): 58–61.

Huang Zheng and Guo Chenyang. "Chinese Private Bookstores Face Shuffling" (Minying Shudian Mianlian Xipai). *China Business and Trade* 20, no. 7 (2012): 16–17.

Hudon, Edward. "Literary Piracy, Charles Dickens and the American Copyright Law." *American Bar Association Journal* 50, no. 12 (1964): 1157–1160.

Hui Zhi. "The Craziness Behind the Swill-Cooked Edible Oil" (Digouyou Beihou De Fengkuang). *Prosecutional Review* 19, no. 12 (2013): 42–44.

Huibao Wen. "History of Tong Ren Tang." *Weihui Daily*, January 19, 2015.

Ji A. "The Influence of Public Opinion Rapidly Increases in China's Legislation Process" (Minyi Lifa Wendu Biaosheng). November 18, 2005. Available online at http://www.xinhuanet.com/report/media/mzfz.htm (accessed November 7, 2012).

Jia Zhangke. "Jiang Zhangke et al.'s Letter to the MORFT" (Jiazhangke Deng Shangshu Dianyingju). *Remote Corner of the Earth* (Tianya) (January 2004): 189–190.

Jiang Dunxiong and Yingjiang Zeng. "There Are Too Few Bookstores in the Cities: What Should We Do?" *People's Daily*, January 4, 1981.

Jiang Jianguo. "Grasp the Main Spirit of Comrade Xi Jinping's Speech, Practise Socialist Core Values" (Shenke Bawo Xi Jinping Tongzhi Jianghua Jingsheng, Jianxing Shehui Zhuyi Hexin Jiazhiguan). *China Press and Publication News*, April 21, 2014.

Jiang Ying. "Ten Years of China's Patent Review System" (Zhongguo Zhuanli Shencha Zhidu Jianli De Shinian). *Intellectual Property Rights* (Zhishi Chanquan) no. 2 (1995): 23–30.

Juran, Joseph. *Quality Control Handbook*. New York: McGraw-Hill, 1962.

Kenez, Peter. *The Birth of the Propaganda State: Soviet Methods of Mass Mobilization, 1917–1929*. Cambridge: Cambridge University Press, 1985.

Kent, Ann. *Beyond Compliance: China, International Organizations, and Global Security*. Stanford, Calif.: Stanford University Press, 2007.

Khoon Tan Loke. *Pirates in the Middle Kingdom: The Art of Trademark War*. Hong Kong: Sweet & Maxwell Asia, 2004.

Khoon Tan Loke and Clifford Borg-Marks. *Trademark Law in the People's Republic of China*. Hong Kong: Oxford University Press, 1998.

Kong Xiangjun. "Law, Policy, and Politics in IPR Legal Trial." *People's Adjudication* no. 13 (2008): 24–27.

Landreth, Jonathan. "Xi Jinping's Film Deals: Search for a Walt Disney of China?" *Christian Science Monitor*, February 18, 2012.

Li Heping. "From 'Ticket Economy' to 'Credit Card Life'" (Cong Piaozheng Jingji Dao Shuaka Shenghuo). *Beijing Archives* (Beijing Dang'an) 28, no. 3 (2012): 11–13.

Li Jizhong. "Improve Trademark Work to Adapt to the Request of Economic Reform" (Shiying Gaige Xuyao Wanshan Shangbiao Gongzuo Tixi). *Industrial Property Rights* (Gongye Chanquan) 2, no. 1 (1989): 80–84.

Li Jizhong. "Speech on the National Trademark Work Conference" (Zai Quanguo Shangbiao Gongzuo Huiyi Shang De Jianghua). *Industrial Property Rights* (Gongye Chanquan) no. 2 (1990): 4–13.

Li Mingde. *Special 301 and China-US IPR Dispute* (Tebie 301 Tiaokuan Yu Zhongmei Zhishi Chanquan Zhengduan). Beijing: Social Science Publishers, 2000.

Li Mingshan. *Modern History of Chinese Copyright* (Zhongguo Jindai Banquan Shi). Zhengzhou: Henan University Press, 2003.

Li Peng. "Counterfeit Double Black Pencils: The Curse for Chinese Exam Takers" (Jiaqianbi Fanlan: Kaofen Zhihuo). *Beijing Science and Technology Daily* (Beijing Kejibao), March 30, 2009.

Li Shunde. "Concrete Problems Confronting Chinese Patent Regime" (Zhongguo Zhuanli Zhidu Mianlin De Xianshi Wenti). *Intellectual Property Rights* (Zhishi Chanquan) no. 4 (2015): 6–13.

Li Wei, ed. *Report on Independent Innovation of Central State-Owned Enterprises.* Beijing: China Economic Publishing House, 2012.

Li Wentao. "Some Thoughts on Deepening Reform and Transforming the A.I.C.'s Functions" (Dui Dangqian Gongshang Bumen Shenhua Gaige He Zhuanhua Zhineng De Sikao). *China Study of Administration of Industry and Commerce* (Zhongguo Gongshang Guanli Yanjiu) 11, no. 7 (2014): 61–62.

Li Yuanchao. "Three Priorities on Our Policy Agenda: What Can We Do to Develop Our Cultural Industry" (Zuohao Sanjianshi: Women Nengwei Fazhan Wenhua Chanye Zuoshengme). *Chinese Reform* (Zhongguo Gaige) no. 5 (2000): 3–5.

Liao Wang Journal Reporting Team. "A Comprehensive Discussion on Managing the Cultural Market" (Wenhua Shichang Lilun Yanjiu Zongshu). *Liao Wang Journal* (Liaowang Zhoukan) 38 (1988): 21–23.

Lieberthal, Kenneth. *Managing the China Challenge: How to Achieve Corporate Success in the People's Republic.* Washington D.C.: Brookings Institution Press, 2011.

Linlin Fang. "Duan Ruichun on IPR Protection." *Science and Technology Daily*, June 10, 2007, 5.

Liu Anwei. "Three Milestones of Fair Trade and Market Competition Legislation in China: Interview with Ning Wanglu, Head of A.I.C. Anti-Trust and Fair Trade Division" (Gongping Jiaoyi Zhifa De Sange Lichengbei: Fang Guojia Gongshang Zongju Gongping Zhifa He Fanlong Duan Zhifasi Sizhang Ning Wanglu). *Administration on Industry and Commerce* (Gongshang Guanli) no. 19 (2008): 25–27.

Liu Gao. "China's Accession to the International Copyright Conventions: Before and After" (Woguo Jiaru Guoji Banquan Gongyue De Qianqian Houhou). In *China Copyright Yearbook*, 114–19. Beijing: China National People's Congress Press, 2009.

Liu Gao. "China's Accession to the International Copyright Conventions: Before and After" (Zhongguo Jiaru Guoji Banquan Gongyue De Qianqian Houhou). In *Two Decades of Chinese Intellectual Property Rights* (Zhongguo Zhishi Chanquan Ershi Nian), ed. Chuntian Liu, 54–69. Beijing: Patent Literature Press, 1999.

Liu Hanwen and Linming Zhang. "Analysis Report of China Film Industry in 2012" (2012 Nian Zhngguo Dianying Chanye Baogao). *Contemporary Cinema* (Dangdai Dianying) 29, no. 3 (2013): 19–26.

Liu Jiyang. "Working Report of Chinese Industrial Property Studies Association" (Zhongguo Gongye Chanquan Yanjiuhui Gongzuo Baogao). *Industrial Property Rights* (Gongye Chanquan) no. S1 (1989): 129–131.

Liu Ming. "In Memory of Liu Yuanzhang, My Dear Father" (Zhuiyi Wode Fuqin Liu Yuanzhang). *China Quality* (Zhongguo Zhiliang) 20, no. 7 (2014): 81–85.

Liu Minxue. "Speech on the Third Conference of the All-China Industry and Commerce Society" (Zai Disanci Quanguo Gongshang Xuehui Huiyishang De Jianghua). *China*

Study of Administration of Industry and Commerce (Zhongguo Gongshang Guanli Yanjiu) 1, no. 2 (1992): 59–61.

Liu Peizhi. "The Vibrant Development of Chinese Trademark Affairs During the Reform and Opening Era" (Zai Gaige Kaifang Zhong Pengbo Fazhan De Shangbiao Shiye). In *Chinese Intellectual Property Work in the Past Two Decades*, ed. Chuntian Liu, 123–145. Beijing: Patent Documentation Press, 1998.

Liu Ren. "Chinese Trademark Application and Registration Ranked as the World's No. 1 for Six Consecutive Years" (Zhongguo Shangbiao Zhuce Shenqing Liang Lianxu Liunian Ju Shijie Diyi). *Chinese Intellectual Property News* (Zhongguo Zhishi Chanquan Bao), December 5, 2008.

Liu Yuanzhang. *A Record of Gratitude: My Career in Chinese Quality Work* (Gan'enlu: Wode Zhiliang Shengya). Beijing: Science Press, 2011.

Liu Zhongde. "The Emphasis of Cultural Reform in 1994 Will Be Laid on the Management of Performing Arts Troupes" (Jinnian Wenhua Tizhi Gaige Jiangzuo Zhongda Gaige,Yishu Biaoyan Tuanti Shi Gaige De Zhongzhong Zhizhong). *China Theatre* no. 2 (1994): 19.

Liu Zhongde. "Quicken the Step of Reform, Make Our Movie Industry Prosper" (Jiakuai Gaige Bufa, Fanrong Dianying Shiye). *Chinese Movie* no. 2 (1993): 4–6.

Lu Dingyi. "Speech on the Closing Ceremony of the National Publishing Conference" (Lu Dingyi Zai Quanguo Chuban Gongzuo Huiyi Bimushi Shang De Jianghua). *People's Daily*, October 21, 1949, 1.

Luginbuefl, Stefen, and Peter Ganea, eds. *Patent Law in Greater China*. Cheltenham, UK: Northampton, 2014.

Luo Gan. *A Significant Strategic Move* (Zhongda De Zhanlue Juece). Beijing: Chinese Politics and Law University Press, 1992.

Luo Jianhua. "Shanghai SOE's Lost Nearly 90 Percent of IPR Disputes." *Shanghai Morning News*, April 27, 2013.

Luo Ruiming. "The Direction of 90 Million Poisonous Capsules Cannot Afford to Remain Unknown" (9000 Wanli Dujiaonang Quxiang Buneng Chengmi). *China Business News* (Zhongguo Shangbao), September 12, 2014.

Lynch, Daniel. *After the Propaganda State: Media, Politics, and "Thought Work" in Reformed China*. Stanford, Calif.: Stanford University Press, 1999.

Ma Weiye. "A New Chapter of Chinese Patent Protection." In *Historical Decision, Great Choice: Commemorative Volume of the 30th Anniversary of the Establishment of SIPO*, ed. Lipu Tian, 57–67. Beijing: Intellectual Property Press, 2010.

May, Christopher, and Susan Sell. *Intellectual Property Rights: A Critical History*. Boulder, Colo.: Lynne Rienner, 2006.

McDowell, Eric. "Lack of Copyright Disturbs US Authors." *New York Times*, January 10, 1984.

Mertha, Andrew. "Pirates, Politics, and Trade Policy: Structuring the Negotiations and Enforcing the Outcomes of the Sino-US Intellectual Property Dialogue, 1991–1999." Ph.D. diss., University of Michigan, 2001.

Mertha, Andrew. *The Politics of Piracy: Intellectual Property in Contemporary China*. Ithaca, N.Y.: Cornell University Press, 2005.

Na Lei and Liao Hui. "A Study of FDI in China During the Past Three Decades: Influence and Development" (Gaige Kaifang 30nian Woguo Yingjing Waizi De Yinxiang Yu Fazhan Yanjiu). *Modern Business, Trade, and Industry* (Xiandai Gongmao Shangye) nos. 134–135 (2008).

Netanel, Neil W. "Copyright and a Democratic Civil Society." *Yale Law Journal* 106 (1996): 283–387.

Ni Zhifu. "Report to the Standing Committee of National People's Congress on the Implementation of Anti Unfair Competition Law, Consumers Rights Law, Product Quality Law, and the Decision on Punishing the Production and Retailing of Counterfeit Goods" (Quanguo Renda Changweihui Guanyu Zhixing Sanfa Yijueding Qingkuang De Jiancha Baogao). *Gazette of Chinese National People's Congress* no. 8 (1994): 63–71.

"Notice by the State Council on the Establishment of Leading Group on Intellectual Property Rights Strategy" (Guowuyuan Bangongting Guanyu Chengli Guojia Zhishi Chanquan Zhanlue Zhiding Gongzuo Lingdao Xiaozu De Tongzhi). *Gazette of the State Council of the People's Republic of China* 8 (2005): 14.

Ou Wanxiong. "Protect Foreign Registered Trademarks in China According to Chinese Law: Some Notes by a Trademark Examiner" (Yifa Baohu Waiguo Zai Woguo De Zhuce Shangbiao: Yiwei Shangbiao Shenchayuan De Zhaji). *Law Science Magazine* 11, no. 4 (1991): 38.

Ou Wanxiong. "A Recollection by a Veteran Trademark Examiner." In *Intellectual Property Rights and the 30th Anniversary of Opening and Reform*, ed. Editorial Board, 365–374. Beijing: Intellectual Property Rights Press, 2008.

"Patent: The Pain for Chinese Companies." *China Invention and Patent* no. 4 (2012): 42–43.

Pfanner, Eric. "King of PCs, Lenovo Sets Smartphone Ambitions." *New York Times*, December 27, 2013.

"Please Prove with Concrete Facts That Chinese Anti-Trust Law Is Not Selectively Enforced" (Yong Shiji Xingdong Zhengming Zhongguo Fanlongduan Bushi Neiwai Youbie). *IT Times Weekly* 13, no. 17 (2014): 6.

Policy Research Department of Chinese Supreme People's Court. "The Historical Repositioning of Mediation Work by People's Court." *People's Adjudication* no. 17 (2009): 65–69.

Qixue Wei. "Ren Jianxin: Trailblazer of the Cause of Chinese Intellectual Property Rights" (Ren Jianxin: Woguo Zhishi Chanquan Shiye De Kaituozhe). *Chinese Trademark* (Zhonghua Shangbiao) 19, no. 2 (2014): 33–37.

Qu Chunhai. "The Evaluation of Some Historical Facts About the Experimental Regulations on Chinese and Foreign Trademark Registrations During the Late Qing Dynasty" (Qingmo Guanyu Zhongwai Shangbiao Zhuce Shiban Zhangcheng Jiaoshe Shishi Kaoping). *Historical Records* (Lishi Dang'an) 31, no. 4 (2012). Available online at http://www.cssn.cn/ddzg/ddzg_ldjs/ddzg_zz/201310/t20131030_786173.shtml (accessed May 21, 2016).

Rao Shuguang. *History of the Development of Movie Market in China* (Zhongguo Dianying Shichang Fazhanshi). Beijing: China Movie Press, 2009.

Reichman, Jerome. "Compliance with the TRIPS Agreement: A Scholarly Debate." *Vanderbilt Journal of Transnational Law* 29, no. 3 (1996): 363–390.

Ren Zhonglin. "Explanation of the PRC Trademark Law (Draft): Address Before the Standing Committee of the National People's Congress." August 19, 1982. Available online at http://www.legalinfo.gov.cn/zt/2005–01/19/content_183660.htm (accessed April 13, 2012).

Richards, Donald G. *Intellectual Property Rights and Global Capitalism: The Political Economy of the Trips Agreement.* Armonk, N.Y.: M. E. Sharpe, 2004.

Ringer, Barbara. "The Role of the United States in International Copyright: Past, Present, and Future." *Georgetown Law Journal* 56, no. 6 (1968): 1050–1079.

Risse, Thomas, Stephen Ropp, and Kathryn Sikkink, eds. *The Power of Human Rights: International Norms and Domestic Change*. Cambridge: Cambridge University Press, 1999.

Rosen, Stanley. "The Wolf at the Door: Hollywood and the Film Market in China." In *Southern California and the World*, ed. Eric J. Heikkila and Rafael Pizarro, 49–77. Westport, Conn.: Praeger, 2002.

Rostow, Walt. *The Economics of Take-Off into Sustained Growth*. New York: St. Martin's, 1964.

Ruan, Victoria. "Americans Echo Gripes on China's Business Climate." *South China Morning Post*, September 3, 2014, 3.

Rueschemeyer, Dietrich. "Can One or a Few Cases Yield Theoretical Gains?" In *Comparative Historical Analysis in the Social Sciences*, ed. James Mahoney and Dietrich Rueschemeyer. Cambridge: Cambridge University Press, 2003.

Ryan, Michael P. *Knowledge Diplomacy: Global Competition and the Politics of Intellectual Property*. Washington, D.C.: Brookings Institution Press, 1998.

Ryan, Michael P. *Playing by the Rules: American Trade Power and Diplomacy in the Pacific*. Washington, D.C.: Georgetown University Press, 1995.

Sadleir, Michael, and Frederick Page, eds. *An Autobiography of Anthony Trollope*. New York: Oxford University Press, 1980.

Selection of Historical Inscriptions on Stone Tablet in Shanghai (Shanghai Lishi Beike Ziliao Xuanji). Shanghai: Shanghai People's Press, 1980.

Shadlen, Kenneth, Andrew Schrank, and Marcus Kurtz. "The Political Economy of Intellectual Property Protection: The Case of Software." *International Studies Quarterly* 49 (2005): 45–71.

Shen Rengan. "Some Recollections About the Drafting of Chinese Copyright Law" (Youguan Zhongguo Zhuzuoquanfa Zhiding De Huigu). In *Chinese IPR System in the Past Two Decades* (Zhongguo Zhishi Chanquan Ershinian), ed. Chuntian Liu, 27–53. Beijing: Patent Documentation Press, 1998.

Shen Rengan. "The Unforgettable Past: Comrade Hu Yaobang and Chinese Copyright Work" (Buneng Wangque De Guanhuai: Ji Hu Yaobang Tongzhi Dui Banquan Gongzuo De Guanhuai). *China Publishing Journal* no. 12 (2005): 16.

Shi Yigong and Yi Rao. "China's Research Culture." *Science* 329, no. 5996 (September 2010): 1128.

Shuo Qin. "Declaration of China's Intangible Assets" (Zhongguo Wuxing Zichan De Xuanyan). *Window of South Wind* (Nanfengchuang) no. 9 (1993): 1.

Sidel, Mark. "Copyright, Trademark and Patent Law in the People's Republic of China." *Texas International Law Journal* 21 (1985): 251–289.

Simmons, Beth. *Mobilizing for Human Rights: International Law in Domestic Politics*. Cambridge: Cambridge University Press, 2009.

Song Jian. "Science and Technology Reform and China's Economic Modernization." *Today's China* 33, no. 1 (1985): 13–15.

Song Muwen. "The Hard Earned Progress: Some Reflections on the Revision of Copyright Law" (Laizhi Buyi De Zhongyao Jinzhan). *Study of Press and Publication* no. 12 (2001): 5–6.

Song Muwen. "Promote the Reform and Development of Chinese Publishing Industry in the Spirit of the 14th CCP National Congress" (Anzhao Shisida Jingsheng Jiakuai Chubanye De Gaige Yu Fazhan). In *My Thirty Years in Chinese Publishing Cause* (Qinli Chuban Sanshinian), ed. Song Muwen, 377–408. Beijing: Commercial Press, 1992.

Song Muwen. *My Three Decades' Experience with Chinese Publication Cause* (Qinli Chuban Sanshinian). Beijing: Commercial Press, 2007.

State Council Development Studies Center. "Our Country's Patent Regime Should Make Timely Adjustment" (Woguo Zhuanli Zhidu Xuyao Jishi Tiaozheng). *China Economy Times* (Zhongguo Jingji Shibao), September 5, 2013, 5.

"State Council's Guideline Opinion on Revitalizing the Movie Industry" (Guowuyuan Guanyu Fanrong Dianying Chanye De Zhidao Yijian). *China Film News* (Zhongguo Dianying Bao), February 4, 2010, 1.

State Intellectual Property Office. "Explanation About the Revision of Chinese Patent Law" (Guanyu Zhonghua Renmin Gonghe Guo Zhuanli Fa Xiugai Cao'an De Shuoming). 2015. http://www.sipo.gov.cn/tz/gz/201504/t20150401_1095939.html.

State-Owned Assets Supervision and Administration Commission. "SASAC Leadership Studied the Important Spirits of Comrade Xi Jinping's Important Speeches on SOE Reform" (Guoziwei Dangwei Xuexi Xi Jinping Tongzhi Guanyu Guoqi Gaige Zhongyao Jianghua Jingsheng). *Bulletin of Propaganda Department of SASAC* 12, no. 1 (2015): 21.

State QTSB Quality Supervision Division. "Promote Product Supervision Work to a New Level According to the Product Quality Law" (Yifa Tuidong Chanpin Zhiliang Jiandu Gongzuo Yueshang Xin Taijie). *China Quality News*, September 23, 2013.

Sun Hui, Hanwen Liu, and Jiawei Song. "Analysis Report of China Film Industry in 2013" (2013nian Zhongguo Dianying Chanye Fenxi Baogao). *Contemporary Cinema* (Dangdai Dianying) 29, no. 3 (2014): 21–28.

Taihong, Lu, Xie Biao, Luo Shuling, and Liang Zhihong. "The Progress and Prospect of Chinese Home Grown Brands" (Woguo Zizhu Pinpai De Jinbu Yu Zhanwang). *Journal of Dr. Sun Yat-sen University* (Zhongshan Daxue Xuebao) 34, no. 3 (1996): 1–10.

Tao Xinliang. "Analysis of the Current Situation of the Recognition and Protection of Well-Known Trademarks in China and Policy Recommendations." In *Several Issues in the Third Amendment of Chinese Trademark Law*, ed. Chinese Academy of Social Sciences IPR Center, 183–205. Beijing: Intellectual Property Rights Press, 2009.

Tian Lipu, ed. *Historical Choice, Great Practice: Commemorative Volume of 30th Anniversary of SIPO's Establishment*. Beijing: Intellectual Property Press, 2010.

Wan Jihong and Richard Kraus. "Hollywood and China as Adversaries and Allies Hollywood and China as Adversaries and Allies." *Pacific Affairs* 75, no. 3 (2002): 419–434.

Wang Jianglian. "Legal Constraint on Chinese Movie Industry: The Perspective of Movie Rating System." *Movie Script* no. 21 (2008): 9–11.

Wang Jun. "The Proposed Revision of Copyright Law Aroused Strong Doubts Among Chinese Musicians" (Zhuzuoquanfa Xiugai Cao'an Yinfa Yinyuejie Qianglie Zhiyi). *Shenzhen Special Economic Zone Daily* (Shenzhen Tequ Bao), April 16, 2012, B05.

Wang Liming. "Research on the First Intellectual Property Negotiation Between China and Foreign Countries in Late Qing Dynasty" (Wanqing Zhongwai Shouci Zhishi Chanquan Tanpan Yanjiu). Ph.D. diss., Soochow University, 2008.

Wang Ruiju. "Two Issues That I Encountered During the Quality Supervision Work" (Wozai Zhiliang Jiandu Gongzuo Zhong Yudao De Liangge Wenti). *Science Forum* (Keji Luntan) 25, no. 4 (2010): 102–103.

Wang Shengjun. "Report by the People's Supreme Court to the National People's Congress on the Judicial Protection of IPR." *Gazette of Chinese National People's Congress* no. 1 (2013): 94–98.

Wang Xinrong. "I Should Be in Charge of My Own Copyright" (Wode Zhuzuoquan Wo Zuozhu). *China Art News* (Zhongguo Yishu Bao), April 13, 2012, 1.

Wang Zhengfa. "The People Who Opened the Gate of Chinese Patent System." *China Invention and Patent* no. 3 (2009): 8–15.

Wang Zhongfu. "Strengthen Law Enforcement, Safeguard Market Order: Speech on the National Conference of A.I.C. Directors" (Jiaqiang Zhifa Lidu, Weihu Shichang Zhixu: Zai Quanguo Gongshang Juzhang Huiyi Shang De Jianghua). *China Study of Administration of Industry and Commerce* (Zhongguo Gongshang Guanli Yanjiu) 3, no. 2 (1995): 3–6.

Webb, Alysha. "GM Probes Alleged Case of Car Theft; Local Maker Chery Says Its QQ Is Not Chevrolet Spark." *Automotive News*, July 14, 2003, 4.

Wei Wei. "The Biggest Lawsuit Concerning Online Piracy Was Born" (Wangluo Shipin Zuida Suopei an Dansheng). *Beijing Business Daily* (Beijing Shangbao), November 14, 2013.

Wu Chuanzheng. "Coca-Cola's 25 Years in China" (Kekou Kele Zai Zhongguo de 25nian). *Nanfang Weekend* (Nanfang Zhoumo), November 18, 2004.

Wu Haimin. *The Contest Between Great Powers* (Daguo De Jiaoliang). Wuhan: Changjiang Wenyi Press, 2009.

Wu Haimin. "Investigation Report of Chinese Underground Cultural Market" (Zhongguo Wenhua Shichang Anfang Baogao). *Beijing Literature* (Beijing Wenxue) no. 1 (1996): 21–32.

Wu Haimin. *The Magic Cube of Book License: Incremental Suicide of Chinese Publishing Houses* (Shuhao Mofang: Chuban Yezhe De Manxing Zisha). Beijing: Huayi Press, 1995.

Wu Handong and Chaozheng Wang. "Revision of Trademark Law Under the Greater Scenario of Chinese Economic Development" (Zhongguo Jingji Fazhan Daju Zhongde Shaobiaofa Xiugai). *Chinese Studies of Administration for Industry and Commerce* (Zhongguo Gongshang Guanli Yanjiu) no. 2 (2013): 23–25.

Wu Heng. *Five Decades on the Front of Science and Technology* (Keji Zhanxian Wushi Nian). Beijing: Science and Technology Documentation Press, 1992.

Wu Hua and Zheng Wenjie. "Jianlibao De Fazhanzhilu" (Jianlibao's Road of Development). *People's Daily*, August 28, 1987, 3.

Wu Hui. "Leading Case on IPR Between China and the US Ended Up in Reconciliation." *China Intellectual Property News*, July 31, 2004.

Wu Jinna. "Do Not Turn Patent Work into a New 'Face Project.'" *Science and Technology News*, March 7, 2013, 3.

Wu Lisi. "Behind the Third Revision of Chinese Copyright Law" (Zhuzuoquanfa Xiugai Muhou). *Xinmin Journal* no. 6 (2012): 62–64.

Wu-Ohlson, Mark. "A Commentary on China's New Patent and Trademark Law." *Northwestern Journal of Law and Business* 6 (1984): 86–147.

Wuhan University Institute of Quality Supervision. *2012 Observation Report on Quality Development in China* (2012nian Zhongguo Zhiliang Guance Baogao). Beijing: China Standard Press, 2013.

Xiang Bing. "Pull Through Troublesome Situation, Re-Create the Glory: The First Anniversary of China's Movie Distribution Reform." *People's Daily*, May 5, 1994.

Xie Peng. "State Q.T.S.B. Publishes the Result of National Quality Supervision and Spot-Check in 2013" (Zhijian Zongju Fabu 2013 Nian Chanpin Zhiliang Guojia Jiandu Choucha Qingkuang). *China Quality News*, March 3, 2014.

Xinhua News Agency. "GM and Chery Reached Reconciliation over Their IPR Dispute." November 19, 2005. Available online at http://news.sina.com.cn/o/2005–11–21/10537497253s.shtml (accessed May 1, 2012).

Xinhua News Agency. "Symposium on Deng Xiaoping's Thoughts on Literature and Artistic Work." *People's Daily*, December 23, 1989, 1.

Xu Dixin. "The United Front Work with the Private Entrepreneurs Under the Leadership of Comrade Zhou Enlai." In *Endless Remembrance: Zhou Enlai, the People's Leader*, ed. Central Documentation Research Office. Beijing: People's Press, 1988.

Xu Jialu. "The Importance of Revising Copyright Law" (Xiugai Zhuzuoquan Fa Yiyi Zhongda). *Democracy* (Minzhu) no. 8 (1998): 5–6.

Yang Ming. "Institutions and Texts: A Historical Examination of Copyright Law of Qing Dynasty" (Zhidu Yu Wenben: Daqing Zhuzuo Quanlu De Lishi Shengshi). *Journal of Huazhong University of Science and Technology* (Huazhong Keji Daxue Xuebao) no. 5 (2013): 58–66.

Yang Yang. "Making Profits Through Online Piracy Is No Longer Tolerated" (Daoban Zhifu Buzai Beiyunxu). *Economic Observation News*, May 26, 2014.

Ye Haiying. "Three Footprints in Wang Kuang's Life" (Wang Kuang Rensheng Zhong De Sange Jiaoying). *Wind of South Guangdong Sea* 10, no. 6 (2007): 46–49.

Ye Xiao. "How Zhou Enlai Saved Chinese Aviation Industry During the Cultural Revolution" (Wenge Zhong Zhou Enlai Zhenjiu Zhongguo Hangkong Gongye Jishi). *History of the Chinese Communist Party* (Dangshi) 12, no. 1 (2006): 11–15.

Yin Xiao. "Chinese Movies in 2013: Domestic Challenges and External Threats" (2013nian Zhongguo Dianying De Neiyou Waihuan). *Literature and Artistic News*, January 18, 2014.

Yongfeng Gao. "Running the Tide of Hearts" (Xinchao Zhulang). *China Quality: 10000 Miles of Journey* (Zhongguo Zhiliang Wanlixing) 1, no. 1 (1995): 6–10.

Yongqin Wang. "How Zhou Enlai Resisted the Ultra Leftist Trend During the Cultural Revolution" (Zhou Enlai Zai Wengezhong Shi Zenyang Pi Jizuo De). *Science of Leadership* (Lingdao Kexue) 26, no. 12 (2001): 22–23.

Yu, Peter. "The Copyright Divide." *Cardozo Law Review* 25, no. 1 (2003): 331–445.

Yu, Peter K. "From Pirates to Partners: Protecting Intellectual Property in China in the Twenty-First Century." *American University Law Review* 50 (2000): 131–243.

Yu, Peter. "The Global Intellectual Property Order and Its Undetermined Future." *WIPO Journal* 1, no. 1 (2009): 10–15.

Yu, Peter. "Rise and Decline of the Intellectual Property Powers." *Campbell Law Review* 34, no. 3 (2012): 525–580.

Yu, Peter. "The U.S.-China Dispute over TRIPS Enforcement." 2010. http://www.law.drake.edu/academics/ip/docs/ipResearch-op5.pdf

Yu Qiuyu. "Yu Qiuyu on Piracy" (Yu Qiuyu Shuo Daoban). *Shandong Library Journal* no. 1 (1999): 68–70.

Yu Youxian, ed. *China's Publishing Industry in 50 Years* (Xinzhongguo Chuban 50 Nian). Beijing: People's Fine Arts Press, 1999.

Zhang Huibin. "Achievements, Limitations, and Future Trends of Chinese Trademark Legislation" (Zhongguo Shangbiao Lifa De Chengji Wenti Yu Zouxiang). *Hubei Social Science* (Hubei Shehui Kexue), no. 12 (2012): 149–152.

Zhang Lin. "Chinese Individual Ownership Economy: Those People, Those Events." *Glory* no. 6 (2011): 34–42.

Zhang Mao. "Deepen Industry and Commerce Reform, Vitalize Chinese Economy" (Shenhua Shangshi Zhidu Gaige, Jifa Jingji Huoli). *Administration Reform* (Xingzheng Gaige) 6, no. 5 (2015): 10–11.

Zhang Mao. "Steadily Push Forward Reform on Administration of Industry and Commerce, Vitalize Various Market Entities" (Wenbu Tuijing Gongshang Guanli Gaige, Jifa Shichang Zhuti Huoli). *China Market* (Zhongguo Shichang) 19, no. 43 (2013): 3–6.

Zhang Naigeng. "Intellectual Property Law in China: Basic Policy and New Development." *Annual Survey of International and Comparative Law* 4, no. 1 (1997): 1–17.

Zhang Xi. "Several Words: Recollecting My Experience at the China Authors Association" (Zhiyan Pianyu: Zai Zhongguo Zuoxie Gongzuo De Huiyi). Beijing: Shiyue Wenyi Press, 2002.

Zhang Xuan. "Haier Group: Build Famous Brands Overseas" (Hai'er Jituan: Guomen Zhiwai Chuang Mingpai). *Chinese Foreign Trade* (Zhongguo Duiwai Maoyi) 7, no. 7 (1998): 31–32.

Zhao Jianguo. "The Fourth Revision of Chinese Patent Law Attracts Great Attention" (Zhuanlifa Disici Xiugai Beishou Guanzhu). *China Intellectual Property News* (Zhongguo Zhishi Chanquan Bao), April 10, 2015.

Zhao Ping. "Enormous Stake Is Tied to the Result of Cisco vs. Huawe: If Huawei Loses, the Consequence Can Be Serious." *China Business News*, March 3, 2003.

Zhao Wei. "Anti-Trust Operations with Chinese Characteristics" (Zhongguo Shi Fanlongduan). *Zhejiang Economy* (Zhejiang Jingji) 26, no. 3 (2011): 30–31.

Zhao Yuanguo. *The Conceiving and Birth of Chinese Patent Law* (Zhongguo Zhuanli Fa De Yunyu Yu Dansheng). Beijing: Intellectual Property Rights Press, 2003.

Zheng Chengsi. "On Several Features of Chinese Patent Law" (Lun Woguo Zhuanlifa De Jige Tedian). *Journal of Graduate School of Chinese Academy of Social Sciences* (Zhongguo Shehui Kexueyuan Yanjiushengyuan Xuebao) no. 6 (1984): 53–56.

Zheng Xiaojun. "A Recollection of Pizza Hut vs. New Vision Global." *China Trademark* no. 10 (2006): 19–21.

Zhong Chengxiang. "A Philosophical Thinking on Certain Trends in TV and Movie Production" (Dui Dangqian Yinshi Chuangzuo Yizhong Sichao De Zhexue Sikao, Xuexi Dangde Shisida Zhengzhi Baogao De Tihui). *China Television* (Zhongguo Dianshi) no. 1 (1993): 32–34.

Zhou Lin and Mingshan Li, eds. *Documents on the History of Chinese Copyright* (Zhongguo Banquanshi Yanjiu Wenxian). Beijing: Zhongguo Fangzheng Press, 1999.

Zhou Yubo. "The Development Process and Future Perspective of Chinese Enterprises' Intellectual Property Rights Work." In *Intellectual Property Rights and the "Reform and Opening to the Outside" Policy*, ed. Lipu Tian, 231–241. Beijing: Intellectual Property Press, 2010.

Zhu Zheng. *Summer 1957: From the Debates Among One Hundred Schools to the Debates Between Two Schools* (1957nianxia: Cong Baijia Zhenming Dao Liangjia Zhenming). Zhengzhou: Henan People's Press 1998.

Zimei Fu. "Three Questions About the Poisonous Capsules Incident" (Sanwen Dujiangnang Shijian). *People's Daily*, May 7, 2012.

Zuo Xuchu. "Chinese Trademark Management in the Era of the Republic of China" (Minguo Shiqi Zhongguo Shangbiao Guanli Gaikuang). *China Trademark* no. 1 (2012): 52–57.

INDEX

ACKNOWLEDGMENTS

This book is the result of a long intellectual journey, during which I received enthusiastic support and encouragement from numerous individuals. With its publication, I finally have the opportunity to express gratitude for their extraordinary kindness and friendship, which benefited me so much in so many ways.

This project has its origins in the Political Science Department of the University of Minnesota. Kathryn Sikkink and Daniel Kelliher constantly provided me invaluable advice from the very beginning. Both of them observed how this project grew through different stages, developing from a woolly paragraph to its completion. I can never sufficiently express my gratitude for their patient guidance in my intellectual growth. In and outside the Political Science Department, Teri Caraway, Ruth Okediji, Raymond Duvall, Michael Barnett, David Blaney, Colin Kahl, David Samuels, Orin Kirshner, and Zhiqun Zhu also provided extremely helpful comments on and critiques of what eventually became this book.

I benefited enormously from a year at Princeton as a fellow in the Princeton-Harvard China and the World Program (CWP). My discussions with Tom Christensen, Alastair Iain Johnston, Joel Wuthnow, Gregory Chow, May Cheng-Rhinehardt, Xu Xin, and Yinan He made the manuscript stronger. Tina Lee, Susan Kang, Jonneke Koomen, and David Leon generously provided me with insights and friendship and turned an otherwise tiresome publishing process into an exciting growth experience. At Princeton, I was fortunate to live for a year in the beautiful house of Lynn White. The hospitality of Lynn and his wife, Barbara-Sue, greatly contributed to the success of this book. Institutional and financial support from Hamline University proved essential for the book's completion. I thank David Davies, Karen Vogel, Joe Peschek, Alina Oxendine, Binnur Ozkececci-Taner, and David Shultz for their friendship, assistance, and advice.

I was lucky to get help from hundreds of individuals across China during my field research for this book. Due to my assurance of confidentiality, I am not able to name my interviewees, but this project would not have been possible without the information they provided. Staff affiliated with the University Service Center at Hong Kong Chinese University, the Chinese National Library in Beijing, the Municipal Library of Shanghai, and the Johns Hopkins University–Nanjing University Center for Chinese and American Studies provided enormous help in my archival research.

I thank Peter Agree, my editor at the University of Pennsylvania Press, for his interest in my manuscript and his patience as I made revisions. I am grateful to the two anonymous reviewers for their constructive critiques and unsparing professionalism, which significantly improved the manuscript. I am also grateful to Julie Trupke-Bastidas for her excellent job in editing and proofreading. Ultimately, I am responsible for any errors in this book.

During my fieldwork in China, various kind people significantly enhanced the quality of my life by generously offering me lodging, transportation, and heavy input of encouraging words. These wonderful people are Cao Yuening, Chen Donglin, Helen Ding, Chaoyang Gao, Fayne Lin, Qifang Lu, Guangjin Luo, Yonger Tan, Bicheng Zhou, and Zhu Guangli, among others. Without their help, it would not have been able to imagine completing the fieldwork.

Last but not at all least, my family has been a constant source of love and help throughout the years. I wish to thank my parents, elder brother, sister-in-law, and niece for their enduring support during the past years and beyond. I dedicate this book to them.